# The Changing Face of Cricket

For cricket enthusiasts there is nothing to match the meaningful contests and excitement generated by the game's subtle shifts in play. Conversely huge swathes of the world's population find cricket the most obscure and bafflingly impenetrable of sports. *The Changing Face of Cricket* attempts to account for this paradox.

*The Changing Face of Cricket* provides an overview of the various ways in which social scientists have analysed the game's cultural impact. The book's international analysis encompasses Australia, the Caribbean, England, India, Ireland, South Africa, Sri Lanka and Zimbabwe. Its interdisciplinary approach allies anthropology, history, literary criticism, political studies and sociology with contributions from cricket administrators and journalists. The collection addresses historical and contemporary issues such as gender equality, global sports development, the impact of cricket mega-events, and the growing influence of commercial and television interests culminating in the Twenty20 revolution.

Whether one loves or hates the game, understands what turns square legs into fine legs, or how mid-offs become silly, *The Changing Face of Cricket* will enlighten the reader on the game's cultural contours and social impact and prove to be the essential reader in cricket studies.

This book was published as a special issue of *Sport in Society*.

**Dominic Malcolm** is Senior Lecturer in the Sociology of Sport in the School of Sport, Exercise and Health Sciences at Loughborough University and Convenor of the British Sociological Association's Sport Study Group. He has published a number of co-edited texts - *The Future of Football, Sport: Critical Concepts in Sociology, Sport Histories*, and *Matters of Sport*. He is author of the *Sage Dictionary of Sports Studies* published in 2008.

**Jon Gemmell** teaches History and Sociology at Kennet School, Thatcham. He is the author of *The Politics of South African Cricket*, and has written a number of articles exploring the links between race/ethnicity, politics and cricket in South Africa, Australia and Ireland. He is the co-editor of *Cricket, Race and the 2007 World Cup* and is currently working on a history of the ethos of cricket.

**Nalin Mehta** is Founding Joint Editor of *South Asian History and Culture* and Trustee of the South Asia Research Foundation. A Fellow of the International Olympic Museum, Lausanne (2007) he is the author of *India on Television* and *Olympics: The India Story*. He works for the Global Fund, Geneva, and is currently co-writing a history of the Commonwealth Games and Delhi 2010.

# The Changing Face of Cricket

From Imperial to Global Game

Edited by Dominic Malcolm, Jon Gemmell and Nalin Mehta

LONDON AND NEW YORK

First published 2010 by Routledge
2 Park Square, Milton Park, Abingdon, Oxon, OX14 4RN

Simultaneously published in the USA and Canada
by Routledge
270 Madison Avenue, New York, NY 10016

*Routledge is an imprint of the Taylor & Francis Group, an informa business*

Typeset in Times by Value Chain, India
Printed and bound in Great Britain by TJI Digital Ltd, Padstow, Cornwall

*British Library Cataloguing in Publication Data*
A catalogue record for this book is available from the British Library

ISBN10: 0-415-44329-6
ISBN13: 978-0-415-44329-6

# CONTENTS

# Sport in the Global Society – Contemporary Perspectives

Series Editor: Boria Majumdar

## The Changing Face of Cricket
From Imperial to Global Game

**Sport in the Global Society – Contemporary Perspectives**

Series Editor: Boria Majumdar

The social, cultural (including media) and political study of sport is an expanding area of scholarship and related research. While this area has been well served by the Sport in the Global Society Series, the surge in quality scholarship over the last few years has necessitated the creation of *Sport in the Global Society: Contemporary Perspectives*. The series will publish the work of leading scholars in fields as diverse as sociology, cultural studies, media studies, gender studies, cultural geography and history, political science and political economy. If the social and cultural study of sport is to receive the scholarly attention and readership it warrants, a cross-disciplinary series dedicated to taking sport beyond the narrow confines of physical education and sport science academic domains is necessary. Sport in the Global Society: Contemporary Perspectives will answer this need.

*Other Titles in the Series*

# Abstracts

### Cricket and modernity: international and interdisciplinary perspectives on the study of the Imperial Game

Dominic Malcolm, Jon Gemmell and Nalin Mehta

This introductory essay seeks to contextualize the contributions in the volume by comparing and contrasting cricket with other sports. Though not wishing to portray cricket in essentialist terms, or as temporally fixed or uncontested, the essay suggests that cricket has certain peculiar features which are not only celebrated by cricket followers and dumbfound its detractors in equal measure, but make the game particularly interesting for sports studies scholars. More specifically, drawing predominantly on Allen Guttmann's schema of modern sports forms outlined in *From Ritual to Record*, the essay argues that particularly with reference to rationalization, specialization and the importance of equality, cricket could be said to contain many unmodern characteristics. The essay builds on these sensitizing concepts to outline the contents of the volume suggesting that four recurrent themes emerge: the importance of identity; the multiple and overlapping forms of identity; the role of cricket in fostering and challenging competing identities; and the playing out of power relations through sport. Taken together, the contributions expand our understanding of the game by inviting three forms of comparison: cultural, temporal and cross-disciplinary.

### Naturally played by Irishmen: a social history of Irish cricket

Jon Gemmell

This study considers the history of Irish cricket in the context of wider social and political developments. It looks at the origins of the sport, how they came to be associated with a British presence in Ireland and the implications of this during a period of nationalist revival. It considers the rise and decline of cricket in Ireland and provides suggestions for its maintenance and current renaissance. The study is in part a celebration of the success of the Irish team at the 2007 World Cup and a reminder of the contribution to worldwide cricket through the diaspora.

### South African cricket and British imperialism, 1870 – 1910

Dean Allen

During the later years of Queen Victoria's reign, cricket was as popular as ever in the home country while overseas the game's influence had spread to all boundaries of Britain's Empire. It was during this period too that South Africa, one of England's most recent 'cricketing colonies', was experiencing major transition in both society and structure.

This essay will explore the early development of cricket in South Africa and investigate its link to British imperialism and colonialism. It will highlight how key agencies and individuals were pivotal in the process of securing the early cricketing ties between England and South Africa. The essay will also investigate the growth of cricket's political significance during the latter part of the nineteenth century – a time when within Britain and her colonies, the game came to symbolize the very essence of an exclusive white, Victorian society.

## Irish Australians, postcolonialism and the English game

Alan Bairner

Members of the Irish diaspora have made a significant contribution to Australian cricket. In seeking to unravel the cultural and political implications of that contribution, this essay considers the character of Irish migration to Australia, comments on the historical status of cricket in Ireland, and discusses the contribution of the Irish to Australian sport in general and to cricket in particular. The main focus of the discussion is on the careers of Bill O'Reilly, Jack Fingleton and Lindsay Hassett. More generally, the essay is intended to shed light on the problematic relationship between imperialism and the experience of being colonized, not only in Australia but also in Ireland.

## 'From far it look like politics': C.L.R. James and the canon of English cricket literature

Anthony Bateman

Is cricket is cricket in yuh ricketics
but from far it look like politics[1]

This essay juxtaposes C.L.R. James's cricket writings with the canon of English cricket literature, and particularly the work of Neville Cardus. It demonstrates that James's writing was immersed in cricket's literary canon even while it sought to subvert it in the cause of an alternative, postcolonial cultural politics. James's cricket writing both transcended the politics of English cricket discourse and attempted to offer an alternative. A telling example of his technique can be found in his essay 'Garfield Sobers'. Writing about Sobers allows James to find the hybrid literary styles and forms through which a postcolonial West Indian cricket could be represented. The essay concludes with a critique of James's aesthetic of cricket, arguing that his theorization of the relationship between cricket as discourse and cricket as embodied performance constitutes *Beyond a Boundary*'s major contribution to an understanding of the game as both an instrument of, and resistance to, colonialism.

## 'Fiery Fred': Fred Trueman and cricket celebrity in the 1950s and early 1960s

Jack Williams

Fred Trueman was a hero and anti-hero of English cricket in the 1950s and 1960s. His celebrity reflected his great ability as a fast bowler and flair for self promotion but reveals much about cultural values and social relations in England at that time. Trueman often appeared to be a working-class man victimized by the upper-class cricket establishment because he made it clear that he thought himself as good as his social betters and had little time for what he considered the hypocrisies of cricketing etiquette. His pride in his Yorkshire roots and what he perceived as unfair treatment by southern cricket authorities resonated with widespread assumptions of the South being prejudiced against Yorkshire. Trueman's brushes with cricket authority and his conduct in general made him appear to be challenging the traditionalism of English society and culture but Trueman's political outlook was essentially conservative.

## Rebellion, race and Rhodesia: international cricketing relations with Rhodesia during UDI

Charles Little

This essay examines the dynamics of Rhodesian cricket during the period of that state's Universal Declaration of Independence (UDI) from Britain (1965–79). During this period of international isolation under the white minority regime of Ian Smith, Rhodesian sport was subject to a variety of pressures and influences. Most significant amongst these were the various attempts to impose an international sporting boycott upon it. The principle purpose of this essay is to analyse the impact of this campaign on cricket, both domestically within Rhodesia and its impact on the wider cricketing world. Particular attention is given to the role of the British Government in instigating and promoting this boycott and the responses of cricketing authorities to such calls, including the MCC's decision to avoid playing in Rhodesia on their planned 1969 tour of Southern Africa and the responses of various governing bodies and national governments to private tours of the republic.

## A national(ist) line in postcolonizing cricket: Viv Richards, biographies and cricketing nationalism

Malcolm MacLean

West Indies cricket writing has presented readers with, at times, challenging and provocative politics: C.L.R James's *Beyond A Boundary* concurrently asserts an appreciation for the cultures of the Imperial homeland alongside post- and anti-colonial politics, while Learie Constantine's *Cricket and I* demonstrates cultural nationalism. More recently, Viv Richards's biography 1991 *Hitting Across The Line* has developed a more explicitly progressive, movement-linked, politics. This paper explores Richards's biography through the lens of cultural nationalism to argue that in the absence of an unproblematically indigenous people, Richards constructs a place-derived sense of indigeneity and hence authenticity in West Indies cricket, and in doing so exposes many of the contradictions of West Indies and other sporting cultural nationalisms in the context of postcolonising tendencies in the former British Empire.

## Brian Lara in poetic form: tradition, talent and the Caribbean 'mwe'

Claire Westall

This essay considers the place of Brian Lara in Caribbean poetry through two literary framing devices. It first situates the iconic image of Lara within the literary frames provided by T.S. Eliot's 'Tradition and the Individual Talent' and Kamau Brathwaite's notion of 'mwe', before unpacking Lara poems composed by writers and performers as well known as Jean Breeze, Howard Fergus and Paul Keens-Douglas. The discussion suggests that by reading these pieces as a collection Lara is shown to represent the Caribbean's ongoing negotiation between the one and the many, as well as the potentially hazardous over-investment in the individual hero. Consequently, the discussion is less concerned with the actions and personality of Lara than it is with his heroic image in poetry and the critical messages West Indies cricket and the Caribbean more generally may take from such literary representations.

## Wunderkidz in a Blunderland: tensions and tales from Sri Lankan cricket

Michael Roberts

The story of Sri Lankan cricket is a tale of great cricketing success within the context of a polity struggling with civil war and great levels of internal violence. Cricket is the one arena in Sri Lankan public culture where Tamils and Sinhalese, locked in a bloody civil war for decades, come together on a national public platform. From being reviled as a Western import in the early years of independence to its gradual embrace and penetration of new catchment areas in less affluent and more rural areas, the story of Sri Lankan cricket in many ways mirrors the development of the post-colonial Sri Lankan nation. This essay fleshes out prominent themes in the history of Sri Lankan cricket within the context of the major socio-political developments in twentieth century Sri Lanka.

## Batting for the flag: cricket, television and globalization in India

Nalin Mehta

Much of the existing literature on Indian cricket identifies the game's inherently political dimension and attributes the pre-eminence of cricket in the Indian imagination to a set of complex and contradictory processes that parallel the emergence of an 'Indian' nation. Yet until the early 1980s, while cricket was popular, hockey was the 'national game' and soccer was equally popular in large parts of the country. From the 1980s onwards cricket assumed centre-stage, not necessarily stemming, as many have written, from some peculiar Indian affiliation for the game, but inextricably linked with the expansion of Indian television and a confluence of other factors: the creation of a large middle class, economic reforms, the politics of identity, the birth of the satellite television industry and broader trends in globalization. This essay maps the growth of Indian television to draw out these linkages and demonstrate the central role of television in making cricket integral to modern notions of Indian identity.

## Different hats, different thinking? Technocracy, globalization and the Indian cricket team

Stephen Wagga and Sharda Ugra

This essay analyses the public debate and the controversies surrounding Australian ex-Test cricketer Greg Chappell during his tenure as coach of the Indian cricket team between 2005 and 2007. It uses the media discourse on Chappell to delineate emerging trends in Indian cricket culture in the context of contemporary Indian society, globalization and relations between East and West within the global economy. Chappell's tenure as coach of Team India emerged as an important marker in the evolution of a global cricket technocracy which flattens out, or threatens to flatten out, what have been perceived as historic differences between national cricket cultures.

## Malign or benign? English national identities and cricket

Dominic Malcolm

This essay examines English cricket discourse in an attempt to expand upon existing analyses of English sporting nationalism. It is argued that there has been a marked strengthening of English national identity in recent years, both in sport and other spheres, and that certain historical peculiarities stand in the way of the emergence of a coherent, or unified, sense of Englishness. This essay argues that whilst discourses of Englishness and cricket were dominated by a malign sense of Englishness during the 1980s and 1990s, in the early years of the twenty-first century, a benign form of Englishness has come to the fore. It is suggested that this is a manifestation of a growing consciousness amongst those in the media and in administrative and political positions that the openness and tolerance characteristic of benign Englishness is how an increasing number of English people would like themselves to be seen.

### 'Look, it's a girl': cricket and gender relations in the UK

Philippa Velija and Dominic Malcolm

This essay seeks to explain why, despite organizational reforms, the number of females playing cricket in the UK has not significantly increased in recent years. The essay draws upon qualitative research with females playing youth and adult cricket and focuses on four main areas: female cricketers' experiences of playing cricket with males; the reactions of males who encounter female cricketers in everyday settings; female cricketers' experiences of an organizational merger with a male team; and female cricketers' views on the status of women's cricket relative to the men's game. Using a figurational sociological perspective, we argue that these experiences lead to a socially-generated personality structure (habitus) in which the internalization of a negative 'we-group' image of themselves as female cricketers is a prominent feature. Consequently female cricketers are unable to pose a broader challenge to their outsider status in the game and thus female participation has not increased.

### International cricket – the hegemony of commerce, the decline of government interest and the end of morality?

Russell Holden

The issue of whether England should play cricket in, and with, Zimbabwe has dogged both cricket's governing international body and the administrators of the English and Welsh domestic game since the start of the millennium. In seeking to explain and contextualize this ongoing crisis (with particular reference to the period between 2002 and 2005), this essay will consider cricketing relationships in terms of how commercial imperatives are reconciled with principles of morality, ethics and the upholding of fundamental human rights. As governmental authority declines in comparison to that of a small number of multi-national conglomerates, the development of cricket appears to be driven by the ever-more powerful forces of commodification in preference to anxieties regarding morality.

### A legacy deeply mired in contradiction: World Cup 2007 in retrospect

Boria Majumdar

The 2007 cricket World Cup in the Caribbean was hailed as a tournament that would change the economy of the Caribbean islands. CWC 2007, it was argued, was an opportunity to project the image of a united global Caribbean community while also creating opportunities to force more tangible intra West Indian diplomatic and business networks. The tournament itself, marred by the controversial death of Pakistani coach Bob Woolmer, and the negative economic impact of the early exits of Pakistan and India, turned out rather differently than the organizers had hoped. This essay, based on field research in the Caribbean, examines the economic, social and political impact of Cricket World Cup 2007 on the Caribbean islands.

## Burning down the house

Rob Steen

Professional cricket, in terms of playing standards, opportunity, profitability, adaptability and reach, has never been as good, for players, administrators and audience, as it is in 2008. However, administrative greed, and a reluctance to see players' unions as partners, have bred an unrelenting fixture list, making increasingly forbidding demands on the men who make it all possible – the players. 'Burnout' is the buzzword. One solution, however, has emerged: the briefer, three-hour Twenty20 limited-overs format, an historic development whose economic potential was emphasized in September 2007 when India won the inaugural World Twenty20 tournament.

## A strong sport growing stronger: a perspective on the growth, development and future of international cricket

Ehsan Mani

This essay analyses the future direction of international cricket from the point of view of a global cricket administrator. To appreciate how the game has developed from being a very English sport played mainly by the aristocracy in the seventeenth and eighteenth centuries, to its current stage of evolution, it also takes a brief look at the history of the game and its transformation from an exclusive sport to a truly global one. It traces the evolution of cricket's governing structures, the transformation of the International Cricket Council and how cricket is being promoted in countries like China which have no tradition of the game. It also outlines the development of women's cricket and the game's responsibilities to the societies in which it is played. This essay also delineates the impact of television, radio and sponsorship on the promotion of the game.

## 'Bombay Sport Exchange': cricket, globalization and the future

Nalin Mehta, Jon Gemmell and Dominic Malcolm

Cricket's imperial lineage continues to define its meaning in parts of the erstwhile British Empire. Simultaneously, the game is now a metaphor for the forces of globalization and a vehicle for asserting new post-colonial identities. The creation of the lucrative Indian Premier League and India's growth as the financial epicentre of the game is reflective of its rise as an emerging engine of the new global financial structure and as a major market for the consumer economy. India's rise as a new 'cricket capital' is intrinsically linked to the forces of global capitalism and this has significantly changed the game's power structure itself. This essay analyses the discourse around the Indian Premier League, debates around cricket's new 'Asian bloc' and the racism row between the Indian and Australian cricket teams in January 2008 to delineate the shift in the international power dynamics of cricket and its implications for debates about post-colonialism and globalization.

# Cricket and modernity: international and interdisciplinary perspectives on the study of the Imperial Game

Dominic Malcolm[a], Jon Gemmell[b] and Nalin Mehta[c]*

[a]School of Sport and Exercise Sciences, Loughborough University, Loughborough, UK; [b]Kennet School, Thatcham, Berkshire, UK; [c]School of Social Science, La Trobe University, Melbourne, Australia

Cricket is a peculiar sport. Whilst cricket, like the majority of sports, was 'invented' in England, it emerged around a century before the other major international team sports – i.e. football and rugby – that currently compete for public and academic attention. Whilst football and rugby emerged in opposition to each other, a consequence, Dunning and Sheard argue, of the status rivalry between Rugby and Eton public schools,[1] cricket seems to have emerged out of consensus, the 1755 code of rules being 'settled by the *several* cricket clubs, particularly that of the Star and Garter Club in Pall Mall' (emphasis added).[2] Moreover, pupils at Eton, Harrow and Winchester regularly played cricket between themselves and against each other prior to both the nineteenth-century reform of the prefect-fagging system which Dunning and Sheard cite as a precondition to the development of football and rugby,[3] and the development of Muscular Christianity and the cult of athleticism which Mangan, amongst others, has argued was significant in the educational adoption of team sports and their diffusion into wider British society in the nineteenth century.[4] Though currently undergoing significant upheaval (see Mehta, Gemmell and Malcolm's conclusion to this collection), cricket also had a (relatively) undisputed national governing body, the Marylebone Cricket Club (MCC), some 100 years before the conflict-ridden formation of the Football Association (FA) in 1863 and the Rugby Football Union (RFU) in 1871.[5]

The peculiarity of cricket's development extends to the internationalization of the game. As befits the historical roots of the respective games, Scotland and England contested the first international football and rugby matches in 1870 and 1872 respectively (interestingly the latter staged at the West of Scotland Cricket Ground), yet the first international cricket match was played between Canada and the United States in 1844, thus pre-empting the English and Scottish footballers by 26 years. Rather contrarily, whilst the English were reluctant participants in the early bureaucratization of international football and rugby union, they were firmly at the helm of the internationalization of cricket. The English FA declined a number of requests to assume leadership of the fledgling international governing body in the 1890s, joining a year after FIFA was established. The relationship continued to be acrimonious, with the FA twice resigning its membership during the inter-war years.[6] Similarly the RFU was not an original member of the International Rugby Football Board (initially consisting of Scotland, Ireland and Wales) but joined in 1890, four years after its formation. In contrast to this, when, in 1907, Abe Bailey, the President of the South African Cricket Association, suggested that an Imperial Cricket Board be established, the President of the MCC, Lord Chesterfield, and the redoubtable Lord Harris, were instrumental in placating initial objections from Australia and hosted the meetings which led to the formation of the Imperial Cricket Conference (latterly the International Cricket Council or ICC) in 1909. The involvement and dominance of the English in this international venture was formally cemented with the President and Secretary of the MCC installed as the ICC's ex-officio Chairman and ex-officio Secretary respectively.

Thus cricket has developed along a somewhat different trajectory to that of many of the team games which currently dominate our sporting landscape and, not surprisingly, the game's peculiarity remains today. Whilst cricket, like football and rugby, is a fully professional sport, closely integrated with media companies and commercial sponsors and part of, and subject to, the broad set of social processes we describe as globalization, its relative popularity is confined to distinct populations (and as the contents of this collection illustrate, primarily the residents of the nation-states of the former British Empire). For some, cricket engages the passions like no other sport. For enthusiasts there is nothing to match the tension and excitement generated by subtle shifts in the game (and its longer versions in particular). For many people in cricket (test) playing nations, no other sport throws up such meaningful contests, which resonate so closely with identity and history. This has much to do with cricket's place in the British colonizing mission. Equally, cricket has taken on new meanings in the post-colonial world. In this context, for instance, the Indian sociologist Ashis Nandy has famously argued that 'cricket is an Indian game, invented accidentally by the English',[7] and the Indian historian Ramachandra Guha has noted, only partially in jest, that only five things have kept India united: the army, the railways, the English language, bollywood and cricket.[8] Conversely, it remains the case that huge swathes of the world's population find cricket the most obscure and bafflingly impenetrable of sports.

**Modernity and modern sports forms**

Given these brief observations, a more systematic comparison of the similarities and differences between cricket and other sports (and team games in particular) is perhaps warranted. Before introducing the contents of this collection, therefore, we will use this introduction to compare and contrast the structural properties of cricket as a game form with what others have suggested are the dominant characteristics of modern sports. To begin with, however, we need to establish what we mean by 'modern', and what distinguishes modern sports from their pre-modern counterparts?

'Modern' can be taken to mean 'up to date' or 'contemporary', but analytically it is more useful to use the term to mean 'not traditional'. Modern, in this sense, sums up the distinctiveness, complexity and dynamism of a range of social processes which developed in Western Europe during the eighteenth and nineteenth centuries and which, cumulatively, marked a distinct break from traditional ways of living. Some of the more commonly cited features of this transformation include: the development and application of more efficient forms of food production and the subsequent replacement of agriculture as the dominant form of productive activity by industrial manufacture (the industrial revolution); the growth of the capitalist mode of production, capitalist organizations and capitalist ways of thinking; population growth and migration from the countryside to the city (urbanization); new (largely 'democratic') forms of government, the growth of the state and secularization; Western colonization of the rest of the world; and, stemming from the *Enlightenment* movement of the eighteenth century, the emergence of new, rational scientific ways of understanding the natural and social worlds which heralded an era of great medical, scientific and technological innovation and the belief in the inevitable and continual progress and advancement of humanity. At the risk of offending postmodernists, sport as we know it today constitutes an explicitly modern institution. Most sports developed in the same time and space as modernity more generally (nineteenth-century Western Europe), are structured by the same set of ideas (progress, rationality, individualism) and have been influenced by the same social processes (industrialization, urbanization, colonization and globalization).

Two of the most useful schema for delineating the specific characteristics of modern sport have been provided by American historian Allen Guttmann and British sociologists, Eric Dunning and Kenneth Sheard. In *Barbarians, Gentlemen and Players*, Dunning and Sheard list 15 characteristics which distinguish modern sports from their folk game antecedents. These are: specific, formal organization; elaborate, written rules, legitimated by rational-bureaucratic means; rules changed on a rational-bureaucratic basis; national and international standardization of rules; fixed participant numbers and spatial and temporal boundaries to play; importance of fairness and equality rather than natural or social differences; high role differentiation between players (e.g. between defence and offence); strict distinction between playing and spectating roles; high structural differentiation of (i.e. little overlap between) game forms; formal social control of players, with outside agencies to enforce rule compliance, etc.; relatively low levels of socially tolerated violence; the generation of controlled, sublimated 'battle excitement'; an emphasis on skill rather than physical force; participation through individual choice rather than obligation to community; contests which are nationally and internationally meaningful rather than just locally significant; and recognized hierarchies of playing standards, often rewarded through monetization.[9]

Guttmann, in *From Ritual to Record*, identifies seven interdependent characteristics of modern sport: 1) secularism – participation in modern sport is rarely related to formal aspects of religious worship; 2) equality – in modern sports considerable stress is placed on the importance of equal opportunity for participation (in the sense that nobody is formally barred) and on literally and metaphorically providing participants with a 'level playing field'; 3) specialization – in modern sports we clearly distinguish between game forms and increasingly expect elite participants to specialize in terms of one particular sport, and a particular role within that sport; 4) bureaucratization – modern sports are not spontaneously organized or *ad hoc*, but are administered centrally, often by people who are not themselves participants; 5) rationalization – modern sports are underpinned by an instrumental rationality which leads events to be staged in specially constructed venues with increasing human control over environmental conditions, equipment which is standardized and regulated, and participants who are prepared using the latest scientific techniques and advances in knowledge; 6) quantification – in modern sport actions are translated into numerical data and participants' performances are measured, recorded and compared; and 7) the quest for records – spectators expect participants in modern sports to produce increasingly advanced performances through which we can see the progression of humanity.[10]

It is not our intention to explore the differences between these two models, or to make a claim for the superiority of one over the other. Indeed, there is a great deal of overlap between these two works and perhaps the one major difference – the role of Elias's theory of civilizing processes in the work of Dunning and Sheard and the emphasis they place on the level of violence in modern sports compared to their folk antecedents – is embraced by Guttmann who has argued that 'the evolution from premodern to modern sports can be construed as an instance of a civilizing process'.[11] Taken together, however, these descriptions of the characteristics of specifically modern sports forms provide a useful framework through which to examine the peculiarity of contemporary cricket.

## Cricket as a modern sports form

Cricket, of course, exhibits many of the characteristics of a modern sport. Though particularly in India cricket may evoke the passion and commitment more traditionally associated with established religions, since its codification in the eighteenth century, cricket has been a secular game in the sense that it is not formally played in honour, or with the blessing, of gods. It has a long history of a bureaucratic control over rule changes,[12] and the recent relocation of the ICC from London to Dubai shows that the game is subject to the same hard-nosed commercialism that influences the dealings of other international sports federations (see Mani in this collection).[13] Currently running to 115 pages, cricket is governed, in Dunning and Sheard's terms, by elaborate written rules (or laws as they are called in cricket), and indeed many critics of the game argue that the complexity of these rules is a significant barrier to developing the popularity of the game.[14] Moreover, as Dunning and Sheard suggest, cricketing success depends rather more on skill than physical force and, again, critics of the game sometimes comment on the body shape of certain cricketers which suggest a lack of physical fitness. The contemporary game also exhibits relatively low levels of socially tolerated violence compared to its premodern antecedents.[15]

Indeed, in some respects cricket is the archetypal modern sport. Cricket publications are replete with quantified data and it is perhaps only baseball which fosters a similar veneration of statistics and records. Few match commentaries pass without the mention of any number of records; the highest partnership for a particular wicket against a particular country, the best bowling figures at a particular venue, etc. The average edition of *Wisden* contains approximately 1,000 pages of numerical data and 50 pages of text and its main competitor, the *Playfair Cricket Annual,* provides much of the same. That *Wisden* is described as the 'bible' of cricket demonstrates the traditional importance of quantification to followers of the game. That cricket-orientated websites are similarly packed with statistics shows the extent to which this tradition continues and has been internationally diffused.

Similarly few sports are as widely accredited as being infused with an ethos of fair play and no sport has provided as many phrases to the English language which encapsulate honour and fairness (e.g. 'it's not cricket'). No doubt aspects of this ideology of fairness are based on myth and romanticism. Bodyline is perhaps the most often cited example in this regard but, given that cricket is so clearly tied to the colonizing mission of the British Empire, few would argue that its history is not also inextricably tied to the subordination and exploitation of subaltern populations. Some would also claim that commercialization has eroded these values to the extent that cricket is 'not what it was', whilst others argue that such changes are not worth mourning (see the comments of Jagmohan Dalmiya in the concluding contribution to this collection). It remains the case, however, that only in cricket (though golf comes close in this respect) do the laws of the game contain a section which explicitly addresses the importance of sportsmanship and formally prescribes the required 'Spirit of the Game'.

Yet in other respects cricket is peculiarly *un*modern. To begin with we can point to the non-standardized nature of the laws. This is not to say that laws are re-negotiated before every contest for, as noted above, cricket has a comprehensive, complex and relatively fixed set of laws. However cricket has multiple and co-existing game forms; that is to say, 'test' or 'first class' matches, the so-called one-day game consisting of one innings per side of approximately 50 overs,[16] and most recently Twenty20 cricket (see Steen's contribution to this collection for a discussion of their co-existence). Whilst football and rugby union also have competing game forms ('5-a-side' and 'Sevens' respectively) their relationships to the main game form are qualitatively different. First, these games use standardized equipment (albeit with a smaller pitch and goals for '5-a-side' football) whilst one-day cricket may be played under artificial lights (to date, first class matches have only been played under lights in South Africa) using a white ball which many believe behaves differently to the red ball used in the longer version of the game. Second, and most importantly, the hierarchy of game forms in football and rugby is much clearer and more widely agreed upon. Whereas FIFA produce a single table ranking the football playing nations of the world, the ICC produce two, one each for both test matches and one day internationals (ODIs). Moreover, the differential status and popularity of the two forms of cricket is reflected in the playing calendars of the different nations. For instance, whilst England's most capped one-day player is Alec Stewart with 146 appearances, it is not unusual for players from the Indian subcontinent to play between 300 and 400 ODIs. In contrast Stewart (133) has played a similar number of test matches to Sachin Tendulkar and Surav Ganguly (140 and 96 respectively at the time of writing), clearly indicating where the preferences of the English authorities (and public?) lie. It is an anomaly that the premier cricketing competition – the Cricket World Cup – is based on the one-day format but that the nomenclature of cricket formally defines this as the secondary form of the game. Except perhaps in England, one-day cricket – the form of the game not considered 'first class' – is more popular.

Cricket is also peculiarly *un*modern in terms of what Guttmann describes as rationalization and what Dunning and Sheard more specifically note in terms of the fixed character of spatial boundaries and the duration of play. An aspect of cricket which is celebrated by the game's followers and confounds outsiders in equal measure is the peculiarity of its timing. Few sports take as long to complete as test cricket and indeed advocates of the longer form of the game decry the one-day game and Twenty20 cricket for their lack of subtlety and inability to create variety and meaningful tension. But more *un*modern than the extended length of the game, is the *flexibility* of time in cricket. Give or take a few minutes to compensate for injuries and stoppages, a football match lasts 90 minutes and a rugby match 80 minutes, but test matches are scheduled for *up to* five days, and they may end at any point before that. This not only makes revenue from ticket sales unpredictable, but it clashes with the rigid schedules of modern television companies and the demands of sponsors and advertisers who want some control over the quantity of exposure and the context in which their product will be placed. Moreover, no other game so completely embraces the possibility of a contest having no clear outcome. A draw is possible in many sports but only in cricket are two words used – a tie and a draw – to differentiate between the ways in which a match can finish without an undisputed winner. Indeed, as Rob Steen's contribution to this collection shows, a draw has traditionally been the most likely outcome of a cricket test match, with 179 more draws than positive outcomes up until 2004. The combination of the length of matches and the frequency with which contests remain undecided is, again, an aspect of cricket which confounds non-followers of the game brought up to expect the rationalized characteristics of modern sports.

Similarly cricket has not been subject to the same degree of spatial rationalization as other sports. Though the dimensions of the wicket are specified within the laws of the game, the maximum and minimum sizes of the playing area are not regulated. This leads to a greater variation in the conditions under which teams play than in any other modern sport. Moreover, diversity is not simply tolerated by cricket followers, it is positively celebrated. Different grounds are notorious for different conditions. It is written into the folklore of cricket that whilst the pitch at the Kennington Oval in London has pace and bounce, Wanderers in Johannesburg helps seam bowlers and spin bowlers will profit at Galle and Chennai's Chepauk stadium. Perhaps the best example of the way this diversity is valued, relates to the 'spiritual home' of cricket, Lord's Cricket Ground. In autumn 2002 the playing surface at Lord's was excavated to enable the installation of a new drainage system which would allow a speedier return to play following rain (and thus more 'product' for spectators and media alike). Lord's was, however, famous for its 'slope' which entailed the south-east side of the playing surface being approximately eight feet (2.5 metres) lower than the north-west. It was, perhaps, not surprising that a sports stadium established in 1814 should not conform to the kind of rationalized playing conditions which predominate in modern sport, but the decision to restore the slope to its *original form* when the playing surface was re-laid in 2003, shows how closely cherished are the 'premodern' characteristics of contemporary cricket. Here, at the premier cricketing venue, was an explicit rejection of the opportunity to create a 'level playing field'. As former Indian opening batsman Aakash Chopra notes, the effect that this slope has on the bounce of the ball makes playing at Lord's 'a whole different ball game'.[17]

These environmental variations are just some of the ways in which inequality forms a central feature of cricket, or at least the extent to which the game's administrators have not sought to regulate for the provision of equal playing conditions with the same vigour as their counterparts in other sports. For instance, no sport is quite as subject to the vagaries of the weather as cricket. Other sports may stop due to rain (tennis, golf), or even because the light is poor (tennis), but the competitors in other sports normally expect that, when they return to play, conditions will approximate to what they were before, or at least that their opponents will also face new environmental conditions. But in cricket rainfall can effect the speed of the outfield, humidity can affect the extent to which the ball moves in the air, and dampness can increase movement off the pitch, all of which may disadvantage the batting side. As the light is not artificially standardized, players must accept that, within limits, they will bat in differing light qualities. Light quality varies both according to time of day, and from country to country. Most significantly, the quality of light disproportionately affects the batting team.

Almost regardless of weather conditions however, longer games of cricket have the in-built inequality of a pitch which (generally) deteriorates over time and thus presents different challenges to opposing teams. Invariably fewer runs are accumulated in the final innings of a first class match than in any of the other innings in the game. Conventionally the pitch initially favours fast bowlers whilst an older pitch favours spin bowlers. As in other sports a coin is tossed at the beginning of a match and the winning captain gains an advantage (through choice of ends, kick off, etc.), but in cricket there are no further mechanisms for the equalization of playing chances, such as swapping ends at half time, or allowing the other team to kick off in the second half. Rather, in cricket the advantages of this initial success may exert a significant influence over the entire match. Only cricketers talk of a 'good toss to win' because only in cricket is this chance element potentially so central to the outcome of the game. Only cricketers talk of a 'good toss to lose', because only in cricket are the environmental conditions so difficult to predict.

On the one hand it could be argued that these aspects of inequality are unavoidable, a consequence of playing a game of this length in an outdoor environment and, indeed, it should be noted that some measures are taken to equalize the playing conditions, such as the use of protective covers on pitches. On the other hand, there seems to be less enthusiasm to investigate equality-enhancing measures in cricket than in many other sports. For instance, even at stadia where artificial lighting is installed in most of the cricket world (the exception being South Africa) it is not routinely used when the natural light is deemed too poor to play. Similarly, there has been little interest in investigating the advantages of using artificial surfaces in elite cricket, with the view that grass is best largely uncontested. This is in direct contrast to sports such as football and American football, but most notably field hockey where artificial surfaces have been welcomed for the standardized and more predictable manner in which they enable the ball to travel.

Cricket's laws regarding substitutions are again unusual in providing little scope for teams to equalize playing chances (see Mani in this collection). Though individual sports such as boxing and tennis are, for obvious reasons, different in this respect, all modern team sports allow injured and unfit players to be substituted. Whilst substitutes for injured players are also permitted in cricket, the incoming player is uniquely limited, barred from the central aspects of the game (namely batting or bowling) and a substitute may not field in the specialist position of wicketkeeper. Most team games also allow for tactical substitutions but, again, cricket differs in this regard (even though tactical substitutions would be one mechanism by which the inequality stemming from the toss might be corrected). Teams must be selected prior to the toss and personnel cannot be altered to adjust for the conditions that teams subsequently face. Indeed a further *un*modern characteristic of cricket is what Guttmann calls specialization, for cricket is unusual in exalting the all-rounder rather than the specialist, and expecting players to fulfil a variety of positions on the field rather than just one. The laws regarding substitutions in cricket are designed to reinforce this ethos, ensuring that players are valued according to a rounded assessment of skills, and partial or selective involvement in the game cannot be used to compensate for weaknesses. In baseball's American League, by way of contrast, a 'designated hitter' bats instead of the pitcher throughout the game, without otherwise entering the field of play.

Thus, particularly with regard to what Guttmann calls rationalization, specialization and the importance of equality, cricket consists of a number of features which do not conform to the ideal-type of modern sport. In addition to this, whereas notions of modernity are inextricably linked to urbanization and the nation-state as the primary political unit, many cricket teams represent distinctly *un*modern formations. In Britain the domestic game is not based upon cities and towns as it is in football and rugby but, rather, on 'counties'.[18] One of these, Glamorgan, is seen by many as the representative of a nation (namely Wales), although 'Wales' itself competes in the ECB tournament for so-called 'minor counties'. Similarly representation at the international level lacks the standardization seen in other sports. Most international sports federations only recognize and grant membership to nation-states. In a number of sports Ireland (which is sometimes represented by players drawn from both north and south of the border) and England, Scotland and Wales (being nations but not nation-states) are the exception to this rule but here at least member nations are distinct and based on mutually exclusive geographical areas. In cricket, the team that plays under the title of 'England' nominally represents the England and Wales Cricket Board. Yet in addition to England, the 'England' team may include players from both Wales, which is not recognized as a cricketing 'nation' in its own right, and Scotland, which is. To compound matters, joining nation-states with full test match playing status such as Australia, Bangladesh and India, is the West Indies, a multi-state confederation. Though it has often been hoped that this joint venture in cricket might lead to greater Caribbean unity, as Majumdar notes in his contribution to this collection, the Caribbean's staging of the 2007 Cricket World Cup is just the latest in a long line of failures in this regard. The *ad hoc* character through which teams in cricket are drawn up is another feature of the game which contrasts with the underlying process of rationality characteristic of modernity.

There are some other peculiarities of the game that we might have mentioned, such as test match cricketers wearing kits which are almost indistinguishable from each other, the prevalence of competitions and league tables in which teams do not play each other an equal number of times, and the rigid hierarchies which dichotomize domestic and international cricket teams into full and second class members thus disregarding modernist ideas about democracy. Our intention, however, is not to present some kind of definitive list, or to argue that cricket should not be classed as modern, still less postmodern. Indeed, as noted above, there are many aspects of cricket which firmly locate it as a globalized sport of the twenty-first century and there is a danger, having undertaken an exercise such as this, that we will appear to be abstracting cricket from the other sports studied in our disciplines. This is not our intention and we recognize that for many of the points that we have made about the peculiarity of cricket one could point to parallels in other sports. However, taken together the characteristics of cricket highlighted do suggest that, whether one loves or hates the game, there is something unusual about cricket and therefore something about the game which should be of interest to scholars of sport. We hope through this that we have provided some thought-provoking comments which will enable the reader to think about the broader context in which we analyse the game, and locate the chapters which follow in this collection.

**International and interdisciplinary perspectives on cricket**

While there might be something unusual about cricket, it has not been our intention to portray cricket as fixed in time or as having some 'essential' characteristics. Despite our different backgrounds and interests in the game, one thing which beyond all others unites us as editors is the belief in the desirability of studying changes over time, or social processes. Our task and desire in bringing this collection together is to attempt to understand the balance between what *appears to be* the uniqueness and unrepeatability of particular cricket-related events, and the structured character of the social changes manifest in the game. To this end the game needs to be studied in its broader social context, as so many of our contributors have done in relation to their specific subject matters. More than this, however, there are knowledge gains to be had from undertaking a broadly comparative approach. The content of this collection implicitly invites three forms of comparison: cultural, temporal and cross disciplinary.

One way to organize this collection would be along geographical lines. To this end it would have been possible to assemble discrete sections on cricket in the UK/Ireland (with contributions from Gemmell, Malcolm, Velija and Malcolm and Williams), Africa (Allen, Holden, Little), the Caribbean (Bateman, MacLean, Majumdar and Westall), the subcontinent (Mehta, Roberts and Wagg and Ugra), and Australia (Bairner). Indeed it is the case that cricket literature is often organized on this basis. In this vein we might cite: Derek Birley's *A Social History of English Cricket* and Jack Williams' *Cricket and England: A Cultural and Social History of the Inter-war Years*; Jon Gemmell's *The Politics of South African Cricket*, Bruce Murray and Christopher Merrett's *Caught Behind: Race and Politics in Springbok Cricket* and Jonty Winch's, *Cricket in Southern Africa*; volumes 1 and 2 of Hilary Beckles' *The Development of West Indies Cricket* and Hilary Beckles and Brian Stoddart's *Liberation Cricket: West Indies Cricket Culture*; Ramachandra Guha's *A Corner of a Foreign Field: The Indian History of a British Sport*, and Boria Majumdar's *A Social History of Indian Cricket: Twenty-Two Yards to Freedom* and *An Indian Cricket Reader*. Tellingly, even texts such as Brian Stoddart and Keith Sandiford's *The Imperial Game: Cricket, Culture and Society* which attempt to analyse 'the forms and fortunes' of the game as it 'spread to various segments of the old British Empire and beyond',[19] and Stephen Wagg's *Cricket and National Identity in the Post Colonial Age*, are essentially organized along national lines. On the one hand we thought that there was little to be gained by following this much trodden path but, in addition to this, the content of this collection shows the limitations of such an approach. For instance, Dean Allen's piece tells us as much about Britain as it does about South Africa, Anthony Bateman draws comparisons between English and Caribbean cricket literature, and Alan Bairner's work is predicated on the conflation of Australian and Irish identities. Humans are not constrained by geographical boundaries and neither should be our scholarship.

A second way to organize this collection is along disciplinary lines. To this end the collection includes contributions from those whose training has been in anthropology (Roberts), history (Allen, Little, MacLean, Majumdar and Williams), literary studies (Bateman and Westall), political studies (Bairner, Gemmell, Holden and Mehta), sociology (Malcolm, Velija and Wagg) and through their employment in the media industry (Steen and Ugra). Again one would have to question the value of such distinctions. The trend towards the blurring of traditional academic disciplines is relatively widespread, and in this regard we have in mind anthropologists' and historians' increased use of social/sociological theory in recent years, sociologists' embrace of historical analyses and the infiltration of academic concepts and viewpoints into the media. This trend, however, is particularly pronounced in relation to the academic study of sport. In part this is because sport-related subdisciplines are relatively new (and hence less constrained by traditional disciplinary divisions), but it is also a consequence of being taught in interdisciplinary departments, defined by the object of study (sport) as opposed to the approach.

A third possibility is a thematic organization of contributions. Here the peculiarity of cricket was again significant because, in contrast to say football for which there are a number of edited works with contributions addressing a broad range of subjects,[20] cricket scholarship is tightly focussed around the key themes of imperialism, nationalism and globalization and their respective impacts on identity formation. Moreover, these themes are closely merged. As the contributions illustrate, we can no more understand the development of 'Caribbean nationalism' without reference to imperialism and the construction of English national identity, than we can understand contemporary trends in English national identity without reference to that nation's imperial past, post-colonial legacies and the commingling of cultures characteristic of more recent phases of globalization. In short, the abiding legacy of cricket's status as the imperial game par excellence is that it remains almost impossible to undertake an analysis without some reference to the importance of this experience and the extent to which it structures both historical and contemporary relations.

As a consequence of these considerations this collection has been loosely organized on a chronological basis. In what remains of this introduction, we will attempt to illustrate some of the relationships between the different pieces and the convergence of themes.

The collection starts with Jon Gemmell's social history of cricket in Ireland, a country not normally associated with the game. Triggered by Ireland's shock success in the 2007 Cricket World Cup, Gemmell seeks to examine the origins, growth, decline and contemporary condition of Irish cricket. As in so many territories which the British invaded, cricket was used to foster unity amongst the military and administrative colonizers and to proselytize to the indigenous population. The Irish gentry adopted the game as an expression of their 'civilization' and their suitability for collaboration, and the game spread geographically and socially until, in 1860, it was thought to be the country's most popular sport. This was the basis for Irish immigrants to play the game in settler colonies like Australia, but a game so closely connected to the cultural expression of Englishness was, of course, bound to suffer as Irish nationalism grew. Cricket remained a marginal, but island-wide, activity. This provides the foundations of Irish playing strength today but, most importantly for present purposes, Gemmell argues that what he identifies as the two key chapters in the country's history – nationalism and the diaspora – are fundamental to an understanding of Irish cricket.

Dean Allen illustrates the enduring pattern of the diffusion of cricket, examining the game's role in the colonization of South Africa. In contrast to Britain's relatively early domination of Ireland, Allen describes the contestation of Southern Africa as perhaps the last major act of British colonization, noting that the Boer War coincided with the Golden Age of English cricket. Thus while the cultural context from which the game was diffused was radically different to the Irish case, Allen's analysis focuses on similar processes to those identified by Gemmell thereby pointing to a cross-cultural continuity.

Alan Bairner's contribution supplements Gemmell's work in particular, but advances our understanding of the diffusion of the game more generally, with an examination of the role of Irish-Australians in cricket. The case study of the Irish diaspora in Australia throws into sharper relief the problematic relationship between imperialism and the experience of being colonized and is particularly useful in highlighting the fluidity of these processes, with Ireland best conceived of as both imperial and colonial at the same time. In answering the question, 'Why have the "Irish" been manifestly more prominent in Australian (rather than Irish) cricket?', Bairner notes that Irish emigrants encountered a 'schizophrenic' sporting culture in Australia. Cricket was rooted in the national landscape of Ireland and an Irish national habitus, but used as a vehicle through which immigrants could foster Australian identity via a demonstration of anti-Britishness.

From Bairner we move to an analysis of perhaps the first, and certainly the most famous, statement on cricket and colonialism/postcolonialism, C.L.R. James's *Beyond a Boundary*. While much has been written about James's immersion in English literature and his relationship with other Marxist cultural theorists, his work's correlation to, and indeed his reverence for, English cricket writing has largely been overlooked. Anthony Bateman corrects this oversight and thus alerts us to another problematic feature of the commingling of cultures inherent in the process of cultural diffusion. As Bateman notes, the discursive conventions of English cricket writing were the only available means for depicting the Caribbean game. However, they were wholly unfit for purpose, unable to convey the distinctiveness of Caribbean styles of play. Bateman adds to our picture of cultural diffusion by illustrating the importance of linguistics in shaping postcolonial politics.

Jack Williams returns our focus to the 'mother country', which thus reminds us that just as colonial cultures need to be conceived of as complex and dynamic, so the culture of the imperial power is in process, adapting to internally driven factors as well as external forces. Williams' examination of Fred Trueman, an English cricket celebrity of the 1950s and 1960s, reveals the importance of changing attitudes towards regionalism, social class and youth in post-war Britain. Trueman's challenge to the cricketing (and wider political) establishment shows us that the cultural product of the imperialists was neither homogeneous nor accurately depicted in stereotypes of the game.[21] As with previous contributions, however, Trueman's case reveals a tension between continuity and change – the influence of tradition on revolution – for his desire was to facilitate access to the social elite rather than to upturn the social order.

Continuity and change, colonial and imperial relations, similarly form the backdrop to our next contribution. Charles Little's essay, 'Rebellion, Race and Rhodesia', provides some historical context to recent debates over Zimbabwe's participation in international cricket (see Holden in this collection), by reviewing the 1965–79 period when Rhodesia (as it was then called), 'existed as an international pariah state'. Little argues that the early cricketing boycotts of Rhodesia were, and have been, overshadowed by events in South Africa. In some respects this is unfortunate for, as Little points out, the campaigns against Rhodesia were more overtly politically-orientated (i.e. aimed at changing the political regime) and less sports-orientated (i.e. protesting against racism within a particular sport) than has often been the case with sports boycotts. We could conclude that the 'amnesia' over Rhodesia has allowed UK governments to continue to propound the view of 'no politics in sport' and escape charges of hypocrisy. This allows the colonial power to suggest that it is the challengers to, rather than the defenders of, the status quo who infringe the conventions of sports diplomacy and therefore lack legitimacy.

One such challenger to British cricketing and cultural hegemony, Vivian Richards, is discussed in our next contribution. Like so much West Indian cricket literature, James is a prominent reference point here, and Malcolm MacLean argues that Richards' idea of West Indian nationalism was just as much a product of its time – post-Black power, post-civil rights movement, and in the context of an emerging neo-liberal global order – as was James's nationalism. MacLean focuses on Richards' autobiography, *Hitting Across the Line,* a title which has both literal and metaphorical connotations. Hitting across the line refers to both a type of batting stroke for which Richards was renowned and which may, in part, have been a consequence of playing in Caribbean environmental conditions, and a kind of cultural resistance which Richards' embodied, a notion of the importance of doing one's own thing in contrast to the prescriptions of the colonial period. Richards therefore emphasizes the importance of place, and Antiguan cricket pitches in particular, whereas James emphasizes the impact of English cultural mores. Temporally this essay comes between Bateman and Westall (and latterly Majumdar), but theoretically it most closely links with Bairner's work and ideas about the multiplicity of identities in particular. As MacLean notes, 'Cricket is one of the few, if not the only, site of a singular West Indies-ness, even if it is restricted only to the British West Indies. West Indies sporting nationalism is therefore asserted as a West Indian thing in some contexts, or as of a specific island or island group in others'.[22]

In the next contribution, Claire Westall considers Brian Lara, the West Indian who is perhaps the most natural heir to Viv Richards in a cricketing (if not necessarily nationalistic) sense. In an argument which parallels MacLean's, Westall suggests that a reading of Lara poems reveals the Caribbean's ongoing negotiation between the one and the many – hence *mwe*. Moreover, just as MacLean argues that Richards' nationalism was just as much a product of its time as was James's, Lara is at one and the same time, both an agent in, and a product of, the commercialized and globalized social structure in which he is historically located. Westall draws on T.S. Eliot and Edward Said to suggest that both the individual and the broader populations in imperial and post-colonial societies are contoured by 'perpetual (re)negotiations between past, present and future'.[23]

In the next reading Michael Roberts provides what is, essentially, a history of Sri Lankan cricket. However, whilst his approach is not explicitly couched in these terms, he charts many of the tensions relating to colonialism and post-colonialism already discussed. Roberts identifies nine thematic threads to cricket in post-independent Sri Lanka, including: the diffusion of the game within Sri Lanka (geographically, across different social classes and across different schools) and by Sri Lankan's globally (particularly to the English county game and in cities like London); the rather paradoxical combination of anti-Western attitudes and interest in the game; and the developing media interest in cricket. He notes, however, that internal political conflicts and status battles within Sri Lanka may have harmed the game's development and reflects on recent international success which, ironically, he largely accredits to the coaching of Tom Moody; that is to say, the (re-) importation of cricketing skills from the West which may be interpreted as a new form of (technocratic) colonialism (see also Wagg and Ugra in this collection). What we see in this reading, therefore, is another illustration of the role of cricket in identity formation.

We continue with the theme of identity in the next two contributions whilst shifting geographical focus to India. For Nalin Mehta, the well-documented argument that cricket's growth was closely connected to the development of Indian national identity is a point of departure. Mehta charts how the pre-eminence of cricket in India was far from inevitable, with hockey and also football vying for supremacy prior to the 1980s. Cricket's relationship with Indian national identity owes much to the somewhat serendipitous convergence of the development of television in India, the declining fortune of India's hockey team, and India's first major international cricketing victory, the 1983 World Cup win. These factors sparked the intense relationship between cricket and television, and cricket has subsequently been a central feature in all the main debates about the further development of television in India, and satellite television in particular. In turn, the finance provided by media companies has been instrumental in cementing India's place as the hub of the international game in the early twenty-first century.

Read in conjunction with Wagg and Ugra's contribution, Mehta's essay further illuminates our understanding of imperial and post-colonial relations. The finance provided by the Indian media is in many ways one of the preconditions to the employment of an Australian, Greg Chappell, as coach of the Indian cricket team. Whilst on the face of it this development might appear to be a manifestation of India's growing power in the international game, Wagg and Ugra argue that the more widespread and growing trend of 'eastern' cricket nations employing 'western' coaches is an example of the tendency towards technocratic cultural imperialism evident as a consequence of broader globalization processes. Debates about Chappell's coaching philosophy centred around ethnic stereotyping of Australians and Indians, characteristic of what Barker has called 'new racism',[24] but interestingly there was considerable convergence between 'eastern' and 'western' perceptions of each others' 'group charisma and group disgrace' (see Velija and Malcolm for an exposition of these terms). On the one hand Wagg and Ugra point toward a homogenization/Americanization thesis of globalization, while on the other, through the forceful reassertion of cultural distinction, and examples of Indian corporate harnessing of Chappell as a source of commercial profit, they point towards a model of globalization characterized by elements of hybridity.

Shifting, hybrid and commingling senses of national identity are also the focus of Malcolm's contribution, 'Malign or Benign? English National Identities in Cricket'. Malcolm argues that there has been a marked, or more overt, strengthening of English national identity in recent years in response to both internal (the devolution of power to a Scottish parliament and Welsh assembly) and 'external' or international pressures (closer European integration, increased rates of migration, Britain's waning position as a world power). In the context of these, and indeed many of the post-colonial struggles outlined in other contributions in this collection, discourse about what it means to be English, and the characteristics which English people would like to see themselves as possessing, have altered. Malcolm argues that whilst the English media depicted a 'malign' nationalism in the 1980s and early 1990s (closed, defensive, insular) more recent coverage of cricket has becoming increasingly reminiscent of a benign Englishness (open, tolerant, cosmopolitan and multicultural).

Malcolm's essay concludes by questioning just how tangible this shift in identity is, and provides some evidence of the continuity of exclusionary practices in the next essay, co-authored with Philippa Velija. Velija and Malcolm chart the grassroots conservatism of English cricket, identifying the mechanisms by which increasing female participation is resisted by the 'established' males. In addition to highlighting the masculinist-orientation of so much cricket scholarship, Velija and Malcolm connect with this collection's recurrent themes: the importance of identity; its multiple and overlapping forms; the role of cricket in fostering and challenging competing identities; and the playing out of power relations between dominated and dominating groups through the sport.

Our next three essays take us back to a focus on the elite end of the game, and draw our attention to the changes invoked by the increasing commercialization of the game. Russell Holden examines British cricketing relations with Zimbabwe in recent years (extending Little's historical analysis) and suggests that governmental authority is declining in comparison to that of multi-national conglomerates. He suggests that cricket administrators' desires to expand the game lead them to ignore questions of morality.

Commercialization is also a guiding theme of Boria Majumdar's account of the impact and likely legacy of the 2007 Cricket World Cup. Drawing on his experiences and travels as a journalist, Majumdar suggests that the ICC's rather successful pursuit of profit at this event led to the neglect of the local populations and smaller businesses within the Caribbean. In local terms, therefore, the event has come to be seen as an economic failure. Majumdar further laments the somewhat sanitized, 'un-Caribbean' character of proceedings and, ultimately, he concludes that hosting the mega-event will have had little positive impact in fostering greater unity among the peoples of the Anglophone Caribbean nations.

Rob Steen further reflects on the impact of commercialization on the players themselves. He questions whether increasing demands on the world's leading players will lead to an increase in burnout and proposes a blueprint such that the game can retain the strengths of its historical legacy whilst successfully exploiting the ever developing financial opportunities for sports at the beginning of the twenty-first century. Of course, what drives the public demand for cricket, and indeed any other sport, is not simply a matter of what is entertaining, but the degree to which events are deemed to be meaningful. As this collection of essays demonstrates, cricket is meaningful for so many people because they rely on it for the construction of a core component of their identity. In this regard nation, imperialism, post-colonialism and globalization are the key sensitizing concepts for an understanding of the social role of the game.

Ehsan Mani, former President of the ICC, develops these sensitizing concepts in the penultimate essay in this collection. Reflecting on the future challenges and prospects for the game, Mani adds to this broader perspective by addressing the importance of bridging the gulf between the emerging and the leading (and finance generating) cricketing nations, the importance of developing women's cricket internationally, and of recognizing the game's social responsibilities (e.g. harnessing the popularity of cricket and cricketers to develop AIDS awareness programmes). His reflections on the exclusionary aspects of the game's early development contrast with his claim that cricket is the second most popular sport in the world today. Together, however, these points neatly underscore the central theme of this introductory essay: that contemporary cricket possesses, at one and the same time, both highly modern and peculiarly *un*modern characteristics.

The volume concludes with a piece that examines the rapid changes going on in the cricket world as this volume was being put together. Nalin Mehta, Jon Gemmell and Dominic Malcolm describe the establishment of the Indian Premier League (IPL), complete with its player auctions and franchises, and two of the key international crises in world cricket in recent years: the Darrell Hair and the Harbajan Singh affairs. Linking these disparate events are notions of colonialism, post-colonialism and the rising economic power of Indian cricket. Whilst the collection opens with a discussion of the multifaceted nature of the colonial diffusion of the game, it ends by reflecting on just how far the process of independence and national self-assertion have come: are the colonized (or at least some colonized populations) embarking on a new process of (largely economic rather than military) colonization?

## Notes

[1]   Dunning and Sheard, *Barbarians, Gentlemen and Players*.
[2]   Cited in Rait Kerr, *The Laws of Cricket*, 91.
[3]   Dunning and Sheard, *Barbarians, Gentlemen and Players*.
[4]   Mangan, *Athleticism in the Victorian and Edwardian Public School*.
[5]   See Rait Kerr, *The Laws of Cricket*; Brookes, *English Cricket*; Birley, *A Social History of English Cricket*.
[6]   See Tomlinson, 'FIFA and the Men who Made It'. For an extended discussion of the development of FIFA see Sugden and Tomlinson, *FIFA and the Contest for the Global Game*.
[7]   Nandy, *The Tao of Cricket*, 1.
[8]   Guha, 'The Miracle that is India'. *Outlook*, May 7, 2007.
[9]   Dunning and Sheard, *Barbarians, Gentlemen and Players*, 30–1.
[10]   Guttmann, *From Ritual to Record*.
[11]   Guttmann, '*From Ritual to Record* (and the Paradigm of Modern Sport)'.
[12]   The degree to which this has been rational is a rather moot point. The administration of the domestic game in England and the international game has not, historically, matched the wider trend towards democratic representation that we've seen in other governing bodies of sport. In England the ceding of powers by the MCC and the establishment of the Test and County Cricket Board in 1968 can be seen as a significant event in this regard, and whilst the MCC no longer has de facto control over the ICC, the system of having full, associate and affiliate member nations neatly circumvents the moral obligation towards a 'one member one vote' system that we see, e.g., in FIFA, the IOC, athletics etc.

[13] Huw Richards, 'Cricket: As Cricket Grows Up, its Panel Leave Home'. *International Herald and Tribune*, August 1, 2005.

[14] See http://www.lords.org/laws-and-spirit/laws-of-cricket/.

[15] Malcolm, 'Cricket and Civilizing Processes'.

[16] Note that the one-day game is itself not a unified entity, with games having taken place on the basis of between 40- and 65-over innings. In recent years, largely driven by member nations' desire for international success in the Cricket World Cup, the format of the game has standardized at around 50 overs per side.

[17] Aakash Chopra, 'Mind the Slope Boys'. Cricinfo, July 20, 2007. http://content-usa.cricinfo.com/columns/content/story/302207.html.

[18] Whilst other sports in England have had competitions based on the county system, most notably rugby union in recent years, it is interesting to note that the GAA is the other sports governing body to retain the county as its central unit of representation.

[19] Keith Sandiford, 'Introduction', 1.

[20] Garland, Malcolm and Rowe, *The Future of Football*; Brown, *Fanatics*; Magee, Bairner and Tomlinson, *The Bountiful Game*.

[21] This point is similarly made in Malcolm, 'The Diffusion of Cricket to America'.

[22] MacLean, 'A National(ist) Line in Postcolonizing Cricket', 527.

[23] Westall, 'Brian Lara in Poetic Form', 537.

[24] Barker, *The New Racism*.

## References

Barker, Martin. *The New Racism*. London: Junction Books, 1981.

Beckles, Hilary. *The Development of West Indies Cricket: Volume 1, The Age of Nationalism*. London: Pluto Press, 1998.

Beckles, Hilary. *The Development of West Indies Cricket: Volume 2, The Age of Globalization*. London: Pluto Press, 1998.

Beckles, Hilary, and Brian Stoddart. *Liberation Cricket: West Indies Cricket Culture*. Manchester: Manchester University Press, 1995.

Birley, Derek. *A Social History of English Cricket*. London: Aurum Press, 1999.

Brookes, Christopher. *English Cricket: The Game and its Players through the Ages*. London: Weidenfeld and Nicolson, 1978.

Brown, Adam. *Fanatics: Power, Identity and Fandom in Football*. London: Routledge, 1998.

Dunning, Eric, and Kenneth Sheard. *Barbarians, Gentlemen and Players: A Sociological Study of the Development of Rugby Football*. 2nd ed. London: Routledge, 2005.

Garland, Jon, Dominic Malcolm, and Mike Rowe. *The Future of Football: Challenges for the Twenty-First Century*. London: Frank Cass, 2000.

Gemmell, Jon. *The Politics of South African Cricket*. London: Frank Cass, 2004.

Guha, Ramachandra. *A Corner of a Foreign Field: The Indian History of a British Sport*. London: Picador, 2002.

Guttmann, Allen. *From Ritual to Record: The Nature of Modern Sport*. New York: Columbia University Press, 2004 (1978).

Guttmann, Allen, '*From Ritual to Record* (and the Paradigm of Modern Sport)'. In *The Sage Dictionary of Sport Studies*, Dominic Malcolm, 107–9. London: Sage, 2008.

MacLean, Malcolm. 'A National(ist) Line in Postcolonizing Cricket: Viv Richards, Biographies and Cricketing Nationalism'. *Sport in Society* 12, no. 4/5 (2009): 537–50.

Magee, Jonathon, Alan Bairner, and Alan Tomlinson. *The Bountiful Game? Football, Identities and Finances*. Oxford: Meyer and Meyer, 2005.

Majumdar, Boria. *An Indian Cricket Reader*. Oxford: Oxford University Press, 2005.

Majumdar, Boria. *A Social History of Indian Cricket: Twenty-Two Yards to Freedom*. London: Routledge, 2006.

Malcolm, Dominic. 'Cricket and Civilizing Processes: A Response to Stokvis'. *International Review for the Sociology of Sport* 37, no. 1 (2002): 37–57.

Malcolm, Dominic. 'The Diffusion of Cricket to America: A Figurational Sociological Examination'. *Journal of Historical Sociology* 19, no. 2 (2006): 151–73.

Mangan, James A. *Athleticism in the Victorian and Edwardian Public School – The Emergence and Consolidation of an Educational Ideology*. Cambridge: Cambridge University Press, 1981.

Murray, Bruce, and Christopher Merrett. *Caught Behind: Race and Politics in Springbok Cricket.* Johannesburg and Scottsville: Wits University Press and University of KwaZulu-Natal Press, 2004.

Nandy, Ashis. *The Tao of Cricket: On Games of Destiny and the Destiny of the Games.* New York: Viking, 1989.

Rait Kerr, Rowan S. *The Laws of Cricket: Their History and Growth.* London: Longmans, Green and Co, 1950.

Sandiford, Keith. 'Introduction'. In *The Imperial Game: Cricket, Culture and Society*, edited by Brian Stoddart and Keith Sandiford, 1–8. Manchester: Manchester University Press, 1998.

Stoddart, Brian, and Keith Sandiford. *The Imperial Game: Cricket, Culture and Society.* Manchester: Manchester University Press, 1998.

Sugden, John, and Alan Tomlinson. *FIFA and the Contest for the Global Game.* Oxford: Polity Press, 1998.

Tomlinson, Alan. 'Fifa and the Men who Made It'. In *The Future of Football: Challenges for the Twenty-First Century*, edited by Jon Garland, Dominic Malcolm, and Mike Rowe, 55–71. London: Frank Cass, 2000.

Wagg, Stephen. *Cricket and National Identity in the Post Colonial Age.* London: Routledge, 2005.

Westall, Clare. 'Brian Lara in Poetic Form: Tradition, Talent and the Caribbean 'mwe'. *Sport in Society* 12, no. 4/5 (2009): 551–65.

Williams, Jack. *Cricket and England: A Cultural and Social History of the Inter-war Years.* London: Frank Cass, 1999.

Winch, Jonty. *Cricket in Southern Africa.* Rosettenville: Windsor, 1997.

# Naturally played by Irishmen: a social history of Irish cricket

Jon Gemmell*

*Kennet School, Thatcham, Berkshire, UK*

One of the few memorable features of a disappointing 2007 World Cup was the efforts of the Irish cricket team, initially in the group stages in which they tied with Zimbabwe and beat Pakistan, and then with a victory over a second Test-playing side – Bangladesh – in the second stage, guaranteeing them a place on the ICC one-day international championship table. In the longer form, Ireland subsequently crushed Canada by an innings and 115 runs in the ICC Intercontinental Cup to assume the lofty heights of champion associate member and a claim, following Zimbabwe's rapid descent, for being in the world's top ten in both formats of the sport. Unfortunately, comparisons with Test-playing sides end here, as the Irish could not be more remote from the wealthy athletes who enjoy lucrative contracts for India, Australia and England. Theirs is a return to a bygone age when cricketers combined sport with holding down a job. The team that went to the Caribbean, for example, included a postal worker, an electrician, a van driver, a storeman and two students, one of whom is a farmer in the off-season. Twenty-four hours after Phil Simmons took over as coach following the World Cup he lost his assistant Matt Dwyer, who cited financial pressures as a key reason for his departure. The best native players such as Ed Joyce are lured by the prospects of international cricket and seek their fortunes with England, whilst the likes of Eoin Morgan and Boyd Rankin are forced to consider professional commitments to their counties alongside those of playing for their country.[1]

In the face of many obstacles, Irish cricket boasts a lengthy heritage that compares favourably with any national side outside of England. This inevitably draws one into the consideration of the elements that permit growth and dissemination of sporting culture in some situations, or restricted growth and rejection in others. Mass preference is difficult to measure outside of attendance figures, participation rates or viewers, but why do the aesthetics of a sport prevail in one society and not another? In the age of mass communications, one is inclined to seek answers in the manipulation of the mass media by marketing strategists that enable sports such as basketball to set root and then flourish.

On a historical basis, though, the factors that contribute to the expansion and longevity of sport are linked to culture and are therefore social above all else. This makes the task of this essay the consideration of Irish cricket in the social context of its past. By this, I mean an examination of historical, political and cultural phenomena, and these areas underlie the following four sections exploring the origins, growth, decline and contemporary condition of Irish cricket.

## A direct link to a political role

The origins and early roots of any sport are usually steeped in mystery and mythology, none more so than cricket. *The Oxford Dictionary of English Etymology* (1966) suggests that the words 'cricket', 'wicket' and 'crease' first appeared in the English language during Anglo-Saxon times and many of the terms familiar with the sport today derive from the Old French dialogue.[2] We have to shape a picture from scant evidence and this, of course, leads to inaccuracy and incompleteness. It does seem plausible, though, to suppose that games involving balls and some form of hitting implement existed before the arrival of their documentation. Indeed, Altham and Swanton's *A History of Cricket* actually opens with the line: 'The instinct to throw and to hit is the basis of man's primitive armoury'.[3]

Is there any reason to suppose that ancient games in Ireland were different to those of her neighbours? We know that there were myriad of bat and ball folk games in England, that each was accustomed to their own regulation and that many would provide certain ingredients for the sport that cricket would become. We know of many of these because of their prohibition, usually as they clashed with the dictates of Church or State. Similarly, in Ireland games such as 'feat of Cat' and 'shoot at the hole' are mentioned in the story of the legendary character Cu Chulainn whilst 'krickett' was banned in 1656 by Cromwell's Commissioners who burned 'sticks made of ash'. Hurling had been proscribed in the Statutes of Kilkenny in 1366 as a covert means of military training and a pamphlet on the origins of cricket claims that the young men of Kilkenny took up the game 'cattie'. Folklore relates how some English landlords supported the game and maintained playing fields on their estates.[4] Recruited into the British Army from as early as the twelfth century the spectacle of young Irish soldiers playing cattie would attract the attention of their British colleagues. According to James Caulfield, these games would be modified and brought home to England where it was recognized as 'cat', 'old cat' or more often 'cricket'.[5] The historian Rowland Bowen had already suggested that Irish cricket would have taken on its own folk-forms being 'a game naturally played by Irishmen as a natural thing'.[6] It is possible that one of the games to which he is referring is 'cattie' which comes from the Irish word 'caith' or 'cat', though it is also conceivable that what we think of as cricket has been misidentified as a form of the ancient Irish sport of hurling. It is however likely that a form of cricket would have been played in Ireland long before its introduction in its codified form by the British at the end of the eighteenth century.

In its modern organized format, cricket is an imperial sport, carried in the boats that took settlers to new lands and spread by the missionary and teacher alongside other cultural traits supposedly designed to transform lives for the better. This link with colonialism is further marked by cricket's written history starting as an activity between military sides. A.M.C. Thorburn, the official historian of the Scottish Cricket Union, considers the 1745 Jacobite Rebellion as playing a key role in popularizing the sport because of the introduction of the army into Scotland.[7] The military were also the first to play cricket in the Caribbean at the end of the eighteenth century, and in Southern Africa during the occupation of the Cape in 1795–1802. As a military presence denotes either conquest, fear of rebellion or invasion, it implies for cricket a link to the power mechanisms and hence a political role. Stanley Bergin and Derek Scott wrote in their contribution to the prestigious *Barclays World of Cricket* that 'to gain a true picture of the history of cricket in Ireland it is necessary to relate the game to the political and social life of the country in the eighteenth century'.[8] They are referring to the presence of the British who had traditionally seen Ireland as a threat, due primarily to a reluctance to follow the conversion to Protestantism. Ireland was ruled through a Dublin executive and a gentry dominated by Anglicans whose descent derived from Norman, Old English, Cromwellian or even ancient Gaelic. Anglicanism conferred exclusivity and this elite monopolized the law, politics and 'society'.[9] They also provide the earliest reference to an organized cricket contest at Fifteen Acres in Phoenix Park in 1792, when 11 of the Garrison played an All-Ireland side for 1,000 guineas. An examination of the cast reinforces the link to authority with the Irish including the later Duke of Wellington,[10] and Major Hobart, Secretary at War, member of both Irish and English Commons and between 1789–93 Chief Secretary to the Lord Lieutenant of Ireland,[11] the most powerful figure in Irish politics. Edward Cooke, the under-secretary at Dublin Castle opened the batting with Hobart while the ranks were swelled by five MPs from the Irish House of Commons. The Garrison side was captained by Lt-Colonel Lennox, a founder of the MCC, who would return to Ireland in 1807 as Lord Lieutenant.

Encouraged initially as a means to replicate the home environment in the colonies, cricket provided a vessel through which the ruling authorities could instil values firstly into settler communities and through them to the indigenous population. If we consider that by 1792 the British aristocracy faced the dual threat of revolt from below alongside an intellectual onslaught via the French revolution, then it allows us at least a context for the introduction of organized cricket into Ireland. The Society of United Irishmen, founded in 1791, outlined its objectives as the removal of both religious distinctions and the British obstacle to true representation in a national parliament, whilst other oath-bound organizations sought redress for enclosure, harsh taxation and high rents. They were countered with repressive legislation that sought to suppress a population through flogging, torture and the threat of transportation, further helping to push an increasingly hostile people towards union with the French and wider social upheaval. The union between Ireland and England was a consequence of the 1798 rebellion and provides organized cricket's revolutionary backdrop. Yet it started as an exclusive preserve played amongst the army, civil servants and a few MPs – hardly the stuff from which foundations are established – and for the next 40 years there were only brief references made to it in the records.

## Designed for civilized gentlemen

After a slow start, by 1840 there were dozens of cricket clubs scattered around the country. Initial impetus came from a military presence of up to 30,000 soldiers garrisoned in the aftermath of the 1798 rebellion and the subsequent act of union that formally incorporated Ireland into the British State. Early reports in 1800 had spoken of contests between military teams in Cork, where cricket took root among several garrison towns – Mallow, Fermoy, Bandon, Kinsale and Cobh – and in Kilkenny and Ballinasloe. Their presence in Ireland though was not to just protect British commercial interests, but also those of the Irish gentrified class – whose wealth derived from the confiscations and plantations of earlier centuries. The gentry saw themselves not as colonials, but as Irishmen who enjoyed English civil rights,[12] and partook in civil life, becoming allies with the English to the extent that allowed the Dublin cricketer and entrepreneur John Lawrence to note that cricket 'formed a bond of union between the country gentlemen of the day'.[13]

The country mansion was a symbol of improved returns from agriculture, and the additional ownership or association with a cricket ground brought with it status. The first documented club, Ballinasloe, County Galway was founded by Lord Dunto in 1825. Dunto was also a member of the Dublin Club formed in 1830, which became the Phoenix Club, one of Ireland's most famous and oldest sides, which also included Lord Clonbrook as a member. The Lord Lieutenant, the 7th Earl of Carlisle, had a cricket field installed next to his official residence, the Viceregal Lodge in Phoenix Park and established the Viceregal XI. The Viceregal establishment involved all the excesses of a small court and was the centre of the 'fashionable' world. By endorsing cricket it further encouraged aspiring gentlemen to patronise the sport and certain matches became more than mere contest, being important social occasions in which those interested in cricket intermingled with those whose greater concern was the latest styles and mixing with the right people. The highlight of the season involved contests against I Zingari who made several visits to Ireland. Being founded by a group of old Harrovians, the intention of the invitation-only membership was to own no ground of their own but to play at any country house where they would be provided suitable hospitality. Membership included key individuals in the cricketing, political and financial elites, ensuring an accommodation at the Viceregal Lodge where the sides combined playing cricket with attendance at luxurious balls and banquets. An Irish equivalent, 'Na Shuler', formed in 1863 by members of the gentry, was listed alongside the Free Foresters, Incogniti and Etceteras as leading amateur clubs with resemblances to I Zingari and continued until the First World War.

Cricket carried with it an ethos that not only governed the sport, but set out a social code designed for the civilized gentleman to pass down to those under his tutelage. The imperialist Sir Hercules Robinson[14] argued that the promotion of sport was amongst the duties of a governor, because 'a similarity of taste in amusements is a guarantee for common sympathy in more important matters'.[15] Rules, authority and the notion of fair play were all concepts favoured by a conquering power, and therefore should be learned by all. Fair play represented a standard of honesty and the correct way to do things in civilized society, whilst 'playing the game' as a moral activity was seen as an exercise in being English. The rules of conduct stated that the umpire (the authority) had to make many difficult decisions, and whilst he occasionally got it wrong, he was impartial and should never be questioned or doubted. A true gentleman would always observe the spirit as well as the letter of the law, and should conduct himself with dignity and honour even in the face of injustice. This ensured not only a moral ascendancy over established rules, but also a means to infuse the sport with a set of norms and values, even when the laws do not account for them.

Dissemination of this ethos was worked through a variety of forms, such as the club and the media, though it would be in the classroom where its essence would be evaluated and promoted as fact in the interests of the 'common good'. As late as the 1890s, one Derry headmaster noted that sports, including cricket, taught 'lessons of courage, of modesty, of command of temper, of consideration for the weak, of self-respect and respect for others, of obedience to lawful authority, of power to govern as well as to obey'.[16]

Cricket was played at Trinity College, the training centre of the Anglican ruling-class, by English school students from 1820, and later at elite establishments such as Clongowes, County Kildare, Portora, Royal School Dungannon and the Royal Belfast Academical Institute. These institutions challenged local clubs and invited English public schools to visit. Queens College (now University College, Cork) regularly opened seasons with a contest against the Cork City Club, whilst College Park Dublin became the centre of Irish cricket, promoting fixtures against top English sides and playing touring Australians (1880 and 1905), South Africans (1894, 1901, 1904) and West Indians (1923).

According to the *Oxford Companion to Irish History*, by 1860 cricket had probably become the most popular sport in Ireland.[17] This expansion would not have been possible if it was merely a sport exclusive to an elite. If the instinct to 'play' lies within each of us, then it is only reasonable to suppose that the enjoyment of sport will attract observers and imitators. W.J. O'Neill Daunt, a Catholic landowner, spoke of 'the social rendezvous it promotes', where aristocrats, squireen and Protestant clerics rubbed shoulders with Catholic peasants. According to Daunt, cricket provided a community spirit throughout Ireland and great matches aroused corresponding interest in the lower classes.[18] In his book *Proud and Upright Men, The History of Tuam Stars Gaelic Football Club*, Noel O'Donoghue wrote of how the footballers had their beginnings in Tuam Cricket Club.[19] The publication in 1865 of the *Handbook of Cricket in Ireland* further confirms this broader interest, and demonstrates that, for the 15 years of the annual's publication at least, cricket was being played in workplaces as well as schools, colleges and universities, and by the military.[20] Tom Hunt's research showed that even where teams were put together by wealthy estate holders, labourers and farmers would be used to make up the eleven on the field, so that by the early years of the last century, cricket was also 'a working man's game'.[21]

Industrial expansion naturally accentuates the development and diversity of cultural activities. The railway allowed Irish villages to forge greater links with the centres, initially through trading, but ultimately in cultural fields such as dialects, literature, political attitudes and sport. The rise of literacy, the telegraph, the printing press and subsequent advertising permitted the propagation of ideas and tastes. The expansion of urban centres provided further stimulus for working-class sport. In Belfast, where the growth of the linen and shipbuilding trades saw a population increase from 120,000 in 1861 to 350,000 40 years later,[22] industrialists sought to influence the leisure activities of their workers and many provided grounds such as Sion Mills and Donacloney. Playing for the company helped to reinforce loyalty, whilst being associated with an English sport helped to ensure a sense of commonality with the industry's largest market.

The extent of cricket's popularity was underpinned by the overseas tour. The English professional Charles Lawrence, employed by Phoenix Cricket Club in the early 1850s, used his contacts to organize a visit by the Marylebone Cricket Club (MCC) in 1853. Two years later the fixture against the Gentlemen of England became Ireland's first representative game, which they duly won.[23] The Gentlemen of England exacted their revenge the following year, and it looked as if the fixture would become a regular one. In 1858, the Irish travelled to England for the first time and defeated the MCC by an innings at Lord's, followed by further victories at the home of cricket in both 1862 and 1868. International opponents were not restricted to England. The first Australian team visited in 1880 and the South Africans visited three times between 1894 and 1914. Links were also established with North America and the Canadians visited in 1887, the Philadelphians in 1879, 1884 and 1908, whilst the Irish toured the continent no less than four times during a 30-year period.[24]

By the 1870s cricket had become a 32 county sport and whilst the number of clubs fluctuated, there was little reason to suppose that the game would not benefit from the increasing demand for leisure that was a consequence of social and economic development. Research by Tom Hunt on cricket reveals that between 1880 and 1905 there were 130 different cricket clubs in Tipperary alone, and that 940 matches featuring 173 different teams were played in the county of Westmeath.[25] However, you cannot study the evolution of cricket in any country without considering its social backdrop. As resistance to an imperial presence grew, it took on forms that were cultural as much as anything else.

*The Handbook of Cricket in Ireland* highlighted not only the spread of cricket to all classes, but also to both Catholic and Protestant communities. The most prominent cricketing school in the 1840s and 1850s, for example, had been the Church of Ireland's St Columba's, where the sport flourished in a nationalist environment.[26] Some of the earliest clubs had been established in Ballinasloe, Carlow and Kilkenny, all of which would subsequently become strongholds of Gaelic sports. However, being associated as the sport of the English, cricket did not fit an emerging nationalist consciousness that lamented the neglect of the old ways. In 1857, an Irish observer mourned the 'passing away' of the games of football and hurling, and their replacement by 'the stupid game of quoits or the more prevailing one of cricket'.[27] In 1873 in County Limerick, a local newspaper grudgingly noted the popularity of 'the English game of cricket' at the expense of hurling, whilst by 1904, it was simply condemned as 'a thoroughly English game', controlled from London and therefore fostering a mental dependence upon England.[28]

Yet, as with the nationalist movement in India, the emerging political opposition proved to have been enthusiastic proponents of the sport. In 1843, for example, the *Nation,* an organ of Daniel O'Connell's Repeal Association, regretted that 'this manly game' of cricket was making insufficient progress in Ireland. This was attributed to sectarian hostilities, the failure of Irish landlords to sponsor cricket amongst their tenants, and the misery of the ordinary people that left them without the stamina necessary for the game.[29] John Redmond, the leader of the Irish Parliamentary Party, 1900–18, and former honorary secretary of the Clongowes College Cricket Club, remarked on a visit to his old school, that during his days there he had learned simply 'that the highest duty of a gentleman was . . . to play the game'.[30] His brother Willie Redmond also played at Clongowes, as did James Joyce and Irish Party MP Tom Kettle. Political legend Charles Stewart Parnell played for Avondale as a boy, Magdalene College, Cambridge as a student, County Wicklow for a decade and finally Phoenix. While he ceased to attend cricket matches after entering parliament, his passion for the game continued to such an extent that his mistress and later wife Katherine O'Shea had a private pitch laid out for him at her house at Eltham.[31] Republican Cathal Brugha was a fast bowler at Belvedere, whilst future prime minister and president of the Free State, Eamon De Valera applied his talents at Blackrode College.

This affection for the sport has to be considered alongside the fact that Ireland's nationalist leaders were recruited from the middle class and so would have had greater exposure to cricket. This attachment, though, would be challenged by a rising consciousness that firstly distrusted, and then disapproved, of association with anything English. Cricket had enjoyed a wide range of support and though it was associated with the elite and middle class there was evidence that it was also widely enjoyed by workers and agricultural labourers. There was, therefore, nothing intrinsically alien about the sport, yet its progress faltered and whilst we can attribute this to the structure and characteristics of the sport and increased competition from other leisure activities, any analysis of retardation requires broader social and political consideration.

**Vehicles for Irish nationalism**

Cricket was carried to the colonies, not merely as a means of entertainment or to maintain cultural links with home, but also because within its ethos lay the fundamentals of the 'civilized' life and the ways of the educated Englishman. Cricket was the quintessential game of the English, for 'wherever Englishmen go', proclaimed Lord Hawke, 'they take cricket with them'.[32] As a cultural expression of Englishness it is not difficult to see how it would become embroiled in any wider cultural struggle, and thereby in a greater political campaign for independence.

There are two ways that anti-colonial movements have tended to approach cricket: ignore it as the sport of the conqueror and colonialist, refuting both foreign rule and its cultural associations; alternatively imbue the sport with 'national' sentiments, overwhelm the colonialists at their own game, and use sports in the process of asserting independence and identity. Whilst in the US cricket fell victim to an alien code of norms and values and was replaced by baseball as something more 'American', in Australia it proved a motivating force for defeating the English, and in the Caribbean formed part of the political struggle for national self-determination.

Nationalism is expressed as both a set of ideas and a form of behaviour. As a political ideology, it is associated with belonging to a community, most principally the nation, from which are believed to derive certain common attitudes that stem from the experience of common traditions and historical development. Benedict Anderson has argued that, culturally, the nation emerges with the arrival of the printed language and is therefore a relatively recent phenomenon, though it frequently draws its inspiration from the past.[33] National literatures arise to express popular customs and the so-called common spirit of the people, whilst emphasis is given to national symbols of all kinds. A common language is an obvious defining characteristic of the nation, and an ideal in any nationalist's repertoire, so for Irish nationalists the salvaging of the Gaelic tongue and customs provided the cultural fusion to a political programme that demanded severance from Britain. A nation had a unique character, argued the nationalist Thomas Davis, and was defined by its culture, notably its literature, its history and, above all, its language. A nation should therefore 'guard its language more than its territories', for a people without a language of its own were 'only half a nation'.[34] Cultural nationalists sought to construct notions of identity and community out of the old Gaelic traditions in order to restore self-respect and self-confidence considered under threat from the forces of modernism, principally a political class, a legal system, an industrializing north-east and a Church that all considered conducting relations in English as a sign of progress. By 1845, 50 per cent of the population spoke Gaelic as their first language, but to the Irish themselves the language had become the mark of poverty, illiteracy and social backwardness.[35] Forces that had existed as far back as the eighteenth century re-emerged revitalized in the last two decades of the nineteenth century as part of attempts to revive and uphold an Irish consciousness built upon the mythological tales, heroes and noble deeds of a bygone age.[36] This resurgence of interest in Gaelic culture could be viewed as a threat to British hegemony, and the encouragement of Anglophile sports alongside the prohibition of Gaelic games seems to have been deliberate British policy. Throughout the empire, certain cultural practices were prohibited where they stood in the way of the colonial project. Indigenous populations would be weaned away from ancient power structures and traditional economic patterns to be socialized into the ways of the colonists. Allies were sought from among elite groups who stood to benefit from an exclusive power structure and from middling groups who had been educated on the merits of political economy and liberal philosophy. The middle-class leadership of the Home Rule Party had long immersed itself in British political and cultural life, being admirers of its liberal-democratic ideals. However, British responses to the rise of Fenianism and agrarian agitations revealed an anti-Catholic bias so that rather than pursue the issue of power based on British ideals, nationalists were forced to exploit traditional religious and agrarian grievances in order to sustain support.[37]

In 1884, at a time when other important vehicles for Irish nationalism were taking shape, Michael Cusack founded the Gaelic Athletic Association (Cumann Luthchleas Gael – GAA) in Thurles. It formed a mainstay of the revival of Gaelic culture, and subscribed to the wider ideals of national allegiance. 'If any two purposes should go together they ought to be politics and athletics', wrote the *Irishman* in 1884, 'our politics being essentially national, so should our athletics'.[38] Cusack noted the descent into physical and moral apathy following the famine in the 1840s and consequent mass emigration, and sought to promote the merits of sport, not simply for their own sake but as a means to raise a new national consciousness.[39] He argued that English influence had destroyed Irish pastimes and sports, and if the late nineteenth-century trend for Irish people to play so-called 'garrison games' continued, there would be no indigenous Irish culture left.[40] Douglas Hyde, the founder of the Gaelic League, argued that Irish sport must be brought back to everyday use, and an attack must be mounted on their English counterparts, so that the Irish cease to be 'a nation of imitators'.[41]

Whilst cricket had once provided a cover for Fenian activities,[42] it was now portrayed as the recreational activity of the adversary and therefore taboo. Alongside other pastimes associated with the British – tennis, polo and croquet – it was to be boycotted whilst military personnel and their collaborators were prohibited from Irish sports under the notorious Rule 21. Politically, the GAA espoused the cause of a 32-county Irish Republic and came to be seen as a covert political body, providing an administrative structure and reservoir of manpower for radical nationalists to tap into. Its promotion of both physical and cultural attributes allowed it to provide a bridge between cultural and political nationalisms, which helps to explain why the historian Bill Mandle argued that 'no organisation had done more for Irish nationalism than the GAA'.[43]

An all-Ireland sporting movement stimulated the drive for Irish national identity. Cultural nationalists saw their struggle as a promotion of all things Irish – names, language, literature, sports and manufactures – to be adopted at the expense of their English equivalents. Membership of the nation was defined as 'an active participation in the nation's cultural, economic, social and political development'.[44] This meant that the Irish national flag would be flown at Gaelic games and branch meetings in Ulster would be held in Gaelic. The boycott of British sports placed cricket as part of the nationalist struggle.

The emergence of cultural nationalism accentuated the demise of cricket as a popular sport, though its initial decline was due more to social and political factors that were exaggerated by particular rural problems in the mid-nineteenth century. Cricket's exclusivity had became an obstacle to progress in the US and Canada as well as Ireland.[45] Whilst there is evidence of cricket being played by Irish workers, there is little to confirm that they mixed with the social elites. In reality cricket was 'a bond of union' between the country gentry, or landlords, in the foxhunting off-season. John Lawrence, author of the *Handbook of Cricket in Ireland,* recommended the game to landlords as a substitute for coercion in the struggle against anti-establishment secret societies. Club cricketers were overwhelmingly drawn from the middle classes as shown by the prominence of public schools, banks and hospitals in Lawrence's annuals. In its final edition in 1880, Lawrence noted that 'here in Ireland, cricket is unfortunately not the pastime of the masses, as it is in England'.[46] However, recent research has suggested that where it became embedded in the cultural activities of the labourers and peasantry, cricket survived longer than where it was dominated by landowners. Michael O'Dwyer's *The History of Cricket in County Kilkenny* shows that the sport had spread beyond the big houses and was played in every town and village, and as late as 1896, there were 50 teams in Kilkenny. In contrast, Patrick Bracken's *History of Cricket in Tipperary* writes of a sport tainted by association with the garrisons and affiliation to the big houses. Whereas cricket had all but died out in Tipperary by 1905, it survived until the Second World War in Kilkenny.[47]

An isolated rural people would have been less influenced by changing cultural tastes and were further ransacked by famine and political agitation. Death and emigration reduced the population from eight million at the start of the Potato Famine in 1845 to just five million by the time Parnell became President of the Land League in 1879, a populist organization with the objective of defending tenants who refused to pay 'unfair' rents. The threat of implicit violence, actual attacks on those who attempted to evict tenants and prolonged campaigns to ostracize unpopular landlords widened the chasm between landowner and tenant and put paid to many small clubs that had developed in spite of class antagonisms. The famine affected the middle classes less than the labouring and further concentrated cricket in the hands of the privileged. It also affected the areas of Ireland where Gaelic was more widespread and by 1900, only a few counties had a large Irish-speaking population and they faced a political agitation process geared to Westminster and the conducting of affairs in English and a Catholic Church that had long considered the old ways a bulwark to progress.[48] The emphasis of the home rule movement was on political action rather than cultural matters. The Irish Republican Brotherhood condemned those it called 'dilettante patriots' who thought they could rejuvenate the country through native literature and art.[49] The literary revival was an affair for intellectuals and there was no substantial middle class outside of Dublin or Belfast to sustain such a movement. In the struggle for the ascendancy between cultural and political nationalisms, sport became a means around which both could unite in opposition to the British way of life. In a society in which complex social divisions had evolved, nationalists sought issues on which they could claim the general support of the whole population. This has to raise the question of whether sport, in the absence of other forms of agreed contention, became by default a focal point of opposition to the British.

The 1916 Easter Uprising marked an intensification of the struggle against British rule. Many of the great houses that had provided homes for cricket pitches were later attacked and burned by republicans – Castle Bernard in Bandon, a regular stop on I Zingari tours, was burned down, as was Timothy O'Briens's Lohort Castle, County Cork, believed to have been occupied by the military. At Croke Park in November 1920 the notorious 'Black and Tans' fired indiscriminately into a crowd at a Gaelic football match, killing a player and 11 other men and women, while wounding 60 others. In retaliation, gunmen fired at British officers, fielding at College Park, Dublin, in a match against the Gentlemen of Ireland, the Irish representative team.

The disruption of the First World War and subsequent departure of the British from southern Ireland affected the clubs that relied on the military, civil service and members of the Viceregal courts for membership. The dismantling of the British state apparatus in the south and the antagonisms generated by the construction of Northern Ireland out of six Protestant-dominated counties, meant that victories against the British need not be confined to the sports field, but increasingly occurred on the military front; national heroes were no longer to be athletes but guerrilla fighters. Whereas in Australia cricket assisted the development of a national consciousness by providing a forum in which Australians could define themselves as a distinct group (against a common opposition) within the broader entity of the British Empire, for many in Ireland identity was shaped by the question of the border, and victories over the 'old enemy' took on different forms.

**The foundations of success**

Nationalist texts had spoken of the cultural benefits that would befit an independent Ireland, but despite the perceived range of forces stacked against a sport inherently associated with the English, cricket did not descend into obscurity following the establishment of the Free State in 1922. Irish rural society maintained the same social patterns and attitudes of the later nineteenth century and a wider conservatism ensured that change was little more than a different political regime. The administration in Dublin adopted a business-like persona, rather than the liberation regime for which revolutionaries had hoped. This was shown through the adoption of rural symbolism, such as the animals and wildlife used on Ireland's first coinage in 1928, rather than the symbols associated with Irish nationhood such as the Celtic cross and shamrock. Against this social setting and lacking the British context through the withdrawal of its state apparatus, cricket survived. In the 1920s, Leinster and Phoenix were particularly strong, and the historian Clarence Hiles claims the inter-war period as the halcyon days for the Northern Cricket Union with large crowds for matches and several star players. Sion Mills dominated the period, with rivals coming from Derry in the 1920s and Strabane in the 1930s.[50] Urban cricket benefited from the migration to the major towns of those seeking a career in the professions and did best in parts of Ulster and Dublin, in places like Trinity College where Anglophile sympathies had resisted the nationalist influence. An Irish XI still played an annual contest against Scotland, there were frequent visits from the MCC, and occasional tourists from further afield.[51]

Cricket maintained a presence throughout the twentieth century and though it failed to become a mass sport, it avoided many of the sectarian controversies that seeped into other areas of social life. The Irish Cricket Union (ICU), which united all provinces under one national body, was formed in 1923 three years after the political division of the country, recognizing cricket on an all-island basis. Controversies over selection for the national side have largely been free of religious affiliation and grievances tend to have been geographical. Early Irish sides, for example, were dominated by players from Dublin and Cork, and it was not until 1924 that Ireland played its first home game outside of these centres when Wales visited Ormeau (Ireland's 111th international).

Eamon de Valera's administration (1937–48) amended aspects of the 1921 Treaty considered an affront to Irish nationhood, notably the Oath of Allegiance to the crown, downgraded the role of the governor general and withheld certain annuities due to Britain. The policy of economic nationalism protected Irish industry and agriculture behind tariff walls, language revival was pursued and traditional music promoted. Yet during de Valera's spell in office, Ireland continued to play regular fixtures with Scotland, the MCC and English counties, as well as against Australia and South Africa. Once the British influence had been expunged, there remained little beyond personal preference with which to condemn cricket. Intellectuals spoke of the authentic Gaelic life in which an Irish resurgence would be born devoid of the overseas influences that sought to absorb Ireland, but the numbers speaking the old language continued to decline and whilst the pursuit of Gaelic was carried out in the classroom, on the streets the daily language of most Irish was English, something that must have aided the development of a 'national' body of any sort. Censorship restricted not just literature but also ideas as Ireland sought to hold back the tides of modernism, an effort inevitably doomed to failure as shown after the Second World War when emigration once again became a serious problem. Enticed into a different way of life through the cinema and radio, many urban young sought to move away from dwellings with few facilities and seek their chances in England. In the period

1936–46, an estimated net emigration of 187,000 was recorded, by 1951–56, this had risen to 197,000, and in the period 1956–61 it was 212,000.[52] As the emigrants were disproportionately young, this will have had a significant impact on the development of Irish sport in general and cricket in particular.

Critics argued that Ireland needed to adapt itself to overseas influences if it hoped to prosper. Identity in the south had been defined in terms of religion, language and culture and presented the Irish as distinct, especially from Britain. In reality, Irish social life was widely influenced by its neighbour. Those English newspapers and books that passed by the censor were widely distributed, while the BBC was audible throughout most of the country. Architecture, furnishings and fashions were all influenced by English tastes, transportation brought the two countries closer together, and most emigration was to Britain. Economic protection was eventually rejected in favour of opening up Ireland's markets in the drive for economic growth. Taoiseach Seán Lemass (1959–66) maintained the national card by arguing that economic renewal was the most practical means to attract the Northern unionist population who had little to gain from a Gaelic identity in a country that was struggling to maintain its own population. By the 1970s, Ireland's social transformation was underway with the majority of its population now residing in urban areas – a third of them in the greater Dublin district. The expansion in the ownership of television sets allowed for the wider dissemination of American and British cultural tastes, the dominance of English-speaking commercials and the availability to a wider audience of English favoured sports.

Attitudes to identity were polarized by the onset of the 'Troubles' in 1968, which further antagonized nationalist and loyalist communities and sharpened cricket's English connotations. For nationalists the security forces were akin to a colonial administration and resistance would take many forms. Cricket clubs in nationalist areas suffered attacks and teams such as Derry's Brigade and City of Derry,[53] and Instonians and Cliftonville in Belfast, were forced to withdraw from their respective leagues. The tense political situation also affected the number of English sides who were willing to travel to the province and meant that competition had to be sought instead against the likes of Denmark and Holland. The Troubles served to reinforce traditional loyalties and cement notions of 'national' identity around ideas of Irishness or Britishness with obvious effects on international sport. It proved difficult, for example, for both Catholics and Protestants to embrace international competition in the way of other nations, for there was no accepted notion of what constituted the nation, no 'national' anthem or flag, and in many cases no single sporting body.

In the South, Ireland was coming to terms with the fact that, rather than being a singular people united under a common culture and identity, it was in reality a multi-faceted nation with a range of differing people and identities. In 1974, RTE broadcast a series of television lectures entitled *A Question of Identity* and in 1977, *The Heritage of Ireland* presented the country as a mosaic of cultures and social forces, remote from the earlier ideologically charged versions of the national story.[54] The New Ireland Forum Report enforced this in 1983, arguing that 'Society in Ireland as a whole comprises a wider diversity of cultural and political traditions than exists in the South, and the constitution and laws of the new Ireland must accommodate these social and political realities'.[55]

In the 1970s fixtures were arranged against Holland, Denmark, the West Indies and Australia, and tours made to the US, Canada and England. In 1980, Ireland was granted admission to the Gillette Cup, the leading one-day English domestic tournament, and has featured in European Championships, other English one-day tournaments, and the ICC Trophy that saw them advance to the World Cup in the Caribbean. In 2007, Ireland could also claim to be champions of Europe at every age level, from Under-13s through to the seniors. The foundations of this success are built on a series of club competitions organized at local and provincial levels and the Senior Cup, a knockout tournament bringing together sides from the entire 32 counties. There are some 18,000 registered players in all of Ireland,[56] and an array of clubs have links to feeder schools. Two-thirds of these cricketers ply their trade in the six counties, where cricket has developed as a working-class Protestant sport, perhaps in contrast to a more middle-class feel in Dublin, although the journalist Ian Callender notes a remarkable revival in North County Dublin, where cricket has become the sport of the common man.[57]

## Ireland's contribution

The different phases of cricket's progress in Ireland have to be assessed against the backdrop of its political history – namely, the presence of a British ruling authority, political and cultural opposition, the construction of post-independent Ireland and the Troubles – and the changing sense of national identity. Identity, though, is a contested and fluid concept, and where territory, language, ethnicity and political allegiance are key to group identification we have to talk of identities in the plural rather than a set of beliefs in nationhood to which a majority subscribe. Nations are defined subjectively and national consciousness encompasses a sense of belonging to a particular community.[58] In a fractured society, though, one looks for synthesis and draws inspiration from sports.

Ireland's contribution to the history of cricket might pale in comparison to its neighbour, ranking say alongside that of the Philadelphians as a force of expectation that failed to live up to early potential. However, once we unravel the interconnectedness of Irish cricket with its history then a more complete assessment is possible. If we say that the key chapters in recent Irish history have been the rise of nationalism and the diaspora, we see both have helped to shape the wider Irish involvement in the sport.

Following the failed insurrection of 1798, hundreds of Irishmen were transported to Botany Bay where they would add to the anti-British sentiment felt by the first Irish sent to inhabit the outpost in 1788 as convicts. Between 1840 and 1914, about a third of a million Irish emigrated to the Australian colonies and up until the Great War were the second largest immigrant group after the English.[59] According to Patrick O'Farrell, the relationship of resistance of the Irish minority to the conservatism of the English provided Australia with its distinct national identity.[60] Sport became a major vehicle for the expression of an Australian character with cultural institutions formed way before Federation in 1901. Australia's sporting motivation became the defeat of the English, providing a key driving force for the assertion of its place in the Empire. Whereas in Ireland political nationalism became the dominant type, for many Irish settlers, with a mythical attachment to an imaginary Irish homeland, exertion through sport provided the opportunity to challenge the English on cultural terms and to justify abstention from the wider political struggle for Irish independence.[61]

This Australian setting allowed the Irish to make their greatest contribution to the sport of cricket. The batting all-rounder Tom Horan hailed from County Cork and played in both the first ever Test against England in 1877 and in the historic Ashes match at the Oval in 1882. He was joined by John Blackham, also of Irish descent, who kept wicket in both games and, like Horan, became Australian captain. The stroke play of Irish-descended Stan McCabe is said to have brought tears to Don Bradman's eyes when he saw him score a double century against England in 1938, whilst another cricketer with Irish blood, Bill O'Reilly, was considered by Bradman to be the best bowler he ever faced.[62]

Other players whose families were part of the great migration include the fast bowler Ray Lindwall, left-arm spinner Chuck Fleetwood-Smith and key batters Leo O'Brien, Jack Fingleton and Lindsay Hassett.

Up until the Civil War, cricket was the most popular sport in the US, but was soon replaced by baseball. A leading reason for its demise was the inability to expand beyond its English base. The *American Cricketer* declared in 1877 that Americans and English 'don't mix well at cricket'.[63] The link with the homeland was stronger amongst the Irish in America than it ever was in Australia, perhaps explained by the need to assert identity in a land of greater competing nationalities. Political values held that emigration was not simply an economic necessity but an act of political oppression,[64] and resistance would come in the shape of rejecting English values such as the notion of deference, the 'normality' of social segregation or the sanctimony of authority and law – qualities that were essential to cricket's ethos.

This is not to say, however, that American cricket was devoid of Irish influence. There were a number of tours by Irish XIs, encouraged and sponsored by an emerging Irish middle class, and Irish teams such as the Queens County Cricket team were amongst the best in New York going into the twentieth century.[65] However, the evidence shows that the Irish took to baseball. By the late 1850s, hundreds of Irish names appeared on the rosters of major and minor clubs, especially in Brooklyn, Newark, Jersey City and Orange, New Jersey and they were the dominant ethnic group well into the twentieth century.[66]

Of course, most Irish migration was to England and included the Dublin-born Leland Hone, who had never played for an English county, but kept wicket for England in a Test match against Australia in 1879. Dublin also provided Timothy O'Brien who won the first of his caps against Australia in 1884. Joseph McMaster (County Down) played his only first-class game for England in South Africa in 1889, whilst Frederick Fane (County Kildare) would be the only Irish-born to captain England, winning 14 caps in the first decade of the twentieth century. Other Irish cricketers of note include S.S.J. Huey, who headed the English bowling averages in 1954 with an average of 6.92, including 14 wickets in a performance against MCC in Dublin, 'Jimmy' Boucher, who headed the averages in 1931, 1937 and 1948 and Dublin's Ed Joyce who has played 17 one-day internationals for England.

Cricket most probably began in one of the myriad folk-forms that it had done elsewhere. We know that it was formalized and codified by a British presence that cast a shadow on the sport, but one from which a native form could evolve and become popular until that influence became an opportunity for resistance to an alien presence. That it survived independence is a statement that cricket posed no threat to the formation of a wider Irish identity, though its association with England, be it through Trinity College, the bureaucracy or by Unionists playing it during the Troubles certainly would have stunted growth. It was not helped that cricket was seen as a game for the 'toffs' and the 'west Brits' and players have been accused of a failure to promote the sport, perhaps in order to maintain an exclusiveness. Bemoaning the lack of media coverage, an article in the *Irish Times* noted that most clubs are content to continue unheralded and unknown outside of the realms of cricket.[67]

Economic growth in the last decades of the twentieth century meant Ireland became a net importer of labour. Immigrants from South Africa, Pakistan, India, Sri Lanka, Australia and New Zealand have brought the love of cricket and their own particular skills to Irish clubs, helping to bolster the numbers playing and improve standards. 'In no other discipline', wrote the *Irish Times*, 'can Catholics, Protestants, Hindu or Muslim sportsmen and women so liberally interact, irrespective of their creed'.[68] This has consequences for the dissemination of identity in an increasingly multicultural society and a globalized world in which Ireland plays its part on the neoliberal stage. The national team will become less 'Irish' as players whose birthplace is not Ireland qualify, placing the side on a similar level to its competitors, like the US who won the Six Nations Challenge in the United Arab Emirates in 2004 with only a handful of American-born players, and Canada with just a couple of native-born members in their squad at World Cup 2007.

As we ponder the future for cricket in Ireland, we think less in terms of political and cultural nationalism, and more about economics and sustainability in the face of increasing competition from other sports. The ultimate problem is the pressure on an amateur side in a professional world, in which the main Test playing nations grow increasingly wealthy as TV deals and sponsorship arrangements scale new heights. Ireland now competes in both forms of the game, in World Cups, the World Cricket League, Inter Continental Cup, European Championships, English County one-day competitions and one-day internationals. Cricket has suddenly become a full-time pursuit, but the fortunes of Irish cricket do not lie solely in the hands of the ICU. Their relationship with the England and Wales Cricket Board could herald more lucrative one-day internationals, but the eligibility of players when county interests conflict with those of country needs a more satisfactory resolution, for the Irish at least. Their connection to politics remains an intriguing one in the light of how South Africa has used the peace and reconciliation process as an opportunity to remould a national identity inclusive of the ethnic makeup of the nation. Sport can allow an area whereby national considerations can be played out away from the day-to-day distractions of party politics and religious division. Ireland's successful World Cup has reinvigorated an old and popular sport, and a national team being endorsed by Ireland's Sports Minister John O'Donoghue as well as the Democratic Unionist leader Ian Paisley and Sinn Fein's Martin McGuinness makes cricket an unlikely unifier among traditional adversaries and also suggests that the future holds promise.

## Notes

[1] Only seven members of the World Cup squad were in the group chosen to take on India and South Africa in Ireland in July 2007. In addition to a number of injuries and one retirement, Jeremy Bray and Eoin Morgan failed to make themselves available.
[2] See, Brookes, *English Cricket*, 15 for a brief account of the origins of cricketing words.
[3] Altham and Swanton, *A History of Cricket*, 15.
[4] Caulfield, *Cricket is an Ancient Irish Game*, 25–6.
[5] Ibid., 32.
[6] Bowen, *Cricket*, 118.
[7] Mair, 'Scotland', 556.
[8] Bergin and Scott, 'Ireland', 554.
[9] Foster, *Modern Ireland*, 170.
[10] Siggins, *Green Days*, 10.
[11] Later Governor of Madras, Secretary for War and the Colonies, had capital of Tasmania named after him.
[12] Foster, *Modern Ireland*, 248.
[13] Garnham, 'The Roles of Cricket in Victorian and Edwardian Ireland', 40.
[14] President of Montserrat in the West Indies in 1854 and lieutenant governor of St Kitts in 1855; he administered Hong Kong between 1859 and 1865, and was appointed governor of Ceylon (now Sri Lanka). He was made governor of New South Wales in 1872; governor of New Zealand (1879–80); and finally of the Cape Colony and high commissioner in South Africa.
[15] Quoted in Hyam, *Britain's Imperial Century*, 295.
[16] Garnham, 'The Roles of Cricket in Victorian and Edwardian Ireland', 36.
[17] Connolly, *The Oxford Companion to Irish History*, 523.
[18] Davis, 'Irish Cricket and Nationalism', 84.

[19] Karl Johnson, 'Bowling Over the Sub-continent'. *The Irish Times*, August 10, 2002.

[20] Garnham, 'The Roles of Cricket in Victorian and Edwardian Ireland', 30.

[21] 'Why it's "Wicket" to play Cricket (Honest!)'. *Irish Independent*, June 24, 2004.

[22] Pollock and Parkhill, *Made in Belfast*, 5.

[23] Technically speaking this was not a full Irish side. Members included the Hon. F.G.B. Ponsonby, one of the founders of I Zingari and the Liverpool-born W. Buttress McCormick, who would become the Honorary Chaplain to Queen Victoria.

[24] 1879, 1888, 1892 and 1909. Full details of these contests are available on the Cricket Archive website: http://www.cricketarchive.co.uk/index.html.

[25] 'Why it's "Wicket" to play Cricket (Honest!)'. *Irish Independent*, June 24, 2004.

[26] Sugden and Bairner, *Sport, Sectarianism and Society in a Divided Ireland*, 49.

[27] 'Carolan' [Charles Kickham?], 'Old Sports and Pastimes'. *The Celt*, X (October 1857), 151. Quoted in Garnham, 'The Roles of Cricket in Victorian and Edwardian Ireland', 28.

[28] Garnham, 'The Roles of Cricket in Victorian and Edwardian Ireland', 33.

[29] Davis, 'Irish Cricket and Nationalism', 83.

[30] Garnham, 'The Roles of Cricket in Victorian and Edwardian Ireland', 36.

[31] O'Shea, *Charles Stewart Parnell*, 209.

[32] Owen Conway, 'Lord Hawke at Home', article in *Windsor Magazine*, 1898. Quoted in Rayvern Allen, *Cricket's Silver Lining*, 241.

[33] Anderson, *Imagined Communities*.

[34] Boyce, *Nationalism in Ireland*, 155.

[35] Lyons, *Culture and Anarchy in Ireland*, 8–9.

[36] Brown, *Ireland*, 69.

[37] Hutchinson, *The Dynamics of Cultural Nationalism*, 152.

[38] Quoted in Holt, *Sport and the British*, 238.

[39] David Greene, 'Michael Cusack and the Rise of the GAA', in O'Brien, *The Shaping of Modern Ireland*, 78.

[40] Cronin, 'Catholics and Sport in Northern Ireland', 30.

[41] Lyons, *Culture and Anarchy in Ireland*, 41–2.

[42] Foster, *Modern Ireland*, 394.

[43] Mandle, *The Gaelic Athletic Association and Irish Nationalist Politics*, 221.

[44] Hutchinson, *The Dynamics of Cultural Nationalism*, 153.

[45] Cooper, 'Canadians Declare "It isn't Cricket"', 74–5; Seymour, *Baseball*, 31.

[46] Quoted in Siggins, *Green Days*, 27.

[47] 'An Irishman's Diary'. *Irish Times*, March 29, 2007.

[48] Daniel O'Connell had argued that, 'It would be of vast benefit to mankind if all the inhabitants of the earth spoke the same language ... I can witness without a sigh the demise of Irish'. Murphy, 'The Gaelic Background', 9.

[49] Boyce, *Nationalism in Ireland*, 177.

[50] Siggins, *Green Days*, 58.

[51] The West Indies visited in 1928 India in 1936, New Zealand 1937 and Australia in 1938.

[52] Brown, *Ireland*, 174.

[53] John Hume, founding member of the Social Democratic and Labour Party, bowled his left-arm 'twisters' for them.

[54] Brown, *Ireland*, 280.

[55] New Ireland Forum, *Report of Proceedings, Irish Episcopal Conference Delegation*, 15. The New Ireland Forum was an attempt to bring political parties from the North and the South together to discuss proposals for unity. Unionist parties and the British rejected it.

[56] Ed Power, 'They Think it's all Overs ... It is Now'. *Irish Independent*, August 26, 2005.

[57] Ian Callender, 'There's no Rest for the Wicket'. *Newsletter* (Belfast), August 11, 2003.

[58] Heywood, *Political ideas and Concepts*, 58.

[59] Fitzpatrick, *Oceans of Consolation*, 6.

[60] O'Farrell, *The Irish in Australia*, 11.

[61] Horton, 'The "Green" and the "Gold', 71. See also Bairner in this volume.

[62] Bradman, *Farewell to Cricket*, 300, 287.

[63] Quoted in Melville, *The Tented Field*, 33.

[64] Foster, *Modern Ireland*, 359.

[65] Ridge, 'Irish County Societies in New York, 1880–1914', 290.

[66] Kirsch, *Baseball in Blue and Gray*, 81–2.
[67] 'A Game Selling Itself Short'. *The Irish Times*, May 22, 2002.
[68] 'Irish Cricket no Longer on a Sticky Wicket'. *Irish Times*, March 24, 2007.

## References

Altham, H.S., and E.W. Swanton. *A History of Cricket*, 3rd ed. London: George Allen & Unwin Ltd., 1947.

Anderson, Benedict. *Imagined Communities. Reflections on the Origin and Spread of Nationalism.* London: Verso Books, 2006.

Bergin, S. and D. Scott. 'Cricket in Ireland'. In *Barclay's World of Cricket*, edited by E.W. Swanton and George Plumtree, 554–56. London: Willow Books, 1986.

Bowen, Roland. *Cricket: A History of its Growth and Development Throughout the World.* London: Eyre and Spottiswoode, 1970.

Boyce, D. George. *Nationalism in Ireland.* New York: Routledge, 1995.

Bracken, Patrick. *History of Cricket in Tipperary.* Kilkenny: Kilkenny People Printing Ltd, 2004.

Bradman, Don. *Farewell to Cricket.* London: Pavilion Library, 1988.

Brookes, Christopher. *English Cricket. The Game and its Players Through the Ages.* London: Weidenfeld & Nicolson, 1978.

Brown, Terence. *Ireland: A Social and Cultural History, 1922–2002.* London: Harper Perennial, 2004.

Caulfield, James. *Cricket is an Ancient Irish Game.* Wexford: Jestherellen & Co.

Connolly, S.J. *The Oxford Companion to Irish History.* Oxford: Oxford University Press, 1999.

Cooper, David. 'Canadians Declare "It isn't Cricket": a Century of Rejection of the Imperial Game, 1860–1960'. *Journal of Sports History* 26, no. 21 (1999): 51–81.

Cronin, Mike. 'Catholics and Sport in Northern Ireland: Exclusiveness or Inclusiveness?' *International Sports Studies* 22, no. 1 (2001): 25–41.

Davis, Richard. 'Irish Cricket and Nationalism'. *Sporting Traditions* 10 (1994): 77–96.

Fitzpatrick, David. *Oceans of Consolation: Personal Accounts of Irish Migration to Australia.* Ithaca, NY: Cornell University Press, 1994.

Foster, R.F. *Modern Ireland, 1600–1972.* London: Penguin, 1988.

Garnham, Neal. 'The Roles of Cricket in Victorian and Edwardian Ireland'. *Sporting Traditions* 19 (2003): 27–48.

Heywood, Andrew. *Political ideas and Concepts: an Introduction.* Basingstoke: Macmillan Press, 1994.

Holt, Richard. *Sport and the British.* Oxford: Clarendon Press, 1989.

Horton, Peter A. 'The "Green" and the "Gold": The Irish-Australians and their Role in the Emergence of the Australian Sports Culture'. In *Sport in Australasian Society: Past and Present*, edited by J.A. Mangan and John Nauright, 65–92. London: Frank Cass, 2000.

Hutchinson, John. *The Dynamics of Cultural Nationalism: The Gaelic Revival and the Creation of the Irish Nation State.* London: Allen & Unwin, 2003.

Hyam, Ronald. *Britain's Imperial Century, 1815–1914. A Study of Empire and Expansion.* Basingstoke: Palgrave Macmillan, 2002.

Kirsch, George B. *Baseball in Blue and Gray.* Princeton, NJ: Princeton University Press, 2003.

Lyons, F.S.L. *Culture and Anarchy in Ireland.* Oxford: Clarendon Press, 1979.

Mair, N.G.R. 'Scotland'. In *Barclay's World of Cricket*, edited by E.W. Swanton and George Plumtree, 556–59. London: Willow Books, 1986.

Mandle, W.F. *The Gaelic Athletic Association and Irish Nationalist Politics, 1884–1924.* London: Christopher Helm, 1987.

Melville, Tom. *The Tented Field: A History of Cricket in America.* Bowling Green, KY: Bowling Green State University Popular Press, 1998.

Murphy, G. 'The Gaelic Background'. In *Daniel O'Connell. Nine Centenary Essays*, edited by Michael Tierney. Dublin: Browne and Nolan, 1949.

New Ireland Forum. *Report of Proceedings, Irish Episcopal Conference Delegation.* Dublin: Stationary Office, 1984.

O'Brien, Conor Cruise, ed. *The Shaping of Modern Ireland.* Toronto, ON: University of Toronto Press, 1960.

O'Dwyer, Michael. *The History of Cricket in County Kilkenny: The Forgotten Game.* O'Dwyer Books, 2007.

O'Farrell, Patrick. *The Irish in Australia*. Kensington, NSW: New South Wales University Press, 1993.

O'Shea, Katharine. *Charles Stewart Parnell: His Love Story and Political Life*. London: Cassell, 1973.

Pollock, Vivienne, and Trevor Parkhill. *Made in Belfast*. Stroud: Sutton Publishing, 2005.

Rayvern Allen, David. *Cricket's Silver Lining*. London: Guild Publishing, 1987.

Ridge, John T. 'Irish County Societies in New York, 1880–1914'. In *The New York Irish*, edited by Ronald H. Bayor and Timothy J. Meagher, 275–300. Baltimore, MD: John Hopkins University Press, 1996.

Seymour, Harold. *Baseball: The Early Years*. New York: Oxford University Press, 1960.

Siggins, Gerard. *Green Days: Cricket in Ireland, 1792–2005*. Stroud: Nonsuch Publishing, 2005.

Sugden, John, and Alan Bairner. *Sport, Sectarianism and Society in a Divided Ireland*. Leicester: Leicester University Press, 1995.

# South African cricket and British imperialism, 1870–1910

Dean Allen*

*School of Psychology and Sport Sciences, Northumbria University, Newcastle upon Tyne, UK*

## Introduction

The history of cricket in South Africa is about more than sport. Within the preface to his study of *The Games Ethic and Imperialism*, J.A. Mangan expressed the wish that he:

> would not like [the] study of cultural diffusion to be naively and erroneously catalogued under 'Games'. It is concerned with much more: with ethnocentricity, hegemony and patronage, with ideals and idealism, with educational values and aspirations, with cultural assimilation and adaptation and, most fascinating of all, with the dissemination throughout the Empire of a hugely influential moralistic ideology.[1]

Arguably, nowhere more than in South Africa have such processes been played out through sport. The 'cultural diffusion' of which Mangan talks relates to the ideology of British imperialism that arrived in South Africa during the nineteenth century, and Gemmell remarks in his recent book that the politics of South African cricket is about the game as it has reflected South African society. South African cricket has been concerned with what lies 'beyond the boundary',[2] drawing our attention to the period of British domination in South Africa – the late 1800s, of Victoria, of Empire – that laid the foundations upon which the sport and society structures of today are being contested.

The Victorian age was a period of expansion. By the beginning of the twentieth century, the British Empire contained around 460 million people and was spread over an area of more than 12 million square miles.[3] Occupying nearly one quarter of the world's area and including almost one quarter of its total population,[4] Britain's Empire was 'by far the most enormous imperial system that the world had known'.[5] According to Sandiford, 'The Victorians were inordinately proud of this empire which they regarded as tangible proof of their racial and moral superiority'.[6] As much to do with commercial and industrial growth as with race or morality, competition from newly industrialized European nations saw Britain accelerate its expansionist policy in the last decades of the nineteenth century.[7] Coinciding with cricket's development within South Africa, almost 5 million square miles of additional territory and about 88 million new subjects were 'acquired' worldwide by imperialist Britain between 1870 and 1900.[8]

The population explosion which the British Isles witnessed during 1750–1900 left room for mass emigration as British subjects were encouraged to seek new opportunities in the colonies. By the time of Queen Victoria's death in 1901, there were approximately 100 million people of 'British stock' occupying territories beyond the United Kingdom.[9] As Britons moved abroad so did cricket.[10] As this essay demonstrates, cricket in South Africa developed at a time of imperial expansion within the regions and, as it had done elsewhere, the game became intertwined with notions of empire throughout the country. As part of the cultural imperialism designed to cement ties between Britain and her dependants, cricket's development in South Africa mirrored the progression of British influence throughout the territories.[11] Indeed, it was not long before South Africa was accepted into imperial cricket's exclusive 'club of empire'. As Williams explains:

> Test cricket was played only between England and colonies or former colonies. As cricket was believed to express a distinctively English morality and as apologists for the Empire stressed the moral obligation to extend the benefits of British rule, the nature of cricket as an imperial game meant that cricket and imperialism became mutually supporting ideologies.[12]

This essay will explore the early development of cricket in South Africa while investigating its link to British imperialism and colonialism. As this study will show, a variety of individuals were fundamental in this process of cultural transfer and assimilation, as were the strategies of the authorities in fostering social, economic and political ties between the 'Mother Country' and her dependents. Early cricket relations between England and South Africa will also be examined as sites of a purposeful imperial fellowship set against a South African society still developing its own hierarchies of power and order. The British had after all introduced cricket to South Africa during a period of intense conflict over land and political control. The game, alongside warfare and politics, was set to play its part.

## South Africa, imperialism and empire

Writing in the 1905 *South African Cricketer's Annual*, MCC supremo the 'Right-Honourable' Lord Harris declared how cricket was 'not merely a game, but ... a great educational medium' and how he 'rejoiced' 'that cricket has taken hold as firmly as it has done in South Africa'.[13] For Harris and fellow imperialists the game was significant throughout the Empire in providing a cultural and sporting bond that could not only transmit the important scriptures of British civility but that, in his words, had become 'a strand in the elastic cord which unites the Colonies and the Mother Country'.[14] It was hoped, and indeed expected, that through political, social and cultural coercion British control of Southern Africa could be established as effectively as had been done elsewhere. Within South Africa itself however, many integral struggles were being fought. The region was set to provide the British Empire with its most defining challenge to date.

For most Victorians, the British were inherently, by 'blood', a conquering, governing and civilizing race with the majority of intellectuals and politicians believing in Britain's righteous mission, as the world's greatest nation, to civilize Africa as well as other dark corners of the globe.[15] Perceived racial superiority of white Europeans (and of the English over all other Europeans) justified the subsequent annexation of foreign land and the imposition of British laws and culture. The introduction of cricket came as part of this process. Traditionally associated with conservatism, the ideologies of imperialism were adaptable and could just as easily consort with more liberal attitudes toward domestic issues. British racial superiority was, after all, constitutionally accepted and agreed.

The apologists for imperialism continued to emphasize that the Empire was an exercise in morality; that England was responding to a moral obligation to extend the benefits of British civilization throughout the world. Indeed Joseph Chamberlain began his spell as Colonial Secretary by declaring how 'it is not enough to occupy certain great spaces of the world's surface unless you can make the best of them – unless you are willing to develop them'.[16] And by 1897, his thoughts were of imperialism and world peace: 'This great Empire of ours, powerful as it is, is nothing to what it will become in the course of ages when it will be in permanence a guarantee for the peace and civilisation of the world'.[17]

Despite this, however, the struggle for control of South Africa came at a time when the maintenance of a demanding empire was beginning to tax an already burdened Britain. The military, the schools and the church became major tools in securing the foundations of hegemonic control in the colonies and were vital if British imperial influence was to be sustained.[18] The British were aware, according to Green,

> that if insurrection were to rear its ugly head at two or three outposts simultaneously, then their resources, already stretched to the limit, might snap altogether … The answer, they felt, lay in a combination of psychological warfare, discipline and decorum, good manners and plenty of churches, propaganda by polite pretext.[19]

In South Africa, cricket increasingly played its part in this process – with the number of cricket tours around the time of the Boer War an indication. The relationship between cricket and the expanding empire was already well established by the 1890s, prompting the conservative *Blackwood's Magazine* to imperiously exclaim in 1892 how 'the Englishman carries his cricket bat with him as naturally as his gun-case and his India-rubber bath'.[20]

Sport became an imperial bond of cultural encounters between the controlling British and subordinate groups in the colonies and nowhere was this typified more than on the cricket fields of empire. Encouraged by the sport's ethos, middle-class colonials were steering their sons towards cricket in the hope of furnishing them with the same strength of character and upstanding morals that was being preached back in Britain.[21] As early as 1862, a writer in *Temple Bar* laid claims to cricket being 'a healthy and manly sport; [which] trains and disciplines the noblest faculties of the body, and tends to make Englishmen what they are – the masters of the world'.[22]

## Cricket's institutions: education and religion

The Victorians had transformed cricket into more than a game. As Keith Sandiford explains, the social centrality of Victorian cricket was fostered, nurtured and maintained by key institutions and agencies which regarded the game as a major cultural virtue and, therefore, worth promoting within society.[23] The moral, social and physical attributes of sport were extolled in Victorian times. England had become a true world power and behind its success, many believed, was the national passion for sport:

> Much less than any other nation do the English need to be taught the art of preserving health. They are admitted to be the strongest of races – proof enough that they are the healthiest … Racing, riding, rowing, skating, curling, and among field sports cricket, with the like hygienic agencies, must, and do in great measure, quicken Englishmen, and make them to a great extent what they physically and morally are.[24]

It was in the exclusive schools of the 'home country' where such lessons were being taught. In mid Victorian times both the public school and cricket became avenues of training for England's next generation of the ruling class. The aristocracy and the landed gentry had become firmly convinced of the inherent social value of cricket, and along with the upper middle classes who had emerged from the industrial revolution, there was a move to ensure that cricket's 'school of moral training' would continue for successive generations. Commenting on the public schools matches at Lord's during the 1850s, the *Times* stressed the importance of securing 'a race of young Englishmen who in days to come ... shall retain the grasp of England upon the world'.[25] The country's elite schools and colleges had already begun to fulfil this role.

The public school system compounded the class divisions already prevalent in Victorian society. According to Perkin, 'The class which mattered most, both to the national and international spread of the games and to the emerging and rapidly enlarging Empire was the class educated at the public schools'.[26] Britain's realm was expanding to places like South Africa and there was a real need for men of 'calibre' to govern throughout her Empire. The public seats of learning with their cricket squares and venerated codes of practice had become the training grounds upon which the next generation of imperial administrators could be moulded.[27]

In 1883, C. Gurdon reflected on the importance of investing in a sporting education at England's public schools:

> A very slight reflection will convince us that our Public Schools are the nursery grounds of our cricketers, and that if we neglect to supply our plants with the requirements necessary for their growth and full development, we shall turn out in the end but a sorry stunted crop. Let us pay them every attention in their tender years.[28]

He was, however, preaching to the converted. By this stage, team sports, and cricket in particular, had replaced scholarship, and in many cases, the pulpit, as the primary device used by the guardians of England's public schools to write a cultural code upon their charges. J.A. Mangan has demonstrated that the cricket field became a place where boys were taught the virtues of loyalty, obedience, discipline and conformity which were held to be the characteristic virtues of the English 'gentleman'.[29] Such 'virtues' it was hoped would serve England capably throughout her Empire.

As Taylor has shown, public school athleticism shaped the ideal of manhood and character, differentiating gentlemen from the 'masses' and creating the amateur-professional distinction that dominated British and colonial sport for over a century. 'This high-minded moral guidance was routed in notions of self-discipline and virtue and was indicative of the puritanical strain in nineteenth century British *bourgeois* philosophy'.[30] It found voice in *Athletic News* in 1876:

> Moralists may well give this subject a portion of their consideration. Excellence in athletics is only possible to those who cultivate habits of temperance, and it is the critical period between youth and manhood that habits and inclinations are formed which may influence a person's entire subsequent career. The young athlete is less likely to stray from the right path than those who have no such motive to control them, and hence a great social problem would be in a fair way to be solved.[31]

The 'right path' was to serve one's country and inevitably for many this meant a career in the military. At the time of the Anglo-Boer War in South Africa, many speakers and preachers were visiting the public and preparatory schools to press home the imperial message. One such orator was cricketing enthusiast E.W. Hornung, author of the best-selling Raffles tales and brother-in-law of Sir Arthur Conan Doyle.[32] At Uppingham, Hornung's old school, a cadet corps was thriving. In February 1900 C.H. Jones, the commanding officer, left for active service in the Boer War, and his adventures in Africa were reported in the school magazine in vivid detail: 'We hear that Mr. Jones has killed five Boers single-handed. We congratulate him heartily on the exploit and hope that he will dispose of many more'.[33]

A sense of duty to Queen and Country pervaded the land's public schools and colleges and throughout the Empire old boys were serving the imperial cause. This ethic had been instilled by the educational institutions and reinforced by support from the established Church of England. Many clergy were in fact school masters and academics and, as the religious doctrine of 'fair play' and 'manliness' spread, most of the Victorian educators became ardent apostles of 'Muscular Christianity' which dominated the late Victorian mind set.

Among the leading protagonists of this ethic were Bishop Fraser, Charles Kingsley, Thomas Hughes and Charles Wordsworth. Through their teachings, godliness became associated with fairness, vigour and manliness and by the 1870s such concepts had been cemented within the nation's psyche.[34] With notable churchmen serving as headmasters in the public schools, the relationship between Victorian cricket and religion was reinforced. 'The Victorian clergy gave cricket their unqualified blessings. Churchmen of all persuasions played the game and encouraged others to do likewise'.[35] As the ideals of Muscular Christianity were taught to the next generation of imperial administrators, sports like cricket, rugby and rowing became important mediums upon which to convey the necessary virtues. So important had the physical aspects of Victorian secondary education become that Thomas Hughes, for example, was assigned to teach boxing, cricket and rowing, in addition to law and public health.[36] In the words of Ian Baucom, cricket had become 'the first C in a revised trivium of Cricket, Classics, and Christianity'.[37]

From the 1880s cricket had become an integral part of church propaganda, so by the time of the Boer War, the game had become synonymous with Christianity for millions of Englishmen. In Green's *Wisden Anthology*, English historian L.C.B. Seaman told how cricket had become associated with religion: 'Just as freemasons referred to God as the Great Architect of the Universe, young cricketers were taught to think of Him as the One Great Scorer and almost to regard a Straight Bat as a second in religious symbolism only to the Cross of Jesus.'[38] 'So long as cricket holds its sway, there is not much wrong with England', exclaimed one country vicar, while the game's most venerated clergyman eulogized how 'in the cricket-field, as by the cover's side, the sport is in the free and open air and light of heaven'.[39] By the turn of the century, cricket morality and religion formed an integral part of the Victorian ethos as the publication of Reverend Thomas Waugh's *The Cricket Field of a Christian Life* duly confirmed.[40]

Within the colonies themselves elite schools were established along the lines of Eton, Harrow and Winchester to propagate this message and English games were naturally part of the curriculum. Throughout colonial South Africa, schools such as Bishops in Cape Town and Grey High School in Port Elizabeth produced a generation of cricketers loyal to Empire and as such were an important part of the wider imperial indoctrination process. By spreading the sporting gospel, tours from England to South Africa also cemented the ties of imperial kinship whilst affirming the superior status of the 'Mother Country'. Lord Hawke, for one, was 'certain that a properly-arranged tour does a good deal for the spread of Imperial Federation. Wherever Englishmen go they take cricket with them'.[41] For the British rulers themselves, they considered the enjoyment of 'our' games for 'our' people to be an expression of the naturalness of empire.[42]

## Harris, Hawke and the MCC

With the promotion of cricket in the schools and in the churches the game's iconic guardians, the Marylebone Cricket Club, grew in significance towards the end of the nineteenth century. By the early 1900s, the MCC was 'perceived to be the Vatican of cricket, the very power-house of the game, controlling and arbitrating for Britain and its Empire'.[43] In 1897 the revered Indian cricketer Kumar Ranjitsinhji wrote how, 'the MCC is acknowledged to be the great cricket authority throughout the world ... Its position is unique. As the leading cricket club, it is universally regarded as the supreme authority'.[44] Lord Harris, who became synonymous with the MCC and its corridors of power at Lord's, once referred to the club as 'perhaps the most venerated institution in the British Empire'.[45]

Cricket was flourishing and the club's influence and reputation had grown through increased membership and revenue. In 1873, MCC receipts amounted to £3,012. They rose to £15,065 in 1884, and reached £21,632 by 1890. The club's total income in 1898 had risen to £82,565 – including £37,200 from life memberships, £4,680 from gates and a further £6,905 from the stands.[46] With the formation of the Board of Control for Test cricket in England in 1898, the MCC took responsibility for all future tours by official teams from England.[47] Its place at the heart of the 'imperial game' had been established.

By the start of the twentieth century the role of individual benefactors had diminished while the MCC had become, as one old cricketer exhorted, 'a national institution'.[48] Yet the MCC remained a private club and despite the formal hierarchy of its committee, like all clubs it contained its own cliques. James Bradley had shown that it was the social background of the committee members that defined the MCC's involvement in imperial cricket. The ruling group comprised ex-officio officers of the club and with a membership that was self-perpetuated (through the nomination of its own replacements) the policy of the MCC was thus controlled by a limited number of individuals.[49]

Following his duties in India, Lord Harris had become the dominant figure at Lord's by the mid-1890s and had gathered around himself Lord Hawke, P.F. Warner, H.D.G. Leveson-Gower and the Hon. F.S. Jackson amongst others. Around this time, the MCC and its Long Room at Lord's became bastions of class privilege and political conservatism as the clubs attracted the economic and social elite. Lord Harris is now revered as one of those individuals who shaped the MCC.[50] A conservative and an imperialist, Harris saw cricket as having a wider significance than that of a mere game. From an imperial background – Harris's father was governor of Trinidad and he himself served as secretary for India (1885–86) and Governor of Bombay (1890–95) – Harris came to epitomize the imperialist view of cricket.

Like Harris, Hawke was also a conservative believing in the imperial dream and the maintenance of the class system. Both men would influence what W.G. Grace politely termed, the 'politics of the game'.[51] In fact in 1899 the Champion, failing to see (or admit) the link between cricket and politics wrote how: 'It is the only bad thing I know about Lord Harris ... [that he] permitted political ambition to interrupt a brilliant cricketing career'.[52] By now, however, politics and cricket had become indelibly entwined. Both of Hawke's tours to South Africa during the 1890s for example were bound up in politics,[53] while Harris himself was chancellor of the Primrose League, a Conservative-front organization that argued for the unity of classes and the imperial cause of Britain.[54] Many MPs were members of the MCC and prominent administrators, like Hawke, F.S. Jackson and Pelham Warner, were also known for their support of Conservative policy. In terms of nationalism, imperialism and empire, the game had taken a distinctly political path.

The spread of cricket's imperialist ethos was aided throughout South Africa by a number of wealthy colonial benefactors to the game. Scotsman James Logan, who made his home in the Cape Colony in the late 1870s, has been referred to as 'the second of the three great patrons of [South African] cricket'[55] and was instrumental in the organization of both of Lord Hawke's tours to the Continent during the 1890s.[56] Along with Abe Bailey, Logan represented a new age of colonial 'tycoon' in Southern Africa who recognized the power of the 'imperial game'. In fact Logan and Bailey show remarkable similarities in the roles they played in the sport, politics and society of colonial South Africa at the turn of the twentieth century. Logan's support for South African cricket came primarily in the years preceding the Anglo-Boer War, culminating with his own tour to Britain in 1901. Bailey then took over, following the end of the war, and from 1902 became the game's principle benefactor.[57]

Following his involvement in the foundation of the Imperial Cricket Conference in 1909, Abe Bailey went on to instigate the Triangular Tournament of 1912 – a competition between South Africa, England and Australia, designed to cement South Africa's place in cricket's 'imperial club' of nations.[58] Prior to the Tournament, Bailey proclaimed how, 'the cricket result should be a secondary consideration to all lovers of Empire. That a spirit of true national comradeship will be produced must be the desire of every cricketer throughout the King's Dominions.' He added that he hoped that 'the strengthening of the bonds of Union within the Empire [will be] one of the many outcomes of the great Tournament'.[59] It was all part of the rhetoric that had begun decades earlier with the arrival of British imperialism and cricket to the shores of South Africa.

## Cricket's development in South Africa

Cricket itself first came to the African continent with the military between 1795 and 1802 in the earliest days of the British regime.[60] Members of the garrison which occupied the Cape in 1806 found time to play cricket and two years later the first known reference to a cricket match being played in South Africa appeared in the *Cape Town Gazette and African Advertiser*.[61] However it was not until later that century, with the arrival of British settlers, that the game started to spread elsewhere. 1843 saw the first organized cricket club appear in Port Elizabeth, followed a year later by one at Wynberg in the Cape. Further north, the first 'rush' on the Diamond Fields swept cricket into the Kimberley region, with the Orange Free State receiving its first cricket club in Bloemfontein during 1855.[62] The first Transvaal club opened in 1863.[63]

As elsewhere, cricket's imperialists viewed the spread of the game as an indicator of a colony's cultural and social development. English cricketers were seen as purveyors of the 'enlightening' process in far flung corners of empire and South Africa was no different. Pelham Warner for one associated South Africa's evolution with the spread of cricket throughout the region: 'Step by step we have forced our way up north, and the cricket-pavilions that have sprung up along our track may almost be called the milestones on the road of the nation's progress', he exclaimed in 1900.[64] Despite this rhetoric, closer inspection reveals how organized sport in South Africa was still in its infancy going into the 1870s. Only a few clubs had been established in the larger centres like Cape Town, Pietermaritzburg and Port Elizabeth and with no regional or national associations having been formed there was little in the form of official competitions or leagues. South Africa was fertile ground for Britain's empire builders to exert their cultural imperialism through sport.

Odendaal has shown how British sport became institutionalized in South Africa in the period between 1875 and 1885 coinciding with the rise of sport as a mass leisure activity in post-industrial-revolution Britain.[65] Following the establishment of cricket, this decade saw the formation of the first rugby, soccer, athletics, cycling, horse racing (jockey), golf and tennis clubs in South Africa and the inauguration of regular competitions.[66] Then, from the late 1880s, national associations started to be formed to place sport on an organized footing.[67] The timing of all this is significant as the nature of sport was transformed by the discovery of the richest mineral deposits in the world. As a result, thousands of European fortune-seekers were attracted into the interior, stimulating industrialization, urbanization as well as opportunities for imperial expansion. As Odendaal explains: 'South Africa's industrial revolution set the stage for the rise of sport as a modern phenomenon with mass appeal in much the same way as the British Industrial Revolution had done'.[68]

Imperial cricket's development in the region led to the formation of its own administration in line with the corridors of power in London. Southern Africa's 'imperial club' of white cricketing Colonies had expanded to include Rhodesia into the South African Cricket Association (SACA) on 1 February 1904.[69] The Association itself had been founded some 14 years earlier after it became clear that a governing body was needed to coordinate the different centres.[70] Formed in the 'style of the MCC',[71] draft rules of the new association were passed at the inaugural congress of delegates, held at Kimberley on Tuesday 8 April 1890.[72] 'The object of the Association', it was stated, 'shall be to foster and develop cricket throughout South Africa' with the onus on promoting cricketing links with the Mother Country.[73] With its headquarters in Johannesburg, the Association from the outset expressed its specific duty in 'the management of Currie Cup Tournaments, and the visits of English teams to South Africa, and South African teams to England'.[74]

Cricket's development in Southern Africa followed closely the path of British imperial expansion. A difficult country to administer, the pioneer cricket officials in South Africa were indeed successful in galvanizing the different centres into a sense of shared identity through the sport. Within its 'Articles of Constitution' the newly formed governing body (SACA) confirmed how:

> The area of the Association shall be divided into districts defined by the Government surveys, as the Association in general meeting may from time to time decide, and that the following be recognised as districts for Unions:- Western Province, Eastern Province, Border, Natal, (including Zululand), Transvaal (including Swazieland), Orange Free State (including Basutoland), Griqualand West, Bechuanaland (including Rhodesia).[75]

As politicians divided South Africa into manageable districts, cricket reinforced this British administration through its competition and organization. As it had done in India, cricket would perform the important role in South Africa of imparting a sense of imperial kinship across an otherwise fragmented and disparate nation. Cricket's volunteer administrators were pivotal to this process and represented, as Baker suggests, an ethos which made cricket an ideal vehicle on which to promote the ideals of Victorian British society:

> Closely connected to the amateur ethos of games playing was the principle of voluntarism in sports administration. Unpaid volunteers should run sporting organizations, from individual clubs to national governing bodies. Voluntarism, so it was believed, would assure that sports were run with the interests of the game foremost.[76]

South African cricket, influenced as it was by the English model, was thus administered by an Association comprising ex-players and volunteers who, as guardians of the game's development, were strong proponents of cricket's imperial purpose. G. Allsop, administrator of Transvaal cricket during these early years, was typical of the vast number of loyal volunteers who ran the game throughout the colonies. For men like Allsop the development of cricket became their duty: 'Many of my most cherished recollections are connected with the world of cricket', he wrote in 1915, 'and so long as I am able I will gladly render whatever assistance I can to the promotion of the game which has for so long retained its proud position in the British Empire'.[77]

### White exclusivity

During this era cricket reinforced a white, colonial exclusivity throughout Southern Africa. The 1886–87 inter-colonial tournament included a white team from British Bechuanaland (now Botswana) and as we have seen, Rhodesia became a member of the South African Cricket Association having been admitted to the Currie Cup competition in the 1904–05 season.[78] The inclusion of these white colonial teams from outside of South Africa took precedence over non-white teams from within the country, leading Nauright to argue that 'racial solidarity [became] more crucial ... than national-based solidarities'.[79] Certainly cricket's colonial community preserved a privileged position within South African society. Surrounded by a large local population linguistically constructed as 'uncivilized', the ability to appropriate English culture and pastimes provided this group with a certain sense of moral power and superiority.

However, while English-speaking whites looked to 'home' origins for their cultural lead, aspects of this culture was inadvertently transferred to the local population. Cricket, as Sandiford claims, may have been a vital element in Anglo-Saxon culture, but it would be incongruous not to explore how the game affected the other sections of South African society.[80] In 1900 that great cricketing tourist Pelham Warner exclaimed how 'the natives of whatever race show no anxiety to learn the game, nor do the Dutch, save only those who, from their education, or from their contact with our residents, have grown to be practically Englishmen themselves'.[81] Despite such rhetoric, there is ample evidence to suggest however that cricket was being played by the non-English population in the years prior to the Boer War.

By the late nineteenth century distinct cultural groups had emerged within South Africa. Apart from the two white groups, there existed those of mixed race or 'Coloureds' predominantly found in the Cape; migrant workers brought to Natal from the Indian subcontinent as well as the indigenous African peoples present throughout the country. Although there is relatively little known or recorded about the history of black cricket in South Africa, research by André Odendaal suggests that its origins date back to shortly after the inauguration of the white game in the country.[82] In the Western Cape the standard of cricket was such that a Malay team were awarded a little-known fixture against W.W. Read's English side of 1891[83] while in the Eastern Cape cricket was particularly well developed amongst the African population after the game had been introduced by missionaries and the first British garrisons. Indeed there were reports of Africans playing cricket in Queenstown as early as 1862, while the first African cricket club was founded in Port Elizabeth in 1869.[84]

While black cricketers had proved their proficiency at the game, their involvement in first class competition was however never seriously considered. International fixtures especially remained the realm of the gentleman tourist whose breeding and skin-colour were as fundamental as his cricketing ability.[85] The early tours of empire were constructed to demonstrate a white, imperial solidarity over the 'dark masses' and nowhere was this more salient than in South Africa. Britain's imperial agenda had indeed contributed to the racially-driven construction of colonial South African society. In fact, as Brantlinger has shown:

> Imperialist discourse is inseparable from racism. Both express economic, political, and cultural domination (or at least wishes for domination), and both grew more virulent and dogmatic as those forms of domination, threatened by rivals for Empire and by nascent independence movements … began gradually to crumble in the waning decades of the century.[86]

The game of cricket compounded this process in Southern Africa. As it had done throughout other realms of the British Empire, cricket confirmed the privileged position of the white Anglo-Saxon male over 'other' races within South African society. In this way, it became an important cultural facet of imperialism within the region.[87]

Having taken to the game the majority of blacks were left to fend for themselves and to administer and develop their own cricket in the face of increased colonial arrogance and opposition. Odendaal has highlighted how organizations such as the South African Coloured Cricket Board; the South African Bantu Cricket Board and South African Indian Cricket Union were initiated by the African, Malay, Indian and Coloured communities in South Africa in order to foster their own involvement in the game.[88] 'That they did so at all', suggests Sandiford, 'speaks volumes for the awesome power of cultural imperialism which, historically, has proved as capable of inspiring mimicry as enforcing obedience'.[89] Inevitably, black participation in middle-class sport dwindled as a realization descended that any aspirations of joining the white community as 'equals' would not be realized in sport or in any other sphere of life. White South Africa had created its own hierarchical structure and the native population had been disenfranchised within their own land.

## Conclusions

'It is time', according to Mangan, 'that it was more widely recognised that by the late nineteenth century sport lay close to the heart of Britain's imperial culture'.[90] This study addresses Mangan's concern, with particular focus on the development of cricket throughout South Africa. For, like other forms of British sport, cricket 'formed a distinct, persistent and significant cluster of cultural traits isolated in time and space, possessing a coherent structure and definite purpose. While it had many cultural functions, it had certainly become a means of propagating imperial sentiments'.[91] Certainly, the tours of the English cricket teams to South Africa at the end of the nineteenth century were 'imperialist in nature' and intended, in some part, 'to promote imperial ideology'.[92]

> The history of cricket is a convoluted affair which is inextricably linked to the social and economic history of Britain and its Empire. Indeed, the game served as a symbol of that Empire's ideology … [for] the spread of cricket was bound to the imperial movement as a whole. As the boundaries of Empire pushed forward, so did the cricket frontier.[93]

Nowhere was this more evident than in Southern Africa during the late nineteenth century. Gemmell, for one, has shown how the development of cricket in South Africa has been shaped by politics.[94] Despite claims that sport should be free from political influence, throughout its history, an imperial agenda thrust politics upon South African cricket in much the same way that policies of racial segregation during the apartheid era politicized the sport.[95]

The notion that sport and politics should not mix is not a recent phenomenon. Sport, after all, was considered as an ideal, something distinct from the corruptions of wider society and, especially in the early days of the amateur ethos, was associated with amusement and pleasure, nothing more. 'Outside interests threaten the values which sport propagates', suggests Gemmell, 'by permitting decisions to be made by people – such as judges, politicians or civil servants – whose main concern lies outside of sport; when they become involved they invariably "damage, corrupt, or pervert sport"'.[96] This is precisely why the agendas of the sporting benefactors, diplomats and civil servants who promoted sport throughout the British Empire were carefully concealed. This was an attempt for sport not to be 'corrupted'. It was characterized as the 'Gentleman's pursuit', free from dishonesty and imbibed with the values which had made Britain 'great'. If sport was to be introduced and developed within the colonies (in South Africa's case, as part of a strategy of white colonial exclusivity), it had to be seen to be devoid of politics and only once it had been established, could the moral lessons and subtle forms of coercion begin.

According to James Mangan, it was the British middle classes who elevated cricket to the status of a moral discipline.[97] Late Victorian society witnessed in reverse a deliberate and purposeful hegemonic force which saw the responsibility for Britain's morality and ethics shift downwards from the upper classes. It was during this time that cricket, primarily through the schools, was invested with extra significance by the middle classes as *the* sport of imperial Britain. 'Eventually', as Mangan explains, 'cricket became the symbol *par excellence* of imperial solidarity and superiority epitomizing a set of consolidating moral imperatives that both exemplified and explained imperial ambition and achievement. It became a political metaphor as much as an imperial game.'[98]

Cricket had the added advantage of providing a healthy distraction from the enforced domination of others by Britain in her colonies. By introducing such moral pursuits, the Empire was of course seen to improve the lives of those it colonised and, as Brantlinger succinctly notes, the game became a relaxing couch for conscience.[99] In reality, 'athletic proselytism was a statement of masculine cultural superiority as much as a gesture of general benevolent altruism',[100] and in South Africa cricket was promoted as the exclusive domain of the white colonial executive.

To the imperialists of the late nineteenth century South African cricket represented a tangible link with the 'Mother Nation' and was indicative of the 'progress' being made at that time. 'Our cricket has grown with our country', declared Abe Bailey in 1912.[101] He was not alone in this view. In 1927, A.C. Webber, President of SACA and Chairman of the Board of Control, paid tribute to the 'pioneers' of the 1890s for having 'laid the foundation' for the success of cricket in the country despite innumerable difficulties.[102]

For the British to be successful in South Africa it was important that the other elements of society be 'persuaded' to adhere to a British way of life. 'Sport was an integral part of this whole process of assimilation and mobilisation', explains Odendaal. 'British games, particularly cricket, which the Victorians regarded as embodying "a perfect system of ethics and morals", were taken almost as seriously as the Bible, the alphabet and the Magna Carte'.[103] And eventually of course, these sports would 'supersede traditional, pre-colonial forms of recreation in popularity' as Britain's cultural and political influence became cemented in South Africa in the decades surrounding the Anglo-Boer War.[104]

With the game a cultural bond of the white imperial fraternity, cricket, in the words of Birley, became 'the cornerstone of Empire; the citadel of true sporting values'.[105] Providing a training ground for service to empire, the sport countered the insecurity of colonial society by elevating Britain as the source of all light while at the same time securing its place as a 'sociological and psychological "road map" permitting chosen inhabitants of empire to develop and maintain emotional ties within an ordered, secure environment'.[106] South Africa had seen the sport develop since its early introduction by the military and by the end of the nineteenth century cricket had become an important social institution, fitting in with the structure and relations of the Empire. As elsewhere, cricket in South Africa retained an air of exclusivity with Afrikaner reluctance to adopt the sport a pertinent example of the tensions inherent in all hegemonic relationships.[107] The black population would of course be discriminated against throughout all realms of society – a feature not only of South African society but of British colonization everywhere.

Such were the features of cultural imperialism. The spread of British sport and culture was further galvanized by the sports tours of the late nineteenth–early twentieth centuries. Imperialists, empire builders and sports enthusiasts all argued that sport, and cricket in particular, fostered emotional loyalties between Britain and those who settled in the colonies, with *The Field* claiming in 1896 how:

> The value of international matches at various games between England and her colonies ... will be found to be equal, if not surpass, as a factor in the manufacture of goodwill, any treaty, commercial or political, that ever was drawn up ... our interchange visits for carrying friendly war into another's country by means of bat and ball do eminent service in keeping alive the kindredship of blood.[108]

During the last decades of the twentieth century, cricket had assumed a new level of importance within the British Empire and in South Africa it played a significant part in establishing Britain's cultural dominance up to Union in 1910. While the quest for control of Southern Africa would ultimately signal the last major act of British colonization, the cricket played in South Africa today remains a legacy of the Empire that once created it. British imperialism has indeed left its mark.

## Notes

1. Mangan, *The Games Ethic and Imperialism*, 17.
2. Gemmell, *The Politics of South African Cricket*, 1. A metaphor he of course borrows from C.L.R. James.
3. See Tozer, 'Cricket, School and Empire', 157, and Sandiford, *Cricket and the Victorians*, 144.
4. Muir, *A Short History of the British Commonwealth*.
5. Sandiford, *Cricket and the Victorians*, 144.
6. Ibid.
7. See Kendle, *The British Empire – Commonwealth, 1897–1931*, 2 and Moore, 'The Pan-Britannic Festival: A Tangible but Forlorn Expression of Imperial Unity', 144–5. Derek Birley has described how 'a land-grab had developed with all the European powers competing. Markets; raw materials; reception areas for immigrants; Christianity; exploration – all played their part in making Africa and Asia skirmishing grounds for rival imperialistic ambitions.' Birley, *The Willow Wand*, 85.
8. Lloyd, *The British Empire 1558–1983*, 258.
9. Sandiford, *Cricket and the Victorians*, 144. This despite the fact that the numbers within Britain itself had increased from around 24 million in 1831 to about 41 million in 1901.
10. 'Where the British flag went, so too went cricket', wrote Brian Stoddart. In other words, cricket's 'geographical spread matched that of British expansionists who were part of the direct and indirect British empire'. Stoddart, 'Other Cultures', 135.
11. For a useful examination of sport and cultural imperialism, see Guttmann, *Games and Empires*, 171–88.
12. Williams, *Cricket and Race*, 1.
13. Harris, 'MCC and Cricket', 3.
14. Ibid., 5.

[15] The struggle for Africa occurred largely in the last two decades of the nineteenth century, but intense public interest in the 'penetration' and 'opening up' of the supposedly Dark Continent began, according to Brantlinger, 'seven or eight decades earlier with the abolitionist movement and culminating in Thomas Fowell Buxton's ill-fated Niger Expedition of 1841. Sir Richard Burton and John Hanning Speke's expedition to find the sources of the White Nile in 1856–58 and the publication of David Livingstone's bestselling 'Missionary Travels' in 1857 initiated the final era of African exploration, which led to the carving up of the entire continent into European-ruled colonies and protectorates'. Brantlinger, *Rule of Darkness*, 28.

[16] Quoted in Churchill, 'A History of the English-Speaking Peoples', 121.

[17] Quoted in Garvin, *The Life of Joseph Chamberlain. Vol.3. 1895–1900*, 186.

[18] For a useful examination of the relationship between religion, cricket and empire, see Sandiford, 'England', 9–33.

[19] Green, *A History of Cricket*, 197.

[20] Cited in Holt, *Sport and the British*, 6.

[21] Huggins investigates the role of the 'international middle class' within his analysis of sport during the Victorian age: Huggins, *The Victorians and Sport*, 219–47. See also, Mangan, 'Britain's Chief Spiritual Export: Imperial Sport as Moral Metaphor, Political Symbol and Cultural Bond', 1–10.

[22] Quoted in Rayvern Allen, *Cricket's Silver Lining, 1864–1914*, 19.

[23] Sandiford, 'England', 11.

[24] Box, *The English Game of Cricket*, 72–3.

[25] Quoted in Podmore, 'Public Schools Matches', 60.

[26] Perkin, 'Teaching the Nations How to Play', 212. Demographically, leaving aside Eton, Harrow and Winchester, these public schools catered more for the upper middle class – the sons of the clergy and the higher professions who looked not to business but to professional and Government service for their future careers.

[27] Anthony Kirk-Greene links athletic ability in the public schools to the shaping of the ideal British Imperial administrator. There is a 'direct link', he suggests, 'between the *rites de passage* of a British public school and the self-discipline of fair play … between the system of school prefects and the principles of indirect rule … An important key is to be found in understanding the role and relevance of sport in the making of our-man-on-the-Imperial-spot'. Kirk-Greene, 'Badge of Office: Sport and His Excellency in the British Empire', 180, 191.

[28] Gurdon, 'Public School Cricket', 31.

[29] See for example, Mangan, *Athleticism in the Victorian and Edwardian Public School*, and Mangan, 'Imperialism, History and Education'.

[30] Taylor, 'Play Up, But Don't Play the Game: English Amateur Athletic Elitism, 1863–1910', 78 (italics in original).

[31] *Athletic News*, July 15, 1876, 4. Cited in Taylor, 'Play Up, But Don't Play the Game', 78.

[32] In July 1914, less than a month before the start of the Great War, Hornung had characteristically chosen 'The Game of Life' as the title for one of his last school sermons; 'the way we played for our side, in the bad light, on the difficult pitch, the way we backed up and ran the other man's runs; our courage and unselfishness, not our skill or our success; our brave failures, our hidden disappointments, the will to bear our friend's infirmities, and the grit to fight our own: surely, surely, it is these things above all others that will count, when the innings is over, in the Pavilion of Heaven.' E.W. Horning quoted in Chichester, *E.W. Hornung and his Young Guard*, 31–7. Cited in Tozer, 'A Sacred Trinity – Cricket, School, Empire', 17. This was typical of the cricket–war rhetoric preached within Britain's public schools since the days of the Boer War.

[33] From the *Uppingham School Magazine*, September 1900, 265. Cited in Tozer, 'A Sacred Trinity – Cricket, School, Empire', 18.

[34] See Newsome, *Godliness and God Learning: Four Studies on a Victorian Ideal*. The success of their teachings must be viewed against the backdrop of a general decline in religious conviction. In 1851, for example, a survey indicated that 40 per cent of Britain's population were regular churchgoers. During the time of the Boer War, 50 years later, the figure had fallen to around 25 per cent and as low as 20 per cent in the cities. Birley, *Land of Sport and Glory*, 178.

[35] Sandiford, 'England', 20. Most notably, the Reverend Charles Powlett was the founding member of the Hambledon Club while the Reverend James Pycroft, a curate of Dorset from 1856 to 1895, gave his long life to reading and writing about cricket after having played for Oxford against Cambridge at Lord's in 1836. For 30 years he was a member of the Sussex County Cricket Club

committee. Reverend Archdale Palmer Wickham was wicket-keeper for Somerset between 1891 and 1907 while Reverend A.R. Ward was hugely influential in the development of first-class cricket at Cambridge University. Cardinal Manning, before his ordination, also represented Harrow against Eton and Winchester. Strikingly, between 1860 and 1900, one in three Oxbridge cricket blues (209 amateur players) took holy orders, of which 59 played county cricket. Marqusee, *Anyone but England*, 69.

[36] Ibid., 21.

[37] Baucom, *Out of Place*, 155.

[38] Green, *Wisden Anthology 1864–1900*, 5.

[39] Quoted in Brodribb, *The English Game*, 122; Reverend James Pycroft, cited in ibid., 11.

[40] See Scott, 'Cricket and the Religious World in the Victorian Period', 134–44. For Keith Sandiford, 'it is significant, in analysing the late-Victorian frame of mind, to notice that Waugh chose to write about cricket rather than soccer and thus his Christians were (virtuous) batsmen and not bowlers (Satanic and devious). He adopted, in other words, the Victorian habit of glorifying the bat at the expense of the ball, while also supporting the popular view that soccer led to too many emotional excesses.' Sandiford, *Cricket and the Victorians*, 36.

[41] O. Conway, 'Lord Hawke at Home'. *Windsor Magazine* (1898). Quoted in Rayvern Allen, *Cricket's Silver Lining, 1864–1914*, 241.

[42] See Inglis, 'Imperial Cricket', 155.

[43] Bradley, 'The MCC, Society and Empire', 27.

[44] Ranjitsinhji, *Jubilee Book of Cricket*, 365, 462.

[45] Harris, *A Few Short Runs*, 45. Harris was referred to as the 'big man' at Lord's by Pelham Warner. See Warner, *My Cricketing Life*, 142.

[46] Sandiford, *Cricket and the Victorians*, 72.

[47] See Webber, *The Phoenix History of Cricket*, 86. Until 1969 the MCC chose the captain and the members of England's overseas Test teams.

[48] Knight, *The Complete Cricketer*, 306.

[49] Bradley, 'The MCC, Society and Empire', 30.

[50] Ibid.

[51] Grace, *Cricketing Reminiscences and Personal Recollections*, 349.

[52] Ibid., 344.

[53] See Allen, 'Logan's Golden Age: Cricket, Politics and Empire, South Africa 1888–1910'.

[54] See Gemmell, *The Politics of South African Cricket*, 47.

[55] Altham and Swanton, *A History of Cricket*, 311. (The others being Sir Donald Currie and Sir Abe Bailey).

[56] See Allen, 'Logan's Golden Age'.

[57] In 1907, J.T. Henderson, editor of the *South African Cricketer's Annual*, detailed the contribution of Bailey to cricket in South Africa since 1902: 'It was mainly though his [Bailey's] instrumentality that the Wanderers Club [of Johannesburg] arranged the visit of the Australian Team of 1902. Two years later Mr. Bailey sent a team to England, which cost him over £2,000; in 1905 he materially assisted the Transvaal Cricket Union in the matter of their M.C.C. guarantee; and when the question arose of sending away the present South African Team, Mr. Bailey came forward with financial assistance. For two seasons past he has paid for a professional coach at the Johannesburg colleges and schools.' Henderson, *South African Cricketer's Annual. Season 1906–07*, 174.

[58] Murray and Merrett, *Caught Behind: Race and Politics in Springbok Cricket*, 7–8.

[59] Bailey, 'Cricket in South Africa', 324.

[60] Winch, *Cricket in Southern Africa*, 16.

[61] The notice read: 'A grand match at cricket will be played for 1,000 dollars a side on Tuesday, January 5, 1808, between the officers of the Artillery Mess, having Colonel Austin of the 60th Regiment, and the officers of the Colony, with General Clavering. Wickets to be pitched at 10 o'clock.' *Cape Town Gazette and African Advertiser*, January 2, 1808.

[62] See *The Diamond Fields Advertiser*, 'Sport and Pastime in South Africa', 19.

[63] Archer and Bouillon, *The South African Game*, 81.

[64] Warner, *Cricket in Many Climes*, 176.

[65] Odendaal, 'South Africa's Black Victorians: Sport and Society in South Africa in the Nineteenth Century', 197–8.

[66] Ibid.

67  For a discussion on this see Archer and Bouillon, *The South African Game*, 22–4.

68  Odendaal, 'South Africa's Black Victorians', 198.

69  See South African Cricket Association, *Minute Book*, February 1, 1904, 67. After an application letter dated 21 December 1903 was received from the Secretary of the Rhodesian Cricket Union, Rhodesia's affiliation to SACA was approved 'unanimously' by the governing body.

70  A letter to the *Cape Times* in August 1888 from 'CEJ' had suggested the formation of a 'South African Cricketers' Congress' or a 'Representative Union'. *Cape Times*, August 28, 1888.

71  The view of contemporary cricket journalist Charles Finlason writing in the *Daily Independent*, November 23, 1888. Quoted in Winch, *England's Youngest Captain*, 185.

72  See Henderson, *South African Cricketer's Annual. Season 1889–90*, 140. The delegates met at Glover's Athletic Bar in Kimberley and voted William Hopley to the chair. He was a respected figure, being a Cape Town advocate with a strong cricket background. Cricket writer and administrator Harry Cadwallader was elected as Hon. Secretary of the new Association.

73  See Parker, *South African Sports. An Official Handbook*, 47 and Transvaal Cricket Union, *Yearbook 1898–99*, 5.

74  Parker, *South African Sports*, 47.

75  Cited in Transvaal Cricket Union, *Yearbook 1898–99*, 5.

76  Baker, 'Whose Hegemony? The Origins of the Amateur Ethos in Nineteenth Century English Society', 2.

77  Allsop, 'Reminiscences of Cricket', 134.

78  See Duffus, *Play Abandoned*.

79  Nauright, *Sport, Cultures and Identities in South Africa*, 26.

80  Sandiford argues that apart from dress and language, some observers in the nineteenth century termed cricket as the most significant and visible part of Anglo-Saxon culture. See Sandiford, 'Introduction', 2.

81  Warner, *Cricket in Many Climes*, 176.

82  Key works by Odendaal on the subject include *Cricket in Isolation*; 'South Africa's Black Victorians', and *The Story of an African Game*.

83  The match was arranged as an 'additional' fixture on the itinerary of the tourists and remained the only match to be played in South Africa between a black side and a 'white' touring team until the African XI met Derrick Robins' side in 1973. See Odendaal, *Cricket in Isolation*, 325.

84  See Archer and Bouillon, *The South African Game: Sport and Racism*, 79.

85  All internationals in South Africa's pre-1990s history were against white sides. See Gemmell, *The Politics of South African Cricket*.

86  Brantlinger, *Rule of Darkness: British Literature and Imperialism, 1830–1914*, 39.

87  According to Brantlinger, 'after the mid-Victorian years the British found it increasingly difficult to think of themselves as inevitably progressive; they began worrying instead about the degeneration of their institutions, their culture, their racial "stock"'. Ibid., 230. The promotion of British forms of sport during this period was an attempt to alley this trend. Cricket was fundamental in this process.

88  Odendaal, *The Story of an African Game*.

89  Sandiford, 'Introduction', 3–4.

90  Mangan, 'Britain's Chief Spiritual Export', 1.

91  Ibid.

92  Murray and Merrett, *Caught Behind: Race and Politics in Springbok Cricket*, 7.

93  Bradley, 'The M.C.C., Society and Empire', 44–5.

94  See Gemmell, *The Politics of South African Cricket*.

95  Even as recently as 2003 when the Cricket World Cup was held in South Africa, the game has continued to be affected by issues of politics. See Majumdar and Mangan, *Cricketing Cultures in Conflict: World Cup 2003*.

96  Gemmell, *The Politics of South African Cricket*, 8. Here he quotes Polley, *Moving the Goalposts*, 12.

97  Mangan, 'Britain's Chief Spiritual Wxport', 2.

98  Ibid.

99  Brantlinger, *Rule of Darkness: British Literature and Imperialism, 1830–1914*, 11.

100  Mangan, 'Britain's Chief Spiritual Export', 6.

101  Bailey, 'Cricket in South Africa', 324.

102  See Webber, 'The Control of Cricket in South Africa', 21.

103  Odendaal, 'South Africa's Black Victorians', 196.

[104] Ibid.
[105] Birley, *Land of Sport and Glory. Sport and British Society, 1887–1910*, 16.
[106] See Mangan, 'Britain's Chief Spiritual Export', 6.
[107] For a discussion on this, see Allen, 'Logan's Golden Age'.
[108] *The Field*, June 27, 1896.

## References

Allen, D. 'Logan's Golden Age: Cricket, Politics and Empire, South Africa, 1888–1910'. PhD Diss., University of Brighton, 2008.

Allsop, G. 'Reminiscences of Cricket'. In *The History of South African Cricket*, edited by M.W. Luckin, 123–34. Johannesburg: W.E. Hortor & Co., 1915.

Altham, H.S., and E.W. Swanton. *A History of Cricket*. London: George Allen & Unwin, 1948.

Archer, R., and A. Bouillon. *The South African Game: Sport and Racism*. London: Zed Press, 1982.

Bailey, A. 'Cricket in South Africa'. In *Imperial Cricket*, edited by P.F. Warner, 311–24. London: The London & Counties Press Association, 1912.

Baker, N. 'Whose Hegemony? The Origins of the Amateur Ethos in Nineteenth Century English Society'. *Sport in History* 24, no. 1 (2004): 1–16.

Baucom, I. *Out of Place: Englishness, Empire and the Locations of Identity*. Princeton, NJ: Princeton University Press, 1999.

Birley, D. *Land of Sport and Glory. Sport and British Society, 1887–1910*. Manchester: Manchester University Press, 1995.

Birley, D. *The Willow Wand*. London: Aurum Press, 2000.

Box, C. *The English Game of Cricket*. London: The Field Office, 1877.

Bradley, J. 'The M.C.C., Society and Empire: A Portrait of Cricket's Ruling Body, 1860–1914'. In *The Cultural Bond: Sport, Empire, Society*, edited by J.A. Mangan, 27–46. London: Frank Cass, 1992.

Brantlinger, P. *Rule of Darkness: British Literature and Imperialism, 1830–1914*. Ithaca, NY: Cornell University Press, 1988.

Brodribb, G., ed. *The English Game: A Cricket Anthology*. London: Hollis & Carter, 1948.

Churchill, W.S. 'A History of the English-Speaking Peoples'. In *Our Island Heritage*, edited by A. Briggs. London: Reader's Digest, 1988.

Diamond Fields Advertiser. 'Sport and Pastime in South Africa'. Kimberley: Diamond Fields Advertiser, 1899.

Duffus, L. *Play Abandoned*. Cape Town: Timmins, 1969.

Garvin, J.L. *The Life of Joseph Chamberlain, Vol.3. 1895–1900*. London: MacMillan, 1934.

Gemmell, J. *The Politics of South African Cricket*. London: Taylor & Francis, 2004.

Grace, W.G. *Cricketing Reminiscences and Personal Recollections*. London: James Bowden, 1899.

Green, B., ed. *Wisden Anthology 1864–1900*. London: Queen Anne Press, 1979.

Green, B. *A History of Cricket*. London: Guild Publishing, 1988.

Gurdon, C. 'Public School Cricket'. In *James Lillywhite's Cricketer's Companion for 1883*, 30–8. London: James Lillywhite, 1883.

Guttmann, A. *Games and Empires: Modern Sports and Cultural Imperialism*. New York: Columbia University Press, 1994.

Harris, Lord. 'MCC and Cricket'. In *South African Cricketer's Annual. Season 1905–06*, edited by J.T. Henderson. Pietermaritzburg: Times Printing & Publishing Co, 1906.

Harris, Lord. *A Few Short Runs*. London: John Murray, 1921.

Henderson, J.T., ed. *South African Cricketer's Annual. Season 1889–90*. Durban: Robinson, Vause & Co, 1890.

Henderson, J.T., ed. *South African Cricketer's Annual. Season 1906–07*. Pietermaritzburg: Times Printing & Publishing Co, 1907.

Holt, R. *Sport and the British*. Oxford: Oxford University Press, 1989.

Huggins, M. *The Victorians and Sport*. London: Hambledon, 2004.

Inglis, K.S. 'Imperial Cricket'. In *Sport in History: The Making of Modern Sporting History*, edited by R. Cashman and M. McKernan, 148–79. Queensland: University of Queensland Press, 1979.

Kendle, J.E. *The British Empire – Commonwealth, 1897–1931*. Melbourne: Cheshire, 1972.

Kirk-Greene, A. 'Badge of Office: Sport and His Excellency in the British Empire'. In *The Cultural Bond: Sport, Empire, Society*, edited by J.A. Mangan, 178–200. London: Frank Cass, 1992.

Knight, A.E. *The Complete Cricketer*. London: Methuen & Co., 1906.

Lloyd, T. *The British Empire 1558–1983*. Oxford: Oxford University Press, 1984.

Majumdar, B., and J.A. Mangan, eds. *Cricketing Cultures in Conflict: World Cup 2003*. London: Routledge, 2004.

Mangan, J.A., 'Imperialism, History and Education', In *Benefits Bestowed? Education and British Imperialism*, edited by J.A. Mangan, 1–22. Manchester: Manchester University Press, 1988.

Mangan, J.A., ed. *The Cultural Bond: Sport, Empire, Society*. London: Frank Cass, 1992.

Mangan, J.A. 'Britain's Chief Spiritual Export: Imperial Sport as Moral Metaphor, Political Symbol and Cultural Bond'. In *The Cultural Bond: Sport, Empire, Society*, edited by J.A. Mangan, 1–10. London: Frank Cass, 1992.

Mangan, J.A. *The Games Ethic and Imperialism: Aspects of the Diffusion of an Ideal*. London: Frank Cass, 1998.

Mangan, J.A. *Athleticism in the Victorian and Edwardian Public School: The Emergence and Consolidation of an Educational Ideology*. London: Frank Cass, 2000.

Marqusee, M. *Anyone but England*. London: Verso, 1994.

Moore, K. 'The Pan-Britannic Festival: A Tangible but Forlorn Expression of Imperial Unity'. In *Pleasure, Profit, Proselytism. British Culture and Sport at Home and Abroad, 1700–1914*, edited by J.A. Mangan, 144–62. London: Frank Cass, 1988.

Muir, R. *A Short History of the British Commonwealth*. London: G. Philip, 1962.

Murray, B., and C. Merrett. *Caught Behind: Race and Politics in Springbok Cricket*. Johannesburg: Wits University Press, 2004.

Nauright, J. *Sport, Cultures and Identities in South Africa*. London: Leicester University Press, 1997.

Newsome, D. *Godliness and God Learning: Four Studies on a Victorian Ideal*. London: John Murray, 1961.

Odendaal, A. *Cricket in Isolation*. Cape Town: Don Nelson, 1977.

Odendaal, A. 'South Africa's Black Victorians: Sport and Society in South Africa in the Nineteenth Century'. In *Pleasure, Profit, Proselytism. British Culture and Sport at Home and Abroad 1700–1914*, edited by J.A. Mangan, 193–214. London: Frank Cass, 1988.

Odendaal, A. *The Story of an African Game*. Cape Town: David Philip, 2003.

Parker, G.A. *South African Sports. An Official Handbook*. London: Sampson Low, Marston & Co, 1897.

Perkin, H. 'Teaching the Nations How to Play: Sport and Society in the British Empire and Commonwealth'. In *The Cultural Bond: Sport, Empire, Society*, edited by J.A. Mangan, 211–19. London: Frank Cass, 1992.

Podmore, A. 'Public Schools Matches'. In *The M.C.C. 1787–1937, The Times*, 58–63. London: The Times Publishing Co., 1937.

Polley, Martin. *Moving the Goalposts*. London: Routledge, 1998.

Ranjitsinhji, K.S. *The Jubilee Book of Cricket*. London: William Blackwood, 1897.

Rayvern Allen, D., ed. *Cricket's Silver Lining, 1864–1914*. London: Guild Publishing, 1987.

Sandiford, K.A.P. *Cricket and the Victorians*. Aldershot: Scolar Press, 1994.

Sandiford, K.A.P. 'Introduction'. In *The Imperial Game*, edited by B. Stoddart and K.A.P. Sandiford, 1–8. Manchester: Manchester University Press, 1998.

Sandiford, K.A.P. 'England'. In *The Imperial Game*, edited by B. Stoddart and K. A. P. Sandiford, 9–33. Manchester: Manchester University Press, 1998.

Scott, P. 'Cricket and the Religious World in the Victorian Period'. *Church Quarterly* 3 (July 1970): 134–44.

South African Cricket Association. *Minutes 1898–1905*. United Cricket Board collection, AG 2912/A1. University of the Witwatersrand, Johannesburg.

Stoddart, B. 'Other Cultures'. In *The Imperial Game*, edited by B. Stoddart and K.A.P. Sandiford, 135–49. Manchester: Manchester University Press, 1998.

Taylor, H. 'Play Up, But Don't Play the Game: English Amateur Athletic Elitism, 1863–1910'. *The Sports Historian* 22 (November 2002): 75–97.

Tozer, M. 'Cricket, School and Empire: E.W. Hornung and His Young Guard'. *International Journal of the History of Sport* 6, no. 2 (1989): 156–71.

Tozer, M.. 'Sacred Trinity-Cricket, School, Empire: E.W. Hornung and his Young Guard'. In *The Cultural Bond: Sport, Empire, Society*, edited by J.A. Mangan, 11–26. London: Frank Cass, 1992.

Transvaal Cricket Union. *Yearbook 1898–99*. Johannesburg: M.J.Wood, 1898.

Warner, P.F. *Cricket in Many Climes*. London: William Heinemann, 1900.

Warner, P.F. *My Cricketing Life*. London: Hodder & Stoughton, 1921.

Webber, A.C. 'The Control of Cricket in South Africa'. In *South African Cricket, 1919–1927*, edited by M.W. Luckin, 21–9. Johannesburg: M.W. Luckin, 1927.

Webber, R. *The Phoenix History of Cricket*. London: Phoenix Sports Books, 1960.

Williams, J. *Cricket and Race*. Oxford: Berg, 2001.

Winch, J. *Cricket in Southern Africa*. Rosettenville: Windsor, 1997.

Winch, J. *England's Youngest Captain*. Windsor: Windsor Publishers, 2003.

# Irish Australians, postcolonialism and the English game

Alan Bairner*

*School of Sport and Exercise Sciences, Loughborough University, Loughborough, UK*

## Introduction

As noted elsewhere, the history of cricket in Australia is liberally sprinkled with Irish names.[1] Other leading Australian cricketers such as Chuck Fleetwood-Smith (middle name O'Brien) and Jack Fingleton, even though their surnames do not indicate their Irishness, were also prominent members of Australia's Irish diaspora. Furthermore, there is nothing new in the Irish contribution to Australian cricket. The Australian team which played the first ever international test series against England in 1877 included two native Irishmen, Thomas Kelly, born in County Waterford, and Thomas Patrick Horan, born in County Cork, who went on to play in 15 test matches between 1877 and 1885, as well as John McCarthy Blackham whose father and mother were natives of Newry and Tralee respectively. This Irish contribution to Australian cricket is in sharp contrast to what one uncovers in the annals of English test cricket in which scarcely an Irish name is to be found. To date, only five Irish-born players – Leland Hone, Sir Timothy O'Brien, J.E.P. McMaster, F.L. Fane and Martin McCague – have represented England in test cricket.[2] More recently, Dublin-born Ed Joyce played for England, for the first time, ironically in a one-day match against Ireland that took place in Belfast on 14 June 2006, and subsequently in one-day games in Australia in 2007.[3]

Why have the 'Irish' been manifestly so much more prominent in Australian cricket? Did the original Irish immigrants only take up this quintessentially English game when they came to Australia? Did subsequent generations of the Irish diaspora community develop a fondness for the game precisely because it offered an opportunity to engage in anti-imperial struggle against the English using sporting means? Did playing cricket help the Irish to become recognized as real Australians, thereby allowing them to jettison their former colonized selves? In seeking to answer these and other related questions, this essay will consider the character of Irish migration to Australia, comment on the historical status of cricket in Ireland, and discuss the contribution of the Irish to Australian sport in general and to cricket in particular. The aim is also to shed light on the problematic relationship between imperialism and the experience of being colonized, not only in Australia but also in Ireland.

### Ireland: postcolonial and post-imperial?

It is one thing to state that the modern world is postcolonial, but as Moore-Gilbert comments, 'such has been the elasticity of the concept ... that in recent years some commentators have begun to express anxiety that there may be a danger of it imploding as an analytic construct with any real cutting edge'.[4] Certainly in terms of discussing Irish cultural politics, its value is necessarily restricted. As ní Fhlathúin observes, 'the question of national identity is more difficult and ambiguous on the periphery of the British Empire than at its centre'.[5] Yet, one could also argue that Ireland, together with Scotland and Wales, which are so close to the English centre that in the eyes of many they are inextricably linked to that centre, have encountered at least as many difficulties in relation to national identity as other, more peripheral, former component parts of the British Empire have experienced in the postcolonial phase. According to Loomba, 'postcolonial studies have shown that both the "metropolis" and the "colony" were deeply altered by the colonial process',[6] and arguably the situation is rendered even more complex when we are dealing with countries that were both part of the metropolis and also colonized in a unique relationship described by Michael Hechter as 'internal colonialism'.[7] The Irish case confirms the truth of Murray's assertion that the postcolonial order is 'one characterised by fluidity and hybridity, a cultural criss-crossing, what has been referred to as the "in-between"'.[8] It has even been argued that Ireland was both 'imperial' *and* 'colonial'.[9] Indeed, Kibberd argues that 'only a rudimentary thinker would deny that the Irish experience is at once postcolonial and post-imperial'.[10] Similar thoughts have been expressed in relation to Australia which, as Hay notes, 'is an offshoot of European imperial expansion, yet part of that expansion itself, with its own colonies such as Papua New Guinea and its own internal colonization of its aboriginal ... population'.[11] Thus, according to Loomba, white settlers in countries such as Australia were agents of colonial rule and, 'no matter what their differences with the mother country, white populations here were not subject to the genocide, economic exploitation, cultural decimation and political exclusion felt by indigenous peoples or other colonies'.[12] We should note however that many of those who arrived in Australia had already played the part of indigenous people subjected at the very least to cultural imperialism, thus ensuring that their status as white settlers was problematic. In fact, in both Australia and Ireland, the antisyzygy – the yoking of opposites – of imperialism and colonialism has had major repercussions.

According to Quayson, postcolonialism 'is as much about conditions under imperialism and colonialism proper as about conditions coming after the historical end of colonialism'.[13] One reason for this is that there may exist important continuities that connect the two periods. So it was that during the colonial epoch, Australians and the Irish took up games that were to remain central to their respective sporting cultures long after a measure of political and cultural independence had been achieved, whilst simultaneously presiding over the emergence of distinctive ludic traditions.

In Ireland, this involved playing (and continuing to play) games such as rugby union, field hockey, soccer and cricket even after the Gaelic Athletic Association had come into existence in 1884 with its clearly stated objective to protect and promote native Irish sports and pastimes. Inevitably many of those who were most active in British (or, according to the GAA, 'foreign') games were stalwart defenders not only of the constitutional relationship between Britain and Ireland but also of the British imperial project. The so-called Anglo-Irish establishment was connected to England through familial and educational ties whilst the working-class advocates of soccer were almost equally well connected as a result of the constant coming and going between the industrial cities of Belfast, Glasgow and Liverpool.[14] However, unlike Gaelic games, these British activities also made possible a form of anti-colonial resistance through sporting competition which, along with personal habitus derived from schooling and upbringing, helps to explain the attraction of British games for Irish nationalists such as Parnell and the Redmond brothers (cricket) and Kevin Barry and Eamon de Valera (rugby union). In sport, as in much else, the Irish, at a time when many of their number were embarking on the perilous journey to Australia, were both imperial and colonized. In their new home, the emigrants were to discover a sporting culture which was at least as schizophrenic as the one they had left behind.

## Irish immigrants in Australia

At no point in time did Irish immigrants to Australia form a homogeneous group. Their experiences differed, according to O'Brien and Travers, 'depending on the date of their arrival, the region in which they settled, the amount of money they brought with them or later made in Australia, chance encounters, tragedies or even just bad luck'.[15] However, the historiography of the Irish in Australia has often been insufficiently nuanced to do justice to a more complex reality. Thus, as McConville notes, 'A myth that the transported Irish had been pure and upright, and had nothing in common with the convict herd, had grown up around the history of the Irish in Australia'.[16] They were presented as either honest farmers who had been convicted for defending their land or else rebels who had sought nothing more than their democratic rights. This was perhaps the inevitable consequence of the fact that, according to Reece, 'Writing about the Irish in Australia began as an act of filial piety or nationalist and religious affirmation on the part of Irish-born Australians'.[17]

One section of the Irish-Australian community that was certainly ignored in this sort of history were the Anglo-Irish although, as Forth observes, 'in both early nineteenth-century Ireland and Australia it was Protestant Irish gentlemen rather than the native Catholic peasantry who were regarded, and regarded themselves, as the true Irish'.[18] Small in number but influential, they came to Australia 'with dreams of freedom and harmony'.[19] Furthermore, 'In colonial Australia, as in Ireland, representatives of the surviving "Old English" Catholic aristocracy obviously had more in common with Protestant gentlemen than with their co-religionists of peasant background'. For that reason, it is argued that prominent Irish Catholic colonists such as the Trinity-educated lawyers Sir Roger Therry and Sir John Hubert Plunkett can also be categorized as 'Anglo-Irish'.[20] For many reasons, one might easily conclude that these immigrants had more in common with the Empire than with those who were actually colonized by it.

However, even the so-called rebel element amongst the Irish immigrant community did not form an entirely homogeneous group since many of the 'political' convicts sent to Australia were Ulster Protestants who had been heavily involved in the United Ireland movement – not imperialist themselves but arguably possessing at least as much in common with the Anglo-Irish elite than with fellow 'rebels' from a Catholic background. In time, indeed, just like the Anglo-Irish, they became 'quietly absorbed in the Protestant mainstream'.[21] Within ten years, as Reece notes, many of the rebels of 1798 had become 'prosperous pillars of society in colonial New South Wales'.[22]

It was not only the Protestant Irish, however, who found themselves increasingly assimilated into the culture of their new homeland. Commenting particularly on the earliest Catholic migrants, McConville argues that, 'Whatever the myths surrounding the first Irish in Australia, in reality they had escaped to a system hardly more brutal than that of Ireland, to a place of comparative material comforts where they were safe from the horrors of the Famine which took so many of their compatriots'.[23] Indeed, as Akenson points out, 'The great complication is the fact that free (that is, non-criminal) settlers began migrating to Australia at a very early date and therefore a society evolved in which the free community intertwined with the society of the convicts (many of whom worked for the free settlers)'.[24] Furthermore, the immigrants who arrived in the 1850s and 1860s looking for gold soon outnumbered the convict Irish and in so doing, according to McConville, 'brought a new Ireland to Australia'.[25] As Akenson has it, 'The triumph of those good ordinary Irish migrants was that they became good ordinary Australians'.[26] In all of this, we should bear in mind that, above all else, these people shared the fact that they were not aboriginal. Regardless of their attitude to the British Empire, all of them had become colonizers in their own right. This did not mean, however, that the Irish necessarily abandoned each and every aspect of their Irishness, including, for many, an anti-imperialist/anti-British perspective.

Certainly none of the preceding discussion should be taken to imply that the relations between the Catholic Irish and the Anglo-Protestants were at once and thereafter cordial. As Reece records, 'Confrontations between Green and Orange certainly marked the history of most Australian colonies in the nineteenth century'. The Irish continued to be viewed with suspicion and their relationship with the wider society was inevitably affected both by events in Ireland and domestic political issues, the latter ensuring that 'the worst sectarian excesses were not just a continuation of the old struggles that had scarred Ireland'.[27] From the 1860s until the 1880s, 'in many places, the harmony between Catholic and Protestant, and Irish and English, came under threat, firstly through the Fenian scare, then through the education issue, and lastly through the campaign for Home Rule'.[28] With Catholic schooling a constant source of friction, relations between Catholics and Protestants would also be affected in subsequent years by the Easter Rising of 1916, the debate about conscription for the First World War and ongoing accusations of 'masonry and wire-pulling' in relation to the job market.[29] Irish Catholic involvement in Australian labour politics was also a consistently emotive issue.

## Cricket and the Irish

The familiarity with cricket of the Anglo-Irish section of the diaspora cannot be in doubt. The first cricket match to be played in Ireland had taken place on grounds adjacent to the home of the Viceroy, Lord Westmoreland, and featured on one side members of the British Army garrison and, on the other, a number of Anglo-Irish gentlemen, including, almost certainly, the future Duke of Wellington.[30] So embedded in Anglo-Irish life had cricket become that one might easily assume that only Protestants and those with a strong attachment to the union of Ireland and Britain would have favoured this most English of pastimes. Certainly there was a perception amongst some of the Irish in Australia that cricket was not their game although, paradoxically, this point is particularly well made by one of the great Irish-Australian cricketers, Bill O'Reilly, who writes, 'Cricket did not come naturally to Irish people who, as I found out later, regarded it more or less as a foreign game which was somewhat beneath their dignity'.[31] It is true that, until relatively recently with the emergence of Ed Joyce (Middlesex), Eoin Morgan (Middlesex) and Niall

O'Brien (Northamptonshire), those few Irishmen who have played county cricket in England have tended to be from what might loosely be described as an Anglo-Irish background. Even Samuel Beckett, celebrated Irish writer and the only Nobel Prize winner to feature in the pages of cricket's 'bible', *Wisden*, was a Protestant, educated at Portora Royal School in Enniskillen, County Fermanagh.

It is, however, too simplistic to associate cricket with only one section of the Irish population. In terms of schools' cricket, for example, although St Columba's College, a (Protestant) Church of Ireland establishment was prominent in the development of the game, so too was Clongowes Wood College, a Jesuit institution and Alma Mater of James Joyce.[32] More significantly, as Hunt reveals, cricket was commonly the chosen summer sport of Gaelic footballers despite subsequent attempts by the Gaelic Athletic Association (GAA) to proscribe participation in 'foreign' games.[33] Although de Búrca suggests that 'the rapid growth of the GAA also brought to a halt the spread of cricket in rural areas where the game had gained a foothold',[34] in Westmeath at least, according to Hunt, 'newspaper analysis reveals that cricket experienced a period of steady growth, both geographic and demographic, throughout the 1880s and 1890s'.[35] Hunt's research shows that cricket was particularly popular amongst the farm labourer and general labouring classes, 'a finding that challenges the traditional perception of Irish cricket as an elitist activity'. Hunt argues that 'Playing cricket presented members of this group with an opportunity to earn respectability, display skill, and win prestige in their own locality'.[36]

Two other studies reveal the strength of cricket among the nineteenth-century Irish in the counties of Tipperary and Kilkenny, both strongholds of Gaelic games in subsequent years. Patrick Bracken reveals that there were as many as 43 cricket teams in the former in 1876.[37] Michael O'Dwyer demonstrates that, in the nineteenth century, Kilkenny cricket had spread far beyond the big houses to be played in every town and village, by labourers and peasantry alike.[38] At its peak in 1896, 12 years after the founding of the GAA, there were 50 teams in the county. This evidence would suggest that many of the Irish who emigrated to Australia in the nineteenth century would have been familiar with the game of cricket.

As mentioned earlier in passing, 'the great Parnell ... inherited his father's taste for the English game ... and he captained the Wicklow team for many years before entering nationalist politics'.[39] Other luminaries of the Irish nationalist movement such as John Redmond and his brother, Willie, both educated at Clongowes, were also enthusiastic cricketers, whilst Tom Kettle, another Clongowes old boy, retained a great affection for the game throughout his life. It is worth noting that the Redmonds were also the leading Irish nationalists to enjoy strong personal links to the Irish in Australia.[40]

From all of this we can readily assume that some of those Irishmen who arrived in Australia had already played cricket. This was not simply a case of people adopting a game that had been denied to them whist living under the colonial yoke but which could now be taken up as a means whereby to confront the English. Furthermore, such was the discrimination which many Irish immigrants faced, that it was no easy matter for the Irish to become good Australians, if that meant accepting the authority of an Anglo-Protestant establishment. To their distinct advantage, however, was the fact that the English had been keen to distinguish Australian cricket and cricketers from notions of Englishness, a process of 'othering' with which the Irish had long since come to terms.[41]

## Sport and the Irish in Australia

The Irish undeniably made a considerable contribution to the emergence of a distinctive Australian sports culture. Indeed, according to one historian, 'The collective impact of the

Catholic Irish Australians on the development of Australian sport was so marked that many of what may be called typically "Irish" behavioural traits have become part of the sporting personality of Australia'.[42] Passing quickly over the unabashed essentialism implicit in this assertion, it is certainly worth commenting on the role played by the Irish (particularly through the major Catholic schools including St Joseph's College in Sydney, St Joseph's, Gregory Terrace in Brisbane, and Xavier in Melbourne) in the growth of sports such as rugby union. It is ironic, of course, that these schools were in numerous ways modelled on English examples – a point not lost on C.L.R. James when recalling his own schoolboy introduction to cricket in Trinidad:

> At school we learnt not only to play with the team. We were taught and learnt loyalty in the form of loyalty to the school. As with everything else in those days, I took it for granted. It was only long afterwards, after gruesome experience in another country, that I saw it for the specifically British thing that it was.[43]

And so it was that young Australians learned to play the English game, absorbing in the process, no doubt, some of the values of the imperialist masters whilst simultaneously becoming good Australians, ready and willing to take on those masters at their own game.

None of this was achieved, however, without controversy. Indeed, it is little wonder, according to Adair and Vamplew, that 'historic Anglo-Irish rivalries and long-standing Protestant-Catholic tensions were played out in Australia'.[44] Real, or just as frequently imagined, evidence of sectarianism has been uncovered within clubs in sports as diverse as rowing, rugby league and Australian Rules Football. Boxers have even fulfilled the time-honoured role of proxy warriors for the rival communities.[45] As O'Farrell points out, 'The fame and fortune of the American boxer John L. Sullivan, and later Jack Dempsey and Gene Tunney, had their parallels in the careers of Larry Foley and Les Darcy'.[46] In March 1871, a prize fight took place between Foley and Sandy Ross, a man with militant Protestant connections. The contest is commemorated in M.J. Conlon's poem, 'The Fight on George's River Ground'.

> They both shook hands, you'd really think
> No ill feeling lay between
> The colours bright that made this fight
> The orange and the green.
> For two long hours that fight did last
> Till Ross's seconds came between
> And threw the sponge high in the air
> In favour of the green.[47]

Other Irish Australian sportsmen celebrated in verse include Darcy, the middleweight boxer who died in the USA in April 1917 at the age of 21 and whose vast funeral 'testified to his extraordinary veneration among Irish Catholics',[48] Tommy Corrigan who was killed on 11 August 1894 when his horse fell during the Caulfield Grand National Steeplechase and cricketers, Tommy Horan and John McCarthy Blackham.[49] Another sport in which the Irish made their mark was rugby league, illustrating that class as well as ethnic background played a significant role.[50]

It is important to note that Gaelic games also had their advocates in Australia. According to O'Farrell, 'Enthusiasts for specifically Irish games were not numerous in Australia, but they were energetic and saw that the only way to ensure a future for such sports was to gain their acceptance by Catholic schools'. However, as O'Farrell reveals, 'Irish campaigners for hurling and Gaelic football made virtually no headway in Catholic schools, at least in New South Wales, against those English games, cricket and rugby football'.[51] Despite the 'Irishness' of these schools, in sport as in much else, the principle of Australianise or perish applied, thereby establishing the foundations upon which the hegemonic power of cricket and rugby could be built. That is not to deny, however, that specific identities have been sustained within the general sporting culture. But what might seem surprising, at least to the uninformed observer, is the extent to which cricket – arguably the most quintessentially English sport and a major element in Anglo-Australian sporting culture – came to play such an important part of the Irish Australian experience.

### 'Irish' Australia and cricket

Australian cricket in the years between 1928 and 1948 has rightly been described as 'the Bradman era'.[52] Donald Bradman dominated world cricket in those years to an extent that had never previously been achieved and that is surely impossible to emulate in the modern era. It is unlikely that Bradman's batting records will ever be wholly erased from the record books – for example, his test match average of 99.94 and his career achievement of scoring 117 centuries in 338 innings. Bradman was unique. Nevertheless he played alongside numerous other great Australian players, notably Stan McCabe and Bill O'Reilly, as well as only slightly lesser figures such as Jack Fingleton. His relationship with these players was however never easy.[53]

Fingleton who, like O'Reilly, was to become a successful cricket writer, salutes Bradman, the cricketer and the captain, for his 'phenomenal career'.[54] He even notes that 'Bradman never allowed success to inflate his ego, he was too modest and sensible for that'.[55] On the other hand, Fingleton observed that O'Reilly, McCabe and he 'talked a similar language' and comments that 'although they had no enmity or "rivalry" with Bradman, they had no real comradeship … They were not on the same wavelength.'[56] These remarks are endorsed by O'Reilly who refers to his respect for Bradman whilst simultaneously drawing attention to their difficult relationship:

> On the cricket field Bradman and I had the greatest respect for each other. I certainly did for him, and I know he did for me, but I might as well come straight out with it and let you know that, off the field, we had not much in common.'[57]

According to O'Reilly, 'You could say we did not like each other, but it would be closer to the truth to say we chose to have little to do with each other'. Why was that? O'Reilly was in doubt that it was largely a matter of upbringing.

> I don't think that this arose from the ego-laden encounters of our younger days. It was more the product of the chemistry arising from our different backgrounds. Don Bradman was a teetotaller, ambitious, conservative and meticulous. I was outspoken and gregarious, an equally ambitious young man of Irish descent.[58]

Irish descent was hugely important to O'Reilly as it was to Fingleton. The opening chapter of the former's autobiography is titled simply 'Ireland' and in it he makes glowing references to a number of leading Irish nationalists, including 'the celebrated Eamon de Valera', Robert Emmett, 'the ill-fated young hero', and Daniel O'Connell, 'the great statesman who stood squarely up to the power of Westminster during his life-long struggle for Home Rule'.[59] In a biography of O'Reilly, written by R.S. Whitington, Chapter Six is headed 'Irish Ingredient', the author describing here the Irish antecedents not only of O'Reilly himself but also of Stan McCabe.[60]

O'Reilly himself describes a visit to Dublin in 1938 by the Australian party that was touring England, a tour that included a game against Ireland at Trinity College Dublin. Reflecting on this experience and, again inadvertently invoking the concept of habitus, O'Reilly recalls that, 'More than once I was struck with a similarity between Irish behaviour and our Australian way of life, but nowhere so powerfully as across the bar'. He goes on to note that,

> An Irishman enters a pub on purpose bent. His approach leaves no doubt in your mind that he is there on business. He slaps his money down, takes up his glass and demolishes his Guinness with the same purposeful intent as any dyed-in-the-wool Australian you meet on the other side of the world.[61]

Yet nothing, one imagines, would have seemed more alien to Donald Bradman. Charles Williams, the great Australian's unofficial biographer comments,

> O'Reilly was in many respects Bradman's opposite: he was of Irish Catholic origin, whereas Bradman was English Protestant; he was tall and lanky, where Bradman was short and dapper; he was a great bowler, where Bradman was a great batsman; and, although each respected the other's ability, the contrast between their two personalities was such that there was never to be much friendship between them, and in the end the distance was to develop into outright hostility.[62]

To paraphrase Fingleton, they simply did not speak the same language.

As noted earlier, both O'Reilly and Fingleton made much of their Irish origins. O'Reilly notes that his paternal grandfather, Peter, had arrived in Australia in 1865 from Ballyconnell, Co. Cavan, and his grandmother, Bridget O'Donoghue, in 1863 from Ballinasloe, Co. Galway. He draws attention to the fact that the latter could read and write and adds,

> You seldom run across an Irish migrant of that period who could neither read nor write, but strangely enough, remarkably few English assisted migrants had those abilities, which makes you wonder about the strange circumstances that forced people to leave their homes forever, in the days when the English [*sic* ] Government no longer held the right to send their convicted felons to our country.[63]

In 1933, O'Reilly married Molly Herbert whose father, Richard, had come to Australia from Longford, Co. Meath and whose mother, Kate Beston, was originally from Co. Clare. For their part, the Fingletons hailed from Portlaoise, Co. Laois.

Both men are equally open about the importance of Catholicism in their education and their later lives. They were both taught at Christian Brothers' schools,[64] thereby establishing a clear link in their minds between Irishness and the Catholic Church at a time when, in the words of O'Farrell, the pupils got 'an Australian education in an Irish-Catholic way'. As a result, 'Pupils were exposed to an Irish conditioning process which conveyed a dimension of difference, a variant on the common English culture'. None of this depended on an alternative curriculum. For O'Farrell, the most Irish thing these Irish-born teachers conveyed 'was themselves'.[65] The fact that the Christian Brothers were so heavily involved not only in ensuring the resilience of embodied Irishness but also in promoting cricket is worthy of comment. In Ireland itself, and especially in the north of Ireland, closer of course to the centre of imperial power, much of their energy went into resisting British cultural influence not least in the world of sport. As Brian Cosgrove recalls,

> Some of us, however, had to stay in Newry; and taught as I was there by a very different kind of religious order from the Jesuits at Clongowes – the Christian Brothers – it was simply inconceivable that we would be allowed to play cricket.[66]

In Australia though, the importance of these teachers in terms of embodied Irishness, regardless perhaps of their promotion of cricket, is underlined by both Fingleton and O'Reilly. The former writes respectfully of his former headmaster at St Charles's Christian Brothers' School in Waverley. 'The headmaster in my time was Denis Benedict Foran; as a young man he had left his native Ireland to work in foreign fields; Australians of my generation owe much to such Irishmen'. Brother Foran, according to Fingleton, 'was a grand inspiring teacher, with a love of his homeland and its history'.[67] 'It was because of his teaching', he adds, 'that I rank, for what it is worth, as the only Australian cricketer who's ever been to Ireland … who can sing "The Wearing of the Green" in Gaelic'.[68] It is obvious that Foran also acted as a father figure for the young Fingleton after his father's early death. He grew up in households where the Rosary was said each evening. His brother, Wally, became a Marist priest. Towards the end of his autobiography, he recalls a visit to Liverpool where he heard Mass in the city's Catholic Metropolitan Cathedral and a short stay in Rome in 1965 where he attended Mass in St Peter's celebrated by Pope Paul VI.[69] None of this is the sort of recollection commonly associated with the life stories of prominent sportsmen.

O'Reilly also refers to his Christian Brothers' education. In 1921, he began boarding at St Patrick's College, Goulbourn which he describes as the second oldest Catholic college in Australia. The school's main supporter of cricket, he recalls, was 'hot-tempered Brother Daly whose lilting accent betrayed the fact that he was fresh from the southwest of Ireland',[70] thus giving the lie to his own expressed opinion and also to conventional wisdom, that 'cricket did not come naturally to Irish people'. The fact is that these descendants of Irish immigrants were learning to play sport as Australians but in an environment in which their Irishness was not only internalized but also embodied and thus projected outwards. Cricket and rugby 'were the avenues through which the Catholic schools related to the rest of the Australian sporting community'. Therefore, 'to drop them in preference for Irish games, would be to opt for the ghetto, to isolate such schools from the mainstream of Australian life, to abandon efforts to compete and win against the world'.[71] Regardless of what they were taught, however, there was nothing to prevent pupils from thinking of themselves as Irish, and indeed much to encourage them to do so.

O'Reilly recalls that during the 1938 trip to Dublin, 'our dressing room door was flung open as a little old white-haired priest in rather shabby clerical gear, together with a round black hat, burst through shouting my name'. The priest continued, '"Welcome to the land of the O'Reillys. Delighted to meet you. Me name's Mick Lacey. Where's McCabe?" And after having given Stanley a similar welcome, "Where's Fingleton? Where's Hassett?"' According to O'Reilly, 'he had picked out the names that left no doubts of Irish lineage'.[72] In fact, in this context, the mention of Hassett is slightly peculiar. A Catholic, educated initially by the Misses Clancy at Geelong Central School, Arthur Lindsay Hassett became a pupil at the non-Catholic Geelong College in 1924 and contributed massively to its growing reputation for sport. His Christian names, unlike those of his brother Vincent Xavier, provide no indication of a Catholic background.

Hassett's biographer also recounts the incident in the Australians' dressing room in Dublin. According to Whitington, also granted entrance to the dressing room, the Dublin priest was taken in tow by Bill O'Reilly, who said, '"Faith, Father, and you'd be wantin' to meet Don Bradman?" The priest replied, "Bradman be bothered … It's a quintet named McCabe, Fingleton, Fleetwood-Smith, Hassett and O'Reilly – particularly O'Reilly –as I'm wantin' to do business with".' According to Whitington, 'Hassett did not play in that game in Ireland. Possibly, having attended Geelong College, not Xavier, he wished to be neutral.'[73] One can only speculate as to the importance of his place of education when the decision was made that he should succeed Bradman as the captain of the Australian team in 1949. What is undeniable though is that neither his Irish ancestry nor his religion loom large in Hassett's life story. How different in that respect from that of O'Reilly who, reflecting on his return trip from England (and Ireland) in 1938, observes,

Sailing away from England on the way home, I felt I was a much better Australian than before I had set out, but at the same time I was certain that I had not seen a better country than my own and that I owed an enormous debt, unpayable, to my grandfather Peter O'Reilly, who had folded up his Irish tent and headed into the southern seas sixty-nine years before.[74]

## Conclusion

There can be no doubt that these Irish Australian cricketers were deeply conscious of their Irish ancestry. This applies to Hassett as well as to the others although, for a variety of reasons, he did not perhaps embody Irishness to the same extent as O'Reilly and Fingleton. In their study of soccer players who were not born in Ireland but who have represented the national team, Holmes and Storey note that 'it seems highly likely that family background may be an issue here'.[75] They argue that there is 'a need to move beyond a conception of national identity that is intrinsically linked to Ireland as a bounded space' and 'to conceive of Irish identity in diasporic terms; an identity that is no longer place-bound or contained by the actual borders of Ireland'.[76] Whilst this is certainly appropriate in the case of soccer players brought up in Britain but willing to play for Ireland, it may seem less directly relevant in relation to cricketers born and brought up in Australia who have gone on to represent their country. However, even though O'Reilly had commented, erroneously, it can be argued, that there was no great affinity between the Irish and the sport that he played, the Irish Australians do not appear to have suffered any unease about playing the English game. Why not?

O'Reilly, Fingleton and others were unreservedly Australian. However, they were also secure in their Irish identity. Indeed, they had internalized their Irishness, not only in their ways of thought but also in bodily practices, thereby making their life-style distinct from that of Bradman and others.[77] A similar point about Irish migrants in the United States is made by veteran Gaelic games commentator, Micheál Ó Muircheartaigh who observes that, 'most of them never saw home again, but it would be true to say that Ireland seldom left their minds'. Indeed, he recalls a telephone conversation with one emigré of whom he had asked why he had never returned home in 50 years:

> His reply was most revealing: 'I have indeed. Every single night before going to bed I walk out the door at home – up Bóthar na Seán and into every single field before returning home and then in my mind going to bed in Dún Síon.[78]

Noting that all social relations are enshrined, not simply reflected, in space, Lefebvre adds that, 'social relations, which are concrete abstractions, have no real existence save in and through space. *Their underpinning is spatial.* In each particular case the connection between this underpinning and the relations it supports calls for analysis.' (original emphasis)[79]

In relation to national habitus, the significant space is often that territory which is contained within national boundaries. For the diaspora, however, the national territory becomes boundless. Within that boundless space though, we must also take account those domestic spaces such as cellars, drawers and wardrobes wherein are located material evocations of the national 'home' – photographs, items of clothing, souvenirs of first holy communions and confirmations, old hurley sticks and so on. It is in 'this material paradise' that we acquire a heightened sense of self[80] – in this case, national self. In such ways are memories of the 'old country' formed for, as de Certeau points out, 'like those birds that lay their eggs only in other species' nests, memory produces in a place that does not belong to it. It receives its form and its implantation from external circumstances, even if it furnishes the content (the missing detail).'[81]

Irish Australian cricketers were also far enough away from England to allay any fears that playing the oppressors' game might culturally contaminate them. Playing cricket in England itself, even though the game had been played widely in Ireland, would have been a very different matter. The 'Irish' in Australia were, for the most part, ready and willing to become Australians almost as soon as they disembarked, although their conception of what made a good Australian was inevitably at odds with that of the pro-British establishment. One way of becoming Australian, at least for male immigrants, was to embrace popular sports such as cricket and rugby. In terms of the maintenance of embodied Irishness, however, it was hugely important that they learned these games in Catholic schools and colleges that were often run by Irish brothers and were redolent of evocations of 'the old country'. Thus, as the likes of Bradman were no doubt aware, they played what were originally British sports as 'Irish' Australians.

With the growth of secularism and major demographic change within the Australian Catholic population, arguably the Irish habitus of cricketers such as O'Reilly and Fingleton is increasingly a thing of the past. Their personal experiences, however, offer fascinating insights into the ways in which members of the Irish diaspora in Australia became assimilated without losing sight of their Irishness. They played the quintessential English game in what was becoming a postcolonial context. In part, this undeniably allowed them to offer resistance towards their former colonial masters. But it also provided them with opportunities to challenge what might be described as a post-imperial view of what it meant to be Australian. Perhaps the antipathy towards Bradman and others was merely anti-Britishness by proxy. However, it may also have reflected a desire on the part of the 'Irish', with their own ancestral memories of colonialism, to ensure that anti-imperialist sentiment should prevail. If that is the case, their contribution to Australian cricket can be said to have lived on long after their playing careers had ended. Furthermore, this may well have formed only a small, albeit significant, part of the legacy of the Irish settlers to postcolonial Australia. As Fanon argued, 'in decolonization, there is … the need of a complete calling in question of the colonial situation'.[82] Arguably, the Irish in Australia, their cricketers included, were far better placed than most of their Anglo-Australian counterparts (and team mates) to ask the question.

### Acknowledgements

For references to work on Irish cricket by Bracken and O'Dwyer, I am indebted to Seamus J. King, author of *A History of Hurling* (Dublin: Gill and Macmillan, 1998).

### Notes

1.  Bairner, 'Wearing the Baggie Green: the Irish and Australian Cricket'.
2.  See Siggins, *Green Days: Cricket in Ireland 1792–2005*.
3.  Paul Weaver, 'Dubliner Joyce begins England Chapter Against Background of Feeble Predecessors'. *Guardian Sport*, June 14, 2006, 13.
4.  Moore-Gilbert, *Postcolonial Theory*, 11.
5.  Ni Fhlathúin, 'Anglo-India after the Mutiny', 67.
6.  Loomba, *Colonialism/Postcolonialism*, 19.
7.  Hechter, *Internal Colonialism*.
8.  Murray, 'Introduction', 4.
9.  Jeffery, 'Introduction'.
10. Kibberd, 'Modern Ireland', 97.
11. Hay, 'The Last Night of the Poms', 18.
12. Loomba, *Colonialism/Postcolonialism*, 9–10.
13. Quayson, *Postcolonialism*, 2.
14. For an extended discussion of these issues, see Bairner, 'Sport, Nationality and Postcolonialism in Ireland'.

15   O'Brien and Travers, 'Introduction', 1.
16   McConville, *Croppies, Celts and Catholics*, 17–18.
17   Reece, 'Writing about the Irish in Australia', 226.
18   Forth, '"No Petty People"', 130.
19   McConville, *Croppies, Celts and Catholics*, 46.
20   Forth, '"No Petty People"', 130.
21   Ibid., 141.
22   Reece, 'Writing about the Irish in Australia', 233.
23   McConville, *Croppies, Celts and Catholics*, 28.
24   Akenson, *The Irish Diaspora*, 95.
25   McConville, *Croppies, Celts and Catholics*, 46.
26   Akenson, *The Irish Diaspora*, 108.
27   Reece, 'Writing about the Irish in Australia', 233.
28   McConville, *Croppies, Celts and Catholics*, 56.
29   Ibid., 100. See also Franklin, 'Catholics versus Masons', 1–15.
30   Hone, *Cricket in Ireland*. See Gemmell in this collection for a further discussion of cricket in Ireland.
31   O'Reilly, *'Tiger' O'Reilly*, 21.
32   Hone, *Cricket in Ireland*.
33   Hunt, 'The Early Years of Gaelic Football and the Role of Cricket in County Westmeath'.
34   De Búrca, *The GAA*, 25.
35   Hunt, 'The Early Years', 39.
36   Ibid., 41.
37   Bracken, *Foreign and Fantastic Field Sports*.
38   O'Dwyer, *The History of Cricket in County Kilkenny*.
39   Hone, *Cricket in Ireland*, 11.
40   See McConville, *Croppies, Celts and Catholics*, 82–4. For information about the Redmond brothers' Australian connections, and for a detailed discussion of the broader issues, see O'Farrell, *The Irish in Australia*.
41   Bradley, 'Inventing Australians and Constructing Englishness'.
42   Horton, 'The "Green" and the "Gold"', 90.
43   James, *Beyond a Boundary*, 42.
44   Adair and Vamplew, *Sport in Australian History*, 73.
45   See, for example, Solling, *The Boatshed on Blackwattle Bay*; Stremski, *Kill for Collingwood*; Williams, *Out of the Blue*.
46   O'Farrell, *The Irish in Australia*, 68.
47   Reproduced in Wannan, *The Wearing of the Green*, 342.
48   O'Farrell, *The Irish in Australia*, 262.
49   See Wannan, *The Wearing of the Green*, 343.
50   See Cashman, *The Paradise of Sport*.
51   O'Farrell, *The Irish in Australia*, 187.
52   O'Reilly and Egan, *The Bradman Era*.
53   For a full examination of the relationship between Bradman and his 'Irish' team mates, see Bairner, 'Wearing the Baggie Green'.
54   Fingleton, *Brightly Fades the Don*, 197.
55   Fingleton, *Batting from Memory*, 110.
56   Ibid., 113.
57   O'Reilly, *'Tiger' O'Reilly*, 53–4.
58   Ibid., 54.
59   Ibid., 2–4.
60   Whitington, *Time of the Tiger*.
61   O'Reilly, *'Tiger' O'Reilly*, 4.
62   Williams, *Bradman*, 21–2.
63   O'Reilly, *'Tiger' O'Reilly*, 7–8.
64   The Christian Brothers were founded in Waterford in 1802 by Edmund Ignatius Rice. Their first Australian colony, consisting of four Brothers, was established in 1868 and was the forerunner of around 50 Christian Brothers' institutions throughout the country, including numerous schools and colleges.

[65]   O'Farrell, *The Irish in Australia*, 189.
[66]   Cosgrove, 'Not Cricket', 61.
[67]   Fingleton, *Batting from Memory*, 45.
[68]   Ibid., 46.
[69]   Ibid., 217–19, 224.
[70]   O'Reilly, *'Tiger' O'Reilly*, 30.
[71]   O'Farrell, *The Irish in Australia*, 187.
[72]   O'Reilly, *'Tiger' O'Reilly*, 5.
[73]   Whitington, *The Quiet Australian*, 51.
[74]   O'Reilly, *'Tiger' O'Reilly*, 141.
[75]   Holmes and Storey, 'Who are the Boys in Green?', 97.
[76]   Ibid., 100.
[77]   In this essay my use of the concept of habitus is influenced primarily by the work of Pierre Bourdieu. See Bourdieu, *Distinction*.
[78]   Muircheartaigh, *From Dún Síon to Croke Park*, 21.
[79]   Lefebvre, *The Production of Space*, 404.
[80]   Bachelard, *The Poetics of Space*, 7.
[81]   de Certeau, *The Practice of Everyday Life*, 86.
[82]   Fanon, *The Wretched of the Earth*, 28.

## References

Adair, Darryl, and Wray Vamplew. *Sport in Australian History*. Melbourne: Oxford University Press, 1997.

Akenson, Donald Harman. *The Irish Diaspora. A Primer*. Belfast: Institute of Irish Studies, The Queen's University of Belfast, 1996.

Bachelard, Gaston. *The Poetics of Space*. Boston, MA: Beacon Press, 1994.

Bairner, Alan. 'Sport, Nationality and Postcolonialism in Ireland'. In *Sport and Postcolonialism*, edited by John Bale and Michael Cronin, 159–74. Oxford: Berg, 2003.

Bairner, Alan. 'Wearing the Baggie Green: the Irish and Australian Cricket'. *Sport in Society* 10, no. 3 (2007): 457–75.

Bourdieu, Pierre. *Distinction. A Social Critique of the Judgment of Taste*. New York: Routledge, 1986.

Bracken, Patrick. *Foreign and Fantastic Field Sports – Cricket in County Tipperary*. Thurles, Co. Tipperary: Liskeeveen Books, 2004.

Bradley, James. 'Inventing Australians and Constructing Englishness: Cricket and the Creation of a National Consciousness, 1860–1914'. *Sporting Traditions* 11, no. 2 (1995): 35–60.

Cashman, Richard. *The Paradise of Sport: The Rise of Organised Sport in Australia*. Melbourne: Oxford University Press, 1995.

Cosgrove, Brian. 'Not Cricket'. In *Ireland (Ulster) Scotland: Concepts, Contexts, Comparisons. Belfast Studies in Language, Culture and Politics 7*, edited by Edna Longley, Eamonn Hughes, and Des O'Rawe, 61–4. Belfast: Cló Ollscoil na Banríona, 2003.

de Búrca, Marcus. *The GAA. A History*. Dublin: Gill and Macmillan, 1980.

de Certeau, Michel. *The Practice of Everyday Life*. Berkeley, CA: University of California Press, 1988.

Fanon, Frantz. *The Wretched of the Earth*. Harmondsworth, UK: Penguin, 1967.

Fingleton, Jack. *Brightly Fades the Don*. London: Collins, 1949.

Fingleton, Jack. *Batting from Memory*. London: Collins, 1981.

Forth, Gordon. '"No Petty People": the Anglo-Irish Identity in Colonial Australia'. In *The Irish in the New Communities*, edited by Patrick O'Sullivan, 128–42. Leicester: Leicester University Press, 1992.

Franklin, James. 'Catholics versus Masons'. *Journal of the Australian Catholic Historical Society* 20 (1999): 1–15.

Hay, Roy. 'The Last Night of the Poms: Australia as a Postcolonial Sporting Society'. In *Sport and Postcolonialism*, edited by John Bale and Michael Cronin, 15–28. Oxford: Berg, 2003.

Hechter, Michael. *Internal Colonialism*. London: Routledge and Kegan Paul, 1975.

Holmes, Michael, and David Storey. 'Who are the Boys in Green? Irish Identity and Soccer in the Republic of Ireland'. In *Sport and National Identity in the Post-War World*, edited by Adrian Smith and Dilwyn Porter, 88–104. London: Routledge, 2004.

Hone, William Patrick. *Cricket in Ireland*. Tralee: The Kerryman Limited, 1956.

Horton, Peter A. 'The "Green" and the "Gold": the Irish-Australians and their Role in the Emergence of the Australian Sports Culture'. *International Journal of the History of Sport* 17, nos. 2/3 (2000): 65–92.

Hunt, Tom. 'The Early Years of Gaelic Football and the Role of Cricket in County Westmeath'. In *Sport and the Irish. Histories, Identities, Issues*, edited by Alan Bairner, 22–43. Dublin: University College Dublin Press, 2005.

James, C.L.R. *Beyond a Boundary*. London: Serpent's Tail, 1994.

Jeffery, Keith. 'Introduction'. In *'An Irish Empire'? Aspects of Ireland and the British Empire*, edited by K. Jeffery, 1–24. Manchester: Manchester University Press, 1996.

Kibberd, Declan. 'Modern Ireland: Postcolonial or European?'. In *Not On Any Map. Essays on Postcoloniality and Cultural Nationalism*, edited by S. Murray, 81–100. Exeter: Exeter University Press, 1997.

Lefebvre, Henri. *The Production of Space*. Oxford: Blackwell Publishing, 1991.

Loomba, Ania. *Colonialism/Postcolonialism*. London: Routledge, 1998.

McConville, Chris. *Croppies, Celts and Catholics. The Irish in Australia*. Caulfield, Victoria: Edward Arnold, 1987.

Moore-Gilbert, Bart. *Postcolonial Theory. Contexts, Practices, Politics*. London: Verso, 1997.

Murray, Stuart. 'Introduction'. In *Not On Any Map. Essays on Postcoloniality and Cultural Nationalism*, edited by S. Murray, 1–18. Exeter: Exeter University Press, 1997.

ní Fhlathúin, Maire. 'Anglo-India after the Mutiny: The Formation and Breakdown of National Identity'. In *Not On Any Map. Essays on Postcoloniality and Cultural Nationalism*, edited by S. Murray, 67–80. Exeter: Exeter University Press, 1997.

O'Brien, John, and Pauric Travers. 'Introduction'. In *The Irish Emigrant Experience in Australia*, edited by J. O'Brien and P. Travers, 1–5. Swords, Co. Dublin: Poolbeg Press, 1991.

O'Dwyer, Michael. *The History of Cricket in County Kilkenny – The Forgotten Game*. Kilkenny: O'Dwyer Books, 2006.

O'Farrell, Patrick. *The Irish in Australia*. Kensington, NSW: New South Wales University Press, 1986.

Ó Muircheartaigh, Micheál. *From Dún Síon to Croke Park*. Dublin: Penguin Ireland, 2004.

O'Reilly, Bill. *'Tiger' O'Reilly. 60 Years in Cricket*. Sydney: Collins, 1985.

O'Reilly, Bill, and Jack Egan. *The Bradman Era*. London: Willow Books Collins, 1984.

Quayson, Ato. *Postcolonialism. Theory, Practice or Process?* Cambridge: Polity Press, 2000.

Reece, Bob. 'Writing about the Irish in Australia'. In *The Irish Emigrant Experience in Australia*, edited by J. O'Brien and P. Travers, 226–42. Swords, Co Dublin: Poolbeg Press, 1991.

Siggins, Gerard. *Green Days: Cricket in Ireland 1792–2005*. Stroud: Nonsuch Publishing, 2005.

Solling, Max. *The Boatshed on Blackwattle Bay: Glebe Rowing Club 1879–1993*. Sydney: Glebe Rowing Club, 1993.

Stremski, Richard. *Kill for Collingwood*. Sydney: Allen and Unwin, 1986.

Wannan, Bill. *The Wearing of the Green. The Lore, Literature, Legend and Balladry of the Irish in Australia*. London: The New English Library, 1968.

Whitington, R.S. ('Dick') *The Quiet Australian. The Lindsay Hassett Story*. London: Heinemann, 1969.

Whitington, R.S. ('Dick') *Time of the Tiger. The Bill O'Reilly Story*. Newton Abbot: Sportsman's Book Club, 1972.

Williams, Charles. *Bradman*. London: Abacus, 2001.

Williams, Terry. *Out of the Blue: The History of Newtown RLFC*. Sydney: Newtown RLFC, 1993.

# 'From far it look like politics': C.L.R. James and the canon of English cricket literature

Anthony Bateman*

*Faculty of Humanities, De Montfort University, Leicester, UK*

## Cardus and James

If John Nyren, the co-author of *The Cricketers of My Time* (1832) has been commemorated within cricket discourse as the sport's Chaucer and Neville Cardus as its Shakespeare, then C.L.R. James is a Miltonic figure, greatly admired for the quality of his prose and knowledge of cricket, but whose politics remain something of an embarrassment. In *Beyond a Boundary* James exceeded the canonical limits of representing cricket by politicizing this avowedly apolitical field. For example, James's reconstruction of Trinidadian cricket in the early years of the twentieth century showed how institutional access to the structure of club cricket, with its finely graded social and racial distinctions, replicated and contributed to the colonial policy of divide and rule.[2] Furthermore, James fearlessly critiqued the colonialist axiologies of English cricket discourse. James understood that such discourse reproduced a colonial value system based upon a racist mind/body binary. His reinterpretation of the great Learie Constantine, for example, is consciously positioned against this opposition:

> Constantine's leg-glance from outside the off-stump to long-leg was a classical stroke. It was not due to his marvellous West Indian eyes and marvellous West Indian wrists. It was due, if you must have it, to his marvellous West Indian brains.[3]

Surprisingly, although James's cricket writings contain numerous references to, and interpretations of, the canon of English cricket literature, little attention has been paid to the way that his work re-articulates this discourse in a manner that is simultaneously profoundly traditional and markedly radical. Critics have correctly identified the relationship of James's work both to the English literary canon (in which he always remained thoroughly immersed) and to the work of other Marxist cultural theorists, but have largely overlooked James's correlation to the tradition of English cricket writing.[4] This critical oversight is particularly serious given that at the beginning of the chapter of *Beyond a Boundary* entitled 'What is Art?', he self-consciously positioned his work in relation to that of Cardus:

> As firmly as I am able and is here possible, I have integrated [cricket] in the historical movement of the times. The question remains: What is it? Is it mere entertainment or is it an art? Mr Neville Cardus (whose work deserves a critical study) is here most illuminating, not as a subject but as object. He will ask: 'Why do we deny the art of a cricketer, and rank it lower than a vocalist's or a fiddler's? If anybody tells me that R.H. Spooner did not compel a pleasure as aesthetic as any compelled by the most cultivated Italian tenor that ever lived I will write him down a purist and an ass'. He says the same in more than one place. More than any sententious declaration, all his work is eloquent with the aesthetic appeal of cricket. Yet he can write in his autobiography: 'I do not believe that anything fine in music or in anything else can be understood or truly felt by the crowd'. Into this he goes at length and puts the seal on it with 'I don't believe in the contemporary idea of taking the arts to the people: let them seek and work for them'. He himself notes that Neville Cardus, the writer on cricket, often introduces music into his cricket writing. Never once has Neville Cardus, the music critic, introduced cricket into his writing on music ... Cardus is a victim of that categorisation and specialisation, that division of the human personality, which is the greatest curse of our time. Cricket has suffered, but not only cricket. The aestheticians have scorned to take notice of popular sports and games – to their own detriment. The aridity and confusion of which they so mournfully complain will continue until they include organised games *and the people who watch them* as an integral part of their data.[5] (James's emphasis)

There are a number of points to be drawn from this crucially important passage. First, James's advocacy of a critical study of Cardus acknowledges and reinforces the importance of this figure within the cricket canon. It also reveals that James himself was an important figure in the critical valorization of Cardus, as other passages in *Beyond a Boundary* reiterate. Second, James's critique of Cardus's aesthetic places cricket and its discourses at the heart of a crucial cultural debate: like theorists such as Raymond Williams and Pierre Bourdieu, James understood the opposition between 'high' and 'popular' culture as a historically specific construction that had arisen as a direct response to the technological and industrial forces of modernity. The reified concept of 'Art' that arose from these conditions, James believed, became the privileged term in a binary opposition between it and the degraded concept of the 'popular'. James fully acknowledged that Cardus rendered cricket as an art form at the level of discourse, but totally rejected his claim that its aesthetic subtleties were beyond the understanding of the sport's mass spectatorship. Indeed, for James the relatively unmediated experience of the crowd was positively constitutive of cricket's meaning as a cultural form. James's statement, therefore, gestures towards a counter-hegemonic discourse of cricket in which proper attention to the experience of mass spectatorship provides a democratic aesthetic which can transcend the exclusive class and racial politics of English cricket writing.

Although aestheticization had been a constant feature of cricket discourse ever since its emergence, in *Beyond a Boundary* James described this process as 'impressionistic or apologetic, timid or defiant, always ready to take refuge in the mysticism of metaphor'. James has in his sights those cricket writers like Cardus who sought to argue for the sport's status as art simply by a process of cultured allusion and intense subjectivity. In James's view the urbane metaphors and allusions amounted to nothing more than a litany of 'literary and psychological responses'.[6] James elaborated this tradition of aestheticizing cricket by offering a more rigorous and historicized theory of cultural equivalence in which aesthetic factors are given a properly historical and materialist context. In this respect Cardus was important for James because his understanding of the relationship between cricket and its social and economic context could be accommodated dialectically within a Hegelian/Marxist schema. For example, in *Beyond a Boundary* James praised Cardus's assessment of W.G. Grace as 'a representative man of his epoch', but notes that he failed to comprehend exactly what Grace represented, particularly to those living in the alienating conditions of Britain's industrial towns and cities:

> As usual, it is Mr Neville Cardus, in his vivid darting style, who has got closest to W.G.: 'The plain, lusty humours of his first practices in a Gloucestershire orchard were to be savoured through the man's gigantic rise to a national renown'. Only it was not the plain, lusty humours of an orchard, but a whole way of life. 'He rendered rusticity cosmopolitan whenever he returned to it. And always did he cause to blow over the fashionable pleasances of St. John's ...' There they needed it least. It was bleak Sheffield, to dusty Kennington and to grim Manchester that W.G. brought the life they had left behind. The breezes stirred by his bat had blown in their faces, north, south and east, as well as in the west.[7]

In this apparently conventional reading (which clearly draws upon the books James consumed voraciously as a boy), Grace is nevertheless represented as an atypical Hegelian/Marxist 'world-historical individual', an embodied synthesis of England's past and present. At the same time the passage is crucial for it establishes James's argument for a popular aesthetic that will cut through the false distinction between 'high' and 'low' culture (the idea of culture is here rendered exactly according to Raymond William's pluralistic definition of 'a whole way of life').[8] Here James simultaneously admires Cardus's prose whilst critiquing his narrow definition of culture in such a way that exemplifies his ambivalent relationship to the English cricket canon.

Cardus's and James's respective analyses of interwar cricket further reveal a sense of an important inter-textual relationship. For example, in a passage in *English Cricket* Cardus tellingly described a sense of aesthetic decline that he believed afflicted cricket after the First World War:

> When first-class cricket was played again after the end of the 1914–1918 war, we were given yet another example of what a sensitive plant this cricket is – how quick to respond to atmosphere, how eloquent at any time of the English mood and temper. It was an age of disillusionment and cynicism; the romantic gesture was distrusted. 'Safety First' was the persistent warning. We saw at once on the cricket field the effect of a dismal philosophy and a debilitated state of national health. Beautiful and brave stroke-play gave way to a sort of trench warfare, conducted behind the sandbag of broad pads.[9]

In this passage Cardus suggests a relationship between a cultural practice and its historical context that explains why, despite his profoundly conservative cultural politics, he remained a literary model for James. Cardus drew upon a tradition of non-Marxian cultural criticism that Raymond Williams has shown was exemplified in the work of Augustus Pugin, John Ruskin and William Morris. According to Williams, these writers sought to demonstrate that 'the art of a period is closely and necessarily related to the generally prevalent "way of life"'.[10] James developed dialectically Cardus's vision of post-First World War cricket by theorizing an inter-war rationalization of cricket, its embodiment in the figure of Donald Bradman and the Bodyline tactic devised and deployed by the English team on the 1932–33 tour, as nothing less than symptomatic of 'The Decline of the West', of 'the violence and ferocity of our age expressing itself in cricket'.[11] In these conditions, argued James, cricket could no longer euphemize aesthetically its violence. Not only did

James correctly identify Bodyline as a moment of imperial crisis, he saw it as the contemporary expression of the emergence of totalitarianism he had interpreted as being foreshadowed in Hermann Melville's *Moby Dick*.[12]

Like Cardus and other English cricket writers, against the fallen present James constructed a pristine point of contrast, a pre-Great War Golden Age of cricket. In this respect *Beyond a Boundary* reveals the tendency of (post) colonial writers to enter into the dominant rhetorical patterns of empire.[13] In his resoundingly canonical view of late-nineteenth-century cricket, James almost completely effaces any sense of the iniquitous systems of exploitation upon which the economies of nation and empire depended. As Gordon Rohlehr has correctly observed, 'one cannot avoid the conclusion that James in his depiction of the Golden Age is engaged in a highly idealised verbal reconstruction of an ethos that he had never actually experienced, but which was part of the nostalgically recalled and abstract world of the books in which as a child he had lived'.[14] Indeed, it is an irony of cricket literature that the conservative Cardus drew more attention to the harsh realities of Victorian social relations than did James. However, both Cardus and James's constructions of the Golden Age of cricket suggest that the discursive meaning of cricket has consistently been produced and reproduced in response to perceptions of socio-economic, political and cultural crisis. Although politically poles apart, both writers constructed and deployed the Golden Age of cricket as a retrospective critique of the conditions of contemporary capitalism.

## 'Garfield Sobers'

Despite James's debt to the canon of English cricket writing, he sought to democratize the notion of a cricket aesthetic and find a suitable, non-racialized literary means of accounting for the embodied performance of West Indies cricket. James was highly conscious of the convention of representation that sublimated matters of cricketing style (or, in James's aesthetic 'significant form') into racialized binaries. James's radical subversion of the tradition of English cricket writing, his re-articulation of the game's aesthetic discourses and his quest for the suitable literary means of representing non-white players were crystallized in his 1969 essay, 'Garfield Sobers' which was originally published in John Arlott's collection, *The Great All-rounders*. This essay exemplifies James's status as an anti-colonial writer, inhabiting colonial literary and cricket discourse, subverting it from within and using cricket as a means of writing about political liberation. Grant Farred has accurately summarized the significance of the work:

> 'Garfield Sobers' is a brilliant piece of writing that is simultaneously cricket commentary, cultural politics, and an articulation of the process of Caribbean nation-building. (Without intending to be reductive, the Sobers piece can in many ways be read as a synopsis of *Beyond a Boundary*, so eruditely does this essay echo the themes of James's most important work.)[15]

In this essay James characteristically situates this phenomenal cricketer in his particular cultural and social space and explicitly positions his own analysis against conventional, metropolitan interpretations of Sobers. As Farred has argued, 'The Sobers essay ... is James's corrective to the "pundits", a code word in this instance for white English cricket critics'.[16] However, Farred's next statement contains an inaccuracy:

> These critics, James holds, are unable to identify in Sobers's unique game the abilities which are representative of their particular 'unit of civilisation'. 'Garfield Sobers', conceptualised in the early years of West Indian independence, is but one Jamesian intervention in a dominant cricket discourse that sublimates questions of race and the effects of colonialism when it considers cultural practices such as sport.[17]

Far from race being sublimated in the dominant discourse of cricket, James identified that Cardus and other English cricket writers misrepresented and misinterpreted cricketers from the colonies precisely because they over-emphasized the issue of race as a means of accounting for a distinctive West Indies aesthetic of cricket. Furthermore, race was frequently cited as an explanation for a supposedly undisciplined colonial approach to cricket, an approach that supposedly codified an apparent West Indian incapacity for political self-determination. As in *Beyond a Boundary*, one of the main themes of James's Sobers essay is to counteract such racialized and reductive accounts of Caribbean players. As a 'text' Sobers is very much a West Indian, but James refuses to account for his West Indianness in terms of race. Instead, Sobers is read as a richly individualized embodiment of historical forces and hence of the West Indian popular consciousness. As in his portrayals of W.G. Grace, James invokes the Hegelian idea of typicality in order to show how Sobers embodies historical currents and forces and thus links the individual to the social whole:

> The pundits colossally misunderstood Garfield Sobers – perhaps the word should be misinterpret, not misunderstand. Garfield Sobers, I shall show, is a West Indian cricketer, not merely a cricketer from the West Indies. He is the most typical West Indies cricketer that it is possible to imagine. All geniuses are merely people who carry to an extreme definitive the characteristics of the unit of civilisation to which they belong and the special act or function which they express or practise. Therefore to misunderstand Sobers is to misunderstand the West Indies, if not in intention, by inherent disposition, which is much worse. Having run up the red flag, I should at least state with whom I intend to do battle. I choose the least offensive and in fact he who is obviously the most well-meaning, Mr Denys Robotham of the *Guardian* of Friday, 15 December 1967. Mr Robotham says of Sobers: 'Nature, indeed, has blessed Sobers liberally, for in addition to the talents and reflexes, conditioned and instinctive, of a great cricketer, he has the eye of a hawk, the instincts and suppleness of a panther, exceptional stamina, and apparently the constitution of an ox'.[18]

To James, Rowbotham's representation of Sobers was typical of the unconscious racism permeating English cricket discourse. James thus sets out to show that Sobers' remarkable cricketing abilities are not racial but 'the fine fruit of a great tradition', a tradition that includes not only great West Indies players such as Constantine and George Headley but English masters such as W.G. Grace and Walter Hammond. A Sobers innings, as much as any poem by Derek Walcott, is thus read as an expression of a cultural hybridity that is the inevitable result of the historical experience of colonialism.

James's aestheticization of Sobers involved an imitation of English cricket discourse through frequent allusions to canonical writers such as Shakespeare and the Romantic poets. With its archaisms and concentration of literary references, the following passage is particularly Cardusian. It also foregrounds the act of literary representation:

> It was jealousy, nay political hatred which prompted Cassius to say to Caesar:
>
> Why, man, he doth bestride the narrow world,
>
> Like a Colossus, and we petty men
>
> Walk under his huge legs and peep about,
>
> To find ourselves dishonourable graves.

> Certainly in the press box watching Sobers a mere scribe is aware of Hazlitt's: 'Greatness is power, producing great effects. It is not enough that a man has great power in himself, he must show it to all the world in a manner that cannot be his or gainsaid'. Of a famous racket-player: 'He did not seem to follow the ball, but the ball seemed to follow him'. Hazlitt would not have minded the appropriation of this acute simplicity for Sobers at short-leg to Gibbs.[19]

This frame of reference is no gratuitous circuit of inter-legitimation but another consciously executed theoretical tactic. In eulogizing Sobers, James pointedly appropriated a literary frame of reference usually preserved in the work of writers such as Cardus for the English amateur batsmen of the Golden Age. The literary works through which Sobers' bodily performance is mediated have been carefully selected for their political, as well as their aesthetic, resonances. Like Shakespeare's Caesar, James's Sobers is a political figure whose 'power', as expressed in the cricket field, is emblematic of the appropriation of political power that was Caribbean independence. The significance of Hazlitt is that, like James, he saw culture in a broad, non-exclusive sense and conceived aesthetic experience as emanating from diverse practices within a broadly defined cultural spectrum. Significantly, Hazlitt's essay on the rackets player, Cavanagh, was greatly admired by James and is discussed at some length in *Beyond a Boundary*. James then interprets Sobers as a direct descendant of the classically orthodox English players of the Golden Age. However, rather than deriving from heredity (as in Cardus), Sobers' classical artistry is interpreted as the dialectical synthesis of the contradictions of the colonial and post-colonial periods. The pervasive cultural effects of British imperialism mean that to be West Indian is, in part, to be British. James's immersion in the English literary tradition and Sobers' brilliance at the English game of cricket are thus held to symbolize the divided consciousness that is the condition of the Caribbean artist.

In providing a historical account of Sobers's emergence as a world-historical individual, James resists the temptation to evaluate the relative skills of players of different eras. Such comparisons are meaningless, believed James, because they fail to take into account the relationship between culture and historical context. James 'reads' Sobers, therefore, as a mediation of the historical moment of de-colonization rather than as an individual genius who, in the bourgeois critical tradition, transcends his historical ground: his all-round talents are 'not so much a quality of Sobers himself. It is rather the age we live in, its material characteristics and its social temper.'[20] Historical 'content' – the inner dynamics of a society at a particular moment – provides the basis for formal achievement. Within the Jamesian aesthetic, great artists such as Tolstoy, Charles Chaplin or Sobers, not only express such particularity but have universal appeal. Cardus is again a point of reference:

> I borrow here a thought from Sir Neville Cardus. Visualise please. Not only in the crowded towns and hamlets of the United Kingdom, not only in the scattered villages of the British Caribbean, people were discussing whether Sobers would make 200 or not. In the green hills and on the veldt of Africa, on the remote sheep farms of Australia, on the plains of Southern and the mountains of Northern India, on vessels clearing the Indian Ocean, on planes making geometrical figures in the air above the terrestrial globe. In English clubs in Washington and in New York, there that weekend at some time or other they were all discussing whether Sobers would make the 200 required from him for the West Indies to win the match.[21]

In the Hegelian tradition of colonial discourse, the absence of written history testifies to the absence of history itself.[22] As shown in his study of the Haitian slave revolt, *The Black Jacobins*, James sought to provide the victims of colonialism with a history denied to them in colonialist discourse. Therefore James's Sobers, this Hegelian/Marxist world-historical individual is 'not something new'; Sobers is a 'consummation', not only of a Caribbean cricket tradition, but the embodiment 'of the whole history of the British West Indies'.[23] To comprehend the double-consciousness embodied in this typically West Indian artist James then places this 'text' within British cultural history:

> For to see Sobers whole one must place him in a wider framework than meets the eye. Research shows that cricket has been a popular game in England for centuries, but the modern game that we know came into its own at the end of the eighteenth century, and the beginning

of the nineteenth. It was part of the total change of an agricultural type of society that was developing into what are now known as the advanced countries. Perhaps a most unexpected and therefore arresting exemplification of the change is to be found in a famous piece of writing.[24]

James then establishes an apparently unlikely inter-textual relationship between Sobers and Wordsworth and Coleridge's preface to *The Lyrical Ballads*. This seminal work of English Romanticism is posited as the key to the interpretation of West Indies cricket of the 1960s. This is no simple act of inter-legitimation but a tactic that justifies the basis of the relationship it establishes. According to James, Wordsworth set out to provide 'an alternative' to a decaying civilization: Wordsworth was certain that there were 'inherent and indestructible qualities of the human mind' which would survive 'this degrading thirst after outrageous stimulation'. In its own way, James argues, cricket 'did what Wordsworth was trying to do'.[25] This assertion derives not only from Wordsworth but from early-nineteenth-century cricket writing, a discourse that had actively produced the meaning of cricket as an organic cultural practice at a time of traumatic social change. However, in relating Sobers to broader historical currents, James then shifts from the idea of cricket as national culture to a post-imperial and global perspective. Sobers is not only 'a West Indian of the West Indies. But he is also a citizen of the world today. James characterizes the late twentieth century as a period of global crisis; thus cricket is 'a most powerful resistant to the "outrageous stimulation" of our age, stimuli far more powerful and far more outrageous than they were in Wordsworth's time'.[26] Thus cricket (again, characterized according to nineteenth century discourse) can counter the dehumanizing effects of 'engineering' – the globalized forces of technology, global politics and economics that degrade the dignity of the individual and weaken social ties. Here, however, there is a typically dialectical understanding of engineering and the 'organic', for forms of technology are held to provide the means by which cricket and its discourses are disseminated nationally, imperially and globally:

> And of all of those who go forth the world over to maintain and develop the beauty and dignity of the human mind which Wordsworth was so certain would survive all challenges, cricketers are not the least. This is the age of Telstar and whatever the engineers do for cricket, there is one all-rounder whom we may be certain will meet their challenge.[27]

Other Marxists such as Theodor Adorno would have regarded such an optimistic view of sport as mythical. To James, however, because the relentless and de-humanizing logic of capitalism had produced an aesthetic paralysis in cricket – firstly in the form of Bodyline and later, in the 1950s and 1960s, in a safety-first mode of play governed by a purely accumulative telos – an artist such as Sobers, appearing at the historical moment of de-colonization, played in such a way as to reflect the rich totality of society, thus counteracting the fragmentation and alienation of global capitalism. Though Sobers is aestheticized through a density of allusions to the canon of English literature, James's rhetorical tactic also involves a dialectically counterbalancing empiricism and a highly controlled textual economy of style. For example, in the following passage nothing, particularly the pithy one sentence paragraphs, could be further from Cardus's purple prose and the belletrist emphasis on style over content:

> In 1964, his last season for South Australia, Sobers, against Western Australia, bowled batsman No. 1 for 12, and had batsman No. 2 caught by wicket-keeper Jarman for 2. Against Queensland Jarman caught No. 2 off Sobers for 5, and Sobers bowled No. 3 for 1. Against the history-making New South Wales side, Sobers had Thomas, No. 1, caught by Lill for 0. He had No. 2, Simpson, caught by Jarman for 0. He then had Booth, No. 4, caught by Jarman for 0. He thus had the first three Australian Test players for 0 each. In the second innings he bowled Thomas for 3 ...

It is impossible to find within recent years another fast bowler who in big cricket so regularly dismissed for little or 0 the opening batsmen on the other side.

His action as a pace bowler is the most orthodox that I know.[28]

As this passage shows, an arid and pointedly un-poetic presentation of empirical observation about Sobers' technique, along with statistical data, is a formal device. James very deliberately positioned himself in relationship to the canon of English cricket writing by fusing the aesthetic rhetoric of Cardus with the scientific rationalism of C.B. Fry, a figure whom he regarded as the one of finest non-intellectual writers of the twentieth century.[29] At the level of literary form, therefore, James challenges the colonialist assumption of much English cricket writing: West Indies cricket was merely 'Carnival Cricket', carefree, spontaneous, but undisciplined. In this respect the keywords in James's description of Sobers are 'orthodoxy', 'discipline' and 'classical': 'He is the most orthodox of great batsmen'; 'His aggressive play is very disciplined'; 'at no time was there anything but orthodoxy carried to the penultimate degree where orthodoxy itself disappears in the absolute'; 'His captaincy has the same measured, one might say classical character.'[30] This rewriting of Sobers debunks the notion – prevalent in English cricket discourse – that West Indies players are lacking in discipline and technique. Whereas English writers such as Cardus interpreted players such as Ranjitsinhji and Constantine as beyond the boundary of the classical metropolitan cricketing tradition, James places Sobers in a tradition of classical batsmanship and bowling – a tradition he holds to be both English and West Indian – and is thus able to pointedly assert, 'There is nothing of the panther in the batting of Sobers'. Even when he claims, 'I have seen the panther in Sobers', the subsequent anecdote relating a spontaneous display of unrestrained stroke play reinforces the sense of discipline in Sobers' cricket at all other times.[31] To be capable of reining in such aggressive tendencies requires immense self-discipline, self-restraint and self-governance. James fully understood that at this moment of West Indies de-colonization that there were metropolitan detractors who regarded the people of the Caribbean as inherently incapable of political self-determination. Sobers' self-disciplined, highly cerebral cricket, and James's controlled, often highly empirical prose, suggest otherwise. Art – as manifest in Sobers' cricket and James's writing – is nothing less than a metaphor of the West Indian aptitude for rational self-governance.

## Constantine and critical practice

Although James's retention of a conception of art as trans-historical is problematic, it is nevertheless far superior to the vague and impressionistic aesthetic of a writer such as Cardus whose work is best understood as part of a broader discourse of inter-war cultural crisis. Nevertheless, by taking Cardus's Ruskinian view of art and society and dialectically incorporating it into a materialist schema, James provided an historical means of accounting for the stylistic specificity of West Indies cricketers that is free from the racial stereotyping of much English cricket discourse.

A passage in *Beyond a Boundary* describing Constantine's batting against an English touring side in 1926 is again crucial for a reading of James that provides an understanding of the practice of cricket (albeit one ultimately mediated through language) as potentially counter-hegemonic at the level of both performance and discourse:

Late one afternoon he walked in to bat to the bowling of Hammond. Hammond bowled him a ball pitching a foot or so outside the off-stump, breaking in. Constantine advanced his left foot halfway to meet the ball and saw the break crowd in on him. Doubling himself almost in two, to give himself space, he cut the ball a little to the left of point for a four which no one in the world, not even himself, could have stopped.[32]

Here James describes a remarkable stroke of complex improvisation enacted within a split second: the checking of an initial reaction in response to the guile of the bowler, the adoption of an unorthodox bodily posture and, from that position, a brilliant re-enactment of a classical stroke – a gesture both from within tradition and external to it. James goes on:

> What made us sit up and take notice was that he had never in his life made such a stroke before ... and he had no premeditated idea of making any such stroke. I do not remember seeing it again. He went in, there was the ball, and on the spur of the moment he responded. Every few years one sees a stroke that remains in the mind, as a single gesture of an actor in a long performance remains in the mind.[33]

This re-articulation of the performative grammar of cricket (a grammar so inextricably bound-up with the disciplinary and identity-forming procedures of empire) is an act of resistance, a complex mediation of *habitus* enacted within the structured field of cricket that gestures towards the possibility that cricket can become both the product and the producer of alternative, post-colonial discourses of nationhood. The stroke is irretrievably enacted at the level of embodied performance but enshrined both in James's memory and in the pages of *Beyond a Boundary* where it and its executor are historicized and afforded symbolic and political significance. As Neil Lazarus has correctly noted, James's description of this stroke is 'reminiscent of, and strictly comparable with, Walter Benjamin's observation that "all great works of literature found a genre or dissolve one"'.[34] But it is not just the innovative performative practices of West Indies players such as Constantine that modified and disturbed the disciplinary discourse of cricket. In *Beyond a Boundary* James quite literally founded a new genre – a hybrid form constituted by autobiography, social history, political tract, treatise on aesthetics and cricket book – that at the level of discourse paralleled the embodied adaptations of cricket's performative grammar enacted by players such as Constantine and Sobers.

Although this sense of the intimate and symbiotic relationship between discourse and practice is at times lost in the Hegelian/Marxist aesthetic explicitly theorized by James, such an approach is nevertheless implied in all of his writings. In the opening chapter of *Beyond a Boundary*, entitled 'The Window', James recalls his first aesthetic experience. As in the corresponding chapter of Cardus's *Autobiography*, the literary recuperation of early aesthetic experience is fundamental to the construction of authorial identity. As a boy, James informs us, his bedroom overlooked an adjacent recreation ground and from his window he would watch the local men play cricket. Whilst the image of the window suggests a relatively unmediated experience of cricket, the bodily performance of the local players is pointedly juxtaposed with James's youthful immersion in literature:

> By standing on a chair a small boy of six could watch practice every afternoon and matches on Saturdays ... From the chair also he could mount on to the window-sill and so stretch a groping hand for the books on the top of the wardrobe. Thus early the pattern of my life was set.[35]

One of the players James watched was a certain Matthew Bondman, the local 'ne'er-do-well', whose dissolute lifestyle and crudeness of manner offended the James family's puritanical values. Yet with bat in hand Bondman was all grace and his majestic stroke play made an indelible impression upon the young James:

> He had one particular stroke that he played by going down low on one knee ... whenever Matthew sank down and made it, a long, low 'Ah!' came from many a spectator, and my own little soul thrilled with recognition and delight.[36]

Here James's recollection of the roguish Bondman's batting is crucial to his view of the meaning of cricket in colonial Trinidadian society. Bondman, so foul-mouthed and dissolute beyond the boundary, was transformed into 'that *genus Britannicus*, a fine batsman' when he entered the identity-forming space of the cricket field.[37] Yet Bondman's stroke play did not neatly conform to the prescriptions of English coaching manuals. As with Constantine, the unorthodoxy of the stroke enacts a revision of cricket's performative grammar; thus it is a structured gesture of resistance, a mediation of the *habitus* of working-class colonial life realized at the level of bodily performance. James then further develops this notion of embodiment by re-emphasizing the idea that particular re-enactments of cricket's performative grammar can constitute modes of social representation. Later in the chapter, the following description of Arthur Jones's cut stroke is deliberately juxtaposed with John Mitford's canonical account of William Beldham, one of the most stylish and innovative of John Nyren's *Cricketers of My Time*:

> My second landmark was not a person but a stroke, and the maker of it was Arthur Jones. He was a brownish Negro, a medium-sized man, who walked with quick steps and active shoulders. He had a pair of restless, aggressive eyes, talked quickly and even stammered a little. He wore a white cloth hat when batting, and he used to cut. How he used to cut! I have watched county cricket for weeks on end and seen whole Test matches without seeing one cut such as Jones used to make, and for years whenever I saw one I murmured to myself, 'Arthur Jones!'[38]

Jones's stylish mastery of this technically difficult stroke emblematizes a West Indies performance of cricket that is counter to the functional English cricket of a contemporary 'Welfare State of Mind'. James then presents the passage from Mitford's review of Nyren alongside bookish recollections and memories of his first bodily response to that work:

> The years passed. I was in my teens at school, playing cricket, reading cricket, idolizing Thackeray, Burke and Shelley, when one day I came across the following about a great cricketer of the eighteenth century:
> 'It was a study for Phidias to see Beldham rise to strike; the grandeur of the attitude, the settled composure of the look, the piercing lightning of the eye, the rapid glances of the bat, were electrical. Men's hearts throbbed within them, their cheeks turned pale and red. Michael Angelo should have painted him'.
> This was thrilling enough. I began to tingle.
> 'Beldham was great in every hit, but his peculiar glory was the cut. Here he stood, with no man beside him, the laurel was all his own; it seemed like the cut of a racket. His wrist seemed to turn on springs of the finest steel. He took the ball, as Burke did the House of Commons, between wind and water – not a moment too soon or late. Beldham still survives ...'[39]

Here the revelatory discovery of a canonical piece of cricket literature confirms and gives literary expression to initial childhood experiences of bodily performance. As James's interjection suggests, such aesthetic discourse heightens the sense of bodily fantasy on the part of the young male reader and has the ability to literarily write itself upon the body. At the same time this entire passage is structured so as to set up a cultural equivalence between cricket and other, more validated art forms. Indeed, James's self-representation in the narrative is constituted by his immersion in English and classical literatures, visual art and the cricket canon:

> By that time I had seen many fine cutters, one of them, W. St. Hill, never to this day surpassed. But the passage brought back Jones and childhood memories to my mind and anchored him there for good and all. Phidias, Michelangelo, Burke. Greek history had already introduced me to Phidias and the Parthenon; from engravings and reproductions I had already begun a life-long worship of Michelangelo; and Burke, begun as a school chore, had rapidly become for me the most exciting master of prose in English – I knew already long passages of him by heart. There in the very centre of all this was William Beldham and his cut.[40]

In this passage a disparate series of texts and artefacts, including Mitford's description of Beldham and the embodied performance of the otherwise ineloquent Arthur Jones, merge into a trans-historical equivalence of cultural status. A cricketer and a particular enactment of cricket's performative grammar (albeit one mediated through a literary text), far from being culturally peripheral, are pointedly placed at the very centre of the aesthetic spectrum. Through his mastery of the cut stroke, Arthur Jones, an obscure Trinidadian cricketer, is placed in a cultural continuum with the great figures and monuments of European culture. Yet, in mediating the *habitus* of his West Indies background through his particular performance of the stroke – a performance untainted by the Keynesian economics that James believed so stifled the liberatory potential of art – Jones enacts a stylized gesture of resistance. James suggests that Jones, like Bondman, did not merely slavishly imitate the technical models of English cricket discourse, but inevitably created something new from both within and outside this tradition. Likewise, James's initial reading of Mitford is mediated via Jones, causing him to create something new from within and beyond the bounded space of the cricket canon. This suggests a relationship between the discursive and the performative that cannot be subsumed into a simple binary; rather, the bodily practice of cricket is both produced by discourse and constantly interrogates and revises its discursive givenness.

James's aesthetic emerged from within the boundaries of the English cricket canon and went beyond the permissible limits of this discourse by refusing to disavow its politics. This was as skilful and conscious an act of position taking within a canon as was James's earlier entry into the field of American Studies.[41] It was a critique of a system of representation that attempted to render the workings of culture invisible. James understood the tradition of English cricket writing (typified in the work of Neville Cardus) as part of a broader discourse of Englishness that functioned aesthetically by concealing its operations and rendering culture no longer a construct to be fought over. Against this James provided a dialectical formulation of cricket as a field in which social contradictions are played out: despite and because of its English provenance; despite and because of the Victorian discursive transformation of it into a moral discipline; despite and because of its important role in the British imperial mission, cricket in the West Indies had been refashioned into a cultural field capable of articulating emerging senses of Caribbean nationhood.

Only a sophisticated popular art form like cricket, James argues, was capable of doing so, and this in turn demands a more sophisticated critical practice on the part of its chroniclers and analysts:

> Mr Neville Cardus circumscribes his vision of Lancashire and Yorkshire professionals within the muse of comedy. Their West Indian counterparts would crack such limitations like egg-shells. Everything they were came into cricket with them.[42]

The bounded discursive practice of English cricket writing is thus wholly inadequate as a means of writing a distinctively Caribbean style of play because this style was a complex mediation of an accretion of shared historical experience. Referring to conventional English interpretations of Constantine, James wrote: 'We are [still] in the flower garden of the gay, the spontaneous, tropical West Indians. We need some astringent spray'.[43] This 'astringent spray' is a method of cricket criticism, both empirical and theoretical, underpinned by a materialist understanding of history and conveyed in a prose style that is itself the dialectically-produced expression of historical processes. For a writer like James who had lived on the other side of the colonial divide, but who nevertheless saw Caribbean identity as intimately bound up with Englishness, the racialized rhetoric of the English cricket canon could not account for the aesthetic specificity of West Indies cricket. West Indian players did indeed create new forms, but these innovations, James showed, were merely in the tradition of Grace, Ranjitsinhji and Victor Trumper: there was nothing 'exotic' or 'primitive' about them. After the West Indies team triumphed in Australia in 1962 under the leadership of their first black captain, Frank Worrell, James wrote:

> Clearing their way with bat and ball, West Indians at that moment had made a public entry into the comity of nations. Thomas Arnold, Thomas Hughes, and the Old Master himself [W.G. Grace] would have recognised Frank Worrell as their boy.[44]

Constantine, Worrell and Sobers were indeed the embodiments of new cultural energies emanating from the colonial peripheries, but their innovations came from within the given grammar of English performativity. Their bodily performances are homologous with the literary enterprise of James who took up a position within the field of cricket discourse in order to reconfigure it radically, to rewrite cricket as a democratic and postcolonial cultural practice.

## Notes

[1] Agard, 'Prospero Caliban Cricket'. The poem is dedicated to the memory of C.L.R. James.
[2] James, *Beyond a Boundary*, 55–71. See also Farred, 'The Maple Man'.
[3] James, *Beyond a Boundary*, 134.
[4] Lazarus, 'Cricket and National Culture in the Writings of C.L.R. James'; Tiffin, 'Cricket, Literature and the Politics of De-colonisation'.
[5] James, *Beyond a Boundary*, 191–2.
[6] Ibid., 192.
[7] Ibid., 179.
[8] Williams, *Marxism and Literature*, 17.
[9] Cardus, *English Cricket*, 81.
[10] Williams, *Culture and Society*, 130.
[11] James, *Beyond a Boundary*, 186.
[12] James, *Mariners, Renegades and Castaways*.
[13] Spurr, *The Rhetoric of Empire*, 99.
[14] Rohlehr, 'C.L.R. James and the Legacy of *Beyond a Boundary*', 152.
[15] Farred, '"Victorian with the Rebel Seed"', 33.
[16] Ibid., 34.
[17] Ibid.
[18] James, 'Garfield Sobers', 379.
[19] Ibid., 383.
[20] Ibid.
[21] Ibid., 383–4.
[22] Spurr, *The Rhetoric of Empire*, 19.
[23] James, 'Garfield Sobers', 384.
[24] Ibid., 385.
[25] Ibid.
[26] Ibid., 386.
[27] Ibid.
[28] Ibid., 380.
[29] Hall, 'A Conversation with C.L.R. James', 27.
[30] James, 'Garfield Sobers', 380–1.
[31] Ibid., 381–2.
[32] James, *Beyond a Boundary*, 109.
[33] Ibid.
[34] Lazarus, 'Cricket and National Culture in the Writings of C.L.R. James', 344.
[35] James, *Beyond a Boundary*, 13.
[36] Ibid., 14.
[37] Ibid.
[38] Ibid., 15.
[39] Ibid., 15–16.

[40] Ibid., 16.
[41] Pease, 'Introduction'.
[42] James, *Beyond a Boundary*, 86.
[43] Ibid., 131.
[44] Ibid., 252.

## References

Agard, John. 'Prospero Caliban Cricket'. *Massachusetts Review* 35, no. 3–4 (1994): 546–8.

Cardus, Neville. *English Cricket*. London: Prion, 1997.

Farred, Grant. '"Victorian with the Rebel Seed": C.L.R. James, Postcolonial Intellectual'. *Social Text* 38 (1995): 21–38.

Farred, Grant. 'The Maple Man: How Cricket Made a Postcolonial Intellectual'. In *Rethinking C.L.R. James*, edited by Grant Farred, 165–86. Oxford: Blackwell, 1996.

Hall, Stuart. 'A Conversation with C.L.R. James'. In *Rethinking C.L.R. James*, edited by Grant Farred, 15–44. Oxford: Blackwell, 1996.

James, C.L.R. *Beyond a Boundary*. London: Hutchinson, 1963.

James, C.L.R. 'Garfield Sobers'. In *The C.L.R. James Reader*, edited by Anna Grimshaw, 379–89. Oxford: Blackwell, 1992.

James, C.L.R. *Mariners, Renegades and Castaways: The Story of Hermann Melville and the Way we Live Today*. London: The University Press of New England, 2001.

Lazarus, Neil. 'Cricket and National Culture in the Writings of C.L.R. James'. In *Liberation Cricket: West Indies Cricket Culture*, edited by Hilary Beckles and Brian Stoddart, 342–55. Manchester: Manchester University Press, 1995.

Pease, Donald E. 'Introduction'. In *Mariners, Renegades and Castaways: The Story of Herman Melville and the Way we Live Today*, by C.L.R. James, vii–xxxiii. London: The University Press of New England, 2001.

Rohlehr, Gordon. 'C.L.R. James and the Legacy of *Beyond a Boundary*'. In *A Spirit of Dominance: Cricket and Nationalism in the West Indies*, edited by Hilary Beckles, 124–62. Jamaica: Canoe Press, 1998.

Spurr, David. *The Rhetoric of Empire: Colonial Discourse in Journalism, Travel Writing and Imperial Administration*. London: Duke University Press, 1993.

Tiffin, Helen. 'Cricket, Literature and the Politics of De-colonisation: the Case of C.L.R. James'. In *Liberation Cricket: West Indies Cricket Culture*, edited by Hilary Beckles and Brian Stoddart, 356–69. Manchester: Manchester University Press, 1995.

Williams, Raymond. *Marxism and Literature*. Oxford: Oxford University Press, 1977.

Williams, Raymond. *Culture and Society*. London: The Hogarth Press, 1987.

# 'Fiery Fred': Fred Trueman and cricket celebrity in the 1950s and early 1960s

Jack Williams*

*Department of History, Liverpool John Moores University, Liverpool, UK*

Fred Trueman was one of the biggest stars of English cricket in the 1950s and early 1960s. The cricket journalist and broadcaster Don Mosey, who knew him well, wrote in 1991 that Trueman, 'was the most colourful and best-known personality in the game' and 'one of cricket's most prominent stormy petrels' whose playing days were 'marked by storm and tempest, fire and fury, argument and controversy ... Fred has always been, and remains to this day, very definitely NEWS'.[1] It was difficult for many to have neutral feelings about Trueman. His persona provoked either affection or loathing. More recently perhaps only Tony Greig, for his support of Kerry Packer's challenge to traditional Test cricket, and Geoffrey Boycott have provoked such divided opinions as Trueman. Exploring the context of Trueman's celebrity provides an unusual but none the less valuable perspective on social and cultural relations in England during the 1950s and first half of the 1960s.

## Trueman as a cricketing great

Without doubt Trueman was among the best fast bowlers of all time. Between 1949 and 1968 he took 1,745 wickets for Yorkshire at an average of 17.13 runs. Only four other bowlers have taken more wickets for Yorkshire and none of Trueman's contemporaries took more. His total of 2,304 wickets in all first-class cricket is the highest for any bowler of very high pace and none of his contemporaries who took more wickets matched his average of a wicket for only 18.29 runs. In 1964 he became the first bowler to take 300 wickets in Test cricket. He played in only 67 of the 118 Test matches which England played between his first Test in 1952 and his last in 1965, and thus his haul of 309 Test match wickets would probably have been much higher had he appeared more regularly for

England. Nevertheless his tally of Test match wickets is the third highest of all England players. Of bowlers who have played for England since the First World War and taken over 100 Test wickets, only Alec Bedser has a better average number of wickets per match than Trueman, but Trueman's average of 4.58 almost equals Bedser's 4.62.

Statistics do not say everything about Trueman's greatness as a bowler. In 2006 Trevor Bailey, who played for England with Trueman, said that, 'On all pitches, and in all conditions, it is doubtful whether there has ever been a more complete fast bowler'.[2] Trueman's side-on action had a classical perfection. His pace was exceptional. Of his England contemporaries, Trueman was considered a shade slower than Tyson but faster than Statham. In his early career Trueman's bowling sometimes lacked direction but he could swing the ball into and away from batsmen like a medium-pace bowler and had a fearsome yorker. Many batsmen feared his bouncer. Brian Close, his captain at Yorkshire for six years, described Trueman as 'a captain's dream. He would bowl whenever you asked, at whatever time of the day you wanted, and would never give less than his all'.[3] Trueman was a big-hitting lower order batsman and regarded as one of the best short-leg fielders of his time.

Trueman's playing abilities would have made him one of cricket's biggest stars in any era but they alone did not fashion the nature of his celebrity. His personality was intertwined with perceptions of him as hero and anti-hero. Trueman's life, John Arlott recalled, was 'recorded in gossip as well as in *Wisden*'.[4] Anecdotes about Trueman were often only rough approximations to the truth. Don Mosey claimed to have heard 'men who have never met Fred telling stories which are totally untrue'.[5] Extrovert by nature, Trueman seems to have needed attention, and after retiring from playing cricket remained in the public eye as a nightclub comedian, an expert summarizer on radio's *Test Match Special* and by appearing as the presenter for the four series of the television pub game programme *Indoor League*. He continued to have a weekly column in the *People* and put his name to 16 books. His demand for the limelight meant that he was often unable to resist playing up to his public image. While in later life Trueman complained that he was very different from his public image, it is hard to resist thinking that he preferred bad publicity to no publicity. He seems to have wanted to appear a 'character', the rough diamond of cricket, and enjoyed the notoriety this brought. In his early cricket career he did not discourage journalists and cartoonists from presenting him as a tough, heavy beer-drinking man from a mining background, though in fact he drank sparingly. David Green, who played for Lancashire and Gloucestershire, recalled that if someone offered Trueman a drink,

> and thousands did – he would generally accept but at the end of the evening ... those clearing up would find numerous pint pots, each with an inch or so sipped off the top, concealed behind curtains, under chairs or behind plant pots. Hence the many occasions on which one would hear a cricket follower say: 'Do you know, I was with Fred Trueman last night. I watched him drink 14 pints, and look at him this morning, fresh as a daisy'.[6]

Trueman was also highly emotional and his demonstrative nature on the cricket field commanded attention. Spectators could see when he was displeased. He glared with ferocity at batsmen when things were not going his way and often indulged in histrionic gestures when elated or disappointed. Some of Trueman's rage may have been simulated because of the attention it brought and was possibly calculated to gain an advantage over the opposing side. Batsmen came to expect a bouncer when he was annoyed but causing them to anticipate a bouncer meant that they would be more likely to be beaten by a yorker.

Part of Trueman's stardom was that there usually seemed to be excitement in the air when he played. He had an innate sense of theatre. His presence and demeanour compelled the attention of spectators. When running in to bowl he exuded ferocity and even those who did not care for Trueman wanted to watch him. Ted Lester, who played for Yorkshire with Trueman, remembered that when Trueman bowled, 'You felt frightened for the batsman'.[7] In 1954 Trueman told the *Sunday Graphic* 'Certainly I get mad with batsmen. I hate 'em ... There's nothing personal in it. That chap might be my best friend, but when he gets a bat in his hand, he's my enemy. I am out to get him and there's no sense in being half-hearted about it'.[8] Cricket journalists often endowed Trueman's bowling with an animalistic, almost primeval, force. His very black hair was often described as a mane. Waiting to bowl, Trueman was compared to a bull or a lion pawing the ground before making a charge. Arlott wrote that his run-up, like the charge of a Spanish fighting bull, was 'a mounting glory of rhythm, power and majesty ... the peak of the charge is controlled violence, precisely applied in a movement of rippling speed'.[9] His bowling had an untamed element. The inaccuracy of his bowling was often described as part of his wild character. When he first played county cricket in 1949, there were 'serious doubts ... his ability to discipline himself and his bowling'.[10] After Trueman's first overseas tour, E.W. Swanton wrote that Trueman needed 'control in all its aspects' while Alex Bannister urged Trueman 'with all my force, to make a serious and determined effort to keep himself in control'.[11]

Trueman was among the first post-1945 stars of English cricket not to have served in the Second World War. Hutton and Compton, the biggest names of English cricket in the immediate post-war years, had played for England in the 1930s and by the early 1950s were approaching the end of their careers. In the early 1950s Trueman seemed to have an aura of youthfulness, and a less deferential youthfulness, than other prominent cricketers whose careers had begun after the Second World War. Brian Close, almost the same age as Trueman, became the youngest player ever to appear for England in 1949, but he never established himself in Test cricket. Post-war batsmen such as May, Graveney and Cowdrey often seemed to be much more like the previous generation than did Trueman.

The dramatic dimension of Trueman's celebrity was related to his capacity to produce sensational bowling feats. In 1952 in his first Test match for England he took three wickets in eight balls as India slumped to four wickets for no runs in their second innings, the worst start to a Test match innings by any side. In the third Test he set a record Test return for a fast bowler of eight wickets for 31 runs in India's first innings. These performances occurred when English cricket was desperate for a bowler of genuine pace. Australia was due to tour England in 1953 and England had not won the Ashes since 1932–33. It was widely believed that Australia's dominance over England since the Second World War had been due primarily to the fast bowlers Lindwall and Miller. Jack Hobbs, or perhaps his ghost-writer, wrote that Trueman had bowled as fast 'as we have seen from any England player in our time' and that 'I can think of no batsman who would have taken up a position confidently'. Hobbs called Trueman a 'five star MUST' for the 1953 series against Australia.[12] Ralph Hadley of the *Sunday People* thought that Trueman looked 'as though he has solved our fast bowling problem for years to come'.[13] Not all judges were so enthusiastic. George Duckworth, who had kept wicket for England between the wars, thought it premature to compare Trueman with Larwood, England's leading fast bowler of the late 1920s and early 1930s, and urged, 'don't let's get too cock-a-hoop because we bowled out India on a cricket wicket on which an ordinary English county would have batted two days against the England attack'.[14] S.C. Griffith, who had played for Cambridge University, Sussex and England as an amateur and was secretary of the MCC from 1962 to 1974, wrote in the *Cricketer* that, 'sensibly handled and coached he might be just what we have been so anxiously looking for' but thought that Trueman was 'somewhat ludicrously hailed as a second Larwood'.[15] Despite the great hopes placed in Trueman in 1952, he was selected only for the final Test against Australia in 1953. In this match England regained the Ashes and Trueman took four vital wickets in Australia's first innings, typically showing his instinct for dramatic timing.

## Trueman as a Yorkshire hero

Not surprisingly Trueman's heroic status was strongest in his home county of Yorkshire. His benefit of over £9,330 in 1962, higher than those of his Yorkshire contemporaries Wilson, Wardle, Watson, Close and Illingworth but lower than Hutton's £9,710 in 1950, was an indication of his popularity in the county. To his admirers in Yorkshire, Trueman personified Yorkshireness and how Yorkshiremen perceived themselves and imagined how others saw them. This was a recurrent theme in his obituaries. Gerald Mortimer wrote that Trueman was 'as Yorkshire as it is possible to be'[16] and Roy Hattersley, the Labour politician proud of his Yorkshire origins, thought Trueman's 'greatest pride was not in playing for England but in playing for Yorkshire'.[17] The umpire Dickie Bird, who played for Yorkshire with Trueman, and the former Yorkshire captain David Byas, each called Trueman 'a great Yorkshireman'.[18] The veteran sports journalist Ian Wooldridge described Trueman as 'a Yorkshireman through and through: proud, opinionated, obsessive'.[19] In the 1960s Harold Wilson called Trueman the greatest living Yorkshireman, and while this could be taken as a very wily politician's attempt to curry public favour, it also reflected an assumption that Trueman was held in great esteem in Yorkshire. Bob Crampsey of the Glasgow *Herald*, however, suspected Trueman of 'playing the professional Yorkshireman',[20] while Brian Statham, another England fast bowler and friend of Trueman, thought that Trueman had 'a typical Yorkshire attitude. Everything Yorkshire do is best and nobody can match them', but he also thought that Trueman had 'a tendency to broaden his accent at times. He puts it on a bit'.[21]

Trueman always believed that he personified Yorkshireness and the Yorkshire approach to cricket. When criticized, his usual defence was to claim that his behaviour represented the Yorkshire way of doing things. Trueman felt that going all-out for victory was the Yorkshire way to play cricket. When Colin Cowdrey told Trueman that, 'The trouble with you Yorkshiremen is that you think cricket is all about winning', he replied, 'It's a pity you don't think winning is as important as I do'.[22] He thought that Yorkshire qualities were the basis of his playing success. When interviewed in 1954 about not being selected for the MCC tour to Australia, he mentioned that his aggressive approach to fast bowling may have counted against him but argued that this was how cricket was played in Yorkshire. The *News Chronicle* reported his comment that in Yorkshire it was said, '"you don't build a fire-eater on lemonade and cream cake". To be a fast bowler you've got to be a fire-eater'.[23] He told the *Sunday Graphic* that, 'I TALK STRAIGHT about my cricket. I TALK STRAIGHT about everything. That's the way we're brought up in Yorkshire'.[24] While admitting to being disappointed at not being selected for the tour, he stressed that he would put all his energies into trying to help Yorkshire win the county championship.

Being omitted from the MCC tours to Australia in 1954–55 and to South Africa in 1956 enhanced Trueman's heroic status in Yorkshire. His treatment confirmed the conviction of a prejudice among cricket administrators in the South against cricketers from Yorkshire and of a more general belief that Yorkshire's true worth in national life was often not recognized. Frank Stainton, cricket correspondent of the Sheffield *Star*, mentioned that that 12 of the

17 tourists were from the South, a point also noted by the *Daily Herald*.[25] A letter to the *Sheffield Telegraph* urged, 'All Yorkshiremen should refuse to take this lying down. It is a slur on Yorkshire's team as a whole'.[26] Trueman said, 'What matters to me is that the people of Yorkshire are right behind me. I know it'.[27] When he took the field at Headingley on the day when the tour party was announced, the spectators were reported to have given Trueman a greater ovation than any Yorkshire player had ever received on a Yorkshire ground, 'a Yorkshire crowd's tribute to a Yorkshireman who, in the opinion of most people, has been given a very raw deal'.[28] Some Yorkshire journalists, and presumably many of their readers, took it for granted that as Yorkshire players Len Hutton, the captain of the touring party, and Norman Yardley, the captain of Yorkshire, both members of the tour selection committee, would have pressed for Trueman to be included in the Australia tour party. Stainton thought it 'no secret to say that both Norman Yardley and Len Hutton were keen on Trueman's inclusion'.[29] Whether they had pressed for Trueman's inclusion is not clear, but Don Mosey believed that Trueman was 'absolutely convinced' that Hutton was instrumental in his not being selected for the Australian tour. Although he made no comment at the time, Hutton said later that he was not responsible for Trueman's non-selection and would have 'dearly loved' for Trueman to have been in the Australia tour party'.[30]

Trueman had detractors in Yorkshire but they were less vociferous than his admirers and it is hard to gauge their numbers. When Trueman was omitted from the Australian tour in 1954, one letter to the *Yorkshire Post* mentioned that many Yorkshire county members did not disagree with the selection of the touring party. Because a touring party had to live 'in the closest association for many months', the letter argued that it was essential for the tourists to 'constitute one happy family' and went on to mention that there had been incidents at Headingley when the tour party was announced which 'could not escape the observation of many spectators nor of, possibly, ten members of the Yorkshire team'.[31]

During his playing career Trueman's relationship with the Yorkshire club was often strained and to his death he felt that he had been treated harshly. In 1997 he said that he had never been 'generously rewarded' either by Yorkshire or England. He felt that he took too long to become established in the Yorkshire first eleven. He was often at odds with the Yorkshire committee and Sir William Worsley, the Old Etonian chairman of Yorkshire, was possibly the only senior committee member with whom he got on well during his playing career. He had rows with the Brian Sellers, a dominant figure at the club, but was not alone in this. Twice he was publicly reprimanded over incidents in which he believed he was the innocent party. Don Mosey pointed out that, 'Fred, in all truth, was never an easy man to handle for any captain or manager',[32] but Trueman seems never to have realized this. Mosey also felt that, 'So numerous and so regular were these complaints citing Trueman as a malefactor when he was not that it is difficult to blame him for his conviction, with hindsight, that he was innocent on all occasions. He was not, of course. The legends did not grow without a certain substance'.[33] Trueman's contretemps with the Yorkshire committee may have boosted his popularity with those followers of Yorkshire cricket who saw all cricket authority as refusing to recognize the merits of Yorkshire players. Despite his pride in being a Yorkshireman and in playing for Yorkshire, Trueman considered playing for Lancashire early in his career when he thought that he was being selected for Yorkshire too infrequently, and in 1972 he came out of retirement to play a few Sunday League matches for Derbyshire.

Trueman's relationship with other Yorkshire players was not always easy but this rarely became public knowledge. Always highly opinionated, always quick to speak his mind, and often unaware of how others perceived his behaviour, Trueman's brashness and self-confidence may have antagonized established first team players. The Yorkshire dressing room was no place for wilting violets. Older players, perhaps worried about keeping their places in the team, gave little praise or encouragement to younger players who were expected to know their place. Don Mosey believed that when Trueman began playing for the Yorkshire first team, established players tried to put him down 'often in cruel and derisive terms'.[34] To survive in the Yorkshire dressing room, young players had to be assertive but Trueman may have been exaggeratedly so. Raymond Illingworth, a year younger than Trueman, recalled that Trueman,

> just didn't give a damn what anybody else thought. That was what enabled him to hold his own against the 'hard men' in the side – Hutton, Appleyard, Wardle. They got both barrels straight between the eyes in any dust-up with Fred and they were *very* hard men.[35]

Trueman felt that the amateur captains Norman Yardley and Billy Sutcliffe did not take a sufficiently strong line with the professional bowlers Bob Appleyard and Johnny Wardle, allowing them to dictate when they bowled and in effect deny Trueman opportunities to bowl. John Arlott wrote that Appleyard did not like Trueman but Stephen Chalke and Derek Hodgson claimed that Appleyard and Frank Lowson tried to make Trueman feel more at home in the environment of county cricket at the start of his career.[36] In 1954, when Trueman and Wardle were both in contention for a prize of £250 for the season's best bowling return, Trueman accused Wardle of deliberately dropping a catch which denied him the prize which was won by Wardle.[37] Trueman seems to have been something of a loner in the Yorkshire team, preferring not to spend time with the other Yorkshire players in the evening.[38] In 1957 he refused to sign a petition supported by other players calling for the captain Billy Sutcliffe to resign.

Trueman approved of the strong discipline imposed by the amateur Ronnie Burnet, who had not played in a previous first-class game and was scarcely worth his place as a batsman or a bowler but who was appointed captain in 1958. Trueman's relations with his next two Yorkshire captains were not easy. According to Don Mosey, Vic Wilson, Yorkshire's first professional captain, had little personal affection for Trueman and with Brian Close, Trueman's contemporary who succeeded Wilson, Trueman had 'a strange sort of love-hate, respect-contempt relationship ... Even the "hate" part had an element of half-amused, half-affectionate regard'. Trueman felt that he ought to have been captain while Close enjoyed winding up Trueman.[39]

**Trueman as a working-class hero**

Much of the controversy surrounding Trueman occurred because he did not behave as cricketers had been expected to behave. Since Victorian times cricket had been a metaphor for traditional authority in England. It emphasized the class distinctions and snobbery of English society. The MCC, cricket's governing body until 1968, was a private members club dominated by those with traditional wealth, very similar to those who controlled the Conservative Party. Lord Monkton, the Conservative Minister of Defence who had been President of the MCC in 1956, said that the MCC committee made Macmillan's cabinet appear 'a band of pinkos'.[40] The upper and upper-middle classes controlled the county clubs. Before 1963 county cricketers were divided into amateurs and professionals. Traditionally amateurs, mostly men educated at public schools, captained the England and county teams. In the 1950s distinctions between amateurs and professionals became a little less marked. In 1952 Yorkshireman Len Hutton became the first professional to captain England since the 1880s and by 1963 14 counties had appointed professional captains. At most county grounds amateurs and professionals ceased having separate dressing rooms. But any relaxation of the amateur/professional divide was as much the result of a shortage of suitable amateurs as any sense among the governors of cricket that amateur authority was out of step with the times. Scrapping the amateur/professional distinction was in part an attempt to enable those with traditional amateur backgrounds to continue playing first-class cricket. When he became England captain Hutton was advised to adopt an Oxford or BBC accent, presumably to indicate a continuity with amateur captains. In 1958 the MCC withdrew its invitation to the Yorkshire professional Wardle to tour Australia after he put his name to newspaper articles which claimed that the Yorkshire side had been carrying the amateur captain Ronnie Burnet whose playing skills were below standard. Burnet had just been responsible for Yorkshire sacking Wardle. For the MCC, supporting an amateur captain was more important than sending the strongest possible side to Australia.

Apologists for cricket, often educated at public schools, argued that cricket had higher levels of sportsmanship than other sports. Cricket, they maintained, promoted ethical qualities such as selflessness, moral and physical courage, resolution, modesty, courtesy and camaraderie, qualities thought to be both consistent with Christian morality and transferable to other areas of life. No doubt those who controlled first-class cricket took it for granted that those with similar backgrounds should captain county teams as they were the boss class in so much of English life, but they also justified amateur authority on the grounds that amateurs were the natural defenders of sportsmanship. In 1967 the former professional Brian Close was sacked as England's captain – and he had not lost one of the seven Tests in which he captained England – because he deliberately wasted time to ensure that Yorkshire did not lose a match and subsequently refused to apologize for this; acts which were considered breaches of sportsmanship. Close's sacking could also be seen as another example of the southern cricket establishment victimizing a Yorkshire cricketer.

Other professionals may have disliked cricket's authority structure even more than Trueman did but no other professional in the 1950s and early 1960s was thought to be as critical of it as Trueman. Arlott noted that in his early career Trueman had 'something of a chip on his shoulder, a mistrust of authority, a feeling that if he did not watch them, "they" would do him some injustice'.[41] In 1993 the *Guardian* columnist Martin Kettle recalled that:

> the great thing about Freddie was that he was a rebel. He wouldn't play the game the southern way. He had no respect for the public school officer class who dominated cricket in his era. The amateur captains of most of the teams in which he played were mostly incompetents. He knew it and we knew it and we knew he knew it … this man once seemed to be the scourge of the establishment.[42]

The broadcaster and cricket writer Michael Parkinson, born in Barnsley in 1935, wrote that 'people of my background and generation saw Fred not simply as a great cricketer but as an emblematic figure; outspoken, bloody-minded, Jack-as-good-as-his-master', and that to a new generation beginning to question the old order, 'Fred – bolshie, outspoken and anti-authoritarian from the start – was a figurehead'.[43] Trueman's obituaries stressed his antagonism to authority. Wooldridge described Trueman and discipline as,

> not compatible. Obsequiousness was far beyond him and he was frequently at Lord's when cricket was still socially divided between amateurs – mostly public school and university men – and professionals. Fred didn't give a bugger for any of them … this contempt for authority, this determination never to be put down, … made Trueman the fearsome opponent he was.[44]

Such qualities no doubt added to the dislike of Trueman among those who thought that the working class needed to be kept in its place.

Assumptions about Trueman's antagonism towards cricket authority spread by word of mouth. Anecdotes suggested that he was especially contemptuous of amateur batsmen. After being congratulated on the quality of a ball by an amateur whom he had just bowled, Trueman was alleged to have said that it had been wasted on the batsman, though in his memoirs he denied saying this. Whether true or not, such stories suggest a widespread assumption of his animosity to those from privileged backgrounds. He expected antagonism between himself and cricket authority. When he first played against Wilfred Wooller, the amateur captain of Glamorgan who had been educated at a public school and Cambridge, he thought that Wooller was, 'the sort of figure that a Yorkshireman from the working-classes, *and* a fast bowler as well, was destined to regard as the natural enemy'.[45] Trueman admitted that, 'I wasn't always able to keep silent and respectful with members of the cricketing establishment. And, oddly enough, no matter how well I was playing following such an incident, invariably I would find myself dropped.' He thought Freddie Brown, the manager of the 1958–59 tour to Australia and who had captained England as an amateur, was 'abhorrent ... a snob, bad-mannered, ignorant and a bigot'. On the 1962–63 tour of Australia Trueman had an altercation with the Duke of Norfolk, the manager of the tour party. Trueman made clear his objection to the Duke addressing him in public by only his surname.[46] Trueman, however, may not have been as antagonistic to amateurs as was often imagined. When Yorkshire were playing Cambridge University he spent a good part of the evening helping a Cambridge fast bowler educated at a public school to overcome a problem with his bowling.[47] This may not have been an isolated incident.

Beliefs about Trueman's bellicosity to established authority were bolstered by the conviction that his omission from the tours to Australia in 1954–55 and to South Africa in 1956–57 was because of his working-class background and rebellious nature. His working-class origins were a recurring feature in press responses to his omission from the Australian tour. Trueman came close to saying that he had been discriminated against because of his background. He said that he had heard that he was not selected because, 'I was a collier's son and worked in the pits myself. I'm not ashamed of my background. I'm proud of it', but added that he did not know whether this was a reason for his non-selection.[48] Alan Hoby of the *Sunday Express* wrote that he could find 'no evidence' that Trueman had been omitted because of 'an excess of "old-school-tie" snobbery' or because as a 'young blunt ex-miner on his first foreign trip, he sometimes unleashed a few torrid words in the heat of the moment',[49] but Hoby's comments imply that many were taking this view. Frank Stainton mentioned 'a school of thought' which considered that 'one of the first qualifications for such a tour is the knowledge that the soup is not taken with a dessert spoon, and that a black tie is customary with a dinner jacket' and 'that such questions are of more importance than cricketing prowess when engaged on an MCC tour'.[50] An article with an editorial tone in the *Cricketer* magazine, which nearly always supported the cricket establishment, mentioned 'murmurings' in some quarters over Trueman's omission, but pointed out that 'selectors have information and facts at their disposal which are not available to the general public ... it is certain that on this occasion every avenue of form and temperament, was closely examined and closely debated'.[51] In general national newspapers with predominantly working-class readerships maintained that Trueman was discriminated against by the MCC, whereas newspapers with upper- and middle-class readers argued that there were valid cricketing reasons for not selecting Trueman. It was explained that Trueman's ability to swing the ball would be as ineffective in Australia as it had been in the West Indies. The *Yorkshire Post*, whose layout and journalistic style suggest that it was aimed at the middle rather than the working class, was guarded in its response to Trueman's omission. J.M. Kilburn, its highly respected cricket correspondent, thought that Trueman's omission would provoke 'the fiercest controversy' and the 'wildest rumours and most startling implications'. For Kilburn, Trueman seemed the 'better bowling proposition for Australia at this moment, but there can be no questioning Tyson's potentiality'.[52]

The unprecedented announcement from Lord's in 1956 that Trueman had been omitted on his current form and that there was no question of discrimination against him suggests that many people must have been saying this. Several newspapers stressed that Trueman had not been selected for the Australian and South African tours because his conduct on the tour to the West Indies in 1953–54 had not conformed to MCC notions of how tourists should behave, a view which could be interpreted as upper-class prejudice against a working-class man. It is, however, almost impossible to separate myth from fact in accounts of Trueman's behaviour in the West Indies. Charles Palmer, the tour manager and amateur captain of Leicestershire, said that Trueman had 'been pulled out of Yorkshire and put in a context which was entirely alien to his upbringing. There was no malice in him, but he spoke as a Yorkshireman would speak in Yorkshire and it didn't go down well in a highly sensitive situation'.[53] In 1956 Swanton wrote in a letter to the England captain Peter May regarding the South Africa tour that Trueman had 'plainly been found wanting for reasons other than cricket'.[54] Crawford White of the *News Chronicle* argued that omission from a second successive overseas tour showed that Trueman *'has indeed paid dearly for the "bad boy" label strung about his neck on the West Indies tour ... the MCC here are in danger of carrying toughness to the point of victimization. Trueman is getting a thoroughly bad deal'.[55]* In 1954 Frank Stainton praised Trueman for being 'steadfastly honest and forthright' and being a man with 'nothing of the smooth diplomatist about him. If he feels he has a good case, he says so – no matter who may be listening.' Stainton wrote 'Misbehaved my foot! ... *Trueman was more sinned against than sinning* [in the West Indies]. He objected to certain things because he had good grounds for objecting'.[56] Ross Hall of the *Daily Mirror* claimed that,

> the West Indies is still a nightmare at Lord's, with Trueman as the villain. How silly! How unworldly of the MCC to hold the faults of immaturity against one who has shown this season that he has learned from his own mistakes in the Caribbean.[57]

Even if one takes the cynical view that such journalists were writing what they imagined readers wanted to read, this confirms that many suspected Trueman was being victimized by the establishment for not knowing his place.

Trueman did not observe the modesty and courtesies which the upper and middle classes thought part of cricket's morality. He was possibly the first big sport star of twentieth-century England who did not at least pretend to be modest and unassuming. In 1987 Swanton claimed that the 'great cricketers of history whom former generations set up as their heroes were, almost to a man, models of modesty and the highest standards of behaviour on the field'.[58] Excessive modesty was one reason why Jack Hobbs had been so idolized in inter-war England. The footballer Stanley Matthews and the jockey Gordon Richards, among the biggest stars of English sport at the start of Trueman's career, were noted for not boasting about their abilities and achievements.

Success at the highest level of sport is probably impossible without excessive self-belief. Trueman had no false modesty and never doubted his ability. At the start of his county career he felt slighted because the Yorkshire club rated Ford, Whitehead and Coxon ahead of him. When he suggested to John Arlott who was writing a biography of him, that its subtitle should be *The Definitive Biography of the Best Fast Bowler Who Ever Drew Breath*, Arlott thought that this was only partially in jest. Trueman also suggested a similar title for a proposed biography to Michael Parkinson who shared Arlott's assessment of the remark.[59] Although in later life Trueman admitted that Frank Tyson bowled faster, he was angered by suggestions in the mid-1950s that Tyson was faster. When they played for the Players against the Gentlemen in 1957 Trueman at first refused to bowl into the wind because this could have made him look less fast than Tyson who would have the wind at his back. Trueman agreed to bowl into the wind only when Godfrey Evans, the Players captain, threatened to take the side off the field. Trueman often thrust statistics about his playing achievements in the faces of other players.

Trueman quickly acquired a reputation for not apologizing to batsmen when they were struck by his bowling and of not enquiring whether they were hurt. In retirement he claimed that he had not tried to hit batsmen, but this is not what many batsmen thought at the time. When Trueman burst on Test cricket in 1952 George Duckworth was impressed most by Trueman's 'fiery attitude towards the opposition'. Some fast bowlers, Duckworth wrote, 'used to apologise when they hit a batsmen. Some just "apologised" – said it and didn't mean it. But Freddy strikes me as the type who, if he really dug one in and inflicted a painful blow, would say "Why apologise?"'.[60] In 1956 the cricket broadcaster Brian Johnston wrote that Trueman seemed to have 'mellowed a lot' in the past year but recalled that he had seen Trueman walk back to his mark and 'scowl in a threatening way at the batsman, as if to say: "Wait and see what's coming to you"'.[61] Don Mosey described Trueman as 'a compulsive *threatener* of batsmen'.[62] On the 1953–54 West Indies tour, Trueman did not join his team mates ministering to the legspinner Wilf Ferguson whom he had just hit. Trueman's next ball was almost a beamer. Trueman maintained that he was incensed by being called 'a white bastard'.[63] First-class cricketers may not have placed much importance on whether a bowler apologized to a batsman. In 1954 Denis Compton explained that when a batsman who had been injured went out to bat again he was signalling his fitness to play and being prepared to face everything 'the other side puts against him'. The fielding side, he thought, should not handicap itself by refusing to bowl bouncers.[64] Such comments, however, suggest that many cricket followers may have taken a different view and would have seen Trueman's reputation for failing to apologize to batsmen as evidence of his disregard for the good manners of cricket.

The etiquette of cricket had always contained a measure of insincerity. Some forms of sharp practice had long been accepted. Bowlers picked the seam and even Jack Hobbs, often regarded as the personification of cricket's tradition of sportsmanship, did not always 'walk' when he knew that he had been caught.[65] Many may have seen Trueman's disdain for the artificialities and hypocrisies of cricket as the expression of an innate honesty. His honesty was also expressed in the forthrightness of his speech. Mosey thought Trueman 'loud, brash, and believed firmly in his God-given right to call spades bloody shovels'.[66] Trueman's speech could be witty but also mordant and personal. Mosey agreed that Trueman could be 'brusque' and that 'there can be no doubt that occasionally he went over the top'.[67] Henry Blofeld, who worked with Trueman in radio, thought that in Trueman's early cricket career 'impulsive brashness often got the better of him' and that 'he was unable to resist telling people what he thought of them'.[68] As Mosey remembered, 'no one – but no one – has the final word in an exchange with F.S. Trueman ... more than one captain took away the lasting impression that Fred was an insubordinate and undisciplined so-and-so'.[69] While Trueman's honesty, when linked to his belief that Jack was as good as his master, made him a hero to some, it created enemies in high places and promoted his reputation as a trouble-maker.

**Trueman in his social and cultural context**

Trueman's heroic and anti-heroic status can also be related to the tensions of anxieties of British, and particularly English, society in the 1950s. Conservative election victories in 1951, 1955 and 1959, full employment and rising real incomes for most of the population suggest that this decade was characterized by social passivity. Yet the 1950s were also a period when the cultural and social forces that were to produce much change by the mid-1960s were fermenting beneath the surface. Westminster politicians regarded Britain as a major world power but the Suez misadventure and the retreat from Empire indicated that Britain was not a super power like the United States or the Soviet Union. Immigration to Britain from the Caribbean and South Asia was transforming the ethnic make-up of inner cities and Britain's first race riots occurred in 1958. Television was becoming a major leisure interest with profound effects for radio and the cinema. Teddy boys had provoked concern about youth being out of control. In 1952 the popularity of American singers such as Johnnie Ray and Frankie Laine prefigured the explosion of rock 'n' roll in 1955 and strengthened alarm about the Americanization of popular culture. Proposals to abolish hanging and decriminalize homosexuality stimulated great controversy.

Peter Hennessey has claimed that it is easy to argue that the long 1930s were coming to an end in the 1950s. Eric Hobsbawm told him that the 1950s were 'the crucial decade. For the first time you could feel things changing. Suez and the coming of rock-and-roll divide twentieth-century British history'.[70] There was a growing awareness, not restricted to the political left, which regarded the high political world as outmoded and removed from the concerns of most people and particularly young adults. In 1955 the political commentator Henry Fairlie coined the expression 'the Establishment' to describe those, almost invariably educated at public schools and Oxbridge, who controlled Britain. Only four of the 21 members of the Cabinet in 1962 had not been educated at public schools. The plays and novels of the 'Angry Young Men'[71] attracted admiration but perhaps even more distaste, and while it must be recognized that they had diverse opinions on many issues, David Cooper detected a 'terrier-like pursuit of all that has a false ring, of all that seems more than it actually is' and 'attacks on superficiality, pettiness and snobbery' as common to their work.[72] The satire boom of the late 1950s and early 1960s registered the spread of this disregard for the establishment and its mores which had been festering in the 1950s. Yet for those who sympathized with such cultural movements in the 1950s and early 1960s, many others, and the Conservative electoral victories suggest they were the majority, felt discomforted by them and remained attached to traditional values and practices.

Trueman's status as hero and anti-hero can be seen as further expressions of these cultural changes in the 1950s. Trueman's challenge to, and victimization by, the snobbery, class distinction and privilege of cricket can be related to the growing fuddy-duddism of English society and politics. Although cricket was not prominent in the work of the Angry Young Men, the social relations of first-class cricket in the 1950s exemplified what the Angry Young Men disliked so much about England. Like Jimmy Porter, the main character of John Osborne's *Look Back in Anger*, Trueman often seemed to seethe with rage against the Home Counties bourgeoisie and what he took to be the hypocrisies of their values and assumptions of superiority and of their entitlement to exercise social leadership. Like Porter, Trueman was a man of strong emotion, acutely aware of his talents going unrecognized and resentful at being patronized yet easily prone to self pity. Parallels can also be drawn with Arthur Seaton, the chief character of Alan Sillitoe's novel *Saturday Night and Sunday Morning*. Seaton and Trueman were provincial, cocksure young men with brash personalities who showed no respect for traditional values and did not defer to their elders or supposed social betters. Trueman's status as a Yorkshire hero victimized by a South of England authority resonated with the emphasis on working-class provincial resentment found in the early novels of John Braine, David Storey's *This Sporting Life* and Shelagh Delaney's play *A Taste of Honey*. Even the physical resemblances between Trueman and the actor Alan Bates, who regularly appeared in stage and film versions of the work of writers regarded as Angry Young Men, were often noted. One suspects that those who were outraged by *Look Back In Anger* would have also have disapproved of Trueman's persona.

Trueman was admired and reviled for challenging and being victimized by the cricket establishment but he was far from a political radical. Most of the Angry Young Men writers supported the Labour Party or some form of socialism in the 1950s. Although he and his father had worked in coal mining, Trueman always voted Conservative and supported the monarchy. He had little time for trade unionism and later detested Arthur Scargill. He embraced economic individualism and from early in his cricket career eagerly exploited financial opportunities presented by his fame and seemed to take it as read that being mercenary was a Yorkshire characteristic. As Stephen Wagg has pointed out so perceptively, while 'the essence of Trueman's philosophy was that Jack's as good as his Master; he never questioned the system itself ... He confronted authority, but wanted to be governed by an iron fist. He angrily demanded to be put in his place.' Trueman 'accepted existing class relations, but not the condescension that went with them'.[73] Trueman seems to have craved the respect of the cricket establishment and of his so-called social betters in general. Don Mosey believed that Trueman was delighted to be designated the senior professional on the MCC tour of the West Indies in 1959–60 after Statham had to return home. Mosey also thought that Trueman believed that he, not Close, should have become captain of Yorkshire.[74] The irony of Trueman's celebrity in the 1950s and early 1960s is that while his personality, sense of self worth and background made him appear a foe of the established order and a hero to many, his political sympathies lay with the establishment. Always convinced that he was as good as his masters, he accepted the social order provided that he was accorded the respect which he believed he was due.

## Notes

[1]  Mosey, *Fred*, ix, 3.
[2]  *Yorkshire Post*, July 3, 2006.
[3]  *Birmingham Post*, July 3, 2006.
[4]  Arlott, *Fred*, 11.
[5]  Mosey, *We Don't Play It For Fun*, 127.
[6]  *Daily Telegraph*, July 7, 2006.
[7]  Cited in Hill, *Brian Close*, 58.
[8]  *Sunday Graphic*, August 1, 1954.
[9]  Arlott, *Fred*, 49.
[10]  Mosey, *We Don't Play It For Fun*, 118.
[11]  *Sunday Express*, August 1, 1954.
[12]  Ibid., July 20, 1952.
[13]  *Sunday People*, June 8, 1952.
[14]  *Empire News*, June 22, 1952.
[15]  *Cricketer*, June 16, 1952, 193.
[16]  *Derby Evening Telegraph*, July 5, 2006.
[17]  *Observer*, July 2, 2006.
[18]  *Daily Post*, July 7, 2006; *Evening Gazette*, July 7, 2006.
[19]  *Daily Mail*, July 3, 2006.

[20] *Herald*, July 3, 2006.

[21] Statham, *A Spell at the Top*, 30.

[22] *Sunday Express*, July 2, 2006.

[23] *News Chronicle*, July 30, 1954.

[24] *Sunday Graphic*, August 1, 1954.

[25] *Star*, July 28, 1954; *Daily Herald*, July 28, 1954.

[26] *Sheffield Telegraph*, July 31, 1954.

[27] *Sunday Graphic*, August 1, 1954.

[28] *Telegraph & Argus*, July 28, 1954; *Star*, July 28, 1954.

[29] *Star Green 'Un*, July 31, 1954.

[30] Mosey, *Fred*, 44; Trelford, *Len Hutton Remembered*, 162.

[31] *Yorkshire Post*, July 30, 1954.

[32] Mosey, *We Don't Play It For Fun*, 134.

[33] Mosey, *Fred*, 53.

[34] Ibid., 23.

[35] Illingworth and Mosey, *Yorkshire and Back*, 55.

[36] Chalke and Hodgson, *No Coward Soul*, 166.

[37] Illingworth and Mosey, *Yorkshire and Back*, 50: Trueman, *Ball of Fire*, 37–8.

[38] Mosey, *Fred*, 65.

[39] Ibid., 59, 95–6.

[40] Swanton, Plumptre and Woodcock, *Barclay's World of Cricket*, 51.

[41] Arlott, *Fred*, 28.

[42] *Guardian*, June 22, 1993.

[43] *Wisden Cricketers' Almanack 2007*, 42.

[44] *Daily Mail*, July 3, 2006.

[45] Trueman and Mosey, *Fred Trueman Talking Cricket*, 132.

[46] Trueman and Mosey, *As It Was*, 2, 219, 249.

[47] I am grateful to Mark Whitaker, the Cambridge bowler whom Trueman helped, for telling me about this.

[48] *Sunday Graphic*, August 1, 1954.

[49] *Sunday Express*, August 1, 1954.

[50] *Star*, July 28, 1954.

[51] *Cricketer*, August 7, 1954, 359.

[52] *Yorkshire Post*, July 28, 1954.

[53] *Wisden Cricketer*, August 2006, 36.

[54] Allen, *Jim*, 199.

[55] *News Chronicle*, August 15, 1956.

[56] *Star Green 'Un*, July 31, 1954.

[57] *Daily Mirror*, July 29, 1954.

[58] *Cricketer International*, February 1987, 16.

[59] Parkinson, *Michael Parkinson on Cricket*, 282.

[60] *Empire News*, June 22, 1952.

[61] *Illustrated*, July 28, 1956, 32.

[62] Mosey, *Fred*, 23.

[63] Ibid., 43.

[64] *Sunday Express*, July 25, 1954.

[65] Williams, *Cricket and England*, 79, 82.

[66] Mosey, *We Don't Play It For Fun*, 132.

[67] Mosey, *Fred*, 55.

[68] *Express*, July 3, 2006.

[69] Mosey, *Fred*, 85.

[70] Hennessy, *Having it so Good*, 490–1.

[71] Angry Young Men was a term widely used to describe a number of young writers whose work provoked controversy in the mid and late 1950s. Those most often identified as Angry Young Men were the dramatist John Osborne, the novelists Kingsley Amis, John Wain, John Braine and Alan Sillitoe and the philosophers Colin Wilson and Stuart Holroyd. The playwright Shelagh Delaney was sometimes called an Angry Young Woman. Not all of them were happy to be labelled Angry Young Men and they never formed an ideologically or aesthetically coherent

movement, but much of their work expressed impatience with established cultural and social values and had a tone of provincial resentment against metropolitan assumptions of superiority.

[72] Cooper, 'Looking Back on Anger', 262, 265.
[73] Wagg, 'Muck or Nettles', 80.
[74] Mosey, *Fred*, 77, 96.

## References

Allen, David Rayvern. *Jim: The Life of E.W. Swanton*. London: Aurum, 2005.

Arlott, John. *Fred: Portrait of a Fast Bowler*. London: Coronet, 1974.

Chalke, Stephen, and Derek Hodgson. *No Coward Soul: The Remarkable Story of Bob Appleyard*. Bath: Fairfield, 2003.

Cooper, David E. 'Looking Back in Anger'. In *The Age of Affluence 1951–1964*, edited by Vernon Bogdanor and Robert Skidelsky, 254–87. London: Macmillan, 1970.

Hennessy, Peter. *Having It So Good: Britain in the Fifties*. London: Penguin, 2006.

Hill, Alan. *Brian Close: Cricket's Lionheart*. London: Methuen, 2002.

Illingworth, Ray, and Don Mosey. *Yorkshire and Back: The Autobiography of Ray Illingworth*. London: Queen Anne, 1980.

Mosey, Don. *We Don't Play It For Fun: A Story of Yorkshire Cricket*. London: Methuen, 1988.

Mosey, Don. *Fred: Then and Now*. London: Kingswood, 1991.

Parkinson, Michael. *Michael Parkinson on Cricket*. London: Hodder & Stoughton, 2002.

Statham, Brian. *A Spell at the Top*. London: Sportsman's Book Club, 1970.

Swanton, E.W., George Plumptre, and John Woodcock, eds. *Barclays World of Cricket: The Game from A to Z*. London: Guild, 1986.

Trelford, Donald, ed. *Len Hutton Remembered*. London: Witherby, 1992.

Trueman, Fred. *Ball of Fire: An Autobiography*. London: Dent, 1976.

Trueman, Fred, and Don Mosey. *As It Was: The Memoirs of Fred Trueman*. London: Macmillan, 2004.

Trueman, Fred, and Don Mosey. *Fred Trueman Talking Cricket with Friends Past and Present*. London: Hodder & Stoughton in association with Scottish Equitable, 2004.

Wagg, Stephen. 'Muck or Nettles: Men, Masculinity and Myth in Yorkshire Cricket'. *Sport in History* 23, no. 2 (2003–04): 68–93.

Williams, Jack. *Cricket and England: A Social and Cultural History of the Inter-war Years*. London: Cass, 2003.

*Wisden Cricketers' Almanack 2007*. Alton: John Wisden, 2007.

# Rebellion, race and Rhodesia: international cricketing relations with Rhodesia during UDI

Charles Little*

*London Metropolitan Business School, London Metropolitan University, London, UK*

The issue of sporting contacts with Robert Mugabe's Zimbabwe has been one of the most contentious and problematic issues facing international cricket in the early twenty-first century. Human rights, morality and commerce became key issues confronting cricketers, the game's administrators and various national Governments. Decisions about these contacts were made in the glare of publicity, none more so than the debates about whether Harare and Bulawayo should have retained their position as co-hosts of the 2003 Cricket World Cup.

One point that was overlooked amongst all of the debate surrounding the issue was that there were precedents of international cricket teams refusing to play in Zimbabwe, and doing so because of opposition to the ruling regime in that country. In that case, however, the regime in question belonged not to Robert Mugabe, but instead to Ian Smith, who led what was then Rhodesia during its period of 'independence' from Britain between 1965 and 1979.

The cancellation of cricketing visits to Rhodesia by England, Australia and a number of county sides were just one part of a long-running international campaign against the white minority Government of Ian Smith. Between 1965 and 1979 Rhodesia existed as an international pariah state, with Britain, the Commonwealth, most African states and the United Nations amongst those ranged against it. This essay aims to examine the ways in which cricket became one of the elements in this campaign.

The sports boycott against Rhodesia is almost totally absent from the historical memory. Not only have media accounts of contemporary controversies ignored their antecedents, but the entire question of the sports boycott against Rhodesia has been almost totally ignored by academics.[1] In spite of this paucity of attention, there are a number of significant reasons why it is deserving of greater attention. Most obviously, it provides additional context to the contemporary debates surrounding sporting relations with Mugabe's Zimbabwe, allowing us to examine the actions of today's cricketers, administrators and politicians from a broader perspective. Another reason is the light that it sheds on the British Government's willingness to use sport as a tool for its wider political objectives. British Governments are usually perceived to have been relatively reluctant, the 1980 Olympic boycott excepted, to mix foreign policy and sport. In the case of Rhodesia, however, not only was Britain extremely heavily involved in unilateral action against Rhodesian participation, it even took the lead in instigating an international boycott against Rhodesian sport.

Thirdly, a crucial issue surrounding cricketing sanctions against Rhodesia, and their key difference from the campaign against apartheid-sport in South Africa in the 1960s, was the essential reason for the boycott. Unlike the case of South Africa at this time, the campaign against Rhodesian participation in international cricket was focused almost solely on the nature of the Rhodesian Government, and not on racial issues in Rhodesian cricket itself. The focus was thus purely in the realm of broader foreign policy, aiming to isolate a racially discriminatory regime, rather than within cricket. In fact, the campaign against Rhodesia foreshadowed the shift in focus of the South African campaign in the mid to late 1970s.

The 1960s marked the 'End of Empire' for the British in Africa. Beginning with Ghana in 1957, Britain granted self-Government and independence to its former colonies. The status of Southern Rhodesia (known from 1964 onwards simply as Rhodesia) emerged as a source of controversy. Rhodesia had a substantial white minority (around 8–10% of the total population), who already enjoyed a substantial degree of self-government, including control of an army and air force. The white Rhodesians indicated an unwillingness to accept independence under majority rule and instead sought to maintain their privileged position into independence.[2]

Granting independence to a white minority government was unacceptable for the British in the international political situation of the 1960s, and they sought to negotiate a solution. The British did not require the immediate transition to majority rule, but instead sought a scheme that would commit the country to eventual majority African rule (albeit after a relatively long transition period). Even this, however, was unacceptable to the white population and, fearful of losing their privileged position, the Rhodesian Government of Ian Smith declared its independence from Britain on 11 November 1965, an action universally referred to as the Unilateral Declaration of Independence (UDI).

The British Government, led by Prime Minister Harold Wilson, declared UDI to be an illegal act of rebellion and claimed that it retained legal authority over Rhodesia. It backed this up with a vigorous campaign to deny any international recognition to the Smith regime, but stood short of taking direct action to replace the Smith Government. These actions, and particularly the failure to take military action, were heavily criticized by the newly independent African members of the Commonwealth, and the ensuing crisis threatened to undermine the very future of the Commonwealth itself.

Stung by this criticism, and fuelled by its own anger at the Smith regime, the British Government took a number of actions against the Rhodesians. These included trade sanctions, an arms embargo and restrictions on the transfer of currency. Although unwilling for the United Nations to take a lead on the issue, the British sponsored a number of resolutions to the United Nations Security Council to further its aims. Above all else, the fundamental aim of the British Government was to deny the legitimacy of the Smith

Government. UDI, it argued, was an unlawful act, and the Smith regime had no legitimate international standing.

These efforts to deny international legitimacy to the Smith regime quickly extended into the realm of sport. The British argued that sporting contacts were a form of 'comfort to the illegal regime in Rhodesia'.[3] These initial efforts succeeded, amongst others, in dissuading the Hockey Association from inviting a Rhodesian team to England in 1966, persuading the Spanish Government to refuse visas for a Rhodesian field hockey team to compete in an international tournament in Madrid in April 1967, and led to the Irish, Norwegian, Swedish and Danish teams withdrawing from the World Ploughing Championships in Rhodesia the following year. Not all efforts were successful: the French rugby team played against Rhodesia in Salisbury in July 1967, and the Mauritian football team also visited later that year. Rhodesia was also successful in gaining admission to tennis' Davis Cup competition in 1968, although its away tie against Sweden was abandoned after anti-racism protestors staged an invasion of the match venue.[4]

What of cricket? The game was the most popular summer sport amongst white Rhodesians, and was well established in the country. Rhodesian cricket was closely aligned with South Africa, with the Rhodesian team playing as a 'province' in the Currie Cup competition. Rhodesian cricketers were also eligible to represent South Africa, with Colin Bland, David Pithey, Jackie du Preeze and John Traicos winning Springbok caps during the UDI period. Rhodesian–South African sporting contacts were unaffected by the sporting boycotts against both parties, and, indeed, international isolation pushed the two closer together.[5]

Institutionally, Rhodesia was a member of the South African Cricket Association (SACA), which had been a member of the Imperial Cricket Conference (ICC) until South Africa became a Republic in 1961. After that date SACA was no longer an official member, but remained in good standing with England, Australia and New Zealand until the 1970s. The reformation of the ICC in 1966 meant that Rhodesia could have sought affiliate membership, although any application would have almost certainly been resisted by India, Pakistan and the West Indies. Such a path was never seriously considered by Rhodesia, however, as doing so would have required breaking its affiliation with South Africa, and most Rhodesians valued this over sporting independence.[6]

In terms of international contacts, Rhodesia's main source came from teams visiting South Africa. As a member of SACA, Rhodesia was granted fixtures against most teams touring the Republic, and playing one or two matches in Salisbury or Bulawayo became an established element of a South African tour. From the 1960s onwards, a number of first class sides had also made tours of Rhodesia, with Rhodesia defeating reigning English champions Worcestershire in Salisbury in March 1965.

The first tour scheduled to take place after UDI was a visit by Bob Simpson's Australians in late 1966, who were due to play two matches in Rhodesia. This slightly preceded the development of the sporting boycott against Rhodesia and, although there was some speculation about whether the tour would proceed, it went ahead as planned, with the Australian Cricket Board claiming that 'our External Affairs Department in Canberra tells [us] that it knows of no reason why the Rhodesian matches should not be played'.[7]

What no one was to know was that this would be the last representative team to tour Rhodesia, save for a low profile visit by the Australian schoolboys' team in December 1967. The first casualty of the boycott was a proposed return visit by the Worcestershire county side in 1967. This visit never moved beyond an invitation from the Rhodesians and following discussions between the British Government and the MCC, Worcestershire quietly abandoned the idea.[8]

Far more contentious was a proposed tour by Yorkshire later that season. Negotiations were well advanced between the two parties before the British Government became aware of the plans, with Yorkshire on the verge of agreeing to tour so long as financial terms were agreeable. Government officials began a lobbying campaign through the MCC, arguing that the tour would 'offer aid and comfort to an illegal regime', to which the *Yorkshire Post* humorously replied that 'the Yorkshire team never goes anywhere to offer aid and comfort to anyone; its object is always to hammer them into the ground'.[9]

Many within Yorkshire cricket reacted with far less humour to the Government's intervention,[10] and there was a similar response from the right-wing press. *The Daily Telegraph* launched a stinging editorial which claimed that,

> For a Commonwealth Office spokesman to suggest now that, in playing cricket with a Rhodesian team, Yorkshire would be offering 'aid and comfort to an illegal regime' is ludicrous ... The next step in this decision will be postal censorship of Christmas cards in case Mr Smith is getting some goodwill message across. Fascist Italy and Germany used to align their athletics closely to their foreign policies, and Britain is in danger of making the same pernicious mistake.

Editorials and letters to the editor in a range of newspapers displayed similar opposition.[11]

In the end, however, the Yorkshire committee bowed to the Government's view, finally announcing that 'as cricketers we would be very willing to accept, but in view of the political pressure which has been exerted [we] have with extreme reluctance decided that there is no alternative but to decline'.[12] The reference to political pressure was a little overstated, as the Government never made any threats against the county. Indeed, throughout the Rhodesian sporting boycott British Governments never ordered any team or individuals to cancel a tour, restricting their efforts to lobbying them to do so voluntarily.

After the acrimony of the Yorkshire cancellation, the cancellation of England's proposed visit to Rhodesia in 1969 proved to be rather low-key. The MCC had customarily played two matches in Rhodesia whenever it toured South Africa, but preventing such a visit on England's planned 1969 tour had been an objective of the British Government since even before the Yorkshire controversy, with lobbying beginning as early as July 1967.[13] In May 1968, after a year of negotiations between the two parties the MCC released a muted press statement announcing that, 'following advice from H.M. Government and in light of the present circumstances it has been decided that MCC will not play in Rhodesia'.[14]

Unlike the media furore over the cancellation of the Yorkshire tour, the reaction by the British press to this decision was extremely understated. No national newspaper appears to have passed editorial comment on the decision, and negative criticism was limited to a mere two letters to *The Daily Telegraph*.[15] This silence was largely the consequence of deliberate efforts by the British Government to prevent any publicity about their efforts to enforce a sports boycott against Rhodesia, mindful of both public support within Britain for the white Rhodesian cause and fearful of accusations of bringing politics unnecessarily into sport. This silence has no doubt contributed to the lack of later historical awareness about this decision. This strategy also relied on the acquiescence of the MCC, which did not follow the lead of their Yorkshire counterparts in complaining to the press over the Government's lobbying.

How are we to understand why the MCC came to its decision, especially given the generally right-wing political views of cricket administrators and in light of their dogged determination to preserve sporting contacts with South Africa? Why did they view Rhodesia as a separate case? The key to understanding the decision lies with Sir Alec Douglas-Home, the former President of the MCC and, at that time, still active committee-member. Douglas-Home was a former Conservative Prime Minister, and still an active Parliamentarian. He was also intimately linked with the broader political issues surrounding Rhodesia, having been Colonial Secretary in the early 1960s (during the period of the Federation of Rhodesia and Nyasaland, which had been the British Government's initial strategy to deal with the 'problem' of Southern Rhodesian independence), and would later serve as Foreign Secretary in the Heath Government, when he would be a key figure in trying to negotiate a settlement with the Smith Government.

On a personal level, Douglas-Home was a strong supporter of 'building-bridges' (i.e. maintaining sporting contacts) with South Africa, and recent works have revealed the extent to which he attempted to prevent the issue of Basil D'Oliveira's selection from compromising the South Africa leg of the MCC's proposed 1969 tour (ironically, the main purpose of his now infamous meeting with South African Prime Minister Vorster, during which the pair discussed the D'Oliveira issue, was to lobby Vorster to implement sanctions against Rhodesia).[16] There is also evidence to suggest that he favoured a lighter touch to any sporting sanctions against Rhodesia than other British politicians.[17] In terms of the situation in 1968, however, his hands were largely tied, and he himself noted, 'I think the committee feel that if the Government asks you not to do something then you don't do it – no matter how much it is against your instincts'.[18] His own position was even more compromised, for as a former Prime Minister, he would have found it extremely difficult to refuse the sitting Prime Minister's request that the MCC abandon the Rhodesian leg of their tour.

Irrespective of their precise motivations, it is interesting to note that English cricket administrators were much more willing to follow the lead of their Government in halting links with Rhodesia than were their counterparts in other sports, most notably rugby union (but also hockey, tennis and golf). Whereas the MCC and the counties bowed to requests to reject invitations to tour Rhodesia, both national and club rugby union teams repeatedly rejected Government requests and undertook tours: the British Lions visiting Rhodesia on their tours of South Africa in 1968 (to the considerable embarrassment of the Government, who were covertly campaigning for the exclusion of Rhodesia from the Mexico City Olympic Games[19]) and 1974, as did national sides from France, Australia, New Zealand, Argentina,[20] and Italy; while there were numerous tours by British club sides.[21]

The divergent positions taken by cricket administrators and their rugby union counterparts can be seen surrounding the Australian cricket team's decision to avoid Rhodesia during its tour to South Africa in early 1970. This visit was a late addition to the Australian tour of India, after Pakistan withdrew from hosting its intended section of the tour. When the itinerary for the South Africa leg was announced, Rhodesia was conspicuous by its absence. The President of the South African Cricket Association, E.R. Hammond, made it clear that this was due to political considerations, noting, 'we tried very hard to persuade the Australians to play in Rhodesia, but you know the position. The visiting side has the right to say who they will play against. There is nothing we could do'.[22] What puzzled many Rhodesians was that this announcement came just two weeks before the Australian rugby union team played a match against Rhodesia in Salisbury.

The decision to omit Rhodesia from the Australian team's itinerary is another example of the sporting boycott of Rhodesia having faded from the historical memory. There was, for instance, no mention of this precedent during the debate that led up to the Australian Government's cancellation of the Australian team's tour of Zimbabwe in 2007.[23]

No mention of the decision appears in any of the published histories of Australian cricket.[24] Even more intriguingly, the matter appears to have been completely overlooked by the Australian media at the time,[25] meaning that the exact machinations behind the decision remain unknown.

After 1970 the growing international campaign against cricketing links with South Africa put paid to any realistic prospects of further representative teams visiting Rhodesia – touring Rhodesia alone was neither financially or politically viable, and now the option of a short visit as part of a wider tour to South Africa no longer existed. Like South Africa, Rhodesia sought to fill this void by organizing private tours.

The first of these was organized by industrialist Jimmy McAlpine (Chairman of Sir Alfred McAlpine and Co.), who visited Rhodesia as part of a Southern African tour in early 1969, playing two matches against a President's XI. It was primarily a private tour for McAlpine and his associates, although there were at least four former County players amongst the touring party. Rather than merely ignoring British Government opposition to sporting contacts with Rhodesia, McAlpine appears to have deliberately chosen to flaunt his contempt for their policies.[26]

Similar motives appear to have been behind the visit of the Tui club from New Zealand in 1974, several of whose members expressed their support for the Smith regime in justifying their decision to tour.[27] The team was a composite side of club players from the Waikato region, only one of whom had played first class cricket, and would be the only team from New Zealand to have any contact with Rhodesia during the UDI period.[28] The side played four matches in Rhodesia, alongside fixtures in South Africa, Malawi and Australia. It was a reflection of how isolated Rhodesian cricket had become that a tour by a side of such low standard received quite significant attention within Rhodesia, highlighted by the visitors being personally welcomed by Ian Smith himself.[29]

By far the strongest of these private visits were three tours arranged under the banner of the International Wanderers in 1972, 1974 and 1975, with the latter two tours also including fixtures in South Africa. These were the only private touring teams that were of first class quality, and the only ones to play matches against the Rhodesian national team. The teams mostly consisted of county professionals, the bulk of whom were English, with a scattering of Australians and New Zealanders, including a fair number of test caps. New Zealand's Glenn Turner was the only player to appear on all three tours, and captained the final party. The 1975 touring party was more diverse, with the inclusion of players from India, Pakistan and the West Indies.[30]

Cricket authorities in England (as well as Australia and New Zealand) took no steps to prevent players making these trips. They did intervene in 1975, however, when initial plans for the tour would have seen a de facto England test team picked to visit both Rhodesia and South Africa. The MCC warned the organizers that any unofficial side that was perceived to be nationally representative would have caused 'considerable embarrassment' to the game and would jeopardize the future careers of the players involved. A significant change of personnel, including the addition of a number of non-English players to the squad, placated the MCC. The tours also benefited from a decision by the Heath Government in 1972 to restrict its lobbying against visits to Rhodesia to only national representative teams, and to ignore the activities of private and club visits.[31]

The other test playing nations, India, Pakistan and the West Indies, took a very different line over these contests, reflecting a wider opposition to any contact with Rhodesia. In 1973 the Indian Government announced that their players would be refused permission to tour Rhodesia with the International Wanderers, and the External Affairs Minister stated that India would not allow its players to play in a country that practised apartheid. As a consequence, former test spinner Budhi Kunderan revoked his Indian citizenship and acquired a British passport to allow himself to join the 1975 tour.[32] Indian Government opposition to cricketing links with Rhodesia had previously been expressed in 1970, when Indira Ghandi threatened to cancel India's tour of the West Indies in the wake of Garfield Sobers visit to Rhodesia, and there have been some suggestions that Indian opposition lay behind Australia's decision to refuse to tour Rhodesia in 1970.[33]

Like India, Pakistan had a long-standing tradition of opposing cricketing links with what it deemed racist regimes. In 1962 it had barred three South Africans (Roy McLean, Neil Adcock and Trevor Goddard) from playing for the Commonwealth XI on the Pakistani leg of its world tour. Ironically, given later events in Barbados in 1966, Rhodesia's Colin Bland was the beneficiary of this decision, as he was called up to join the touring party as a replacement. Although having already been capped for the Springboks, Bland's status as a Southern Rhodesian (as this occurred during the Federation phase) posed no problem for the Pakistani Government.[34] UDI, however, changed the stakes. In 1973 the Pakistani Government followed the lead of India in refusing permission for four Pakistani test players resident in England to accept invitations to participate on the International Wanderers tour. Former test players Younis Ahmed and Mohammed Ilyas would, however, join the 1975 tour, and Ahmed spent three seasons playing club cricket in Salisbury.[35]

It was in the West Indies, however, that the issue of cricketing contacts with Rhodesia were to receive the most prominence. Given the serious divisions that later contacts would bring, it was somewhat ironic that initial linkages between Rhodesian and West Indian cricket were not only positive, but even played some role in breaking down racial integration within Rhodesian cricket. The first suggestion of a cricketing relationship came in late 1958 with the announcement of the planned West Indian tour to South Africa for the following season. Rhodesia's cricket authorities sought to be granted a match against the tourists and, although the matches in South Africa would involve only non-European teams, there were suggestions that any Rhodesian team picked for this match would be multi-racial.[36] Although the tour eventually collapsed due to protests over the segregated nature of the South African matches, Rhodesian interest in hosting the West Indians remained.[37] Negotiations were undertaken to arrange a visit at the conclusion of the West Indian's tour of Australia in 1960–61, but the parties were eventually unable to secure an agreement.[38]

These negotiations were the genesis, however, for the Ron Roberts-led Commonwealth teams that toured Rhodesia in 1961–62 and 1962–63. Roberts had been the key figure in trying to negotiate the 1960–61 tour, and West Indian players formed the foundation of the Commonwealth Squads. The first touring side included Everton Weekes, Roy Marshall and Sonny Ramadhin, whilst Rohan Kanhai, Chester Watson and Wes Hall joined Marshall on the return visit. The teams also included Indian and Pakistani players and the English-based coloured South African Basil D'Oliveira, and were the first multi-racial teams to tour Rhodesia.[39] Despite this pioneering achievement, the tours also revealed racial tensions within Rhodesian cricket. Chesterfield has noted that the West Indian players were subjected to a number of acts of discrimination during the tour, particularly in hotels and bars, while the Queen's club of Bulawayo, the usual venue for first class cricket in that city, refused to allow the team to play at its ground after imposing a colour-bar.[40]

These incidents hinted at the potential for future discord, and UDI would drive a wedge through these cracks. The first apparent consequence of the changed political situation might initially appear to have been the withdrawal of an invitation to Colin Bland to appear in a match in Barbados in 1967. Bland, along with South African test players

Graeme and Peter Pollock, had been invited to play in a Rest of the World XI against Barbados as part of that nation's independence celebrations. The selection of these three white players from Southern Africa caused a controversy within Barbados and the wider West Indies, which eventually led to the withdrawal of the invitations.[41]

There is little evidence, however, to suggest that UDI played a role in the controversy.[42] Instead, it was Bland's status as a South African test cricketer that drew opposition, and the entire debate was framed in terms of opposition to South African racial politics and apartheid. The players were usually referred to as simply South African,[43] and the eventual catalyst for the withdrawal of the invitations was the 'D'Oliveira Affair'.[44] Although Bland's Rhodesian citizenship was noted on occasion, there was no specific debate about the merits, or otherwise, of West Indian-Rhodesian sporting contacts. This was not through any lack of awareness of the political situation in Rhodesia, as UDI and the subsequent political negotiations were front-page news in Barbados.[45] Although in most ways this episode was a false start in terms of West Indian opposition towards Ian Smith's Rhodesia, it is illustrative of the fact that the broader question of international sporting contacts with South Africa during this period often obscured debates surrounding relationships with Rhodesia.

The politics of race in Rhodesia was unequivocally at the heart of events in September 1970, however, when it was announced that Garry Sobers, the West Indian captain, had agreed to participate in a double wicket competition there. Sobers duly participated in the competition, for which he was paid £600, and also lunched with Ian Smith, whom Sobers described as 'a great man to talk to'.[46] Sobers' visit caused a massive uproar in the West Indies, and the issue escalated into a full-blown regional political crisis when Guyana's President, Forbes Burnham, suggested that Sobers could be barred from entering Guyana, jeopardizing a forthcoming Test match against India in Georgetown. Other political leaders from Jamaica and Trinidad and Tobago also weighed into the debate, leading Hilary Beckles to claim that the resulting furore 'was perhaps the major postcolonial regional political crisis' in the Caribbean and that 'no other matter, since the collapse of the British West Indies Federation, had mobilised regional public opinion in this way'. The issue was only resolved when Sobers issued a statement of regret over the matter.[47]

Further controversy and division erupted in West Indian cricket in February 1976 when a Shell Shield match between Guyana and Barbados was cancelled over the involvement of Barbadian batsman Geoffrey Greenidge. Greenidge had toured South Africa with the Derrick Robins XI the previous year, and had been refused entry into Guyana on the eve of the match. The issue again raised divisions within West Indian cricket, with Greenidge receiving the support of the Barbadian authorities, whilst Forbes Burnham continued to take a hard line against sporting contacts with Southern Africa. Greenidge had also toured Rhodesia with the International Wanderers, but, as in 1965, this Rhodesian connection was completely overlooked in the resulting debate.[48] One outcome of this controversy was that it forced West Indian cricket to seek a uniform approach to dealing with this question and led, in May 1976, to the West Indies Cricket Board of Control deciding to impose bans on any West Indian cricketer who coached or played in either South Africa or Rhodesia.[49]

So far this analysis has looked at visits to Rhodesia by international teams, but what of Rhodesian teams playing abroad? There was little tradition of touring within Rhodesian cricket, and prior to UDI only two sides had ever toured outside of Africa. A national junior side, known as the Fawns, had toured England in 1962, whilst Mashonaland Country Districts followed in late 1964. The national side, however, had only ever toured South Africa.[50]

The sports boycott against Rhodesia was to ensure that there was no follow-up to these tours. Amongst a raft of United Nations Security Council-backed sanctions imposed against Rhodesia in 1968, were the non-recognition of Rhodesian passports and travel bans imposed on those deemed to be representative of the Smith regime. The non-recognition of passports issued by the Smith regime had an obvious impact on the ability of sportspeople to travel to international competitions. Colin Bland was amongst the first to feel the impact of these when, in July 1968, he was refused entry to Britain on these grounds. Bland had been travelling to take part as a member of an International XI in an invitational match in Scarborough, but was turned back at Heathrow airport. Later that year Bland was warned by the Australian Government that he would be refused entry if he attempted to enter Australia to take part in an invitation match in Melbourne.[51]

This restriction was not enough, however, to prevent all Rhodesians travelling internationally, as the resolution only applied to Rhodesian passports, whereas the vast majority of white Rhodesians had some form of dual citizenship, usually either British or South African, and were able to travel freely under the passport of these other nations. This meant that individual Rhodesian cricketers were able to travel internationally, which allowed a number to play in Britain. A small few were able to play county cricket in England, whilst Oxford University was captained by five Rhodesians in succession between 1967 and 1971.[52]

National representative sporting teams were less able to exploit this loophole, as they were increasingly defined to be representatives of the Smith regime and thus in contravention of the travel ban. Because it was backed by the power of the Security Council this resolution was widely enforced, and no representative cricket team toured abroad (South Africa excepted) during the UDI period. Although overseas tours by Rhodesian clubs were theoretically possible, they could also be targeted through these measures if they were deemed to be in breach of the spirit of these regulations. A Rhodesian club side, the Ridgebacks, had made a low-key visit to Britain in 1974, but on the verge of a return visit in 1976 they were barred from undertaking their planned 18-match tour. That side contained eight Rhodesian representative players and its costs had been partially met by a public appeal in Rhodesia, which led British Minister for Sport and recreation Dennis Howell to deem it in violation of the resolution.[53]

Having accounted for the outcome of international efforts to exclude Rhodesia from international cricket we must now turn to the reasons for these actions. And it is in this area that the distinctions between the sporting boycotts of Rhodesia and South Africa are most important. Whereas the sports campaign against South Africa in the 1960s and 1970s focused on segregation and racism within South African sport itself, in the case of Rhodesia from the outset it was firmly aimed at opposing the existence and policies of the Smith regime.

Thus, the arguments employed to oppose sporting contacts with Rhodesia included:

- 'offering aid and comfort to an illegal regime' (British Government, 1968)
- 'We cannot but think that against the background of economic sanctions and criticisms levelled at Rhodesia's white minority Government and its apartheid-like policies, Sobers' visit indicated some naiveté and a lack of recognition of the Rhodesian problem' (*Morning Star* newspaper, Jamaica, 1970)[54]
- 'India will not allow its players to play in a country that practises apartheid' (Indian External Affairs Minister, 1973)[55]
- 'we are reluctant to admit to Britain groups from Rhodesia who are seeking to gain publicity or to further the political aims of the illegal regime' (British Government, 1977)[56]

This is not to say that there was no racism within Rhodesian cricket. Indeed, a strong case could have been made for opposing cricketing contacts with Rhodesia on similar grounds to the campaign against South Africa, although the situation was rather complicated. On the one hand, and in distinct contrast to the situation in South Africa, there were no legal barriers to multiracial sport, at least at open-age level, within Rhodesia. Football and athletics were amongst sports that were almost fully multi-racial.[57] There was also at least some multi-racial cricket, notably against visiting teams. As well as the Commonwealth XI tours of the early 1960s, Basil D'Oliveira toured with Warwickshire CCC in 1965, and, in 1975, the West Indian professional John Shepherd was selected in the Rhodesian XI, becoming the first black cricketer to compete in the Currie Cup during the apartheid-era.[58]

On the other hand, the Smith regime had, in 1968, barred all racially mixed sport from taking place within state-funded schools. Within cricket itself there were also a range of racial issues. Well into the 1970s Rhodesian teams competing in South Africa always deferred to 'local custom' by not including non-European players, and Shepherd himself was allegedly dropped from matches in South Africa for this reason.[59] Domestically, a large number of clubs had exclusionary policies, refusing to select Asian and African cricketers,[60] and in some cases preventing any multiracial sport on their facilities. The game was barely played at all by African Rhodesians – there were only two African clubs in 1963, despite Africans making up approximately 85% of the nation's population, with economic inequality amongst the factors influencing this.[61] And non-European cricketers and supporters faced abuse from spectators and the general public, such as the incidents against members of the Commonwealth XI tour and crowd violence the first time that an Asian club played a league match in Bulawayo.[62]

Rhodesian cricket, as an institution, could therefore not claim to be fully multiracial, and indeed in some cases remained deeply rooted in racist practices. Moreover, school sport apart, the racial discrimination that existed within Rhodesian cricket was the consequence of the attitudes and actions of the nation's cricket clubs and bodies themselves, and could not be explained away as the consequence of Government action. However, and this is a very important point, this case against Rhodesian cricket was never made by opponents of sporting contacts. Aside from a few isolated occasions, the justifications given for the boycott of Rhodesia were solely related to the nature of its Government and its policies.

On reflection then, what are some of the broader issues that can be derived from an analysis of these events? Firstly, this analysis has demonstrated that the Rhodesian issue was not merely a footnote to the campaign against South Africa. It was a wholly separate action, waged by separate actors with a separate range of objectives. Secondly, it was also distinct in that it was targeted against the racist nature of the Rhodesian Government, rather than focusing on racial issues within cricket. As such, it certainly provides a direct precedent to contemporary issues surrounding Zimbabwe, with the then British Government and at least some sporting bodies being willing to use sporting boycotts as a means of dealing with rogue political regimes.

**Notes**

[1] For an overview of the historical treatment of sporting contacts with Rhodesia see Little, 'Preventing "A Wonderful Break-Through for Rhodesia"'. The only acknowledgement of the cricketing boycott is a small section in Chesterfield's recent analysis of Zimbabwean cricket. Chesterfield, 'Zimbabwe Cricket', 137–40.

[2] Mansergh, *The Commonwealth Experience*, 163–201; Lloyd, *The British Empire*, 357–80.

3  Chitty (Rhodesia Political Department) to Tupholme (British Amateur Athletic Board), January 10, 1967. Public Record Office (hereafter PRO) Foreign and Commonwealth Office (FCO), 36–316.

4  Little, 'The Sports Boycott against Rhodesia Reconsidered'.

5  For the history of cricket in Rhodesia see Winch, *Cricket's Rich Heritage*.

6  There were some occasional calls for Rhodesia to break its ties with South Africa and seek independent international affiliation, but these never received official backing from the Rhodesia Cricket Union. Moreover, these were usually due to 'provincial squabbles', such as when the SACA refused to reconsider Rhodesia's demotion to the B Zone of the Currie Cup in 1962, rather than over broader political or racial issues. *Evening Standard* (Salisbury), February 13, 1962, 12.

7  *Rhodesia Herald*, February 11, 1966, 22; February 12, 1966, 6; August 25, 1966, 24; August 26, 1966, 25; September 2, 1966, 26.

8  Willcocks (Cultural Relations Department) to Griffith (MCC), July 12, 1967. PRO FCO, 36–316; Young to March, July 21 1967. PRO FCO, 25–549.

9  *Yorkshire Post*, September 13, 1967.

10  Yorkshire's players expressed their support for the tour. Fred Trueman was quoted as saying, 'I don't know what the hell the fuss is about. All I know is that I want to go and play cricket and nowt else'; and captain Brian Close opined, 'Cricket should be above politics and the fact that Rhodesia is said to be an illegal regime means nothing as far as our game is concerned'. *Daily Express*, September 13, 1967; *The Daily Telegraph*, September 13, 1967.

11  *The Daily Telegraph*, September 13, 1967. Other editorials critical of the Government's intervention appeared in the *The Times*, *Sunday Express* and *Sunday Telegraph*, while both the *The Times* and *Yorkshire Post* printed large numbers of letters to the editor with a similar viewpoint.

12  *The Times*, September 19, 1967.

13  March to Young (Rhodesia Political Department), July 14, 1967. PRO FCO, 36–316.

14  *The Times*, May 27, 1968.

15  *The Daily Telegraph*, May 30, 1968; May 31, 1968.

16  Murray, 'Politics and Cricket'; Murray and Merrett, *Caught Behind*; Oborne, *Basil D'Oliveira*.

17  He was on record as saying Colin Bland's exclusion from Britain in 1968 (see details on p. 531 of this article) was 'very much to be regretted', and he took a leading role in the Heath Government's decision to lessen British lobbying against some sporting contacts with Rhodesia in the early 1970s. *The Times*, August 20, 1968, 1; Galsworthy (Rhodesia Department) to Green (Department of the Environment), October 18, 1972. PRO FCO, 36/1293.

18  *Daily Mail*, May 27, 1968, 1.

19  Little, 'Preventing "A Wonderful Break-Through for Rhodesia"'.

20  The planned Test match was, however, cancelled due to the intervention of the Argentine Government.

21  Little, 'No Politics, Mucho Rugby'.

22  *Rhodesia Herald*, July 19, 1969, 24.

23  This was despite the fact that Australian Prime Minister John Howard's justification for his Government's intervention, that 'I'm not going to stand around and allow some kind of aid and comfort be given to [Robert Mugabe] by the greatest cricketing team in the world visiting his country', almost precisely echoed the British Government's entreaty to the Committee of the Yorkshire CCC committee that any visit to Rhodesia would provide 'aid and comfort' to the Smith regime. Australian Broadcasting Corporation News, 'Howard Pulls Plug on Zimbabwe Tour'. ABC News [online]. http://abc.net.au/news/stories/2007/05/13/1921510.htm; *Yorkshire Post*, September 13, 1967.

24  See for example, Cashman *et al.*, *The Oxford Companion to Australian Cricket*; Harte with Whimpress, *The Penguin History of Australian Cricket*; Andrews, *The Encyclopedia of Australian Cricket*.

25  There was no mention of the announcement of the tour's itinerary in the *Sydney Morning Herald* (June 16–28, 1969), *Sun-Herald* (June 1–30, 1969); *Bulletin* (June 14–26, 1969), *Age* (Melbourne) (June 16–30, 1969), *Australian* (June 1–30, 1969), *Courier Mail* (Brisbane) (June 16–30, 1969) or *Advertiser* (Adelaide) (June 24–28, 1969). As well as having been publicized in the Rhodesian press, the itinerary was also widely reported within South Africa.

26  McAlpine, a member of the MCC, voiced his disappointment that the MCC had cancelled England's visit to Rhodesia and dubbed the refusal to grant Colin Bland entry into Britain as 'disgusting'. *Daily Mail*, August 20, 1968; *Rhodesia Herald*, February 15, 1969, 15; *Cricketer*, May 2, 1969.

27  *8 O'Clock*, September 28, 1974; *Bulletin* (Australia), September 21, 1974.

28  The New Zealand team had played in Rhodesia on its 1961–62 tour of South Africa, but would make no further tours to Southern Africa until a 'Young New Zealand' team toured Zimbabwe in 1984–85. A proposed tour to South Africa in 1971 was cancelled at an early stage of planning, negating any potential debate about whether any fixtures in Rhodesia would be included on its itinerary. Test players Bevan Congdon and Bruce Taylor did visit Rhodesia in 1973–74 as the unofficial New Zealand representatives in a double-wicket competition. McConnell and Smith, *The Shell New Zealand Cricket Encyclopedia*, 256; Winch, *Cricket's Rich Heritage*, 123.

29  *Sports Post* (Wellington), August 24, 1974; *Dominion* (Wellington), August 29, 1974; Trevor Richards to K.M. Comber, September 17, 1974. Alexander Turnbull Library, Trevor Richards Papers, 99-278-12/05.

30  Winch, *Cricket's Rich Heritage*, 111–37; Turner, *My Way*, 114.

31  *Rhodesia Herald*, September 12, 1975; September 24, 1975; Galsworthy (Rhodesia Department) to Green (Department of the Environment), October 18, 1972. PRO FCO, 36/1293; Aspden (Rhodesia Department) to Rellie (UNMIS, New York), August 26, 1975. PRO FCO, 36/1775.

32  *Bulawayo Chronicle*, July 13, 1973, 16; *Rhodesia Herald*, September 27, 1975.

33  Sobers and Harris, *My Autobiography*, 295; *Rhodesia Herald*, July 19, 1969, 17.

34  *Sunday News* (Bulawayo), March 4, 1962, 12.

35  *Bulawayo Chronicle*, July 17, 1973, 10; *Rhodesia Herald*, September 16, 1975, 14.

36  Rhodesian cricket remained segregated at this point, so any multi-racially selected team would have been a first. The West Indian tour was being planned by the non-European cricketing bodies in South Africa, who were in negotiations with Rhodesia's Indian Cricket Union about staging a match in Salisbury (the Indian Union had hosted a match against Basil D'Oliveira's South African Non-Europeans team earlier in 1958). An official from the Indian Union said that it would likely grant the right to stage the match to the Rhodesia Cricket Union, on the condition that a multi-racial team were selected. *Rhodesia Herald*, November 25, 1958, 24.

37  Beckles, *The Development of West Indies Cricket*, 151–3.

38  *Evening Standard* (Salisbury), February 21, 1962, 10.

39  *The Times*, January 31, 1962, 4; *Evening Standard* (Salisbury), February 21, 1962, 10; Winch, *Cricket's Rich Heritage*, 81–5.

40  The Queens club had previously turned down the opportunity of hosting a match on the proposed tour in 1961 for the same reasons. Chesterfield, 'Zimbabwe Cricket', 138–9: *Bulawayo Chronicle*, September 16, 1961, 12; February 9, 1962, 16.

41  *Advocate* (Bridgetown), August 24, 1966, 10; August 26, 1966, 12; January 31, 1967, 1, 8.

42  Although the full range of Caribbean newspapers was not available for examination, this was no specific reference to Bland's Rhodesian citizenship being a cause of controversy in any of the newspapers viewed by the author, namely the *Advocate* (Bridgetown), August 21–October 4, 1966, January 1–February 28, 1967; *Daily Gleaner* (Kingstown, Jamaica), August 24–September 11, 1966; *Nation* (Port of Spain, Trinidad), August 1966; and *Guyana Graphic* August 25–31, 1966.

43  Examples of headlines from the *Advocate* newspaper included 'PPM deplores inclusion of South Africans' and 'Sir Learie raps selection of South Africans'. *Advocate* (Bridgetown), August 26, 1966; August 31, 1966.

44  *Advocate* (Bridgetown), January 31, 1967, 1.

45  For example, during the period of 24 August to 10 September 1966 (when the initial debate over the invitations was at its height) reports on the political situation in Rhodesia appeared on the front page of the *Advocate* newspaper in Barbados on no less than five occasions. *Advocate* (Bridgetown), August 25, 1966; August 27, 1966; September 4, 1966; September 5, 1966; September 10, 1966.

46  Sobers and Harris, *My Autobiography*, 292–304.

47  Beckles, '"The Unkindest Cut"', 100–22.

48  Michael Manley claims that Greenidge's Rhodesian connection was the cause of the controversy, but this is not backed up by an examination of contemporary newspaper reports. Manley,

A History of West Indies Cricket, 450; *Guyana Chronicle*, February 5, 1976; February 6, 1976; *Sunday Chronicle* (Guyana), February 8, 1976.

49  *The Times*, May 20, 1976; Beckles, "'The Unkindest Cut'", 112–14.

50  Winch, *Cricket's Rich Heritage*, 91–2, 186.

51  *Rhodesia Herald*, August 19, 1968, 6; September 3, 1968, 1.

52  Winch, *Cricket's Rich Heritage*, 104–5.

53  *The Times*, May 14, 1976, 2; May 15, 1976, 1.

54  *Morning Star*, September 22, 1970.

55  *Bulawayo Chronicle*, July 13, 1973, 16.

56  Herbert (Foreign and Commonwealth Office) to Offen (Department of the Environment), January 18, 1977. PRO AT60/120.

57  For a thorough analysis of race and racism within Rhodesian sport see International Olympic Committee, *Report of the Commission of Enquiry for Rhodesia*.

58  *Rhodesia Herald*, November 25, 1975, 8.

59  *Rhodesia Herald*, December 2, 1975, 1, 18; December 3, 1975, 1, 24; December 4, 1975, 14, 24; and, Shepherd, 'My South African Connection'.

60  For instance, when Peter Chingoka (who is now President of the Zimbabwe Cricket Union) sought to play senior club cricket in 1975 he was refused membership of the Old Georgians club (the old boys club of the school, St George's College, which he had attended) on the grounds of race. *Rhodesia Herald*, January 4, 1975, 15.

61  *Daily Mail* (Salisbury), January 2, 1963, 7; January 11, 1963, 8; *Sports Herald* (Salisbury) September 21, 1968, 6.

62  *Rhodesia Herald*, January 13, 1975, 13.

## References

Andrews, Malcolm. *The Encyclopedia of Australian Cricket*. Sydney: Golden Press, 1980.

Beckles, Hilary. *The Development of West Indies Cricket; Volume 1, The Age of Nationalism*. Barbados: UWI Press, 1998.

Beckles, Hilary. "'The Unkindest Cut". West Indies Cricket and Anti-Apartheid Struggles at Home and Abroad, 1893–1993'. In *A Spirit of Dominance: Cricket and Nationalism in the West Indies*, edited by Hilary Beckles, 100–22. Kingston: Canoe Press, 1998.

Cashman, Richard, Warrick Franks, Jim Maxwell, Brian Stoddart, Amanda Weaver, and Ray Webster, eds. *The Oxford Companion to Australian Cricket*. Melbourne: Oxford University Press, 1996.

Chesterfield, Trevor. 'Zimbabwe Cricket: A Challenge almost Won'. In *Cricketing Cultures in Conflict: World Cup 2003*, edited by Boria Majumdar and J.A. Mangan, 129–43. London: Routledge, 2004.

Harte, Chris, with Bernard Whimpress. *The Penguin History of Australian Cricket*. London: Andre Deutsch, 2003.

International Olympic Committee. *Report of the Commission of Enquiry for Rhodesia*. Vienna: IOC, 1974.

Little, Charles. 'Preventing "A Wonderful Break-Through for Rhodesia": The British Government and the Exclusion of Rhodesia from the 1968 Mexico Olympics'. *Olympika* 14 (2005): 47–68.

Little, Charles. 'The Sports Boycott against Rhodesia Reconsidered.' Paper presented at The New Currency of Sport: Inaugural Political Studies Association Sport and Politics Study Group Conference, Newtown, Wales, February 24–25, 2007.

Little, Charles. 'No Politics, Mucho Rugby: International Rugby Contacts with Rhodesia during the UDI Period'. Paper presented at 'Le Rugby: du village au global' Conference, Paris, October 11–12, 2007.

Lloyd, T.O. *The British Empire 1558–1995*. Oxford: Oxford University Press, 1996.

Manley, Michael. *A History of West Indies Cricket*. London: Andre Deutsch, 2002.

Mansergh, Nicholas. *The Commonwealth Experience: Volume Two; From British to Multiracial Commonwealth*. London: Macmillan, 1982.

McConnell, Lynn, and Ian Smith. *The Shell New Zealand Cricket Encyclopedia*. Auckland: Moa Beckett, 1993.

Murray, Bruce. 'Politics and Cricket: The D'Oliveira Affair of 1968'. *Journal of Southern African Studies* 27, no. 1 (December 2001): 676–84.

Murray, Bruce, and Christopher Merrett. *Caught Behind: Race and Politics in Springbok Cricket.* Johannesburg and Scottsville: Wits University Press and University of KwaZulu-Natal Press, 2004.

Oborne, Peter. *Basil D'Oliveira: Cricket and Conspiracy – The Untold Story.* London: Time Warner, 2005.

Shepherd, John. 'My South African Connection'. In *Cricket in Isolation: The Politics of Race and Cricket in South Africa*, edited by Andre Odendaal, 189–92. Cape Town: The Author, 1977.

Sobers, Garry, and Bob Harris. *My Autobiography.* London: Headline, 2003.

Turner, Glenn. *My Way.* Auckland: Hodder and Stoughton, 1975.

Winch, Jonty. *Cricket's Rich Heritage: A History of Rhodesian and Zimbabwean Cricket, 1890–1982.* Bulawayo: Books of Zimbabwe, 1983.

# A national(ist) line in postcolonizing cricket: Viv Richards, biographies and cricketing nationalism[1]

Malcolm MacLean*

*Department of Sport and Exercise, University of Gloucestershire, Cheltenham, UK*

The role of games and sport in asserting and maintaining the legitimation of power in the British Empire is becoming increasingly recognized in scholarly analyses, yet sport in British colonies of settlement plays a distinctive and complex role. On the one hand it asserts a particular kind of Britishness – football (soccer), with its working-class associations, is nowhere near as popular among men in formerly British colonies of settlement as sports that have traditionally been seen as associated with Britain's middle and upper classes, especially rugby union and cricket. On the other hand, there is an assertion of a cultural nationalism often based in aesthetics – the claims to distinctive styles of play are held to mark New Zealand rugby as not British and Welsh rugby as not English, or West Indies cricket as distinctively like, but not the same as, the English game. These colonial sporting nationalisms are a complex phenomenon that asserts both membership of a community associated with some notion of Britishness through a shared Imperial past, and distinctiveness through its association with forms or ways of nationalism. In the West Indies, with their distinctive politics of settlement, cricket performs a role similar to other colonies of settlement, but the local politics of indigeneity, or its lack, create a distinctive politics of place and space in postcolonising cultural nationalism.

Much of the contemporary literature dealing with nations and nationalism has taken Benedict Anderson's poetic label and set out to critique the idea of 'community'.[2] Much less, however, has addressed the question of how 'imagining' works to create this community. This essay explores how cricket mediates an imagining of West Indies-ness in the twentieth century through a focus on life writing by the former West Indies captain, Viv Richards. Richards's 1991 autobiography *Hitting Across the Line*, described by Beckles as 'a manifesto of the progressive movement',[3] is a text that builds on some of the great West Indies cricket writing to suggest significant changes in the meaning and importance of cricket in West Indies cultural politics.[4] Richards is informative in this context because his career straddles what Beckles characterizes as the ages of nationalism and globalization.[5]

Cricket's significance in West Indies cultural politics is hard to over-estimate. As with many other sports during the later nineteenth century it was seen by colonial-born whites as a sign that they had not been degraded by being colonial. Seecharan, for instance, points to the central role of cricket as a 'civilizing' and pedagogical agent in elite schools in late-nineteenth-century Barbados such as The Lodge and Harrison College, as well to the concurrent burgeoning cultural and political confidence and activism of African- and Indian-West Indians.[6] C.L.R. James has also noted that in the early decades of the twentieth century in Trinidad, he

> had been brought up in the public school code... The striking thing was that inside the classroom the code had little success. Sneaking was taboo, but we lied and cheated without any sense of shame... But as soon as we stepped on to the cricket or football field, more particularly the cricket field, all was changed... [W]e learned to obey the umpire's decision without question, however irrational it was. We learned to play with the team, which meant subordinating your personal inclinations, and even interests, to the good of the whole. We kept a stiff upper lip in that we did not complain about ill-fortune. We did not denounce failures, but 'Well tried' or 'Hard luck' came easily to our lips. We were generous to opponents and congratulated them on victories, even when we knew they did not deserve it.[7]

More recently, cricket has been a site of struggle over the politics of decolonization, such as during the campaign in the late 1950s for a black captain to be appointed to lead the West Indies representative team. This debate replicated, in many ways, the situation in the two decades before the First World War, when blacks were excluded from Barbadian and Demararan/Guianan representative teams during English tours in 1895 and 1897, but included in Trinidadian teams. Despite this apparent liberal outlook in Trinidad, their teams in the Inter-Colonial Challenge Cup competition were almost all-white with most of their black players being spuriously declared professionals (the indisputably middle class and amateur Lebrun Constantine, father of Learie, later Lord, Constantine, was the most notable exception), it seems in deference to Barbadian and Demararan/Guianan wishes. This situation prevailed despite the membership of elite clubs (such as the British Guiana's Georgetown Cricket Club [GCC] and Trinidad's Queen's Park Cricket Club) of light-skinned blacks (coloureds, in the West Indies parlance of the time) such as the businessman D. Ouckama, member of the British Guiana Legislature and Vice President of the GCC.[8] Furthermore, the smaller islands – such as Grenada, Antigua or St Kitts – that could not field a competitive team that did not include blacks and coloureds were excluded from the Challenge Cup competition.

Like body cultural practices in other colonial settings, cricket was not as straightforward as many colonials liked to think, and as some later analysts have suggested.[9] It was neither indisputably a mechanism of imposed colonial culture, nor an unsullied site of subaltern cultural resistance. Rather, it is best read through the lens of great and little traditions: of localized reinscription, innovation, and distinctive, even unique, practice within a broader coherent epistemological and ontological system, although this should not be read as necessarily meaning that colonial cultural practices make colonies into part-societies in the manner of Redfield's views of peasant societies.[10] As James has shown, West Indies cricket was run through with Englishness, but its players were often only slyly civil.[11] In his analysis of cricket during the slave era (until the 1830s), Seecharan notes, 'this activity, like other forms of play, was necessarily dichotomous: infused with the potential for containment, as the plantocracy saw it, as well as subversion, from the standpoint of the enslaved'.[12] It is this dichotomous nature, as well cricket's Englishness – where Englishness was seen as the marker and medium of civilization – in the context of the colonial relations of the British West Indies that makes the sport such a complex cultural practice.

During the later half of the twentieth century, British West Indies cricket became increasingly culturally complex. The politics of decolonization affected the British West Indies in ways similar to the rest of the British Empire: the local subaltern leadership sought to increase their influence and power; the colonial elites sought to retain their power; the subaltern masses, in many cases, sought more fundamental political change.[13] Cricket's role as one of the markers of West Indies-ness alongside its cultural dichotomousness meant that developments in the game could have significant and widespread social impacts – hence the campaign for a black captain, and the resistance to such a move from the colonies' cricket authorities and many white West Indians.[14] The eventual outcome of that campaign was the appointment in 1960 of Frank Worrall as captain. Worrall was one of the dominant players in West Indies cricket in the later half of the twentieth century. He joins other batters – Everton Weekes, Clyde Walcott, Garfield Sobers and Viv Richards – as among the West Indies' greats: all five received knighthoods, along with cricket a marker of colonial tradition, yet all five were among the leading batters during the nationalist, decolonizing era. It was during this era that the West Indies' team became a dominant force in world cricket, through a combination of outstanding batters, of which these five with the addition of Brian Lara in the 1990s were just the most outstanding and globally recognized, and a series of exceptional fast bowlers with a lineage reaching back to the 1890s. (Singling out these batters admittedly does a disservice to other outstanding players such as Conrad Hunte, Rohan Kanhai, Clive Lloyd and Gordon Greenidge – all with over 40 test matches and batting averages of over 45 runs per innings.) Yet by the time Richards joined this elite – in the late 1970s – the West Indies colonies had become politically independent. They were charting an increasingly self-directed role in global politics and were asserting, through musical forms such as calypso and reggae, a growing impact on popular cultures around the world. Through writers such as V.S. Naipaul, Derek Walcott and Phyllis Shand Affley, the West Indian societies also had a significant impact on global high culture. These cultural and political shifts that became most obvious in the 1960s and 1970s led to questions about the place and role of cricket, with all its tradition and Englishness and its culturally and politically dichotomous function, in a West Indies that is, at least temporally, post-colonial.

**What and when is the postcolonial?**

The notion that the 'postcolonial' is a single thing is confounded by the power and profile of the broad theoretical approach that is postcolonialism. Leaving aside the impact of ~ism on a term, the 'portmanteau'[15] characteristics of 'postcolonial', and the tendency of the missionaries of post~isms to denigrate and deny any usefulness in what went before,[16] the most confounding part of the term is the post~, which tends to be interpreted temporally rather than metaphysically or meta-ethically. That is, the post~tends to be seen as something coming after colonialism, rather than something that reflects on and critiques the cultures of colonialism. Part of the problem here is a laxity of language use where 'post-colonial' is seen as a state of existence after the political process of decolonization rather than a cultural process of a critique of colonialism's cultures. There is a consequential confusion of temporality: in short, postcolonization as a cultural dynamic is less linearly temporal than decolonization as a formal political practice. To suggest to many indigenous peoples in colonies of settlement that they live in a time after colonialism is to invite derision if not ridicule: these peoples, and the post-settler states within which they live, are struggling to come to terms with their colonial histories of alienation, of dispossession, and of the marginalization of the indigenous from social power.[17] As Sissons notes, 'the cultural politics of indigeneity continues to exert its greatest force in relation to the imagination of post-settler nationhood and the legitimacy of post-settler states'.[18] These complexities mean that a clear grasp of West Indies cricket in the time of Richards, in the time after formal colonial rule ended and after colonial cultures had begun to weaken, requires an exploration of the 'what' and 'when' of the post-colonial, and a concern with indigeneity.

The 'when' of the postcolonial, as the evidence from indigenous peoples noted above suggests, is a major difficulty in the usefulness of the concept: the same limitations do not apply to the theory known as postcolonialism or, adapting Harvey, to the condition of postcoloniality.[19] As Hall has noted, suggesting that there is a time of the post-colonial denies the complexity of colonial political and cultural relations, and that 'disengagement from the colonizing process has been a long, drawn-out and differentiated affair'.[20] Schwartz suggests much of this complexity in his analysis of James's post-colonizing of self.[21] There is a problem with Hall's assertion of a post-colonial process in this claim, and it may be a slip of the keyboard: his use of the past perfect 'has been' allows this sentence to be read as if we are in a time of the post-colonial. This reading is at odds with the broader case being made, but shows the very difficulty of discussing 'The' post-colonial when a scholar such as Hall makes such a slip. Hall's overall case is accepted: there is no post-colonial time, but there is a process of post-colonization – a disengagement from being colonized (note the present continuous 'being', not the past perfect 'having been', in keeping with the principles of the cultural politics of indigeneity, and the realpolitik of post-settler societies). This acceptance of Hall's case then raises the problem of the meaning of post~ if it is not a temporal moment after colonialism.

There is little in contemporary social theory that has excited the passions of analysts more than the meaning of post-modern's post~ : postmodernism, postmodernity, post-modern itself. Despite the length of this debate – there is now seldom an introductory text addressing post-structuralism or post-modernism that does not outline its principal contours – Appiah has cautioned against assuming that post-modern post~ and post-colonial post ~ are the same thing.[22] His case raises two key points for understanding the nature of postcoloniality in the British West Indies. The first is that in attempting to grasp the character of the post-modern he suggests that in a range of cultural 'domains there is an antecedent practice [form of knowledge or ontology] that laid claim to a certain exclusivity of insight, and in each of them postmodernism is a name for the rejection of that claim to exclusivity'.[23] That is to say, whether the post-modern is a critical extension of the modern as in Lyotard, or a taming of modernism's oppositional forms as in Jameson, there is in all cases an assertion of the legitimacy of pluralism.[24]

In colonial contexts, if the post~ is to incorporate this 'rejection of that claim to exclusivity', a fundamental shift in knowledge systems is necessary – a shift that grants the colonial subaltern subjectivity and agency. In the British West Indies, cultural and political practices – from literature to history to political activism – have since the 1930s been active in public assertions, with subaltern voices leaving a record that challenges the authenticity of that left by the colonial and political elites. This may be seen, for instance, in James's wider body of work, and in texts by Meeks, by Hall and by Williams.[25] Meeks and Hall each place the major shifts in the reconfiguration of power in the period of decolonization. Seecharan's linking of the 1900 West Indies cricket tour of England and the 1900 Pan-African Congress in London suggests a longer pedigree for the assertion of black subjectivity and agency than is often assumed, as does James's history of the Haitian revolution and his life of Arthur Cipriani. In this sense then, the posts~ are similar in that they clear space for other, but not necessarily counter-hegemonic, voices and practices.[26]

Appiah's second point is more difficult, and concerns the question of who it is that lives in a state of postcoloniality. This is the problem of who has agency, whose subaltern voice is recognized as a voice, and which of the colonized are granted a degree of subjectivity. In this, his assessment is harsh: 'Postcoloniality is the condition of what we might ungenerously call a *comprador* intelligentsia: of a relatively small, Western-style, Western-trained group of writers and thinkers who mediate the trade in cultural commodities of world capitalism at the periphery.'[27] In this he extends Spivak's case that the subaltern cannot speak because as soon as their voices are recognized as voices they are no longer subaltern but accepted, in part, into the hegemon.[28] In much of the West Indies, this group of comprador intelligentsia is referred to disparagingly as 'Afro-Saxon'. A problematic implication of Appiah's case and the designation 'Afro-Saxon' is that they do not allow for the existence of a *national* intelligentsia who may also occupy a space of postcoloniality. This denial means that the nature of the British West Indies focussed non-colonial intelligentsia remains unclear.

The cases made by Hall and Appiah point to a further question centred on the content of the cultural process of postcolonization. Appiah's analysis, with its grounding in an investigation of the use of 'African' art in North American museums, is quite firmly linked to the commodification of colonized cultural practices, texts and artefacts, and critiques the primitivist discourses of authenticity. Thomas's analyses of South Pacific art suggest a different, more subtle, and more dynamic process of postcolonization, where the 'antecedent practice[s] that laid claim to a certain exclusivity of insight' are challenged by the inclusion of parts of those 'antecedent practices' into post-colonial artistic practices.[29] Thomas's case is significant for a further reason: in his analyses the foundation for those challenges lies in the cultural politics of indigeneity: that is, these are national, not comprador, cultural practices. In a place where the colonial subalterns are not indigenous, the authenticity of any postcolonial critique – often understood as a critique of the 'foreign' – may be challenged. In these settings then, such as the British West Indies, there remain significant doubts over the epistemological and ontological basis of postcoloniality, even after political decolonization. The prioritization of indigeneity in postcolonization causes problems for understanding the process in the British West Indies, and for the subsequent construction of a cultural nationalism for the West Indies and its constituent parts.

## Constructing cultural nationalism

The dissolution of empires in the twentieth century has been framed by a language of nationalism, be it the Austro-Hungarian and Ottoman empires in 1919–20, the British and French empires in the 1950s and 1960s, or the final collapse of the residue of the geographically delimited Tsarist Russian empire in the 1990s. The rationale for decolonization, in most cases, was asserted through a claim to a right to national self-determination. The twentieth-century processes of de- and post-colonization were intended to lead to a creation of independent nations, often assumed to be unproblematically linked to political states. This creation of nations, however, is not a once and for all action.

As Smith has shown, nations have five key cultural characteristics.[30] The first key point, and the one that in this context is most important in making postcolonization a process, is that nations are and must be continually redesigned, reasserted and reinvented: that is to say that the meaning and content of the nation is in a state of almost continual change.

Whereas this aspect of nationhood causes some political and cultural difficulties, there is little in those that are specific to the British West Indies. Smith's next three characteristics, however, are particularly difficult for these former colonies where everyone is an immigrant. For, as Smith notes, 'nations require ethnic cores if they are to survive. If they lack one, they must re-invent one. That means discovering a suitable and convincing past which can be reconstructed and re-presented to members and outsiders.'[31] Construction of an ethnic core for the collective called the British West Indies or for each of the colonies confronted the problem of indigeneity: the various migrant peoples in the British West Indies had to find a way to 're-belong'.[32] Along with the myth of the destruction of the indigenous peoples of the Caribbean islands goes the extinguishment of these peoples – the Taino, the Carib, the Arawak and others – from the national cultural memories, or where they are remembered the distinctiveness of indigeneity is marginalized. Sherlock and Bennett in an otherwise sympathetic consideration of the Taino in Jamaica claim that the 'story of the Tainos is woven into the story of the African-Jamaicans, the "old indigenous" melding with those who became the "new indigenous"', while at the same time asserting and celebrating African cultural roots.[33] Although in Guiana there is no myth of an extermination of the mainland indigenous, these indigenous peoples are also marginalized in cultural-political consciousness. The eradication of the indigenous from British West Indies cultural and historical consciousness means that the task of creating a distinctive and unique foundation for postcolonial cultural consciousness has been much more demanding than in many other colonies of settlement. For much of the twentieth century this task centred on reinscriptions and modifications of either a sense of Britishness or a Pan-African consciousness, both of which as international modes of cultural consciousness required significant adaptation to create either collective or island-specific West Indies cultural codes.

The significant aspect of this ethnic core of nation, for Smith, is that these *ethnie* are demotic – they have depth, they have vertical relationships so the masses feel a link to the cultural and political space of the nation, and they carry with them a sense of autochthony or indigeneity. The problem with Sherlock and Bennett's claim that African-Jamaicans are the 'new indigenous' is that in making the claim, the ethnic homeland is located elsewhere – in Africa. This 'homeland' is essential to the binding together of the ethnic core of the nation, but as Smith notes this homeland is not 'just terrain on which to nurture … identities, unities and autonomies, but [is an] historic [territory] in which "our ancestors" lived and which "we carry in our hearts".'[34] To achieve this, the nation emerging and taking shape through a postcolonizing process must confront and reshape the historicisation of territory and territorialisation of history that was so essential to state and nation, the cultures of colonialism.[35] A vital element in this spatial cultural politics was the grounding of particular practices in the place and space of the new nation – something Richards does in his presentation of West Indies cricket.

## Sporting cultural nationalism

Finally, as part of these cultural politics of nationalism all nations construct golden ages and claim heroes, some ancient, some modern.[36] In much of the former British Empire with limited access to the ancient many of these heroes and golden ages were sporting. The tactics of colonial sporting nationalism are varied, but often centre on assertions of indigenousness: a style of play, a body culture, a set of movements that are naturalized and are grounded in ways of being that are often linked to cultural forms associated with – either claimed by or imposed upon – indigenous peoples.[37] These cultural claims then may be used to emphasize nationalism by way of an assertion of indigeneity: it becomes a cultural rather than a political claim. In West Indies cricket this tactic is complicated by two dynamics: the politics of West Indies nationalism, and the problems of indigeneity and colonization. Despite attempts at federation building in the late 1950s and early 1960s, nationalism in the British West Indies has tended to be island focussed rather than British West Indies focussed; Seecharan points to a long history of island insularity.[38] Most cricket and other sports in the region are island centred, although teams from the Windward and Leeward Islands play in regional competitions. In competitions centred on International Cricket Conference divisions, however, the team is 'The West Indies': it is likely that most non-British West Indies cricket supporters fail to acknowledge the island-based teams. Cricket is one of the few, if not the only, site of a singular West Indies-ness, even if it is restricted only to the British West Indies. West Indies sporting nationalism is therefore asserted as a West Indian thing in some contexts, or as of a specific island or island group in others: it is similar to some of the complexities of British and Irish rugby union, but arguably more intense.

The absence of indigenous peoples from collective memory seems to have fed into a sense of nation in the British West Indies that is less clear about its claims to nation-hood, that has had to look hard to find authentic markers of distinctiveness, and that, for the most part, has settled on cultural markers: argot, music styles, dance, styles of sport performance in cricket and netball, and related aesthetic characteristics, although there are clearly complex cultural politics surrounding these practices.[39] The British West Indies is not alone in claiming or deploying sport as one of these cultural markers: it is one of several forms of movement culture regularly used alone or in combination to assert national distinctiveness. The cultural ambiguity of sport in former British colonies as marking both Britishness and colonial distinctiveness makes sport, most notably cricket, in the British West Indies particularly complex, with its lack of an indigenously-derived authenticity. There is, for instance, no ground to incorporate first nations' movement cultures into colonial nationalist sports practice to mark distinctiveness, as New Zealand rugby has done with its various haka since the late 1880s.

These ambiguities, these complexities of colonial national distinctiveness pervade West Indies cricket writing, but they are not its only difficulty. The core challenge for West Indies cricket writers is the dominance of one text – C.L.R. James's *Beyond a Boundary*.[40] This text, often presented as one of the great (if not *the* great) text of colonial and postcolonial sports writing, dominates the field. It seems to shape both writing about, and analyses of, West Indies cricket. It is, however, one of the most complex literary texts to address sport. In one possible reading, it seems that James is arguing that Trinidadian cricketers are better at being British than the British, because they are better at the cultural codes of cricket. In another reading, the text embodies many of the traits Homi Bhabha identifies in postcolonial culture 'sly civility'.[41] There is little doubt that it is a superb piece of sports writing, but it is not the unremitting anti-colonial text often imagined or expected. Subsequent books about West Indies cricket may not be written in the shadow of James, but they are likely to be read in the shade he casts.

James depicts West Indies cricket as a 'weapon of the weak' where a cultural practice of the dominant group is deployed as a site of guarded and ambiguous resistance. In Bhabha's terms, this is sly civility. Because the resistance is not recognized by the colonizers, it is a hidden transcript of resistance.[42] According to the dominant views of the colonialist project, the West Indies' mainly African subalterns were intellectually inferior and incapable either of ever, or of yet, governing themselves. This colonialist ideology held that in adopting or mimicking the colonists' practices the subaltern failed to grasp the subtle cultural or social meanings of those practices: in Bhabha's terms this is ironic mimicry. The evidence from James is that the slyly civil British West Indies subaltern knew exactly the politics of resistance involved in their ironic cricket. It was a resistance articulated through Britishness: these were, after all, the *British* West Indies.

## Cricket, Britishness and nationalism

It is this shadow of a focus on cricket's Britishness as well as a forthrightness that signals a textual break from the ambiguity of colonial nationalism that makes Viv Richards's autobiography *Hitting Across the Line* so significant.[43] It is devoutly and unremittingly nationalist, even if that nationalism is both confused and complex. As Beckles notes, even the title of the book 'is a declaration of a new sense of sovereignty and independence, a rupture with an imperial tradition and a legitimization of an indigenous methodological approach'.[44] Ideal cricket, as prescribed by the aesthetic principles of nineteenth-century English cricket, accentuated hitting the ball with a perpendicular bat along the line of the ball: to hit across the line of the ball using a less than perpendicular bat was considered bad form and poor cricket. It was also a risky style of play – the line and direction of the ball is easier for the batter to predict than is the height of ball above the ground when it gets within striking distance, meaning that the more perpendicular the bat, the more likely the batter is to hit the ball. English captains against the West Indies in the 1970s and 1980s would often position their fielders in such a way that the batter either had to play along the line and attempt through slow attrition and careful placement of the ball to beat the field, or hit across the line to a less populated part of the field and enhance the chances that the bowler would hit the wicket. Richards was one of several West Indies players who regularly defied aesthetic convention to play across the line.

The text breaks with many of the conventions of sports autobiographies, in that the ghost writer (Mick Middles) is an active voice, providing scene-setting opening and closing sections to many chapters. The paradox of this technique is that it makes more authentic the sections that Middles has not explicitly written. Richards, however, struggles with authenticity throughout. The text is peppered with an oxymoronic discourse of learned instinct and learned naturalness, such as where Richards notes that he 'learned to respond in an instinctive manner'.[45] Richards' invocation of the nation at times refers to the West Indies, but equally to Antigua. Richards is intensely proud of being Antiguan, and makes no effort to gloss this. His affinity with place, however, shifts – at times he celebrates and claims an Antiguan identity, less often he is clearly of the West Indies, and occasionally he asserts his place in the Leeward Islands. At times the rhetoric becomes extremely complex, with Antigua functioning as a metonym of and for the West Indies, but noting also that West Indies unity exists only when it is outward looking.

There is one element of his narrative where a sense of authenticity is powerful – the origins of a West Indies cricket style. He describes childhood pitches as often being only 'roughly playable' but also notes that the 'unpredictability of those pitches provided us with the best possible cricket training'.[46] Players in games on these pitches often had minimal or non-existent protective equipment, and sometimes no proper bats. While recognizing the dangers to wicket-keepers in this form of play, the player in the greatest danger was the batsman [*sic*]. He just had to be able to see the ball at a very early stage. The ball would move all over the place. It was full of surprising bounces. It made the batsman instinctively want to go for the big hit, to get rid of the thing. Playing defensively was pretty pointless and just as dangerous, so the batsman might as well try to hit the ball into the surrounding undergrowth. The hook shot was a particular favourite. And there was no point in telling a batsman not to hit across the line, in fact that was the way everyone *had* to play.[47]

Richards's point here is clear – playing across the line, with all its metaphorical meanings – was part of the sense of survival that is essential to the game and is the basis of West Indies cricket philosophy. These childhood wickets, he suggests in this passage, are the basis of the non-Englishness of Antiguan, and by connotation, West Indian cricket. A West Indies cricket style, then, was autochthonous – it was authentically West Indian because the place and space of West Indies cricket required it: there was no alternative and the characteristics of place and space made 'the batsman instinctively want to go for the big hit'. The indigenously-derived authenticity of West Indies cricket then is a product of *where* it was played, not *who* played it. Despite this place-based sense of authenticity, the aesthetics of West Indies cricket was not limited to those from the place – Richards, for instance, grants Ian Botham an 'approach to cricket [that] seemed more West Indian than English'.[48]

This is a very different view of West Indies cricket from that advanced by James, for whom its core, meaning and its cultural politics lie in its Englishness. It is this accentuation of Englishness that causes problems for many readers and analysts of James – where some readers think they have (as one colleague said to me) 'picked up the wrong book', while others see James's adherence to cricket as an ideological blind-spot.[49] Equally, this attachment to Englishness and James's extension of it to argue that the thing about Trinidadian, and by connotation West Indies, cricket is that colonials, black, brown and Creole, do Englishness-via-cricket better than the English lends itself to a Homi Bhabha-esque inspired reading of *Beyond a Boundary*. It also provides the basis of James's case that cricket taught him a culture of sacrifice and collective activity that is essential for Party work in the Marxist left.

In contrast, Richards's cricket is significant for the very reason that it is not English. Like James, an exploration of cricket grants insights into its context, into the society in which it is played. As Richards notes, cricket 'is not some irrelevant, eccentric sport played by a handful of countries but a game that gets right to the root of the societies involved'.[50] About a quarter of the way through the narrative (not counting the career record) Richards and Middles recount an outing to an Antiguan football match. The chapter is notable for two primary things: it is the most sustained discussion of the West Indies as not-England, and the voice is explicitly shared. It is the only chapter where Middles's 'contextualizing' voice accounts for more than half the text (in most it makes up less than 10% of the text). This excess of contextualization does two things. First, it marks the space of football as different – Middles opens with an account of the drive to the match which presents roads as ill-maintained tracks yet celebrates the ability of taxi drivers to negotiate those thoroughfares, even if it involves 'bouncing from side to side'.[51] At the same time, he depicts Richards in his Range Rover as gliding in an unproblematic manner across the terrain. He finishes with a description of the ground immediately after the match where winning and defeated team fans (from St Kitts and Antigua) mingle in an 'enjoyably partisan atmosphere'.[52] In between Richards talks of his first visit to Anfield where he thought a riot had broken out when a referee disallowed a goal in the Liverpool-Manchester United match. He writes that he 'had never seen sporting passion displayed so openly and fiercely … the hostility was so blatant'.[53]

The second effect of the structure of this chapter is that it denaturalizes English football as a cultural experience, and allows Richards to make some universalist claims for elite athlete's attitudes. This universalist language sees him call on what he saw as Liverpool's ethos to state that the West Indies cricket team also 'expect to win … [and] to perform with dignity, professionalism and dedication'.[54] The textual form here is complex. In asserting the distinctiveness of West Indies cricket, the ethos of the nationally representative version of the game is linked explicitly to an English soccer club in a way that denigrates that distinctiveness by claiming that it is just like a football team from the imperial centre. This linkage also celebrates hierarchy and elitism by linking the nationally representative players to the upper echelon of English football. The rhetorical effect is two-fold: although the chapter denaturalizes English football, it universalizes the ethos of at least part of its upper echelon. The second is that it elevates the West Indies through this shared elite ethos to a global elite, but in doing so separates the style of play, the need to hit across the line, from an authentic and ontological spatially-derived need to become a question of survival in the unfair, uneven, 'roughly playable' setting of world cricket.

The third paradox is based in this tendency to marginality. This is the contradiction between an emphasis on the vital role of cricket in his communities and his celebration of commercialization. Ghost writer Mick Middles stresses the 'master blaster's' status in Antigua, and of the role that sport plays in uniting and celebrating the island. Richard's celebrates Rishton, his Lancashire League town, as a place where he was made welcome and to feel at home, sees Glamorgan as inclusive, and despite being unceremoniously dropped by Somerset speaks fondly of the people of Taunton and Bath. At the same time, Richards praises Kerry Packer for driving the commercialization of cricket during the later 1970s, and as being the sort of 'forward-minded' entrepreneur cricket needs, claiming that he does not want to be 'involved in a nostalgia sport'.[55] This appears alongside the sense of awe so often expressed by players arriving at Lords for the first time.[56]

This paradox points to the final contradiction of the autobiography. This commercialized global future for cricket coincides with a contradictory celebration of 'hitting across the line' that may be seen as a cry against a neo-colonialist demand for a radically instrumentalist performance orientation in cricket. The place-derived indigenously authentic style of West Indies cricket that metaphorically and actually hits across the line cannot be incorporated into a performance orientation: when it works well, and in the 1970s and 1980s, it is almost unbeatable, but when it does not work, as in the late 1990s and early 2000s, it fails dismally. Richards writes of feeling constrained by his youth experience at an English coaching camp where his 'authentically' Antiguan style was constrained, because 'coaching can restrict … uniqueness'.[57] As a result he found himself torn between an offer of contracts to play with Somerset, with all the 'straight bat' conservatism that county cricket embodies, and with Oldham in the Lancashire League, where league cricket accepts forms of flair and innovation that were against the conventions of acceptability in the county game. The tensions between the two are similar to the purists' rejection of one day cricket and Kerry Packers' World Cricket Circus in the late 1970s. Despite taking the Somerset contract, and praising Packer, Richards seems to realize that an increasingly commercialized and commodified cricket constrains and limits the variation and personalities he praises, and certainly does not allow for the resistive ethos of hitting across the line that he endorses throughout.

The contrasts between James's and Richards's invocations of West Indies cricket rest in large part on their contexts: the boundary between the West Indies wickets and outer has always been extremely permeable. For James, the West Indies were without doubt part of a British sphere of politics and of cultural influence. Whatever his vision of a socialist West Indies in a socialist world, there is no sense that James would seek to reject the entire cultural sphere. For Richards, however, the context is less clear: he lives and works in a more intensely global and emerging neo-liberal world, but more importantly, he lives and works in a post-civil rights, post-Black Consciousness setting. His West Indies are independent states, the federation project had failed, and Britain had withdrawn from rule. Whereas for James, there was a sense of West Indies connectedness to a larger socio-cultural sphere of Britishness, in Richards's case there is a potent sense of insularity, which he acknowledges with concern, but also of a distinct Antiguan-ness in larger West Indies cultural setting, just as in James there are hints that his case is Trinidad-specific. Richards celebrates Blackness, and associates it with pride.[58] He is also aware, however, that there are times when the West Indies team, with its representative connotations, were 'made to doubt ourselves'.[59] There is a strong sense of marginality that runs through the text – from West Indies cricket, to being a captain from Antigua 'rather than one of the larger islands'.[60] The marginality is intensified by the English experience, from feeling constrained by English coaches, to playing for Somerset – not a powerful county – and then into league cricket in Lancashire. Whereas James seemed secure in his Britishness, Richards articulates a series of insecurities that reflect the struggles of the post-Black Consciousness discourses of the meanings of Blackness, of nation, nationality and nationalism, and of the linkages between subaltern experience and a subaltern past in a global sporting practice that was moving, at least economically, out of its subalterneity.[61]

Whereas some of James's cricketers are slyly civil in being more British than the British while also subverting and degrading the culture of cricket, Richards's elite cricketers, and by connotation Antigua, the Leeward Islands, and the West Indies for which this cricket at various times stands, have become alienated from their authentic and 'instinctive', from their 'natural', selves. In doing so, the texts expose two different forms of West Indies cricket appropriate to their cultural times. James provides insights into the ambiguities and cultural politics of cricket during an era of colonial nationalism. It is telling and revealing that *Beyond a Boundary* is justifiably seen as a great piece of sports writing, but it needs to be recognized as integral, and not antithetical, to his overall body of work. Richards's autobiography is problematic in a different way: whereas James points to the sly and subtle subversions of colonialism, Richards reveals the difficulties of exploring a cultural politics of nationalism using the colonizer's tools in an era of Black Consciousness. There are elements of subtle subversion in Richards's text – Botham as West Indian for instance – but the alienation of hitting across the line from its authentic grounding in the place of Antigua to a means of survival in a global sport reveals a sense of West Indies nationalism that is more confrontational than James's, that is the product of its time as much as James's was of his, and that is struggling with a cultural politics that is temporally post-colonial but is not necessarily culturally so: cricket is here exposed as perhaps too complex a colonial cultural practice to become a tool in the effective construction of a form of indigeneity to mark as distinctive West Indies-ness. In a sense, then, Beckles is right to call it 'a manifesto of the progressive movement', but it is a manifesto that reveals many of the contradictions in a cultural nationalism that relies on critical, postcolonizing, engagement with such a core Imperial practice as cricket.

**Notes**

[1] Earlier versions of parts of this essay were presented to the Political Studies Association's *Sport and Politics* workshop, Newtown, Wales, February 2007; The Institute of Commonwealth Studies, March 2007; and *Sport in a Global World: Past, Present and Future*, International

Sociology of Sport Association and International Society for the History of Physical Education and Sport, Copenhagen, July–August 2007. I am grateful to participants in those sessions, and especially Dr Alun Hardman, for comments that have greatly improved the essay.

2   Anderson, *Imagined Communities*.
3   Richards, *Hitting Across the Line*. Beckles, *The Development of West Indies Cricket Vol.1*, 91.
4   Beckles, *The Development of West Indies Cricket Vol. 1*, 91.
5   Beckles, *The Development of West Indies Cricket Vols 1 and 2*.
6   Seecharan, *Muscular Learning*, 20–46.
7   James, *Beyond a Boundary*, 26.
8   Seecharan, *Muscular Learning*, 131–2.
9   Bale, *Imagined Olympians*; Bale and Sang, *Kenyan Running*.
10  Redfield, *Peasant Society and Culture*, 40–59.
11  James, *Beyond a Boundary*, 66–71; MacLean, 'Mimesis, Alterity and Colonial Cricket'.
12  Seecharan, *Muscular Learning*, 3.
13  Meeks, *Narratives of Resistance*; Darwin, *Britain and Decolonisation*.
14  Beckles, *The Development of West Indies Cricket Vol. 1*, 75–8.
15  Slemon, 'The Scramble for Post-colonialism', 45.
16  Nash, 'When Isms Became Wasms'.
17  Fleuras and Elliot, *The Nations Within*; Maaka and Fleuras, *The Politics of Indigeneity*; Samson, *A Way of Life That Does Not Exist*.
18  Sissons, *First Peoples*, 8.
19  Hall, 'Introduction'; Harvey, *The Condition of Postmodernity*.
20  Hall, 'When was "the Post-Colonial"?', 247.
21  Schwartz, 'Becoming Postcolonial'.
22  Appiah, 'Is the "Post-" in "Postcolonial" the "Post-" in "Postmodern"?'
23  Ibid., 425.
24  Lyotard, *The Postmodern Condition*; Jameson, *Postmodernism*.
25  James, *The Case For West-Indian Self Government*, James, *A History of the Pan-African Revolt*; James, *The Black Jacobins*; James, *Beyond a Boundary*; Meeks, *Narratives of Resistance*; Hall, 'Negotiating Caribbean Identities'; Williams, *History of the People of Trinidad and Tobago*; Williams, *From Columbus to Castro*.
26  Seecharan, *Muscular Learning*, 221–6; James, *Black Jacobins*; James, *The Case For West-Indian Self Government*.
27  Appiah, 'Is the "Post-" in "Postcolonial" the "Post-" in "Postmodern"?', 432.
28  Spivak, 'Can the Subaltern Speak?'
29  Appiah, 'Is the "Post-" in "Postcolonial" the "Post-" in "Postmodern"?', 425; Thomas, *Possessions*; Thomas, 'Introduction'.
30  Smith, *The Ethnic Origins of Nations*, 212–13.
31  Ibid., 212.
32  Seecharan, *MuscularLearning*, 276.
33  Sherlock and Bennett, *The Story of the Jamaican People*, 2.
34  Smith, *The Ethnic Origins of Nations*, 213.
35  Poulantzas, *State, Power, Socialism*, 114.
36  Smith, *The Ethnic Origins of Nations*, 213.
37  Bale, *Imagined Olympians*.
38  Seecharan, *Muscular Learning*, 230–63, explores this insularity in respect of Jamaican involvement in the 1900 tour of England.
39  Meeks, *Narratives of Resistance*, Featherstone, *Postcolonial Cultures*.
40  James, *Beyond a Boundary*.
41  Bhabha, *The Location of Culture*.
42  Scott, *Domination and the Arts of Resistance*.
43  Richards, *Hitting Across the Line*.
44  Beckles, *The Development of West Indies Cricket: Vol. 1*, 90; Beckles (ed.), *A Spirit of Dominance* is presented as a collection of essays in honour of Viv Richards.
45  Richards, *Hitting Across the Line*, 72.
46  Ibid., 19.
47  Ibid., 19–20.
48  Ibid., 138.

[49] Tiffin, 'Cricket, Literature and the Politics of De-colonisation'.
[50] Richards, *Hitting Across the Line*, 76.
[51] Ibid., 82.
[52] Ibid., 90.
[53] Ibid., 85.
[54] Ibid., 86.
[55] Ibid., 114 and 200.
[56] Ibid., 197.
[57] Ibid., 39.
[58] Ibid., see for instance 217 and 162.
[59] Ibid., 160.
[60] Ibid., 148–9.
[61] Chakrabarty, *Provincializing Europe*, 101, notes that subaltern pasts 'are marginalized not because of any conscious intentions but because they represent moments or points at which the archive that the historian mines develops a degree of intractability with respect to the aims of professional history … Élite and dominant groups can also have subaltern pasts to the extent that they participate in life-worlds subordinated by the "major" narratives of the dominant institutions.'

## References

Anderson, B. *Imagined Communities: Reflections of the Origins and Spread of Nationalism*, rev. ed. London: Verso, 2006 (1983).

Appiah, K.A. 'Is the "Post-" in "Postcolonial" the "Post-" in "Postmodern"?' In *Dangerous Liaisons; Gender, Nation, and Postcolonial Perspectives*, edited by Anne McClintock, Aamir Mufti, and Ella Shohat, 420–44. Minneapolis, MN: University of Minnesota Press, 1997.

Bale, J. *Imagined Olympians: Body Culture and Colonial Representation in Rwanda*. Minneapolis, MN: University of Minnesota Press, 2002.

Bale, J., and J. Sang. *Kenyan Running: Movement Culture, Geography and Global Change*. London: Frank Cass, 1996.

Beckles, H. *The Development of West Indies Cricket: Vol. 1, The Age of Nationalism*. London: Pluto Press, 1998.

Beckles, H. *The Development of West Indies Cricket: Vol. 2, The Age of Globalization*. London: Pluto Press, 1998.

Beckles, H., ed. *A Spirit of Dominance: Cricket and Nationalism in the West Indies*. Kingston: University of the West Indies Press, 1998.

Bhabha, H.K. *The Location of Culture*. London: Routledge, 1994.

Chakrabarty, D. *Provincializing Europe: Postcolonial Thought and Historical Difference*. Princeton, NJ: Princeton University Press, 2000.

Darwin, J. *Britain and Decolonisation: The Retreat From Empire in the Post-War World*. Basingstoke: Macmillan, 1988.

Featherstone, S. *Postcolonial Cultures*. Edinburgh: Edinburgh University Press, 2005.

Fleuras, A., and J.L. Elliot. *The Nations Within: Aboriginal-State Relations in Canada, the United States, and New Zealand*. Oxford: Oxford University Press, 1992.

Hall, C. 'Introduction: Thinking the Postcolonial, Thinking the Empire'. In *Cultures of Empire: A Reader*, edited by Catherine Hall, 1–33. Manchester: Manchester University Press, 2000.

Hall, S. 'Negotiating Caribbean Identities'. *New Left Review* 209 (1995): 3–14.

Hall, S. 'When was "the Post-colonial"? Thinking at the Limit'. In *The Post-colonial Question: Common Skies, Divided Horizons*, edited by Iain Cambers and Lidia Curti, 242–60. London: Routledge, 1996.

Harvey, D. *The Condition of Postmodernity: An Enquiry into the Origins of Cultural Change*. Oxford: Blackwell, 1990.

James, C.L.R. *The Case For West-Indian Self Government*. London: Hogarth Press, 1933.

James, C.L.R. *A History of the Pan-African Revolt*. London: Race Today, 1938/1986.

James, C.L.R. *The Black Jacobins: Toussaint L'Ouverture and the San Domingo Revolution*. London: Penguin, 1938/2001.

James, C.L.R. *Beyond a Boundary*. London: Serpents' Tail, 1963/1994.

Jameson, F. *Postmodernism, or, The Cultural Logic of Late Capitalism*. Durham, NC: Duke University Press, 1991.

Lyotard, J.-F. *The Postmodern Condition: A Report on Knowledge*. Manchester: Manchester University Press, 1984.

Maaka, R., and A. Fleuras. *The Politics of Indigeneity: Challenging the State in Canada and Aotearoa New Zealand*. Dunedin, NZ: Otago University Press, 2005.

MacLean, M. 'Ambiguity within the Boundary: Re-reading CLR James' *Beyond a Boundary'*. *Journal of Sport History*, forthcoming.

Meeks, B. *Narratives of Resistance: Jamaica, Trinidad, The Caribbean*. Kingston: University of the West Indies Press, 2000.

Nash, J. 'When Isms Became Wasms: Structural Functionalism, Marxism, Feminism and Postmodernism'. *Critique of Anthropology* 17, no. 1 (1997): 11–32.

Poulantzas, N. *State, Power, Socialism*. London: New Left Books, 1978.

Redfield, R. *Peasant Society and Culture*. Chicago, IL: University of Chicago Press, 1956.

Richards V., with M. Middles. *Hitting Across the Line: An Autobiography*. Sydney: Macmillan Australia, 1991.

Samson, C. *A Way of Life That Does Not Exist: Canada and the Extinguishment of the Innu*. London: Verso, 2003.

Schwartz, B. 'Becoming Postcolonial'. In *Without Guarantees: In Honour of Stuart Hall*, edited by Paul Gilroy, Lawrence Grossberg, and Angela McRobbie, 268–81. London: Verso, 2000.

Scott, J.C. *Domination and the Arts of Resistance: Hidden Transcripts*. New Haven, CT: Yale University Press, 1990.

Seecharan, C. *Muscular Learning: Cricket and Education in the Making of the British West Indies at the End of the 19th Century*. Kingston: Ian Randle Publishers, 2006.

Sherlock, P., and H. Bennett. *The Story of the Jamaican People*. Kingston: Ian Randle Publishers, 1998.

Sissons, G. *First Peoples: Indigenous Cultures and the Futures*. London: Reaktion Books, 2005.

Slemon, S. 'The Scramble for Post-colonialism'. In *The Post-Colonial Studies Reader*, edited by Bill Ashcroft, Gareth Griffiths, and Helen Tiffin, 45–52. London: Routledge, 1995.

Smith, A.D. *The Ethnic Origins of Nations*. Oxford: Blackwell, 1986.

Spivak, G.C. 'Can the Subaltern Speak?' In *Marxism and the Interpretation of Culture*, edited by Cary Nelson and Lawrence Grossberg, 271–313. Urbana, IL: University of Illinois Press, 1988.

Thomas, N. *Possessions: Indigenous Art/Colonial Culture*. London: Thames and Hudson, 1999.

Thomas, N. 'Introduction'. In *Double Vision: Art Histories and Colonial Encounters in the Pacific*, edited by Nicholas Thomas and Diane Losche, 1–16. Cambridge: Cambridge University Press, 1999.

Tiffin, H. 'Cricket, Literature and the Politics of De-colonisation: The Case of C.L.R. James'. In *Sport, Money, Morality and the Media*, edited by Richard Cashman and Michael McKernan, 177–93. Sydney: University of New South Wales Press, 1981.

Williams, E. *History of the People of Trinidad and Tobago*. London: Andre Deutsch, 1964.

Williams, E. *From Columbus to Castro: The History of the Caribbean, 1492–1969*. London: Andre Deutsch, 1970.

# Brian Lara in poetic form: tradition, talent and the Caribbean 'mwe'

Claire Westall*

*Department of English and Comparative Literary Studies, University of Warwick, Coventry, UK*

## Introduction

At present no full length study of Brian Lara's life or career exists. Brian Scovell's recent biography, *Brian Lara: Cricket's Troubled Genius*,[1] comes tantalizingly close but falls short of depicting Lara's international retirement. The work of historian Hilary Beckles has offered the most nuanced analysis of Lara's cricketing and cultural impact and we can perhaps anticipate that Beckles may expand upon his writings in the wake of Lara's withdrawal from the world stage.[2] For Lara's remarkable career has been inscribed into the popular imagination of the Anglophone, and thereby cricketing, Caribbean and the cricketing world more generally. It has also featured in the literature of the Caribbean and its diaspora. Like a number of other West Indies cricketers, Lara's image and triumphs have been rendered and celebrated in music and poetry as artists investing in the social, political and cultural import of cricket continue to represent the sport and its heroes in their own aesthetic terms. Within the wider tradition of cricket literature seen in the region, a collection or cluster of Lara-based praise poems, calypsos and songs has emerged over the last 15 years. This essay primarily considers the cluster of Lara poems. It first situates the iconic image of Lara within the literary frames provided by T.S. Eliot's 1919 essay 'Tradition and the Individual Talent' and Kamau Brathwaite's poetic notion of the Caribbean 'mwe', before unpacking Lara poems composed by writers and performers as well known as Jean Breeze, Howard Fergus and Paul Keens-Douglas, among a number of others. The discussion suggests that by reading these pieces as a collection Lara is shown to represent the Caribbean's ongoing negotiation between the one and the many, as well as the potentially hazardous over-investment in the individual hero. The essay itself is less concerned with the actions and personality of Lara (though these are interesting in and of themselves and should spur a fully developed study of their own) than it is with his heroic image in poetry and the critical messages West Indies cricket and the wider Caribbean may take from such literary representations.

## Lara's cricketing life

Brian Charles Lara was born in Santa Cruz, Trinidad, in 1969. He dedicated himself to cricket at an early age and was supported in his career pursuits throughout his teenage years by his loyal and loving father, Bunty, who died just as his son was breaking into the West Indies set up. Lara's international playing career began as the curtain was falling on that of Sir Vivian Richards and reached its own end at the 2007 World Cup Finals, when the competition was held for the first time in the Caribbean. Although Lara's prodigious talent was spotted relatively early, and welcomed by cricketing legend Sir Garry Sobers, he experienced something of a false start to his international career.[3] He made his debut in the Third Test against Pakistan in Lahore in December 1990 but did not make another Test appearance until April 1992, against South Africa in Barbados. In his autobiography, *Beating the Field*, Lara talks of this as a faltering and frustrating start and describes how he felt that young players were not respected by older team members or given their chance by the captain (Richards) and management until the stalwarts of past successes decided to retire. He even depicts Lance Gibbs, team manager during the 1991 tour of England, accusationally, declaring: 'You think you can bat like Gary Sobers'.[4] This view of young talent, spirit and desire running up against what he saw as the tradition and hierarchy of West Indies cricket contextualizes all that follows in this autobiographical portrayal of his rise to world record-breaking fame. As is well known, in 1994 the 'Prince of Port of Spain' made 375 against England to surpass Sobers' 365* record for the highest ever Test score.[5] Shortly afterwards he amassed 501* for Warwickshire to secure his superstar status. And perhaps most impressively, almost a decade to the day after he first obtained the world record in Antigua, Lara regained his title by overtaking Matthew Hayden's 380 (scored against Zimbabwe in October 2003) to become the first batsman to accumulate 400* Test runs in a single innings. These incredible feats, along with multiple others, have ensured Lara a unique place in West Indies and world cricket; a place reflected by his unmatched financial attainment as a West Indies player which set him apart both from his immediate teammates and former West Indies legends. Although the amounts he earned appear to have been inflated in the press, it is nonetheless fair to say that the economic truths and dependencies of the Caribbean have been written into Lara's pay cheques with advertisements and endorsements financed from outside his home region accounting for the vast majority of his income.

Importantly, Lara's career historically spans the period from the last days of the domination of West Indies in the early 1990s to their fall into what is at present a sorry state of disillusion and uncertainty which continues to manifest itself in the ongoing conflict between players and the management/board.[6] Lara's individual talent and immense world records were mostly set against the decline of West Indies cricket and as three times captain of the formerly great regional team, Lara was often at the helm of their sinking ship. His batting may have repeatedly help stave off disaster but has not (and perhaps could never have) worked to raise the team to the point of regular success, which Beckles claims the traditional historical paradigms of West Indies cricket demanded of heroes.[7] Also, Lara's behaviour both on and off the field have repeatedly been viewed as running contrary to the accepted image of a 'good' West Indies captain (modelled on Sir Frank Worrell) and against his team's best interests. Incidents such as disputes with captains and team members, missed planes and tours, player strikes and contract disputes, resignations and the declaration that cricket was 'ruining' his life, have soured Lara's public image but sit alongside his powerfully aesthetic stroke play and his professional reputation as one of the few remaining world-class batsmen who 'walk'. These aspects of his career have created a potent and much commented upon tension between the individual batting excellence of Lara, including the rewards it brought, and the predicament of his team, especially their lack of consistency and their struggle to represent a region that is seemingly moving away from the nationalist, collectivizing sentiments of previous generations. Beckles has described Lara as '(Con)testing the Caribbean Imagination' by occupying a critical position within the paradigmatic shift caused by the age of globalization – Beckles's third paradigm of West Indies cricket history.[8] Similarly, Hector has identified how, as a player of his time, Lara is 'trapped between the ways of his raising and the value-less globalizing invasion which assails us all'.[9] It is in the light of these negotiations between individual talent, cricket history and Caribbean unity that Lara can be read through Eliot and Brathwaite.

### Tradition, talent and the Caribbean 'mwe'

T.S. Eliot's famous essay 'Tradition and the Individual Talent' was first published in two separate instalments of the *Egoist* in 1919 and was reprinted in *The Sacred Wood* (1920). In the essay Eliot articulates his view of the relationship between a poet and literature. For Eliot an artist never 'has complete meaning alone' but must participate in, and respond to, tradition. He argues that what defines a great poet is not an ability to express their individuality through originality, as in unique difference, nor is it the skill of recreating, repeating or mimicking past poetic masters or masterpieces. Instead, a poet must know and engage with the past as a living and constantly altering entity which is itself changed by the insertion of new, yet still traditional, forms of poetic excellence. Only then and with 'great labour' can a poet gain Eliot's 'historical sense', that is, a 'perception, not only of the pastness of the past, but of its presence ... , not of what is dead, but of what is already living'. Further, a poet should 'continue to develop this historical consciousness throughout his career' and work through a 'process of depersonalisation' in order to ensure that his art is not concerned with conveying 'personality' but with the expression of new combinations of aesthetic feeling.[10] Eliot is insistent upon the literary past and present existing concomitantly in the mind of a poet so that they can themselves add to the tradition of great literature. Moreover, this is a tradition that must not be lost because, as Eliot says in 'The Possibility of a Poetic Drama', 'by losing tradition, we lose our hold on the present'.[11]

Taking up this point, Edward Said opens his expansive postcolonial text, *Culture and Imperialism*, by transposing Eliot's proposition onto the historical, cultural and literary dimensions of imperialism, arguing that imperialism, including dimensions of anti-imperialism and neo-imperialism, is characterized by perpetual (re)negotiations between past, present and future.[12] This essay contends that Said's move, from Eliot to empire, is one that can be taken forward by looking specifically at cricket. As the game of colonialism and postcolonialism *par excellence*, cricket stands as a testament both to Eliot's insistence on the past and present co-existing in a single socio-aesthetic space and Said's relocation of this co-existence in imperial terms. Approaching cricket through Eliot's poetic frame, we can suggest that a great cricketer would have to know and appreciate the living attributes of the past masters and traditions of the colonial/postcolonial game and recognize how their own actions impact upon the order of tradition. They would possess an intimate understanding of the history of their national game and comprehend its relation to the wider spectrum of (international) participation. In addition, a player's cricketing individuality, his style and mannerisms, would have to be viewed in relation to the historical and aesthetic developments of the game and the key practitioners of the past. Their actions would have to be less about individuality as personality or self interest and more about the execution of new aesthetic combinations of physical performance. As C.L.R. James says, 'Cricketers call it style'.[13]

I also wish to propose that the cricketing application of Eliot's thinking can be seen in the work of James, someone we may identify as linking colonial and postcolonial intellectual and cricketing histories in his writings about players like Learie Constantine, Collie Smith and Rohan Kanhai – all of whom he describes as expressing their 'West Indian heritage' through their play and playing styles.[14] James' proximity to Eliot's position is most obvious in his assessment of Sobers both in his canonical text *Beyond a Boundary* and in his essay on the Barbadian legend entitled 'Garfield Sobers'. To James, Sobers' batting, bowling and fielding 'are a living embodiment of centuries of a tortured history', changing history and tradition as they are performed against the backdrop of Caribbean cricketing imperialism and nationalist, anti-imperial protest.[15] Although James identifies and writes about Sobers' 'individual style' – indeed he places immense value on interpreting all cricketers through their aesthetic performances – he rejects an English journalist's view of Sobers' individualism as exceptionalism. Instead, he asserts that Sobers brought together immense talent, dedicated training and the unique history of the region to make him 'the fruit of a great tradition'.[16] Kenneth Surin has rightly drawn attention to James' rather gendered attachment to such heroic male figures within and beyond cricket. He has also argued against James' assessment of Sobers by positioning himself against James' mobilization of Hegel's world-historical individual, that is, a prodigious man whose individual passions coincide with the unconscious will or spirit of the people. Surin contends that no man or individual, even one as significant as Sobers, can express a fraction of the Caribbean's 'impulses and disposition'.[17] Yet this seems to be the manner in which such visibly successful cricketing heroes, like Sobers and later Lara, are represented within the Caribbean popular and literary imagination and this was something that James appears to have understood.

Beckles has presented Lara as the inheritor of the West Indies tradition that James saw in Sobers, and Sobers himself has described Lara as 'a real West Indian batsman in the time-honoured tradition'.[18] Having watched Lara reach 375, Beckles reports that Lara possesses the 'eye, technique and timing of Gary [Sobers], the ideological contempt for foolishness of Viv [Richards], and the occasional display of Sir Frank's [Worrell] grace and elegance'.[19] In examining Lara's status, Beckles evokes terms that are similar to Eliot's by writing of a 'critical consciousness' that meets with a 'reorganization of information' to be put into 'exceptional social use by individuals at the edge of expectations'. He goes on: 'With Lara we see flashes and we hear sounds of all those who have gone before', but, like the favoured pupil, Lara claims that, 'What has gone before is excellent, but must be improved'.[20] That is, Lara is of tradition thanks to his inheritance, absorption, enactment and manipulation of greatness and his own entrance into the tradition of West Indies and world cricket. Additionally, according to Beckles, Sobers not only helped prepare Lara mentally for his 375 record but had emphasized that Lara focus on West Indies needing 45 more runs rather than just thinking of his own score.[21] Beckles posits that in cricket, particularly West Indies cricket, 'supporting the "whole" motivates more than pleasing the "part"'.[22] Sobers, he claims, had handed Lara the authority to surpass him and had done so through the power of a selfless belief in unity, in the individuality of talent residing within a collectivity of the team and the (regional) nation. However, as noted, Lara has been repeatedly criticized for placing his own interests (often business-related) above cricket and Beckles identifies him as the example of sporting entrepreneurship that will set the way for a new generation.[23] Despite Lara's more mature efforts to speak of himself with Eliot's 'historical sense', to rebuild a West Indies team worthy of the name 'team' and to forge a purposeful role as a captain and leader responsive to communal hopes and fears, his efforts remained largely unproductive in terms of results. While his batting has positioned him as an inheritor of, and entertaining contributor to, the tradition of West Indies cricket, his personal behaviour has worked to separate him from his community and the political intersection of cricket, nationalism and unity of previous generations. He stands as a contemporary example of why, in James' words, 'the cricketer must be returned to the community'.[24]

This concern with the balance between the individual and their community is shared by the Barbadian poet and critic Kamau Brathwaite, who has repeatedly made clear his interest in Eliot's use of the 'voice' to explore the Caribbean idiom of folk language and collective expression in what he calls 'nation language'.[25] Brathwaite captures a localized articulation of the interaction between autobiography and history, between the history of the individual and their awareness of their own position within their locale and community, in his use of the word or phrase 'mwe'. Lawrence Breiner has explained that in Haiti 'official orthography for Haitian creole programmatically works to make written creole look less like French' as when the expression 'for me' is written in creole as 'pou mwe' so as to visually obscure its connection to the French 'pour moi' (though to the ear they are more similar).[26] As Breiner's example shows, 'pou mwe' works to remove the metropolitan influence as it localizes that very influence and inserts a communal 'we' into the singularity of 'me'. This relates to the appearance of 'mwe' in Brathwaite's poetry where it is the 'me' of the poet and the 'we' of his audience, community and people, where it evokes the 'me' of a single island and the 'we' of the islands holding the singular and collective together in a dialectic which speaks of their inseparable opportunities, their unity even in verbal/linguistic/visual difference. It also links back to Breiner's 'Autobiography of the Tribe', the story of the socio-historic group told through a single yet representative voice which is something of supreme importance to Brathwaite's poetry and his view of himself as a communal poet.[27] In Section VII of *Barabajan Poems 1492–1992* Brathwaite uses his largest typescript to convey the essence of the Caribbean 'mwe' across two full pages, using his video style to convey the size and significance of this individual and collective utterance and its relation to the Bajan landspace:

After this it

Became

possible – more

possible? – for

mwe/ for us

to begin to

enter/ repossess

our

Igbo

BaJan

landscape [28]

Brathwaite's uses the 'mwe' as a form of 'us' expressing the improved possibility of individual and communal entrance and repossession as he identifies a reconnection to the god-like power of creation that is the land. Like Eliot, Brathwaite is interested in past and present, but specifically in the individual present negotiating a way with the communal present in their common locality, as caused by the historical journey of their past, toward a new beginning founded upon unity. This is what Hector calls the Caribbean's 'long awaited becoming'.[29]

Perceiving Brian Lara through the idiom of Brathwaite's 'mwe' we can identify the 'me' of individual talent and the 'we' of tradition, as in Eliot, but also a more immediate 'me' of success/prosperity and 'we' of representation/responsibility that are held together in his 'mwe' cricketing position as batsman/hero and leader/captain, connected to and emerging from the Caribbean people and their landscape. Further, we can see that Lara may embody such a 'mwe' phenomenon by bringing crowds of people together in glorious appreciation of his play. At the same time, such adoration of a single player can lead and has led to the down-playing of other team performances and to an over-reliance on the heroic individual. This is pertinent to the reliance of the regional team upon Lara and to the difficulty of maintaining a conception of collectivity against a backdrop of regional factionalism and socio-economic decline. Indeed, as Beckles states, 'a "team" as mental construct, no longer is an easy concept' whether in cricketing or political terms.[30] For West Indies cricket this notion has been all the more problematic given the over-reliance on Lara. As Hector eloquently summarizes, the 'one-manism' of West Indies cricket meant the regional team were 'as dependent on Lara in the 90s as they were on Headley, as Atlas, in the 30s'.[31] However, where Hector sees history as repeating itself, we can identify a notable difference: Headley's talents were set against the beginnings of regional nationalism while Lara's may have been cast against its demise. This tension between the individual and the collective as a 'mwe' formulation, particularly in the negotiation between batsman/captain and team, is embedded within Lara praise poems even as they focus on his heroic image and record-breaking scores.

## Lara in poetic form

In *The Development of West Indies Cricket: Vol. 1* Beckles provides a useful survey of cricket's appearance in Caribbean literature as he explores the sport's impact on popular cultural art forms, including calypso, poetry and drama. Similarly, Gordon Rohlehr engages with cricket's place in Caribbean art as he charts the overlapping cultural, political and aesthetic resources of 'Music, Literature and West Indian Cricket Values', while Douglas Midgett also draws upon the intersection of cricket and calypso.[32] Further, a new anthology, *The Bowling was Superfine*, brings together a comprehensive collection of writings concerned with Caribbean cricket.[33] As each of these works indicate, the Caribbean and its diaspora has established a tradition of representing cricket in various literary forms and this tradition has been especially strong in poetry – the oral poetry of calypso as well as that of written and performance verse. Brathwaite's 'Rites' is perhaps the most famous and critically acclaimed of all Caribbean cricket poems but has been well supported by the likes of 'Cricket' by Bruce St John and 'Prospero Caliban Cricket' by John Agard. As with the cycle of cricket calypsos Rohlehr describes, West Indian cricket poetry has often portrayed cricketing heroes. Notable examples include: 'To Learie' by Eric Roach; 'Sonny Ramadhin' by Cecil Gray; 'Call Him the Babu' by Sasenarine Persaud about Rohan Kanhai; and 'Greenidge' and 'Viv' both by Faustin Charles. Since 1994 a series or cluster of calypsos and poems about Lara has emerged from this tradition.

Calypso and pan tracks have included 'Lash dem Lara' by Alexander de Great, 'Signal for Lara' by Superblue and 'Four Lara Four' by de Fosto, all marking the triumphs of 1994, while Rootsman's 'Lara' rang out around the Caribbean in 2004 and Lara's 400* was captured by de Fosto in his pan sequel (and my favourite) 'He Strikes Again'.[34] It is to such poetic examples that this discussion now turns.

'Song for Lara' by Jean 'Binta' Breeze, a female Jamaican living and working in Britain, is a dense and optimistic performance poem that praises Lara and his 'young generation' as those who refuse to stand 'in awe of Wisden', who refuse to be oppressed by the force of English cricketing institutionalism.[35] For Breeze, writing in the mid-1990s, this youthful West Indies team enjoys a 'fresh clean page' in the book of cricket history where 'de wicket hold no shadows' for those descended from a recent line of world conquerors. Crafted for live enactment, her poetic rendition is a musical ensemble of Caribbean rhythms as she calls on dance, pan and kaiso (i.e. calypso) to answer the cries of collective conviviality. Raising her pace to a frenzy that matches Lara's stroke play, Breeze gambles all. Yet even at this moment of euphoric surrender she works to recall and refute bland, touristic stereotypes of uncontrolled, reckless calypso cricket. She also draws upon David Rudder's famous 1987 calypso, 'Rally Round the West Indies' to identify the versatility of musical forms in the region and to mark the slow rhythmic play which the crowd (and Rudder) can soon turn 'extempo'. By calling on Rudder, Breeze intertextually references the difficulties facing West Indies cricket and Rudder's call for regional solidarity in the face of generational change and defeat. However, she still chooses to concentrate on the young, sensational Lara, situating him as the mediating force between 'we an' de Lord!' as if he is the bridge between the people and their spiritual point of guidance. She identifies the individuality of his batting – 'steady timin'/watchful eye' – but matches this with the combinations of physical pairings – eyes, hands and legs – that he uses to bat. This technique functions to remove the sense of isolated singularity from Lara and instead registers a type of productive unity achieved through synchronized physical action. With a rhythmic overflowing of emotion, Breeze sees Lara as playing himself in, into both his innings and his place in history. He is batting for himself, to express himself, to obtain his own goals but, as she insists in repetition, he does not play 'all hiself'. It is as if he has not given all of himself yet, that he does not play alone but is one of a line of heroes, playing with a team and drawing on the powers of the people. She views Lara's sense of self and the collective Caribbean self as contained and maintained through his cricketing excellence and ends with her claim for Lara's combination of self and selflessness:

> an he playing hiself
>
> he playing hiself
>
> but he doan play all hiself yet
>
>
> he playin hiself
>
> he playin hiself
>
> but he doan play all hiself

In a similar tone, the female Indo-Trinidadian poet Ranjandaye Ramkisson-Chen writes of Lara's world record as a moment of Caribbean carnival.[36] 'On Lara's 375' is an example of what Paula Morgan has noted as the poet's use of a trope of 'intentional hybridity' as a marker of Caribbean integration.[37] Moving through the celebratory crowd Ramkisson-Chen sees the cricketing masses as united in song and dance by the performance of their sporting icon. They 'bowl fists of cheer their arms in line and length' in cricketing exuberance as Lara becomes the object of their joy, the target of their affection and the cause of their party. Having established this Caribbean cauldron of cross-cultural amalgamation, the poem moves downward from the heights of ecstasy to Lara's physical presence on the pitch. In the same way that Breeze references Lara's humility, Ramkisson-Chen conveys how, 'Humbly like a hero/he bows to the wicket' and 'kisses the earth'. This image, one to be repeated a decade later and an important motif in poems about Lara, is an act of connection, of loyalty and locality being expressed to the soil and people of the region to show that he comes from them and belongs to them, that he gives thanks and praise to them and the islands 'instinctively'.[38] Here the 'me' of individual glory performs Brathwaite's sense of entering/repossessing the landscape which has provided an immense and tangible source of support and solidarity defending, in this instance, Lara's wicket and carrying him and his shots 'beyond the boundary', as Ramkisson-Chen says. The crux of the poem becomes the emotional intensity felt by Lara and its reflection in the crowd which coalesces in the wake of his domination of England and the world. Importantly, Lara becomes the body of achievement, the physical enactment of Caribbean glory as 'He walks the victory sign', in that now famous posture with his arms and bat held above his head. Standing as the warrior of the 'red ... flash of runs', he is transfigured into the (young) father and protector of the region, standing with 'arms that unite/beneath an uncertain sun'.

Embedded within this cricketing parade are four less positive dimensions to Ramkisson-Chen's presentation of the event. First, the poem references Lara as 'bubbling like unstoppered cola' which captures the fizz of the batsman's emotional state, the outpouring and overflowing of his jubilation, but also registers the sizeable promotional sums that Lara would attract thereby signalling his proximity to the stream of global wealth and advertising that would subsequently follow him and set him apart. Second, Shivnarine Chanderpaul is characterized as Lara's nameless and juvenile 'little partner', despite Lara's record resting on the batting support of his team mates. In *Beating the Field* and elsewhere, Lara has spoken generously of Chanderpaul's maturity and the encouragement his 19-year-old batting partner offered in the build up to the historic moment. Chanderpaul's belittling may be a gesture of humorous affection or may be said to emerge from the poet's loyalty to Lara and Trinidad first and foremost. Nevertheless, it is worth noting that such silencing and marginalization of Chanderpaul is an obvious consequence of the single focus upon Lara and a nod toward Lara's heroic isolation. Third, and quite significantly, the poet removes Sobers from the scene though it was his embrace, perhaps more than that of Chanderpaul, which signified the moment of self-referential and generationally continuous achievement for the Caribbean in front of a global audience. In fact, each of the poems depicting Lara's 375 discussed here erase Sobers in order to concentrate on Lara alone, writing over the generational point of transfer between the 'King' and 'Prince' of West Indies batsmanship. Consequently, there is a sense in which Lara is being seen in the literary imagination as having broken away, or become distanced, from his cricketing heritage, specifically the records/obtainments of the previous and overtly nationalist generations. Finally, Ramkisson-Chen portrays the 'uncertain sun' under which Lara has united the Caribbean and her tone of ambiguity for the future casts a long and relatively gloomy shadow (one which Breeze denied) over the cricketing future and general fate of the people and region. This sense of uncertainty is echoed in Howard Fergus' depiction of the same event.

Sir Howard A. Fergus, the poet and historian from Montserrat, has penned four poems about Lara and entitled his 1997 collection, which features three of these, *Lara Rains and*

*Colonial Rites*, reiterating the importance and connection between Lara's performances and the colonial history of the region.[39] In 'BC Lara', a poem which playfully praises Lara's 501*, Fergus traces the idea that Lara brings about historical and religious transformation. Identifying 1994 as 'Anno Lari' in a play upon Queen Elizabeth II's description of 1992 as *annus horribilis*, Fergus claims that the arrival of Lara is the 'turning tide of history', a 'watershed' from which a 'New gospel' will be written. For Fergus, time will be divided between before Lara and after him with the player's initials signifying the alteration from 'BC' to 'BL', as the names Brian Charles and Brian Lara are written over that of Christ. With Lara's arrival set to 'eclipse' old empires, Fergus' double-edged attack appears to be directed both at a Christian timeline and imperial cricketing history. In Lara's Christ-like role he is described as a father, 'Papa Lara!', and children call his name in adoration and as an amusing claim to parentage. Meanwhile middle-aged women are 'padding up' their bras in order to have a '500 to 1' shot of becoming Lara's wife.[40] Fergus' poem quite clearly echoes Hector's optimistic sentiments about Lara's impact upon Caribbean social history:

> [I] would want to think that Lara's 375 innings put behind the Caribbean the conditionalities of the IMF [International Monetary Fund] with its structural readjustments that has structured Caribbean people out of their own economy and history. They will return centre stage after Lara because Caribbean history can be divided into BL (Before Lara) and AL (After Lara).[41]

We should recognize though that after more than a decade this has sadly not been the case for the region and, if anything, the distance between the local population and the economics of their subsistence, including the cricketing economy, has only increased: a fact that seemed to be displayed by their general absence from the World Cup venues at the start of the 2007 tournament.

'Lara Rains', Fergus' poem about the 375, emphasizes the brutal demise of England caused by Lara's batting in a cricketing reversal of colonial exploitation. It comes close to the tone of batting violence in Brathwaite's 'Rites' and the poetic brutality of Richards in 'Massa Day Done' by Ian McDonald and Fergus' own poem, 'Conquest'.[42] As in these examples, there is a sense of Paul Gilroy's 'slave sublime'. Although Gilroy examines music as the primary mode in which there is a 'centrality of terror in stimulating black creativity and cultural production',[43] poetic representations of black batsmen by Caribbean artists often mobilize a comparable idiom of anti-colonial or postcolonial violence as part of an attempt to utter and redress the unspeakableness of the past where the terrors of slavery are (re)articulated through aggressive but aesthetic shot making. This is seen in the poetry of Charles, McDonald, Fergus and others who use similar, sometimes blood-thirsty, motifs like cutting and lashing in order to manipulate and/or reverse their loaded historical meanings. (This is also true of many calypsos about cricket and cricketers.) In 'Lara Rains', Lara, cutting the opposition, 'Over and over with a blunt willow', bludgeons England to death until they are buried under a 'ruin of runs' in an 'Antiguan graveyard', the Antiguan Recreation Ground (ARG), the site of both Lara's Test records. The ARG has St John's Catholic Cathedral on its west side and Fergus draws upon Catholic iconography to portray the umpires as priest-like 'ombudsmen', dressed in 'black and white', counting the remnants of a 'broken rosary' and calling 'over and out' as they enact the last 'rites' of England, declaring an end to its cricketing and imperial superiority. It is Lara though who has dug 'their hell' as his batting presents the nightmare of colonial rebellion and defeat causing a massive historical readjustment as the last are now first and the first dead and buried. Again, on this occasion of warrior-like ascension, Lara becomes that famous 'shape of victory', walking with his hands aloft, as Fergus opens a window onto the future of a people who keep faith despite 'an uncertain resurrection/After 375 years of rain under Lara'. Like the 'uncertain sun' of Ramkisson-Chen, Fergus' ambiguity over the people's future asks what currency, what impact, what social value can and will Lara's innings bring. In this fashion, the 'rain' of Lara, as the favourable weather source that breathes life into the lush Caribbean landscape, may also be the monarchical reign that must end which also auratically plays upon his 'reign' and 'rein' as restrictive or limiting forces. This note of concern about what will follow is valid, particularly given that Lara went for two years without scoring a further Test century, but is overcome in the poem by an optimistic insistence on the continuing promise of cricketing and regional collectivity after Lara's passing. As Fergus writes, 'the sun will not set/On the united states of the West Indies/And rain will come again'.

In terms of Fergus' own poetry the 'resurrection' of Lara is seen to have occurred specifically on 15 December 2000 as recorded in 'Lara Again' in *Volcano Verses*. This work captures Lara's first innings of the Third Test in Adelaide against Australia with West Indies already 2-0 down in the series.[44] Three days after having scored 231 against 'Australia A', Lara came in at 52-2, was 136* overnight and went on to make 182 the next day. Although West Indies secured a first innings total of 391 they collapsed to 114 in the second, lost the match and ultimately endured a disastrous 5-0 series defeat. In spite of this reality and by focusing exclusively on the first day's play, Fergus is able to pay homage to Lara's spectacularly commanding performance as the batsman who makes a Christmas 'gift' like 'Santa' to his people. The notion of Christmas during the winter tour is reinforced by the examination of Lara as 'The West Indies Saviour', resurrected, 'born again' and now the Christ-like talisman of a change of fortunes. It is noteworthy that Fergus recognizes the batting efforts of a young Marlon Samuels who stays with Lara at the crease but he insists on identifying Samuels' strength as his ability to 'follow the beat of the master', to act as Lara's 'disciple' or Santa's helper. This is at once due praise to the elder, experienced father in Lara (not captaining at the time) but equally the type of subservient following that younger players may find difficult to accept (as indeed Lara did at the start of his career). It is an irony of history that it was Marlon Samuels who ran Lara out in ignominious fashion in Lara's last international game. During the match commentary and repeatedly afterwards, Viv Richards spoke of Samuels' substantial error of judgement – in not being more careful, quick-thinking or self-sacrificing – as a possible and regretful indicator (conscious or otherwise) of the type of ongoing tension between the players and their star captain that was so often reported in the press. Returning to 'Lara Again', Fergus praises Lara's volcanic, eruptive qualities as a batsman, expressed via his repetitive boundaries against 'terrorists' like Australian bowler Glen McGrath, whilst recognizing that a volcano is unpredictable, unreliable. Fergus manoeuvres this ferocious uncertainty into a threat against the Australians but it is, just as easily, another example of the uncertainty of relying on a single man. Although this may be closer to the historical position of Lara, it stands in opposition to Fergus' presentation in 'Lara Reach' where the ordinary hero worshipping spectator sees the arrival of Lara at the wicket as bringing a certain century while his own cricketing experience of 'singles and dots' is soon ended when he is given out. This poem offers a comedic, and perhaps unintentional, reinforcement of the notion of almost impossible public expectations weighing on Lara and the widening gap between professional and social cricketing experiences.

Trinidadian performance poet and artist Paul Keens-Douglas also addresses the batting of Lara through an attack on ordinary folk's hero-worshipping and idolization of him. Keens-Douglas' first engagement with Lara comes via his pivotal female character 'Tanti Merle' who is at the centre of some of his best pieces about cricket, including his most acclaimed and popular cricket poem 'Tanti at de Oval' which introduced the strong, rambunctious, no-nonsense aunt in the 1970s.[45] By superimposing Tanti upon the otherwise male-dominated space of the cricket ground, Keens-Douglas draws attention to the under-representation of women in cricket and allows an exposure of the 'cool pose' of supposed male freedom which is often displayed by young men at matches. Almost three decades after her first poetic outing, Tanti Merle reappears in 'Tanti Backin' Lara' a short story celebrating Lara's 375.[46] On discovering that Lara can surpass Sobers's 365* Tanti wants everybody in her Trinidad home 'to back de boy' playing out in Antigua. Tanti's notion of 'spiritual support' means everyone putting their hands on Blackie who then acts as an 'aerial' with his hands on the tiny TV which is precariously balancing on a stool on a table. Before and during the game the local viewers (Tanti's guests) offer the usual 'bad talk' criticizing everyone from the selectors and Tony Cozier to Lara's 'winjy' Guyanese batting partner, Chanderpaul (again). They support Lara with calls of 'Yesssss Lara, Nooooo Lara!' until he misses the ball and they cry out, 'Oh Goooooooooood Lara!' Then, with Lara needing only six runs, Tanti's goat curry starts to burn and she heads off to save her dish taking the TV with her. By the time the TV has been resurrected Lara is standing triumphant with his bat in the air and they 'never see ah ting'. As in 'Tanti at de Oval', Tanti's calamitous engagement with cricket frames a historic moment to create an amusing folk story. Her personality seems to overwhelm or consume the cricketing occasion leaving a blind spot in the recollection of those caught up in her adventure.

The Montserrat-born E.A. Markham uses a similar figure in 'Mammie', an elderly Caribbean immigrant in Britain, who insists on the need to support West Indies and offers up her own critical reading of the game and Lara's technique in the poems 'Conversations at Upton Park iii' and 'For Brian Lara'.[47] In the first example, Mammie is calling on her people to enact Rudder's demand to 'Rally Round' (akin to Breeze) as the losses of her own family are set against the bad fortunes of the cricket team. In spite of her age and arthritis she is 'ready to come in at No. 3' but what she really needs is someone to simply 'follow her instruction – like that boy Lara'. Mammie makes Lara her compensation for past losses and her light for the future. His potential becomes her potential and that of their people, at home and around the world. In the second example, a similar situation sees Mammie offering a critique of Lara's technique, especially his backlift 'too high', and though her observations are contradicted by Lara's century she is almost proven right when he is nearly bowled by a straight ball. In both instances, Mammie's love of the game is comedically infectious and carries the weight of her connections to the islands and people she has left behind. Lara is rendered the omen of talented potential but also the danger of uncertainty that challenges her view of the distant Caribbean.

Keens-Douglas's other tribute, 'Lara Fans', offers a poetic critique not of Lara but of those 'die hard Lara' fan(atic)s.[48] He complains that 'Dey eh askin ... bout West Indies,/Or if de wicket takin' spin' but only want to know 'how much Lara make' – as a play on both his run getting and his money making. Worshipping Lara as a kind of 'demi-god' in the way that has come to be expected for cricket heroes,[49] they believe 'Lara alone could win dis match!' and want him to be allowed to 'open' and 'bat twice'. When Lara makes a duck they are discussing luck, fatigue and Obeah (folk magic or mysticism) not concentration, determination or shot selection. This is reminiscent of B.C. Pires' experience at the Queen's Park Oval in 1998 when he attempted to unearth some criticism of Lara on his debut as captain only to discover that at this point in history Lara was 'infallible in Trinidad' and that when he made a mistake 'everyone was immersed in a personal struggle to transform a dropped catch at a critical point into something positive, if not a sign of genius'.[50] This criticism-free experience is one that has not continued for Lara who is now praised and condemned almost in equal measure. Nonetheless, Keens-Douglas' poem remains useful in its rejection of the idolization of a single man as he reveals his concern at the over-investment in Lara and the problems it poses for the West Indies team and regional unity. The poem ends poignantly with his ambition for West Indies cricket:

Ah hope West Indies start makin' runs,

For everybody sake,

Because ah tired hear dem askin',

'How much Lara make?'

This hope for cricket is also Keens-Douglas's aspiration for the Caribbean. Along with cricket's popularity, its relationship to England and the success of West Indies, this dream is why he continues to write about the game. As he has repeatedly shown in his work, cricket has the language, humour, action, structure and beauty that make it a part of the popular and literary imagination in the Caribbean. It also supports the maintenance of both the individual and the collective in a medium that is known to, and appreciated by, the masses. Keens-Douglas hopes that the West Indies team and the Caribbean more generally can and will move beyond their over-investment in the heroic individual, cricketing or otherwise, and toward a new or renewed era of unity in purpose and action.

The tone of unadulterated praise that Keens-Douglas attacks is reflected in the two poems of Eutrice Cowie-Hope which celebrate Lara's 400, namely 'Lara the Brave' and 'Celebrating Brian Lara'.[51] Cowie-Hope proclaims Lara, 'A genius, a hero, a batting master', 'a super hero', 'a son of the soil' who would bat on if his people asked him and whose batting has already brought them to life. She notes the criticism that follows Lara – 'They accused him of indifference, lack of grit/No backbone, a man lacking leadership' – but condemns such claims as unfair on a man who is too often 'given/Out for all the wrong reasons'. Although she notes that it would have been historically crippling for West Indies to endure a 'white wash in 2004', she still rejects the importance of a series defeat against England in favour of Lara's achievement. However, after the 400* record Lara himself said: 'I don't think it's much to rant and rave about. It's a really nice, flat track. It was different last time. Then we were winning and you've got to look at this in the context of the series, which we've lost.'[52]

Lara's mature attempt at modesty and leadership comes to the fore here. His sense of reaching back and recognizing the gap between his own success and his team's position is clearly articulated. His sentiment was taken up by other commentators, including Fazeer Mohammed, who would consider Cowie-Hope as an example of the 'misguided celebrations' at Lara's 400*; celebrations that minimized the team's lack of coherence, solidity and consistency and obscured the more general predicament of cricket in the region. Mohammed does not wish to down-play Lara's achievement but insists that it is capitalized upon in a socially productive fashion which instead of the 'same old platitudes' really 'means a record of success or at least consistent improvements at senior national team level. It means a measurable growth in the number of people playing the game and the attendant increase in the number of clubs and team.'[53] His voice of genuine, critically engaged concern identifies the social value that must be made of cricketing success and collaboration, that the work of heroes such as Lara needs to be used as part of a wider socio-political uprising, part of the improvement of the masses and their communal enjoyment of the game. His sense that hollow praise, wasted money and political self-congratulation are hindering West Indies cricket and economic and political improvements for the region is a clear call to his community for them to build upon the legacy of their cricketing greats, for the traditions and talents of West Indies cricket to be united, especially now that Lara's departure has left them without a cricketing icon.

## Notes

[1]   Scovell, *Brian Lara: Cricket's Troubled Genius*.

[2]   Beckles' key writings on Lara are: *The Development of West Indies Cricket: Vol. 2*; 'The Strife of Brian' and 'Brian Lara'.

[3]   See Sobers, *Garry Sobers*, 276.

[4]   Lara, *Beating the Field*, 33–42.

[5]   The symbol * indicates that a batsman is not out.

[6]   For a discussion of this fall see, among others, Grigg, 'Calypso to Callapso'.

[7]   See Beckles, 'Brian Lara', 245.

[8]   Beckles writes of the three paradigms of West Indies cricket history. He argues that the nationalist sentiments of the first and second paradigms are now in retreat and being overriden by diverse and competing island-based socio-economic interests. See *The Development of West Indies Cricket: Vol. 1*, xviii. Beckles repeats the point about Lara being the 'first hero of a new paradigm' of globalization in 'Brian Lara', 253.

[9]   Hector, 'Lara in Cricket Time and Social Place'.

[10]   Eliot, 'Tradition and the Individual Talent', in *The Sacred Wood*, 42–53.

[11]   Eliot, 'The Possibility of a Poetic Drama', in *The Sacred Wood*, 55.

[12]   Said, *Culture and Imperialism*, 1–3.

[13]   James, *Beyond a Boundary*, 202.

[14]   Ibid., 131.

[15]   James, 'Garfield Sobers', 389.

[16]   Ibid., 379–80.

[17]   Surin, 'C.L.R. James' Materialist Aesthetic of Cricket', 318.

[18]   Sobers, *Garry Sobers*, 277.

[19]   Beckles, *The Development of West Indies Cricket: Vol. 2*, 145.

[20]   Ibid., 150.

[21]   Ibid., 146. Interestingly this information is not conveyed by either Sobers in *Garry Sobers* or Lara in *Beating the Field* but Beckles records his first hand conversations with both players to support his case.

[22]   Beckles, *The Development of West Indies Cricket: Vol. 2*, 146.

[23]   Ibid., 131.

[24]   James, *Beyond a Boundary*, 218.

[25]   See Brathwaite, *History of the Voice*, 13 and 30.

[26]   Breiner, 'Creole Language in the Poetry of Derek Walcott', 30.

[27]   See Breiner, 'Lyric and Autobiography in West Indian Literature'.

[28]   Brathwaite, *Barabajan Poems 1492–1992*, 204–5.

[29]   Hector, 'Lara in Cricket Time and Social Place'.

[30]   Beckles, *The Development of West Indies Cricket: Vol. 2*, 93.

[31]   Hector, 'Lara in Cricket Time and Social Place'.

[32]   Rohlehr, 'Music, Literature and West Indian Cricket Values'; Midgett, 'Cricket and Calypso'.

[33]   Brown and McDonald, *The Bowling was Superfine*.

[34]   See Christopher Martin-Jenkins, 'Scintillating Lara peaks at 400'. *The Times*, April 13, 2004, 70.

[35]   Breeze, 'Song for Lara', in *On the Edge of the Island*, 67–9.

[36]   Ramkisson-Chen, 'On Lara's 375', in *Ancestry*, 101.

[37]   Morgan, 'With a Tassa Blending'.

[38]   In *Beating the Field*, Lara claims that this was action was done 'quite instinctively', 100.

[39]   Fergus, *Lara Rains and Colonial Rites*, 9–11.

[40]   Although Lara himself has a young daughter, Sydney, from a relationship with former Trinidadian model Leseal Rovedas, he has never married and Brian Scovell puts this lack of a partner and the death of his father as the two chief factors shaping Lara's personal life. See, Scovell, *Brian Lara*, 21.

[41]   Hector in the *Outlet* cited in Searle, *Pitch of Life*, 44–5.

[42]   McDonald, 'Massa Day Done', in *Between Silence and Silence*, 87–8; Fergus, 'Conquest', in *Volcano Verses*, 59–60.
[43]   Gilroy, *The Black Atlantic*, 131.
[44]   Fergus, 'Lara Again', in *Volcano Verses*, 61. All citations are taken from these pages.
[45]   See Keens-Douglas, 'Tanti at de Oval', in *Tim Tim*, 26–32.
[46]   Keens-Douglas, 'Tanti Backin' Lara', in *Roll Call*, 33–6.
[47]   Markham, 'Conversations at Upton Park iii' and 'For Brian Lara', in *Misapprehensions*, 77 and 78 respectively.
[48]   Keens-Douglas, 'Lara Fans', in *Roll Call*, 8–9.
[49]   In the 'The Strife of Brian', 87, Beckles describes how, 'The cricket hero became a demi-god, a role model, invested with expectations that suggest iconic 'worship' and idealisation'.
[50]   Pires, 'Emperor of Trinidad', 215.
[51]   Eutrice Cowie-Hope, 'Lara the Brave'. *Trinidad Guardian*, April 26, 2004; and 'Celebrating Brian Lara'. *Trinidad Guardian*, April 28, 2004.
[52]   See, among numerous other sources, Christopher Martin-Jenkins, 'Scintillating Lara Peaks at 400'. *The Times*, April 13, 2004.
[53]   Fazeer Mohammed, 'Of misguided celebrations and misplaced priorities', November 30, 2005. http://content-www.cricinfo.com/ci/content/story/227748.html.

## References

Agard, John. 'Prospero Caliban Cricket'. In *'A Breathless Hush . . . ': The MCC Anthology of Cricket Verse*, edited by David Rayvern Allen with Hubert Doggart, 232–3. London: Methuen, 2004.

Beckles, Hilary McD. *The Development of West Indies Cricket: Vol. 1. The Age of Nationalism*. London: Pluto, 1998.

Beckles, Hilary McD. *The Development of West Indies Cricket: Vol. 2. The Age of Globalization*. London: Pluto, 1998.

Beckles, Hilary McD. 'The Strife of Brian'. In *The New Ball: Volume 2. Universal Stories*, edited by Rob Steen, 79–95. Edinburgh: Mainstream Publishing, 1999.

Beckles, Hilary McD. 'Brian Lara: (Con)testing the Caribbean Imagination'. In *Sport Stars: The Cultural Politics of Sporting Celebrity*, edited by David L. Andrews and Steven J. Jackson, 243–56. London: Routledge, 2001.

Brathwaite, Kamau. 'Rites'. In *The Arrivants: A New World Trilogy*, 197–203. Oxford: Oxford University Press, 1973.

Brathwaite, Kamau. *Barabajan Poems 1492–1992*. Kingston: Savacou North, 1994.

Brathwaite, Kamau. *History of the Voice: The Development of Nation Language in Anglophone Caribbean Poetry*. London: New Beacon, 1995.

Breiner, Laurence A. 'Lyric and Autobiography in West Indian Literature'. *Journal of West Indian Literature* 3, no. 1 (1989): 3–15.

Breiner, Laurence A. 'Creole Language in the Poetry of Derek Walcott'. *Callaloo* 28, no. 1 (2005): 29–41.

Breeze, Jean 'Binta'. *On the Edge of the Island*. Newcastle upon Tyne: Bloodaxe, 1997.

Brown, Stewart, and Ian, McDonald eds. *The Bowling was Superfine*. Leeds: Peepal Tree, 2008.

Eliot, T.S. *The Sacred Wood*. London: Methuen, 1920.

Fergus, Howard. *Lara Rains and Colonial Rites*. Leeds: Peepal, 1998.

Fergus, Howard. *Volcano Verses*. Leeds: Peepal Tree, 2003.

Frank, Kevin. 'Caught in the Slips: Boundaries of C.L.R. James' Imagination'. *Journal of Caribbean Studies* 15, no. 3 (2000): 223–44.

Gilroy, Paul. *The Black Atlantic: Modernity and Double Consciousness*. London: Verso, 2000.

Gray, Cecil. 'Sonny Ramadhin'. In *The Woolgatherer*, 105 Leeds: Peepal Tree, 1994.

Grigg, Gerald. 'Calypso to Callapso: The Decline of West Indies as a Cricketing Super Power'. *Journal of Sport and Social Issues* 30, no. 3 (2006): 306–14.

Hector, Tim. 'Lara in Cricket Time and Social Place.' *Fan the Flame*, April 9, 1999. Available online at www.candw.ag.

James, C.L.R. 'Garfield Sobers'. In *The C.L.R. James Reader*, edited by Anna Grimshaw, 379–89. Oxford: Blackwell, 1992.

James, C.LR. *Beyond a Boundary*. London: Serpents Tail, 2000.

Keens-Douglas, Paul. *Tim Tim: The Dialect Poetry of Paul Keens-Douglas*. Trinidad: Keensdee Productions, 1976.

Keens-Douglas, Paul. *Roll Call: Poetry and Short Stories by Paul Keens-Douglas*. Trinidad: Keensdee Productions, 1997.

Lara, Brian, with Brian Scovell. *Beating the Field: My Own Story*. London: Partridge, 1995.

Markham, E.A. *Misapprehensions*. London: Anvil, 1995.

McDonald, Ian. *Between Silence and Silence*. Leeds: Peepal Tree, 2003.

Midgett, Douglas. 'Cricket and Calypso: Cultural Representation and Social History in the West Indies'. *Sport in Society* 6, nos. 2 and 3 (2003): 239–68.

Morgan, Paula. 'With a Tassa Blending: Calypso and Cultural Identity in Indo-Caribbean Fiction'. *Anthurium: A Caribbean Studies Journal* 3, no. 2 (2005). http://anthurium.miami.edu/home.htm.

Persaud, Sasenarine. 'Call Him the Babu'. In *The Hungry Sailor*, 34–5. Toronto, ON: TSAR, 2000.

Pires, B.C. 'Emperor of Trinidad'. In *The Picador Book of Cricket*, edited by Ramachandra Guha, 215–6. Basingstoke: Picador, 2002.

Ramkisson-Chen, Ranjandaye. *Ancestry*. London: Hansib Caribbean, 1997.

Roach, Eric. 'To Learie'. *Trinidad Guardian*. January 19, 1939.

Rohlehr, Gordon. 'Music, Literature and West Indian Cricket Values'. In *An Area of Conquest: Popular Democracy and West Indies Cricket*, edited by Hilary Beckles, 55–102. London: Pluto, 1994.

Said, Edward. *Culture and Imperialism*. London: Vintage, 1994.

Scovell, Brian. *Brian Lara: Cricket's Troubled Genius*. Stroud: Stadia, 2007.

Searle, Chris. *Pitch of Life: Writings of Cricket*. Manchester: Parrs Wood, 2001.

Sobers, Garry, with Bob Harris. *Garry Sobers: My Autobiography*. London: Headline, 2002.

St John, Bruce. 'Cricket'. In *Bimbatuk 1*, 17–19. Barbados: Cedar, 1982.

Surin, Kenneth. 'C.L.R James' Materialist Aesthetic of Cricket'. In *Liberation Cricket: West Indies Cricket Culture*, edited by Hilary McD, Beckles and Brian Stoddart, 313–41. Manchester: Manchester University Press, 1995.

# Wunderkidz in a Blunderland: tensions and tales from Sri Lankan cricket**

Michael Roberts*

*Department of Anthropology, University of Adelaide, Australia*

*Wunderkidz* in Blunderland: The two metaphors in juxtaposition place the achievements of the Sri Lankan cricketers, *wunderkidz* in qualified measure, within the encompassing context of a blundering polity. The achievements can be a marked by reference to cricketing records: Sri Lankan teams have produced the highest Test total, the two biggest Test partnerships, the Bradman among Test match bowlers (according to Neville Turner's evaluation – two years ago – because of Muthiah Muralitharan's achievement of taking 5 wickets 57 times),[1] and most notably the manner in which Arjuna Ranatunga's team swept to victory at the 1996 World Cup. But more significant than such episodes is the fact that Sri Lanka has been in the throes of an ethnic civil war from 1983 to the present, besides going through a nativist-Leftist insurgency in the southern areas which amounted to a civil war among the Sinhalese during the period 1987–90. This meant that the cricketers lost home country advantage from mid-1987 to 1992; while on at least two occasions foreign tours have been aborted because of major bomb attacks in Colombo effected by the Tamil militants who had the advantages afforded by a considerable Tamil population in the metropolitan environs (perhaps as much as 24% of its population) with substantial segments sympathetic to their cause.

This turbulent context has been compounded by Sri Lanka's system of cricket governance. A board elected annually by the cricketing clubs was set up in 1948. This scheme did not matter too much in the era when cricket bosses sometimes had to dip into their own pockets to help the cricket board's parlous finances. But once the coffers expanded exponentially after 1996, entrepreneurs were attracted to the post of President, Board of Control for Cricket in Sri Lanka (now known as Sri Lanka Cricket or SLC) and have been able to manipulate the elections through a spoils system that set up oligarchic regimes. On top of that the government has stepped in on two occasions to insert gentlemen of its own choice in Interim Committees. The overall outcome has been a game of musical chairs in governance, sometimes aggravated by ministerial whim or changes in the country's government after elections.[2] Changes in cricketing board, of course, mean changes in Selection Committee and its policies. It is therefore a marvel that the cricket team has been competitive in the field during the years 1996–2005, especially when playing at home and, since 2006, even abroad.

However, this does not mean that the previous era was a gentlemen's paradise. It had its share of conspiracies and tensions in the six decades since 1948.[3] A detailed history, episode by episode, is not attempted here. What is presented is a selective outline of some significant strands without any claim to comprehensive coverage. To begin with I highlight nine themes – some intertwined and overlapping with each other. These are not taken up in temporal sequence, but straddle the period 1948–2007 in a logical order deriving from an arbitrary starting point that is an overview anchored in 2005/07.

## I

From the 1960s there has been a process that has progressively reduced the dominance that had been exercised previously at the top-level of cricket by largely English-speaking elites centred within Colombo, a development involving the penetration of these ranks by players from elite Sinhala-speaking schools in Colombo and lesser-known schools along the western seaboard. From the 1970s – and the 1990s in particular – there has been a further broadening to encompass a wide variety of schools in the south western quadrant which has Kandy and Kurunägala at its north eastern edges.

## II

Despite the game's spread, partly for reasons of distance, the schools in the south eastern, eastern, north central and northern areas have still in 2007 to produce a noticeable number of top players. For the Tamil-speaking eastern littoral and the Northern Province, of course, the outbreak of war from 1983 meant that cricket was of declining interest and mostly impossible. When C.E. Anandarajah, Principal of St John's, organized a cricket match between the army and his school he was assassinated by the Liberation Tigers of Tamil Eelam (LTTE) on 25 June 1985 for collaboration with the 'occupying army'. The sentiments on this issue among Sri Lanka Tamils since then have been ambivalent and it is difficult for an outsider to provide a definitive viewpoint on the cricketing loyalties of SL Tamils in Lanka and abroad.[4]

Among the Tamil diaspora staunch Eelamist and/or Tiger supporters seem to side with whoever Sri Lanka's cricket team is playing against – that is, if they do bother with such a frivolous pastime as cricket. Some have also used the world stage of cricket matches to advertise their liberation objectives; indeed, one Canadian Tamil even ran on to the hallowed grounds of St George's in the Caribbean during Sri Lanka's Super Eight World Cup game against the Australians, brandishing the colourful (or 'virulent' according to political persuasion) flag of the Liberation Tigers of Tamil Eelam.

However, various websites indicate a committed line of support for Sri Lanka's cricket team from a sprinkling of Tamils. Again, cricket has been a fervent national pastime for many decades so it is not surprising that migrants have launched their own teams when assembled in sufficient numbers in cities abroad. London has been one such site. The Festival of Cricket, a series of competitive one-day matches played over one summer weekend or one day, was launched in 1989 by Sri Lankans of all shades. Teams of old boys from specific schools competed for a trophy. Remarkably, in contrast to the old 'Ceylon' scene of the period 1948–70s, some of the best alumni teams at this festive competition proved to be from the colleges of the Jaffna Peninsula, whether Hartley, St Johns, Jaffna Hindu or St Patricks. But the more remarkable fact is that even during the height of Eelam War II (1990–95) Sinhalese and SL Tamil migrants were playing friendly cricket matches against each other in London. In effect, there were some keen Tiger supporters who were ready to modify their enmity in qualified ways on the cricket pitch.

But that situation quickly changed for the worse. When, in late-1995, the army broke out of its beachhead in the extreme north and took control of the western half of the Jaffna Peninsula, inclusive of the symbolic centre, Jaffna town, and proceeded, among other acts, to bulldoze the LTTE war cemeteries (*thuyilam illam* or 'resting places'), even these Tamil migrants had enough. Their heartland was no more under their own control and their hearts were sore. These cricketing Tamils broke away and now run their own cricket festival.

Within Sri Lanka there is evidence that the Tamils who watch cricket lean in different directions, with a fair proportion partial to Sri Lanka – except perhaps when the opponent is India.[5] Speculatively, this measure of loyalty can be attributed to several factors: (a) the dominance of white sides in the cricket world and the influence of colour considerations; (b) Sri Lanka's triumph at the World Cup in 1996; (c) vestigial twinges of Sri Lankan-ness among those still residing in the land; (d) the presence from the 1990s of Muralitharan, a Tamil from a plantation worker-foreman lineage, as a star performer in the team; and (e) the general awareness that there has been no manifest ethnic prejudice in team selections.[6]

The issue is not that simple however. Since the late 1970s few Tamils living in the cricketing heartland of south western Sri Lanka and Colombo have been playing for their school teams and thus, *ipso facto*, for the clubs. From the 1970s, in the context of escalating ethnic tension and two pogroms in Colombo in 1977 and 1983, there existed a situation where Tamil boys in these cities were usually discouraged by their parents from playing much sport. They were pushed into studying with an eye on migration out of the country. Thus the Tamil Union C&AC has had only 14 Tamil cricketers in its team between 1979 and 2007 though the administrators are still mostly Tamils of yesteryear. Other than Damien Nadarājah, Muttiah Muralitharan, Russel Arnold and Pradeep Jayaprakāshdaran, in fact, there have been no Tamils pushing for places in the top sides since 1990. Thus, one sees a stark contrast with the context of the 1940s to 1970s when several Tamil cricketers competed vigorously for spots in the best Sri Lankan teams and provided a number of distinguished cricketers, among them the prodigy, Mahādēva Sathāsivam.[7]

## III

In the period stretching from the 1940s to the early 1970s, the SL Tamils were both Tamil and Ceylonese. Many Tamils from the north and a handful from the east had migrated and settled down in the south western quarter, especially in Colombo, though some retained their local roots. Educated in the best schools and entering the more esteemed professions or government service, many of these 'Colombo Tamils' were an integral part of the Ceylonese bourgeoisie and middle class. Their cricketing men emerged from the best regarded schools of Colombo to compete at the highest level. Coomāraswamy, Sathāsivam, Nāgendra, Schāffter, Kasipillai, Dēvarāja, Edward, Chanmugam, Ponniah, Pathmanāthan, the honour roll is long. Every one of these Ceylon players had been nourished in the south. The only Jaffna schoolboy to break into the ranks of the Ceylon side was C. Bālakrishnan, who entered the Medical Faculty in the 1960s and made his mark in the ranks of what was then a powerful University of Ceylon side.

The regional imbalance in source of origin did not sway loyalties. Despite their considerable cultural links with the Tamils of South India, when Sri Lanka and the Madras Cricket Association launched an annual series in 1953 between Madras and Ceylon for the Gopalan Trophy, most cricket-oriented Tamils in Sri Lanka were firmly behind the Ceylon side. This tide of support did not begin to ebb till the late 1970s and notably surged away after the anti-Tamil pogrom of July 1983.[8]

## IV

The influential SL Tamil seam in the tapestry of Sri Lankan cricket in the era 1948–70s had been launched much earlier:[9] it was marked, for example, by the sponsorship of cricket in the 1900s and 1910s by the wealthy entrepreneur, Dr John Rockwood, and by the prowess and influence of the Saravanamuttu family, a lineage that not only produced several great cricketers, but used its social clout and its position in municipal politics to further the cause of cricket. Most notably, the Saravanamuttus were key figures in engineering the construction by the early 1940s of a magnificent cricket ground in the slum quarter of Wanāthamulla in Maradāna, the 'Colombo Oval' as it was called (since renamed the Saravanamuttu Stadium), as the home of the Tamil Union. This ground hosted Bradman's Invincibles in 1948 and other matches with visiting international sides.[10] It was, quite appropriately, Sri Lanka's first Test venue.

However, Sri Lanka's entry to Test status was premised on the creation of other Test venues. The person who was a key figure in securing the island's entry to the highest level, Gamini Dissanāyake (President of the Board of Control for Cricket in Sri Lanka [BCCSL] and a powerful minister in the government of the time), was also the Minister heading the Mahaweli Development Board. He chose the small grounds of his Alma Mater, Trinity College in Kandy, as the next Test venue by twisting the arms of a British construction company, Balfour Beatty, who were party to his major development activities along the Mahaweli River. This 'creative act' was in place by 1983 for Australia's first tour of Sri Lanka under Greg Chappell.[11] Dissanāyake also chose the Sinhalese Sports Club (SSC) ground in Colombo as the site for the BCCSL office headquarters and proceeded to upgrade that ground to Test status. Though directed by necessity there may have been an ethnic tinge as well as personal interest in the latter choice.

The next venue to receive this esteemed position of Test-level ground was a product of supreme power, class-conflict and highly personal interest. Competing with Dissanāyake (who was from an elite Kandy family) in the implicit presidential succession stakes within the ruling United National Party was one Ranasinghe Premadāsa, the Prime Minister, a man who had emerged from the slum quarter of Khettārama in the north of Colombo and had no genteel club connections. By the 1980s cricket was a field that drew popular fame and Dissanāyake was ploughing this terrain. Premadāsa had drive and was successfully furrowing several heart-winning fields of his own; but he decided to add another battery to his belt. He organized the construction of Sri Lanka's first floodlit cricket stadium – in the heart of Khettārama, a symbolic shot directed across the bows of the superior Cinnamon Gardens quarter where the SSC and other *pukka* clubs are located.

The first stage of building a stadium suited for day games was undertaken in the mid-1980s. The momentous creation of floodlights in the late 1980s was part of a construction plan devised on the lines of the Western Australian Cricket Association (WACA) ground and Michael Joachim, a former cricketer[12] and engineer in the Municipal Council, played a key hand in its planning. The ground was ready for day/night matches by 1991 and is now known as the Premadāsa Stadium.[13] Whatever Premadāsa's motives, this was a far-seeing move: in one bold stroke he pushed local cricket into the twenty-first century and enabled the governors of cricket to host day-night games at an early stage.

## V

In the period extending from the 1940s to the 1960s both at the administrative level and within the best Ceylon XIs the Royal-Thomian set dominated the scene in association with cricketers from such Christian denominational schools as Wesley, St Peter's, St Joseph's and St Benedict's in Colombo or Trinity and St Anthony's in Kandy. This was in part due to better facilities (e.g. turf wickets in some cases), but largely due to what can be called 'cricketing capital', namely, a lineage of good coaching sustained by the transmission of good practice from one cohort of boys to those cohorts behind them. The significance of the latter is seen in the tale of S. Thomas College. S. Thomas had a golden asset in the form of Lassie Abeywardena, their Under 16 coach from the late 1940s to the 1970s.[14] From Ian Pieris and Dan Piachaud, the Oxbridge players of the late 1950s,[15] to an outstanding crop of cricketers who adorned the Lankan stage in the period 1958 to the 1970s, S. Thomas marked its cricketing heritage with flair and technique. Of the XI that beat a virtual Pakistan Test team at the Colombo on 28–30 August 1964, six were Thomians: T.C.T. Edward, Mano Ponniah, Buddy Reid, Michael Tissera, Ian Pieris and Neil Chanmugan. Five months later a Ceylon team captained by Tissera and including Ponniah and Chanmugam as well as Darrell Lieversz of Royal went one step further and beat India in an 'Unofficial Test' away from home – at Ahmedabad in early January 1965.[16]

## VI

This Royal-Thomian predominance aroused jealousy. Such motives were exacerbated (a) by the populist and nativist electoral 'revolution' in 1956 that witnessed an attack on the Westernized elites and the English language and (b) by the pre-existing social context involving a 'class divide' – as long as 'class' is read as status of a stratified sort within that amorphous folk category known as the 'middle class'.[17] In a context where fluency in English and a particular lifestyle marked differences at the top level of society, the resurgent Sinhala-speaking elements of the middle class resented the advantages accruing to the Westernized mob and the supreme confidence of their demeanour.[18]

Among the leading ideologues who inspired the political overturn of 1956 were products of Ānanda and Nālanda Colleges in Colombo and other Buddhist denominational schools in the main outstation towns. The political thrusts of 1956 included socialist strands and, ironically, soon led in the 1960s to the take-over of not only most Christian denominational schools, but also all the Buddhist schools. However, the divide in orientation between the allegedly indigenist and the supposedly 'alien Western-cum-Christian' schools remained of some consequence for quite a while after that. The products of Ānanda, Nālanda and such Buddhist schools were usually pro-Buddhist interest and Sinhala nativist in orientation – quite staunchly so. But their younger generations also played cricket with passion. By the late 1950s and the 1960s they were producing excellent cricketers (e.g. Stanley Jayasinghe, Danasiri Weerasinghe, T.B. Kehelgamuwa, Sonny Yatawara, D.H. and D.P. de Silva).[19]

Despite this budding development, cricket was not the flavour of the month in political circles dominated by socialist rhetoric and nativist complexes. An amazing contrast with the present-day can be highlighted. From the late 1950s it was the kiss of death for a political party to support cricket. When the right wing United National Party (UNP) came to power in 1965 under Dudley Senanāyake, a man who had played cricket from S. Thomas in the 1920s, his brother Robert, another ex-Thomian cricketer, was more or less permanent (annually re-elected) President of the BCCSL.[20] It was precisely the moment when Sri Lanka was at the threshold of some recognition from the MCC and ICC. The performances of Goonasena, Piachaud, Jayasinghe, Inman and Co in England, and the Ceylon team's victories over Pakistan and India in 1964/65 encouraged the ICC to admit Ceylon as an Associate Member in 1965.

As critically, the MCC invited Sri Lanka to send a touring team to play the counties in 1968. The financing of such a trip, however, was Sri Lanka's responsibility. This was as much a hurdle as the invitation was a breakthrough. Amazing though it may seem today, Robert Senanāyake could not ask his brother to commit state funds in aid of the enterprise. This was in part due to the country's abject financial circumstances and its shortage of foreign exchange, but it was also because of profound hostility to the Westernized elites and their accoutrements (including cricket) arising from the 1956 political revolution. The most virulent opposition came from the Leftist parties and those left of centre within the Sri Lanka Freedom Party, so the antipathy was as much Marxist as indigenist. The UNP dared not touch cricket with either bargepole or bamboo rod. Thus it was left to interests in the tea trade, including an Englishman, Dusty Miller, to step forward and commit money for the project.

This enterprise then fell apart as the cricketers themselves, that is, a conspiratorial few, shot themselves in the foot. A threesome involving a Wesleyite (Abu Fuard), an Anandian (Danasiri Weerasinghe, who was also a Selector) and a Peterite (H.I.K. Fernando), conspired to depose Michael Tissera from the captaincy and to select a touring squad that was captained by Fernando and included both Weerasinghe and Fuard. When this 'shit hit the fan', as the saying goes, the tour collapsed because sponsors withdrew their promises. Personal ambitions and status jealousies, of course, were behind this ill-advised move. Sri Lanka's rise to the world stage was set back ten years.[21]

## VII

In the meanwhile, the inexorable momentum arising from (a) the burgeoning growth in the number of secondary schools that had begun from the 1940s, (b) the switch-over from the English medium to the vernacular languages in teaching that began around 1951 and (c) the adoption of Sinhala as the principal language of administration, wrought its effects on the context impinging upon cricket. In the late 1960s Neville Jayaweera of the Sri Lanka Broadcasting Corporation, a Thomian no less, took a momentous step by organizing radio broadcasts of the big match between Ānanda and Nālanda. A whole new vocabulary had to be invented for the purpose.[22] This innovative act then promoted the popularization, and the political acceptability, of the game over the next decades.

The second step in this process of popularization was the entry of Sri Lanka into the ICC fold of superior cricket in 1981 at a time when colour TV was introduced into the island – in one step – unlike India where the first stage of television was in black and white. Cricket was the only international sport where Sri Lanka was competing regularly at the top. So sports nationalism focused on cricket, really took off and spread beyond the cities. The final stage of this democratization occurred when the cricket team won the World Cup in 1996: as a result grass roots interest expanded exponentially both in terms of numbers interested and in geographical reach.[23]

## VIII

In the meantime the increase in the number of schools at a time when the opportunity structure within the game was also opening out meant that lads/men from lesser known schools within striking range of Colombo begun to press forward and gain entry to the top XIs. From the 1960s players from the established schools had to 'share space' with those from the two Christian denominational schools in Moratuwa (Prince of Wales and St Sebastian's) that had become government colleges in the 1960s on the one hand and those from the former Buddhist denominational schools Ānanda and Nālanda in Colombo, Dharmarāja in Kandy and Mahinda in Galle. By 1975 and 1979 when Sri Lanka won the ICC Trophy for Tier II countries that was played in England, the squads were a real mix.[24] Anandians and Nālandians were at the cutting edge of this transformation and Bandula Warnapura's accession to captaincy in 1980–81 (succeeding the Thomian, Anura Tennekoon) marked the transformation neatly.[25] The further broadening and democratization was then indicated when Sanath Jayasuriya, a fisherman's son from St Servatius' College further south in Matara, was made captain in 1999.[26]

## IX

As indicated at the outset of this essay, there are still shortcomings in the reach of cricket, partly from the logistics of distance and partly due to the Tamil separatist movement and its war. Moreover, the nature of the political economy and the overwhelming dominance of the greater Colombo area in the island's scheme of things result in the best teams accumulating in Colombo so that the best players from the outstations gravitate into these folds and even build their millionaire mansions within the capital's environs. More lads from the outstations are certainly figuring prominently in the Premier League and in the U-23 and U-19 squads and younger levels, but a sizeable proportion of each squad comes from the schools in Greater Colombo (now including Moratuwa in my adjusted reasoning). Not only does the remedy for this imbalance lie beyond the field of cricket governance, it is a major problem for socio-economic engineers.

### 2005–06 and beyond

The thematic threads in post-independence cricket and its politics can now be capped by a review of developments in the cricket world in the three years 2005–07, commencing with some significant administrative acts.

With the emergence of a new government in Sri Lanka early in 2005 headed by Mahinda Rājapakse yet another change was brought about in the governance of cricket. The cricket body headed by Mohān de Silva, widely regarded as a proxy for the ambitious wheeler-dealer, Thilanga Sumathipāla, was displaced by a body headed by another businessman, Jayantha Dharmadāsa. Sumathipāla had not only fallen foul of the ICC, but had associated himself with the wrong political horse locally, while also having his name besmirched because he was facing serious criminal charges to do with false passports for aides.

Dharmadāsa's team included representatives associated with the Tamil Union which had been subject to Cinderella-treatment by the boards associated with Sumathipāla.[27] The new board included Prakāsh Schäffter and Tryphon Mirando of the Tamil Union with Mirando, an experienced cricket administrator who had served on previous boards, in the important position of Secretary. His premature death in late 2005 has been met by the arrival into board affairs of K. Mathivanan, who quickly became Secretary. A Tamil businessman with a successful company of his own, Mathivanan had recently rejuvenated the Colts CC and made it his 'franchise'. He now inserted these energies into the management of SLC and has been responsible for an ambitious programme to upgrade the cricket pitches in the direction of greater speed and bounce. It is too early to weigh the results of this attempt.

The Dharmadāsa regime also initiated a long-overdue overhaul in the structure of Sri Lanka cricket. For decades it had been widely noted that the top level of the local cricket competition (now called the Premier League) was overblown. There were too many teams and several were weak in resources so that unequal encounters ensued. However, the annual system of elections and its concomitant spoils system had prevented any reforms. Assured of stability and political backing, the Dharmadāsa team has been able to prune the competition in stages so that a two-tier system, with a relegation and promotion scheme, will be in place by the season 2007/08. Whether this sharpens the standard of local cricket remains to be seen.

The Dharmadāsa regime has also secured firm control of Rangiri Stadium (located near Dambulla) for SLC, another momentous step. This stadium was the brainchild of Sumathipāla[28] and was constructed from scratch in record time in 2000/01 for what was then an enormous figure, reported to be 611 million rupees. Dambulla is located in the dry zone and the *raison d'être* of this venture arose from the fact that most international teams find the period May-to-September to be the most convenient window for tours of the island – precisely when the unpredictable monsoon rains can ruin outdoor activities. Sumathipāla's act was a brilliant move, despite its undue haste and the questionable tendering and accounting process.[29]

But the project was also built on sand. SLC did not gain control of the land, which remained in the hands of Inamaluwa Sri Sumangala *Thero*, the incumbent *bhikkhu* (Buddhist priest) at Dambulla Vihāra, another wheeler-dealer and a man of influence. In a strange arrangement the site was leased to a trust in Sumathipāla's personal control. The lease was not for 99 years, but seems to have been an annual one. In effect the site was in the pocket of Sumathipāla and the *Thero*. This context created immense difficulties for the Dharmadāsa Board in mid-2006 when the triangular ODI series involving India and South Africa was rained off. In prolonged and delicate negotiations in 2007 however, with Prakāsh Schäffter at the coalface, SLC persuaded Inamaluwa Sri Sumangala *Thero* to release his hand on the site.[30]

Behind these recent administrative achievements is the relative stability of the Dharmadāsa Board. Behind this in turn is Hambantota District in the extreme south eastern corner of the island. Hambantota has no cricketing schools of distinction and is a poor relative in the cricketing scheme of things. But it has been the political base of the Rājapakse family for several generations, even though the Rājapakse males were educated at prestigious denominational schools such as Richmond of Galle and St Thomas of Mount Lavinia. After Mahinda Rājapakse was elected President of Sri Lanka in late 2004 the Province has shot to the fore. There are ambitious plans to develop a modern airport and a whole new harbour in the region. These schemes may bring about a welcome balance in the long term to the hegemonic weight of Colombo District within the island's political economy.

In the short-term and within the cricketing scene, however, Hambantota has been significant in the manner in which it has encouraged strong business and personal links between the new ruling clique, the four Rājapakse brothers on the one hand and, on the other, (a) the Dharmadāsa family who hail from neighbouring Matara District and have several enterprises in Hambantota, and (b) the former Test cricketer and businessman,

Ashantha de Mel, who has garment factories in Hambantota.[31] De Mel was made Chairman of Selectors in early 2005 (in addition to a leading position in the Ceylon Petroleum Corporation), while the Dharmadāsa team was inserted as an interim Committee after Rājapakse came to power. Grapevine gossip indicates that the personal intervention of Mahinda Rājapakse himself, with all its attendant delays, was one facet within the re-negotiation of the tenurial arrangements for Rangiri Stadium. A powerful saffron robe, it seems, requires a prod from a powerful crown.

In the meantime the SL cricketers have performed excellently at the international level, not only in the results secured, but in their brand of cricket and their demeanour on and off the field.[32] An important springboard for this progress has been the several A Team tours organized by the previous board and the innovative step of having the A Team participate in the Indian provincial tournament for the Duleep Trophy in 2006. The emergence of Chāmara Silva and Mālinda Warnapura to the front ranks was made possible by these steps, and it is now known that Tom Moody insisted on Silva being given an opportunity after a chance moment led him to witness Silva in action at the SSC grounds.[33]

It is the selection of Moody as coach by the Dharmadāsa board that has had the most far-reaching and practical impact on the cricketing performance of the Test and ODI squads. Unlike previous coaches Moody – at his insistence in the pattern he was familiar with at Worcestershire – had overall command of the coaching structure and links with the tiers below the leading squad of players. Here, the clustering of cricket in Colombo worked to advantage and enabled good communication with the other coaches.

Moody noticed that an inordinate number of players, some 80 or so, had been selected for the top teams during the recent past and about 49 had actually played. He suggested greater continuity and a less ad-hoc approach. He also pressed the idea of continuity and simplicity as a maxim in the selection of the top squads. Ashantha de Mel appears to have listened. In the result there have been fewer knee-jerk reactions than in the past.[34]

Mahela Jayawardene has recently evaluated Moody's influence thus:

> Tom challenged every individual. You could not stay in the same place. Every training session, every team talk mattered. We all learned, not just the youngsters but the senior guys too. He certainly didn't allow me to coast and helped me become a better and more consistent player. He pushed us all out of our comfort zones and in the process made us much tougher mentally as individuals and as a team.[35]

Add to this the assessment presented by the well-placed Charlie Austin:

> Moody's success was achieved through the introduction of a new performance-based culture that encouraged self-improvement. He was organised and clear with his communication, insightful in his thinking and able to motivate the team. And there was one characteristic that will be particularly hard to replace: his willingness to stand up to senior players when they stepped out of line. The senior hierarchy are not troublemakers, but their high profile makes them powerful and, like all players, they sometimes need to be confronted. His management of Sanath Jayasuriya, Muttiah Muralitharan and Chaminda Vaas was exceptional. There were no screaming tantrums or chair-throwing theatrics, he was strong in his own careful, methodical, rational manner.[36]

The contrast with tales around the Indian cricket squads during the same period render this picture all the more striking (see Wagg and Ugra's contribution to this collection).

Thus, this policy crystallized in a team that has gelled well and enjoyed considerable success during the years 2006–7. Not only did the ODI squads of early 2005 fare reasonably well in the Antipodes,[37] but Sri Lanka matched England in the Tests in England and then simply whitewashed the English side in the subsequent ODI series during the summer of 2006. They went on to perform well in both versions of the game in New Zealand in the summer of 2006/07 after an erratic Champions Trophy. Many observers predicted that they would make the finals of the World Cup. The squad lived up to this expectation. Contingent circumstances unfortunately intervened in favour of the Australians and prevented an ultimate triumph. Despite a powerful Aussie batting performance after the advantageous winning of the toss, Sri Lanka was within striking distance when heavy drizzle skewed the balance of the match away from them.

Assisting this success has been the arrival of Lasith Malinga as a frontline strike bowler and the rejuvenation of Dilhāra Fernando as a dangerous paceman. The contingent factor of an injury to Marvan Atapattu also saw Mahela Jayawardene take over as captain in late 2006 and Sangakkāra become vice-captain. The two are bosom pals and intelligent, articulate cricketers who work well in tandem. As Tissera noted in a recent interview, Jayawardene is also 'highly organised' – a measured comment that is, in fact, high praise from the manager of the team (mid-2005 to May 2007).[38] A more distant observer, Schoorman, presses this argument even further:

> Jayawardena's [*sic*] captaincy has been a revelation. He has brought a refreshing approach to our entire game, with … inspired changes and is constantly thinking on his feet. His handling … of the superstars has been admirable and he has got the whole team together once again.[39]

In sum, therefore, Sri Lanka's cricketers have recently secured success abroad on a scale that was not achieved before. Central to this process has been the practical hand of Moody, not only in man-management, but also in building on the policy of the previous coach, John Dyson, and gradually nourishing a capacity for players to cope with differing match scenarios. As he told me when I asked him about the language problem of communicating with some players who knew little English, he encouraged them to speak in any language at team meetings and gave them time to ponder over specific scenario questions and come back the next day and tell the squad (and Moody) – in any language of choice—what they would do in that specific scenario.[40] Over time this practice has not only developed self-confidence, but also enabled the players to become familiar with each other's thinking.

With the support of the SLC board Moody also spent liberally on importing Sandy Gordon for spells of psychological motivation.[41] Trevor Penney, an evangelist in the art of fielding, was hired as assistant coach and he has sharpened the fielding skills from its pre-existing levels of 'competent' to that of 'excellent'.

Set against this success story it is significant that when SLC was on the hunt for a new coach in early 2005, India was also on the look-out for one. The two leading contenders then were Greg Chappell and Tom Moody. SLC could not match India's cheque book and waited on the Indian outcome. But it can now be revealed that even had both contenders been available, the Dharmadāsa board and its advisors would have chosen Moody rather than Chappell – probably because they preferred a hands-on approach to high theory and perhaps because of a word from Chaminda Vaas derived from his Worcestershire stint under Moody.[42] Whatever the reasoning, our retrospective advantage indicates sagacity of thought.

## Notes

[1] Turner, 'A Temporary Fracture or a Permanent Breach?' In December 2007, Murali became the highest wicket taker in Test cricket overtaking Shane Warne's record of 708 test wickets.

[2] Roberts, *Forces and Strands in Sri Lanka's Cricket History*, 1–3; Roberts, *Essaying Cricket*, 126–30.

[3] Right at the outset Sathāsivam was made captain of the Ceylon team selected to play the whistle-stop game against Bradman's Australian team in March 1948 when Derek de Saram, who was senior to him and a good batsman and experienced skipper, was the logical choice.

To outsiders it looked as if the Tamil Union trumped the Sinhalese Sports Club, though personal ambitions probably counted for more (Roberts, *Forces and Strands in Sri Lanka's Cricket History*, 20–1).

[4]   For some information, including an assessment conveyed by Nirupama Subramanium, a journalist from *The Hindu*, see Roberts, *Forces and Strands in Sri Lanka's Cricket History*, 7 and Roberts, 'Landmarks and Threads in the Cricketing Universe of Sri Lanka', 125–6.

[5]   Roberts, *Forces and Strands in Sri Lanka's Cricket History*, 7.

[6]   Indeed, the Sri Lankan squads have been the most multi-ethnic and multi-religious international team for some time. The 15 players at the World Cup included 2 Tamils (Arnold and Muralitharan), 1 Moor (Maharoof), 1 Malay-Sinhalese (Dilshan), 1 Sinhalese-Burgher (Atapattu) and 9 Sinhalese on the ethnic front; while on the religious side there were 2 Catholics (Vaas and Fernando), 8 Buddhists, 1 Protestant (Arnold), 1 Muslim and 1 Hindu. When one adds fringe players such as Ian Daniel (Colombo Chetty) and Michael Vandort (Burgher), the spread is even wider.

[7]   Re: Sathāsivam, see Roberts, *Essaying Cricket*, 173–8 and plates 8 and 38.

[8]   For fuller information on the issues in this section, see Roberts, *Forces and Strands in Sri Lanka's Cricket History*, 5–7 and 'Landmarks and Threads in the Cricketing Universe of Sri Lanka', 125–6.

[9]   For historical information on cricket in Sri Lanka during the colonial era, see Foenander, *Sixty Years of Ceylon Cricket*, Perera, *The Janashakthi Book of Cricket, 1832–1996*, and Roberts, *Forces and Strands in Sri Lanka's Cricket History*, 8–17.

[10]   The match against Bradman's team is described by Jack Fingleton in Roberts, *Crosscurrents*, while several pictures taken at this ground appear in that book and in Roberts, *Essaying Cricket*, plates 9, 10, 11 and 134.

[11]   See the pictures in Roberts, *Essaying Cricket*, plates 46 and 82. Also see plate 45 for Dissanāyake's triumphant return to Sri Lanka in July 1981.

[12]   We were colleagues in the University of Ceylon B team in the late 1950s.

[13]   See the striking picture taken by David Colin-Thomē in Roberts, *Essaying Cricket*, plate 153.

[14]   Roberts, *Forces and Strands in Sri Lanka's Cricket History*, 25–7.

[15]   Another Ceylonese who played for Cambridge (and Nottinghamshire too) was Gamini Goonasena of Royal College, who went on to captain the Light Blues and made outstanding contributions in English county cricket as well as MCC tours (see Roberts, *Essaying Cricket*, plate 17–20). The individual achievements of these three men, and subsequently of Jayasinghe and Inman, undoubtedly assisted Sri Lanka's cause in MCC, and thus ICC, circles.

[16]   See Roberts, *Essaying Cricket*, plate 44.

[17]   Roberts, 'The Political Antecedents of the Revivalist Elite within the MEP Coalition of 1956'.

[18]   On the 1956 political revolution by ballot and its far-reaching ramifications, see Mervyn de Silva, '1956: the Cultural Revolution that Shook the Left'. *Ceylon Observer Magazine Edition*, May 16, 1967; Peiris, *1956 and After*; Wriggins, *Ceylon. Dilemmas of a New Nation*; Kearney, *Communalism and Language in the Politics of Ceylon*; K.M. de Silva, *Managing Ethnic Tensions*, 1986; Roberts, 'The Political Antecedents of the Revivalist Elite within the MEP Coalition of 1956'; Roberts, 'The 1956 Generations: Before and After'; Roberts, 'Landmarks and Threads in the Cricketing Universe of Sri Lanka', 126–8.

[19]   D.P. de Silva, Weerasinghe and Jayasinghe can be seen in the group pictures from the Indian tour of 1964/65 in Roberts, *Essaying Cricket*, plates 44 and 21. For Kehelgamuwa, see plate 27. The de Silvas, namely, D.H., D.P. and D.S. de Silva, all from Mahinda College in Galle, provide a rare case of three brothers who played for their country.

[20]   Both Dudley and Robert Senanāyake are in the group picture of the St. Thomas College team that played against St Peters' College of Adelaide in Colombo on 26 March 1928 (Roberts, *Essaying Cricket*, plate 2).

[21]   For fuller information on this unseemly episode, see Perera, *The Janashakthi Book of Cricket, 1832–1996*, 320–6, and Roberts, *Forces and Strands in Sri Lanka's Cricket History*, 23–5 and Roberts, 'Landmarks and Threads in the Cricketing Universe of Sri Lanka', 129.

[22]   Roberts, 'Landmarks and Threads in the Cricketing Universe of Sri Lanka', 131.

[23]   Roberts, *Forces and Strands in Sri Lanka's Cricket History*, 17–20.

[24]   For the squads sent to England in 1975 and 1979 for the ICC Trophy and the World Cup, see Roberts, *Essaying Cricket*, plates 35–7.

[25] Warnapura is seated beside Gamini Dissanayake (President, BCCSL) and J.R. Jayewardene (President of Sri Lanka) in a photograph that was probably taken at the Colombo Oval prior to Sri Lanka's first ever Test Match, that against an England team led by Fletcher in 1982. Roberts, *Essaying Cricket*, plate 79.

[26] Third Eye, 'Sanath Jayasuriya: A Class Act'.

[27] For one, the Saravanamuttu Stadium was not accorded Test matches. For another, when Chandra Schäffter was Manager of the touring SL squad in England in early summer 2002 (appointed by the Interim Board), he was unceremoniously dumped at the end of this trip and subjected to character assassination by members of a new board headed by Hemaka Amarasuriya, a board that was in league with Sumathipāla interests and that in fact paved the way for the latter's return to power at SLC via the electoral process in mid-2003.

[28] Re: Sumathipāla, see articles by Charlie Austin and Michael Roberts in *Essaying Cricket*, 120–2 and plates 61 and 62.

[29] Roberts, 'Rangiri Stadium and Its Tempestuous History'.

[30] Ibid.

[31] De Mel was a bowling all-rounder who played for Sri Lanka in the 1980s and was in fact the highest wicket-taker at the 1987 World Cup. He is also a double international because he has represented Sri Lanka at bridge. In the 1980s he was a bosom friend of Sidath Wettimuny who was both club-mate at the SSC and a member of the SL team. De Mel and Tissera were also appointed to the Interim Board headed by Rienzie Wijetilleke in mid-1999, while Wettimuny became Chairman of Selectors – in a governmental intervention that deposed Sumathipāla and aimed at reforms in the cricket scene. This background suggests that de Mel may occasionally consult Wettimuny on cricketing matters, in part because Wettimuny's non-partisanship is beyond question and in part because he was the Gavaskar of SL cricket, technically-sound in batting.

[32] Note Menon, 'Why do we love to love Sri Lanka?'; and Simon Barnes, 'Put Your Shirt on Sri Lanka to summon their Maverick Match-Winning Spirit'. *The Times*, April 28, 2007.

[33] Charlie Austin, 'Sumathipāla as New President: Hero or Villain?'.

[34] This summary is based partly on Austin's writings in www.cricinfo.com and also derived from an interview with Trevor Penney reported in the same source at the time Moody left at the end of his contract in mid-2007. One illustration has been the story of Chāmara Silva. He made two golden ducks in his debut Test in New Zealand in late 2006. Where earlier tour committees may have dropped him, he was retained for the 2nd Test match and re-paid the faith in his capacities with a striking century in a difficult situation.

[35] Austin, 'Sumathipāla as New President: Hero or Villain?'.

[36] Ibid.

[37] In the VB series in Australia in early 2006 Sri Lanka overturned the local expectations by outplaying South Africa and reaching the finals, where it beat the powerful Aussie side in the first game.

[38] Tissera was the manager of the team from c. August 2005 to May 2007 and was interviewed by Sa'adi Thawfeeq in June 2007 after he ended his stint. The possibility that Tissera himself contributed to good management and selection on occasions should be considered. Moody was clearly the supremo at the outset, but as the team toured and Tissera chaired selection meetings for a spell (till a Selector was sent on tour for this express purpose), it is likely that his opinions were given the weight they deserved both on formal occasions and informally.

[39] Schoorman, 'Sri Lanka's Cricket is on a Firm Footing', 37–8.

[40] During a formal interview (with SLC approval from Duleep Mendis) over breakfast at the Hyatt Hotel in Adelaide in late January 2006.

[41] Note Mahela Jayawardene's qualified endorsement of Gordon's input when Sa'adi Thawfeeq explicitly questioned him on this point (*Montage*, March–April 2007, 11).

[42] An email note from Michael Tissera conveyed this information to me after I sent an email letter to Tissera as well as Duleep Mendis (CEO of SLC) strongly urging them to refrain from considering Chappell. This was based on my own evaluations and grapevine information gathered from the Adelaide cricket circuit. In brief, my advice was *not* required. Note, too, that in recently selecting Trevor Bayliss as Moody's successor after a short-listing and interview process (Trevor Oliver was also interviewed), SLC set up a consultative body of past cricketers that included Tissera, Warnapura, Wettimuny, Aravinda de Silva and others. It follows that similar consultations were deployed in early 2005.

## References

Austin, Charlie. 'Sumathipāla as New President: Hero or Villain?' Wisden Cricket Comment, June 8, 2003. www.cricinfo.

De Silva, K.M. *Managing Ethnic Tensions in Multi-ethnic Societies*. Lanham, NY: University Press of America, 1986.

Foenander, S.P. *Sixty Years of Ceylon Cricket*. Colombo: Ceylon Advertising & General Publicity Co., 1924.

Kearney, Robert N. *Communalism and Language in the Politics of Ceylon*. Durham, NC: Duke University Press, 1967.

Menon, Suresh. 'Why Do We Love to Love Sri Lanka?' *Montage* (May–June 2007): 39–40.

Peiris, Denzil. *1956 and After*. Colombo: Associated Newspapers of Ceylon, 1958.

Perera, S.S. *The Janashakthi Book of Cricket, 1832–1996*. Colombo: Janashakthi Insurance, 1999.

Roberts, Michael. 'The Political Antecedents of the Revivalist Elite within the MEP Coalition of 1956'. In *K.W. Goonewardena Felicitation Volume*, edited by C.R. De Silva and Sirima Kiribamune, 185–220. Peradeniya: Peradeniya University, 1989.

Roberts, Michael. 'The 1956 Generations: Before and After'. In *Exploring Confrontation. Sri Lanka: Politics, Culture and History*, chap. 12. Reading: Harwood Academic Publishers, 1994.

Roberts, Michael. *Crosscurrents. Sri Lanka and Australia at Cricket*. Sydney: Walla Walla Press, 1998.

Roberts, Michael. *Forces and Strands in Sri Lanka's Cricket History*. Colombo: Social Scientists' Association, 2006. Reprint of article in *Cricket and National Identity in the Postcolonial Era*, edited by S. Wagg. Abingdon: Routledge, 2005.

Roberts, Michael. *Essaying Cricket. Sri Lanka and Beyond*. Colombo: Vijitha Yapa Publishers, 2006.

Roberts, Michael. 'Landmarks and Threads in the Cricketing Universe of Sri Lanka'. *Sport in Society* 10, no. 1 (2007): 120–42.

Roberts, Michael. 'Rangiri Stadium and Its Tempestuous History'. www.ozlanka.com, July 2007.

Schoorman, Dion. 'Sri Lanka's Cricket is on a Firm Footing – and the Present Moment can lead to Greater Heights'. *Montage* (May–June 2007): 37–8.

Third Eye. 'Sanath Jayasuriya: A Class Act'. *Montage* (May–June 2007): 40–1.

Turner, J. Neville. 'A Temporary Fracture or a Permanent Breach? Australia and Sri Lanka at Cricket'. In *Essaying Cricket. Sri Lanka and Beyond*, edited by Michael Roberts, 245–8. Colombo: Vijitha Yapa Publishers, 2006.

Wriggins, Howard. *Ceylon. Dilemmas of a New Nation*. Princeton, NJ: Princeton University Press, 1960.

# Batting for the flag: cricket, television and globalization in India

Nalin Mehta*

*School of Social Sciences, La Trobe University, Melbourne, Australia*

## Café 20: *Aaj Tak Bhangra*, cricket and television nationalism

September 24, 2007, began as just another day on *Aaj Tak* [Till Today], India's most popular Hindi satellite news channel. The first news bulletin of the day opened with the news headlines of the hour but when the camera cut to the news, anchor viewers saw a sight they had never seen before. Instead of the usual serious looking news anchor, dressed in a tie and suit, and sitting in the usual news studio, the camera cut to a new special studio with the tagline Café 20 prominently displayed in the background. Eight of Aaj Tak's most prominent news anchors were sprawled out over four separate tables in a café-like setting and they were all wearing the Indian cricket team's official blue cricket uniforms. It was the morning of the India-Pakistan final in the Twenty20 Cricket World Cup in South Africa and India's biggest news channel decided to focus only on the build-up of the game, to the exclusion of all other news.

Significantly, the anchors on display were not the usual sport reporters or commentators. These were men and women who normally presented the channel's mainline political coverage. Prominent among these was the channel's Executive Editor Deepak Chaurasiya, usually seen only outside the offices of the BJP or the Congress. Their dressing up in the Indian team's colours was the equivalent of John Simpson of the BBC wearing the Union Jack and turning up in the news studio to cover an Ashes games between England and Australia. Café 20 was as clear a signal as possible that in an overcrowded satellite television market, Aaj Tak had attached its fortunes to the aspirational nationalism of the Indian cricket fan. To drive the point home further, the Aaj Tak logo was prominently displayed on the Team India jerseys the anchors were wearing, right next to the logo of Team India. The game itself did not begin until 5.30 pm India time but Aaj Tak's Café 20 began early in the morning and continued through the day. There was no pre-match analysis or reporting – simply news anchors in the Indian colours chatting informally about what they felt about the cricket team. There used many props as well. One anchor held up a cricket bat as he showed the viewers his own take on the square cut, another demonstrated the intricacies of leg spin bowling, while a third fondled cricket pads.

When the match ended in an Indian victory after a nerve-wracking thriller that went down to the last over, the Aaj Tak camera cut once again to Café 20. This time the studio had not just the eight anchors who had begun the day's programming but was overflowing with virtually Aaj Tak's entire Delhi staff – all dancing in gay abandon to the tune of a *dholak* (drum) specially brought in for the occasion. Dancing with Aaj Tak was Kapil Dev, the last Indian captain to win a World Cup (in 1983), who had stayed in the studio through the day as a contracted expert. As other news channels went around the country showing instantaneous street celebrations, for 20 minutes, Aaj Tak's viewers saw only one sight: its entire staff doing a Punjabi *bhangra* in concert with Kapil Dev. It was a reaffirmation of television's allegiance to the flag: cricket, nationalism and television mixing in a seamless hue that more than anything else encapsulates how inextricably India's satellite television revolution is entwined with cricket.

Aaj Tak was not an exception. Every other news channel – and India has more than 50 24-hour satellite news networks in 11 languages – focused almost exclusively on cricket that day. An alien landing and watching Indian television would not have been wrong in assuming that cricket was the only news in the country that day. Yet it was a day when the ruling Congress announced the accession of Gandhi scion Rahul to a formal position as General Secretary in the party's top hierarchy and one on which an important Left party supporting the Congress government personally targeted Prime Minister Manmohan Singh as 'immature and inexperienced' for pursuing India's nuclear deal with the United States.[1] These barely featured on television. But news television's tunnelled focus on cricket wasn't just a product of what is now a cliché: the fanatical Indian support for cricket. There was a clear economic dimension to news channels staying on the cricket alone. According to one senior television news manager, his network banked more advertising in the months leading up to the Twenty20 World Cup – advertising targeted specifically for the event – than the entire advertising it received for covering the Union Budget.[2] This, when the concerned channel was not even broadcasting the event – broadcast licensing rules allowed it only limited use of the actual match footage.[3] The economics of the private television business and the heavy advertiser interest in cricket meant that the news channel could not but focus its energies on the game.

I have argued elsewhere that in a land divided at multifarious levels by factors such as language, caste and custom, the unrelenting drive to construct and capture a national market for maximizing profits has led television producers and advertisers to turn to cricket as the lowest common dominator. Channels eventually turned to cricket because of its indelible link with what might be termed 'Indian-ness'.[4] Their focus on cricket, in turn, further augmented its equation with notions of Indian identity. This is a process that unfolded through the 1990s and Aaj Tak's Café 20 was only the latest addition on this palimpsest. There is now a substantial literature tracking how cricket, from the colonial era, has always had a political dimension in India and much of this literature attributes the striking pre-eminence of cricket in the Indian imagination to a set of complex and contradictory processes that parallel the emergence of an 'Indian' nation.[5] As a crucial hinge of the modern Indian nation, cricket is also the easiest way to register on TV ratings.

This is why Indian television embraces cricket, at least economically, but its embrace of cricket is the fuel that has driven the rise of India as the financial centre of the global game. This rise is well documented. In a complete reversal of the earlier power order in the game, 80% of the International Cricket Council's (ICC) earnings are now estimated to come from India[6] and the Board of Control for Cricket in India (BCCI) is now the richest cricket body in the world.[7] India has always had the population numbers but this new-found economic power is a recent phenomenon derived from the muscle of India's burgeoning private television industry. Between 1992 and 2006 the total number of Indian households with television sets tripled to reach an estimated 112 million.[8] It made India the world's third largest television market, just behind China and the United States.[9] It is estimated that more than 60% of these television sets are connected to satellite dishes.[10] While numbers like these have attracted global media corporations, with both India and China gradually turning into new focal points of the global communication industry,[11] this industry has fundamentally changed the nature of cricket, nationally and globally.

Cricket dominates television because its administrators adapted the best to the forces of television and globalization when they took shape in India. In the cases of hockey and soccer, their administrators initially refused to change and by the time they did, they had been left behind. It would be foolhardy to attribute causal effects to television. Television does not explain everything but it is equally impossible to understand post-liberalization India without reference to satellite television. By 2007 India was home to as many as 300 indigenous satellite television networks[12] and television's embrace of cricket is the fuel that has driven the rise of India as the financial centre of the global game.

India's increased power in the global organization of cricket stems from Indian television. This is the link that this essay will sketch out. It seeks to answer two basic questions. The first: why only cricket? This essay argues that cricket's emergence as the new Indian 'national' game does not necessarily stem from some peculiar Indian affiliation for the game but is inextricably linked to the expansion of Indian television and a confluence of factors that came together: the creation of a large middle class, economic reforms, the politics of identity, the birth of the satellite television industry and a whole gamut of forces that fall under the broad rubric of globalization. This essay will map the growth of Indian television to draw out these linkages and demonstrate the central role of television in making cricket integral to modern notions of Indian identity. The second question I address is the impact cricket has had on television itself, not just sport television, but on the Indian broadcast industry as a whole. It is a measure of cricket's embrace of television, in direct opposition to other sports, that it has virtually defined the legal structure of India's satellite revolution. Historically, the story of Indian satellite television is the story of a private industry leap-frogging across stringent government regulations. In a country where the state monopolized television until the mid-1990s, the rise of the private satellite television networks is nothing short of a revolution. Up to the time of writing, successive Indian governments had managed to pass only two Parliamentary Bills pertaining to the challenge of this new industry. As this essay will show, since the early 1990s, the politics of the private television industry have been such that successive governments were forced to back off from virtually every controlling legislation that was mooted. The only two laws that managed enough support from Parliament came about because of cricket. Both these laws provide the legal superstructure of Indian television and in that sense, cricket has defined India's satellite television industry as much as television has defined it. The fact that they were passed by parliamentarians at all demonstrates the power of cricket in the Indian imagination and the wider significance of the game in Indian public culture. Simultaneously, the deep linkages between Indian television and cricket have changed the nature of the global game itself though it is outside the scope of this essay to discuss this in greater detail.

### Cricket's journey to pre-eminence

There is no evidence to show that cricket was any bigger in India than other sports like hockey and soccer before the 1980s. During the colonial period, hockey, soccer and cricket each became important playing fields for the politics of identity and nationalist self-assertion. Some of the greatest nationalist triumphs came not in cricket but in the other two games. Let us first consider soccer. The 1911 victory of the Calcutta-based Mohun Bagan Club over the British East York Regiment is seen by a number of historians as not just a sporting, but also a nationalist, milestone that spurred on the Swadeshi (indigenous) movement.[13] It was celebrated in vernacular popular culture as a fitting reply to the British discourse on Bengalis being effeminate and hence, in the ideology of the period, an inferior race. The victory had a resonance beyond the playing field precisely because it was seen as the Bengali answer to the charge of effeminacy that had become a leitmotif of imperial discourse. Contemporary commentaries on the victory focused more on its social meaning than on the game itself. To cite one example, *Amrit Bazar Patrika* pointed out that mental and physical strength was 'an integral quality of Bengalees' and urged Europeans to cease to consider them 'non-martial'.[14] Similarly, *The Mussalman* commented: 'The victory of Mohun Bagan ... has demonstrated that Indians are second to none in all manly games'.[15] No one caught the nationalist meaning of the 1911 victory for Bengali identity and self-assertion better than the *Nayak* which pointed out the victory would fill 'every Indian with joy and pride to know that rice-eating, malaria-ridden, bare-footed Bengalis have got the better of beef-eating, Herculean, booted John Bull in that peculiarly English sport'.[16]

A measure of the centrality of football in the Bengali consciousness is Swami Vivekanand's oft-quoted remark, 'playing football rather than reciting the Gita will take one near to God'.[17] By the 1930s, the noted literary figure Sajani Kanta Das stated that three things personified Bengali colonial identity: Mohun Bagan, Subhash Chandra Bose and New Theatres.[18] Almost until independence, soccer had a legitimate claim to be among the most popular spectator sports in India. As Mihir Bose has noted:

> While the Indians were fighting the British for their independence, one of the most popular games in the country was football. Logically after independence, football should have become India's number one sport. It is cheaper, it certainly permeated more layers of Indian society – even down to the semi rural areas – than cricket and as in other parts of the world, could have been a metaphor for nationalism.[19]

This essay is not the place to document the story of the decline of Indian soccer after independence. That has been well documented in many fine studies elsewhere.[20] It must be pointed out though that in sharp contrast to India's abysmal position of 128 in the FIFA rankings at the time of writing, the country began independence with success on the soccer field. India won the gold medal at the first Asiad in 1951, barefooted-footballers beating the booted Iranians in the final. Similarly in the 1956 Olympics, India became the first Asian nation to enter the semi-finals, eventually finishing fourth. Its last great international soccer victory came in the Bangkok Asiad of 1970 when Indian won bronze. It has been pointed out that ever since, 'the unresolved dichotomy between the interest of the nation and club as well as the long-term failure of the AIFF/Sports ministry to appreciate the importance of professionalism and commercialism in Indian football'[21] have led to its terminal decline. For our purposes, the point is that soccer always had a strong mass base in India, certainly not less so than cricket, before television arrived and changed everything.

Similarly, the astonishing early success rate of Indian hockey when it won six successive gold medals at the Olympics between 1928 and 1956, turned that game into an icon for Indian nationalism. When the IOC toyed with the idea of dropping hockey as an event in the 1952 Helsinki Olympics, India even offered to host the hockey event separately in New Delhi.[22] The success of Indian hockey teams in beating Western teams demonstrated to the nationalists that Indians could compete on equal terms with the West. The success of the Indian hockey teams was such that after independence the Ministry of Sport, not surprisingly, chose hockey as the official 'national game' of India.

It is significant that the BCCI was only founded as late as 1928, a full four years after the formation of Indian Hockey Federation. By this time, the hockey players had already won India its first Olympic gold medal. In fact, Anthony de Mello, one of the founders of the BCCI, has pointed out that it was the pride of the Olympic gold that first ignited the desire to create an Indian 'national' cricket team:

> Heightened by our hockey success at Amsterdam, our ambitions for Indian sport knew no bounds just then. We visualized our cricketers playing at the Oval, at Lord's ... and straightway was born in those of us connected with the game in India the determination, that sooner or later, it should happen.[23]

Hockey had initially caught the national imagination and it led the way for cricket. Due to lack of popular support, 'cricket in India was far from being a flourishing national sport in the middle 'twenties'.[24] With the exception of Calcutta, Madras and Bombay, there were few facilities for cricket across the country. Compared to other sports, cricket was still dominated by the British, by the royalty or by the elites.[25]

This is not to say that cricket was not popular. Ramachandra Guha, among others, has demonstrated the role cricket played in galvanizing nationalist sentiment from the 1880s onwards.[26] In the early twentieth century, the Bombay Pentagular tournament, for instance, was a huge commercial and popular success until it was shut down in the 1930s.[27] Cricket, however, was never the pre-eminent Indian sport.

Even a pioneer of Indian cricket like Anthony de Mello saw the future of hockey as much brighter until well after independence. Writing in 1959, he saw an equally bright future for soccer as well, observing that, in contrast to cricket, they were both mass sports:

> Soccer in India, like hockey, is a poor man's game. It is a game which most boys around the country play at one time or another – at school or in the maidan ... Thus there is a nationwide understanding of, and liking for, soccer, stronger than that for cricket, which has till now tended to be more a game for the rich man.[28]

Until well into the 1960s, all contemporary observers agreed that cricket certainly always had the 'glamour', due to its aristocratic roots, but its popular appeal in India was never more than that of soccer and hockey.[29]

## Cricket and television

### The Nehruvian legacy

In order to understand the pivotal role of television it is necessary to recount a short history of the medium in India. Independent India's encounter with television during 17 years of Jawaharlal Nehru's stewardship was negligible. Independent India followed the colonial practice of keeping broadcasting a preserve of the state which fitted the larger Nehruvian superstructure of keeping the 'commanding heights' of the economy under state control.[30] Yet in this period, far from being a 'commanding height', broadcasting was barely a molehill. Radio became a government department and the state assumed a monopoly over broadcasting.[31]

The first television broadcasts were put together by All India Radio in September 1959. They were watched by 'teleclubs' organized around the 21 gifted television sets that were installed within a 25 kilometre radius in Delhi.[32] It took another six years for a regular daily one-hour service to appear. India's television encounter of the 1960s remained a developmental exercise and a curiosity restricted only to a few bureaucrats, politicians and a few select localities in Delhi.

For the rest of India, television simply did not exist. The lone transmission from Delhi operated on a weak signal and the state simply did not allow any infrastructure for the development of the industry. When Nehru died in 1964 the country had a grand total of 58 licensed TV sets.[33] The first Indian television factory opened only in 1969 in Kanpur and, indicative of the miniscule size of the existing market, produced just 1,250 sets in its first year.[34]

Television was restricted to the Delhi area until as late as 1972 when a TV transmitter was set up in Bombay, followed by strategic transmitters in the border cities of Amritsar and Srinagar in 1973.[35] This was still nowhere near a national presence and the first semblance of a symbolic India-wide network emerged only in the first year of the Emergency,[36] with the setting up of new stations in Lucknow, Madras and Calcutta in 1975. With severe censorship imposed upon the print media, the Indira Gandhi government saw broadcasting as a crucial tool to direct public opinion.

At the height of the Emergency in 1976 three important things happened: television was separated from radio and put under the jurisdiction of a new entity called Doordarshan (though it remained under the control of the Ministry of Information and Broadcasting); the government reduced excise duties on television sets which encouraged local manufacture; and for the first time advertising was allowed on television. All three measures spurred television's expansion. From just one company producing 1,250 sets in 1969 India had progressed to 40 companies making 250,000 by 1977.[37]

### The great expansion: the 1982 Asian Games, Kapil's Devils and 'Whole New Worlds'

It is possible to date the rise of cricket as the pre-eminent Indian game almost precisely to the date when television began expanding. Television became a mass medium in India only during the 1980s. The 1982 New Delhi Asian Games are widely held to have been the trigger that unleashed television's potential and the decisive leap was possible because a number of policies that had been initiated in the 1970s came to fruition at the crucial moment. The Asian Games was a stage for the government to showcase a shining India to itself and to the world. Television was to be the tool. Appu, the tubby elephant mascot of the Games, was also symbolic of the advancing, prosperous nation-state; but taking Appu to the drawing rooms of its citizens required a unified national service facilitated by enhanced technology. This capacity had to be created if India was to look good internationally and the Asian Games, therefore, became the catalyst for sprucing up television and stitching for it a brand new suit.

The first direct result of the Asian Games was the introduction of colour television and the creation of a 'national' service. As the host broadcaster it was up to India to provide a live telecast of the Games to other participating countries and Doordarshan's technical backwardness was painfully brought home. Doordarshan still operated in black and white and Minister for Information and Broadcasting Vasant Sathe discovered to his horror that even neighbouring Sri Lanka had colour television. Many of the broadcasting organizations from the participating countries demanded colour feeds and to appear backward would be shameful. Despite stout resistance from the Prime Minister's scientific advisors, who cited the traditional argument about India not being able to afford the luxury, the decision was taken to convert to colour transmissions.[38]

The development of the indigenous satellite programme in 1982 provided a viable instrument to realize this vision. The launch of INSAT-1A, and later INSAT-1B, allowed the creation of what became known as the National Programme which was envisaged as a tool for uniting people and developing awareness of the 'oneness of India'. The satellite system allowed a massive expansion of television through a gradual build-up of low power transmitters that could pick up television signals bounced off satellites. Quite symbolically, the 'national' colour transmissions and the National Programme commenced on Independence Day in 1982. For the first time, all of India would see the same image at the same time and the Asian Games could be transmitted to every home across the country in glorious colour.

This was the first sporting event Indians saw on the medium. The only way to follow games previously had been to follow commentary on radio. Now for the first time they could see their sporting heroes. That changed everything. India's dominance in hockey had declined since the late-1960s, but in the showpiece Delhi Asiad, the hockey team lost 7-1 to Pakistan in the finals. This was the first time most Indian viewers had seen the hockey team in action and the camera was cruel. Mir Ranjan Negi, the hapless goalkeeper on that day, later complained that the inexperienced Doordarshan cameramen never showed how he charged at Pakistan's defenders, cutting to the empty goal after he had been beaten in his charge. Negi never played a game for India after that day and for years was hounded as a 'traitor', who had 'sold out'. Someone even cut the electricity at his wedding function, such was the popular anger he faced.[39] His story has since been depicted in the 2007 Bollywood blockbuster *Chak De India*. That loss to Pakistan, on television and watched for the first time by a national Indian audience, did irreparable damage to the image of Indian hockey in the nationalist imagination.

The tragedy of Indian hockey, as Shekhar Gupta points out, was that while television expanded, Indian hockey declined:

> Our last championship, victory, the Kuala Lumpur World Cup in 1975, was telecast live but then all of India had no more than a thousand television sets, all black and white, and in the metros ... A sporting 'product' was needed to sell those wares, to consume the sponsors' and the advertisers' money, and hockey did not make the grade.[40]

Taking 1982 as the cut-off point for television, a detailed breakdown of Indian hockey performances bears out this analysis in Tables 1, 2 and 3. India lost only two games in the first three hockey World Cups. Between 1986 and 1990, it won only one game. While India has consistently performed steadily at the Asian Games, it has languished at the Olympics and in World Cup hockey (see Tables 1–3).

The decline in hockey standards began to turn spectators away at a time when television was providing opportunities for building an entirely new support base. In this

Table 1.   Indian performance at Hockey World Cups, 1980–2006.

| Year | Venue | Position |
| --- | --- | --- |
| 1982 | Mumbai | 5 |
| 1986 | London | 12 |
| 1990 | Lahore | 10 |
| 1994 | Sydney | 5 |
| 1998 | Utrecht | 9 |
| 2002 | Kuala Lumpur | 10 |
| 2006 | Mönchengladbach, Germany | 11 |

Table 2.    Indian performance at Asian Games post-1982, 1980–2006.

| Year | Venue | Position |
| --- | --- | --- |
| 1982 | Delhi | Silver |
| 1986 | Seoul | Bronze |
| 1990 | Beijing | Silver |
| 1994 | Hiroshima | Silver |
| 1998 | Bangkok | Gold |
| 2002 | Busan | Silver |
| 2006 | Doha | 5th |

context, Ramachandra Guha has argued that interest in soccer too began to wane after the television telecast of the 1982 World Cup.

This was the first World Cup telecast live in India; alerted to the gap between their own local heroes and the great international stars, men in Calcutta began to turn away from their clubs. The slide continued; 20 years later, soccer ranks a poor second to cricket in the sporting passions of Bengal.[41]

Significantly the creation of a national network with the Asian Games coincided with India's epochal Cricket World Cup win in 1983. This was not Indian cricket's first great win. The 1971 victory of Ajit Wadekar's team against England in England perhaps ranks higher in cricketing terms. Wadekar's team was welcomed back by huge street parades in Bombay although few had actually seen them play. The 1983 World Cup was different. Unheralded, inexperienced in the one-day format, and led by a new young captain – Kapil Dev – 'Kapil's Devils', as they became known, millions of Indians saw them through their journey to winning the Cup. It is not surprising that this victory was followed by political felicitations that Wadekar's team and even the hockey players of an earlier era had never received.

The 1983 victory was followed by another victory in 1985 in the Benson & Hedges Champion of Champions Trophy in Australia. Again, television was the conduit, as for the first time, Indians saw the Australian tournament live. In fact, it is possible to precisely map the rise of cricket with the increase in television penetration. From 1983 the expansion of the television network became a key governmental priority. Between July and October 1984, for instance, practically one TV transmitter a day was commissioned.[42] As Figure 1 demonstrates, starting from just one transmitter in 1971, 18 had been set up by 1980. The graph leaps spectacularly in the early 1980s with total transmitters rising to 172 in 1985 and 698 in 1995. The expansion of TV transmitters was accompanied with a simultaneous increase in the sale of TV sets. In the first decade of television, the number of television sets increased from 41 to 24,838. It took another 12 years, until 1982, for this

Table 3.    Indian performance at Olympic hockey, 1980–2006.

| Year | Venue | Position |
| --- | --- | --- |
| 1980 | Moscow | Gold |
| 1984 | Los Angeles | 5 |
| 1988 | Seoul | 6 |
| 1992 | Barcelona | 7 |
| 1996 | Atlanta | 8 |
| 2000 | Sydney | 7 |
| 2004 | Athens | 7 |

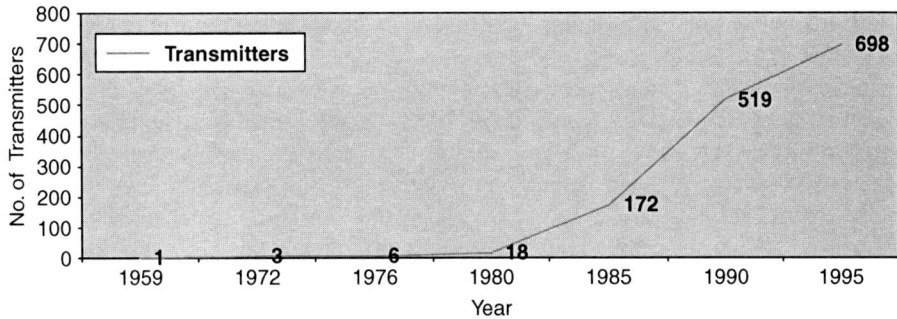

Figure 1.   Growth of television transmitters.
Source: Audience Research Unit, Directorate General Doordarshan, cited in Joshi, *Asia Speaks Out*, 5–8; NRS 2006.

number to cross the two million mark. But from the mid-1980s, the graph suddenly rockets up and we see the makings of a mass medium. By 1986, three million TV sets were being produced in India, including 700,000 colour sets[43] and by 1992 the figure had reached 34 million TV sets. 1992 was a watershed, the year that private satellite television first made its appearance and we examine its influence later in the essay (see Figures 1 and 2).

The rise of Indian television coincided with some of India's greatest cricketing achievements. At a time when other Indian sports were languishing, television made cricket central to the Indian sport fan's imagination.

It is no coincidence that the cricketers of this era, while not necessarily more talented than those of earlier generations, became the first brand names among Indian sportsmen. As television advertising expanded, it looked for heroes, and found them in the national cricket team. Kapil Dev, Sunil Gavaskar, Ravi Shastri and Dilip Vengsarkar were hired to model a whole range of consumer products from shaving cream and toothpaste to clothing and English-language speaking guides. The creation of a 'national' network became a magnet for advertisers because it opened up the possibility of constructing a 'national' market. The focus of this advertising was on the 'exploding new middle classes' and television, in the eyes of the advertisers, enabled their transformation into consumers.

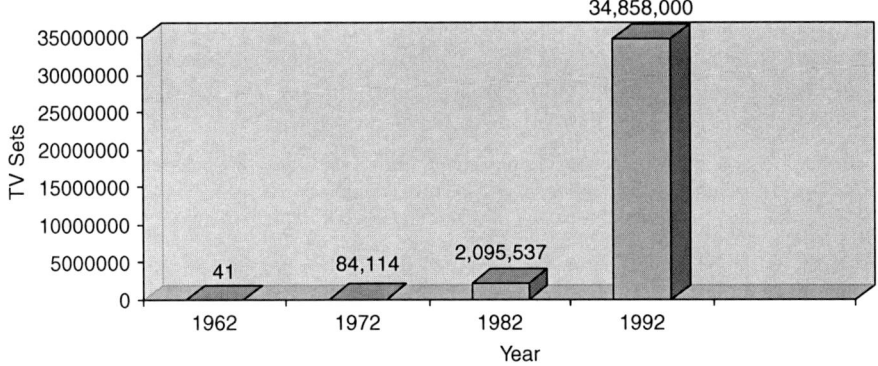

Figure 2.   Television sets in India (1959–92).
Source: Audience Research Unit, Directorate General Doordarshan, 1995, cited in Joshi and Trivedi, *Mass Media and Cross-Cultural Communication*, 16.

Advertising was first allowed on television in 1976 but it only grew in the 1980s with the creation of a national audience. The decision to allow advertising, the push to create a nationwide television network and the spread of colour television after 1982 all combined to create a new consumer spectacle. It has been suggested that the rise of commercial television formed the basis 'for a new notion of collectivity, expressed as "the middle class" and based on the "idea of the democratization of aspiration"'.[44] A number of scholars have focused attention on the intrinsic links between the 'exploding middle classes' of India in the 1980s and state-sponsored commercial television through the 1980s.[45] Certainly, marketing and advertising professionals were in no doubt about what television meant for the new consumer economy. According to Ahmad Khan, Head of Enterprise, Nexus Lowe Advertising:

> I think what television did was that it opened, for a few million people, *whole new worlds* which they never knew existed. And it made them want and need things which they never bought before. So from just saving money for the sake of saving money, I think for the first time people said, 'Oh, I make money so that I can do things with it.' And this is something which I think happened for the first time in our history. I think that's what television did.[46]

Television enabled the circulation of commodity images on a national scale in a way that simply wasn't possible before. Cricket and cricketers were key components of these commodity images. It is no accident that the historical lineage of the Indian middle class as a political category can be traced to 1985. That was the year when Mani Shankar Aiyar, then a Joint Secretary in the Prime Minister's Office, told the *Washington Post* that India contained a middle class of one hundred million and that this class looked up to Rajiv Gandhi.[47] It was the first political articulation of the middle class as a social category and this was only possible in the context of a newly created national television network with an overt middle class agenda, subsuming within it the state's lofty developmental objectives. This perception, in turn, fuelled television advertising and the focus on cricketers as new heroes of the nation. By the 1986 Asian Games, cricket had become so popular that a reader of a national daily could write:

> The disgraceful performance of the 400-strong Asian contingent … is not surprising when the nation's main sport is following the cricket score on radio and television. The result is that city children take to breaking window panes and noses … Village children also have now taken to the Englishmen's game and dropped fast the Indian games … Unless cricket is banished from this country, the rest of the sports would not get any encouragement, people would not do honest work in their work places and youth would not get adequate exercise.[48]

As cricket embraced the new charms of television, hockey, with a combination of bad performances and short-sighted planning, continued to languish until cricket supplanted it in the national imagination. Indian hockey, to its misfortune, failed when television arrived. As Harsha Bhogle points out:

> Television is the seed that breeds sponsorships, ignites passions and carries sport across boundaries. Formula One has shown that. A seemingly monotonous sport with invisible drivers thrives solely due to brilliant television. Hockey can do more, much more, if it chooses to.[49]

Globalization and the new economy were embraced by cricket while hockey administrators remained mired in old ways.[50] The few times that Indian hockey did well, such as at the Bangkok Asiad, its success was followed by administrative wrangling and internal discords. Half the victorious team at Bangkok, for instance, was sacked soon after it won the gold because of internal discords between the players and the IHF.[51] Hockey administrators have made belated attempts to embrace television with, for example, the National Hockey League on ESPN- Star. Hockey, however, has long been supplanted in the popular imagination of India. As Rohit Brijnath put it, 'cricket has settled on the mind and leaves little place and time for other pursuits. As a nation we are [now] guilty of a one-track mind'.[52]

## 'The battering ram': satellite television and the centrality of cricket

This essay is not the place to detail the complex processes through which satellite television penetrated into India. Suffice it to say, from 1991 onwards satellite technology allowed private broadcasters to bypass the shackles of state control and break the state's monopoly over the medium. By 2007 India was home to as many as 300 indigenous satellite television networks. The initial spark was lit by the Hong Kong-based Star TV network that was soon bought over by Rupert Murdoch's News Corporation. Like elsewhere in the world, News Corporation banked on sport as a battering ram to capture the Indian television market. And given the events of the 1980s, by sport, it meant cricket. Murdoch had first demonstrated the immense commercial power of sport when he turned around the ailing Sky TV's fortunes in the United Kingdom by buying telecast rights for the English Premier League in 1992.[53] News Corporation's various entities have consistently followed this strategy ever since – from buying television rights to Major League Baseball and American football to rugby league and rugby union rights in England. Murdoch has since branched out into buying sport clubs themselves, a practice that other media players, like Italy's Silvio Berlusconi, have followed.[54] In a speech to shareholders, soon after News Corporation acquired STAR TV, Murdoch outlined the importance of sport in his business plans for expanding into Asia:

> We have the long-term rights in most countries to major sporting events and we will be doing in Asia what we intend to do elsewhere in the world, using *sports as a battering ram* and a lead offering in all our pay-television operations. Sport absolutely overpowers film and everything else in the entertainment genre.[55]

Accordingly, News Corporation chose cricket as a lynchpin of its strategy in India and ESPN announced its entry into the Indian market in 1993 by acquiring the exclusive rights to telecast cricket in India for five years for US$30 million.[56] This is a lesson that all major Indian broadcasters have also learnt and since the mid-1990s the exponential expansion of the Indian broadcast industry has been accompanied by vicious wars over cricket telecast rights. India's well-documented transformation into the 'spiritual and financial heart of world cricket'[57] during the same period is intrinsically linked to the infusion of television money.

### Confusion and the Supreme Court: the cricket test

As the torch-bearer of satellite television, cricket has played a major role in the history of Indian broadcast reform and was the catalyst for the landmark Supreme Court judgement of 1995[58] that deprived the state of its legal monopoly over the airwaves. That judgement, in one stroke, gave a legal basis to the burgeoning new economy of satellite television. Since then, new stakeholders have arisen and in relative terms the once all-powerful Ministry of Information and Broadcasting, the executive arm of the state in broadcasting matters, has found its power severely eroded. All of this stemmed from a dispute over cricket.

The state's monopoly over broadcasting accrued from the colonial Indian Telegraph Act of 1885 which gave the central government 'the exclusive privilege' of establishing, maintaining and working telegraphs as well as the right to grant licences.[59] The nationalist regime that succeeded the Raj continued to be guided by this nineteenth-century legislation and an amendment to it in 1957 expanded the term 'telegraph' to mean any 'apparatus for the purpose of affording means of telegraphic communication'.[60] In 1991 foreign satellite television expanded in India like the American Wild West for two years before the state made its first serious intervention. Until then satellite broadcasters found ingenious ways to get around the legal restrictions, often with help from 'pro-reform' sections of the state, but this dichotomy led to a serious crisis when the Ministry of Information and Broadcasting first decided to enforce its legal monopoly in the dispute over cricket telecast rights between October 1993 and February 1995.

Until 1993, Indian cricket had always been covered by Doordarshan and the crisis occurred when the Cricket Association of Bengal (CAB) sold the telecast rights of the five-nation Hero Cup[61] to the multi-national television company TWI. Doordarshan, which had failed to match TWI's bid, refused to allow the foreign broadcaster to uplink from Indian soil.[62] Claiming an exclusive right to do so under the Telegraph Act of 1885, Doordarshan accused the BCCI and the CAB of being 'anti-national' and the ensuing legal battle illustrated the complexity of economic liberalization.[63]

TWI and CAB signed the agreement for the Hero Cup in May 1993. Even though Doordarshan saw the granting of rights to anybody but itself as illegal, the Ministry of Home Affairs, on 13 October, approved TWI's application to allow a satellite link-up. TWI even paid $29,640 to the government-owned Visesh Sanchar Nigam Limited (VSNL)[64] as up-link fees and the Finance Ministry allowed it to import its own broadcast equipment, waiving customs and additional duties.[65] Clearly other ministries and departments did not have a problem with the TWI deal. In sharp contrast, the Ministry of Information and Broadcasting condemned it as 'a diabolical move to violate the law of the land'.[66] As a pressure tactic, the Ministry even forbade All India Radio from broadcasting ball-by-ball coverage of the tournament. Soon thereafter, customs authorities in Mumbai, under governmental instructions, confiscated TWI's broadcasting equipment.[67] This was the first serious muscle-flexing by the Ministry of Information and Broadcasting and some media commentators immediately made the link with a larger crisis of the reform process itself:

> CAB will be bludgeoned into submission and somehow Doordarshan and the government will have their pound of flesh … the next time Mr. Narasimha Rao [then prime minister] and Mr. Jyoti Basu [then West Bengal chief minister] go round the world seeking investments and much else besides, they must expect to be asked some searching questions.[68]

With TWI's equipment in the custody of customs officials, the CAB appealed to the Supreme Court of India. The court took the matter very seriously. As Boria Majumdar notes, 'Never before in the history of independent India did a Supreme Court Division bench sit in judgement on a government holiday at 11.30 pm'.[69] In an important ruling on 15 November 1993, the court overruled the government and allowed TWI to generate its own broadcasts.[70] The case was urgent because its significance extended far beyond the game of cricket. Majumdar has argued that the crisis of the Hero Cup seemed to jeopardize the 1996 World Cup, which was to be co-hosted by India, Pakistan and Sri Lanka. The South Africa Cricket Board had threatened to withdraw South Africa's support for the subcontinent playing host to the tournament unless the wrangle over telecast rights was sorted out immediately. Foreign broadcasting corporations were already demanding their money back from the World Tel, which held the World Cup telecast rights,[71] and the wrangle over telecast rights threatened to take away foreign investment, the heart of economic liberalization itself.

The Supreme Court's 1993 ruling, however, was limited to the Hero Cup. It did not solve the basic dichotomy of satellite broadcasters challenging Doordarshan's legal monopoly. Consequently, Doordarshan and the BCCI locked horns again in 1994 when the BCCI granted ESPN the right to telecast India's series with West Indies as part of a $30 million deal which gave ESPN the exclusive right to telecast cricket in India for five years. Cricket was attracting foreign investors to India but the Ministry of Information and Broadcasting was fighting tooth and nail to preserve its fiefdom. Once again, other government agencies opposed Doordarshan. For instance, VSNL, which had granted up-link rights to ESPN, accused the Ministry of Information and Broadcasting of deliberately obstructing its plans. VSNL was forced to return the advance it had received from ESPN[72] and VSNL officials were clearly unhappy at the financial losses: 'We do not need to put in any money for infrastructure because we already possess all the facilities but the Ministry of I&B will not let us do anything, even if it involves earning thousands of dollars for the country in foreign exchange'.[73]

Again, the BCCI appealed to the Supreme Court, which in an epochal judgement on 9 February 1995 ruled that the airwaves cannot be a state monopoly as they constitute public property. The court made it clear that it was the duty of state to see that airwaves were utilized to advance the fundamental right of free speech, something difficult to achieve under a broadcasting monopoly. The broadcast media, the court said, 'should be under the control of the public as distinct from Government. This is the command implicit in Article 19(1)(a). It should be operated by a public statutory corporation or corporations'. The judges further added that the fundamental right to freedom of speech and expression includes the right to communicate effectively, including through the electronic media. Ruling that the Indian Telegraph Act of 1885 was totally inadequate, 'intended for an altogether different purpose when it was enacted', the judges ordered the government 'to take immediate steps to establish an autonomous public authority ... to control and regulate the use of the airwaves'.[74] Thus ended the first Indian battle over broadcast reform. The state lost its monopoly and the Ministry was ordered to develop a new regulatory framework.

### *'National interest': cricket and the last broadcast law*

So central has cricket become to Indian television that it was also at the heart of the second broadcasting law that India managed to pass. More than a decade after the Supreme Court's order, the Indian state has failed to evolve an overarching regulatory body to oversee broadcasting issues. Simultaneously, the Ministry of Information and Broadcasting has periodically tried to fill the regulatory vacuum with draft legislation and summary executive directives, most designed to assert its control. Broadly speaking, it has consistently tried to put the genie of broadcasting back into the bottle. Yet, almost every one of its measures has come up against serious challenges. Almost at every step, the Ministry's controlling instincts have had to contend with either the courts or strong public opinion or heavy corporate lobbying by the new broadcast capitalists. In every case, except for the 2007 law on mandatory sharing of sports feeds, the Ministry has had to cede ground.

This last law is interesting because it is the only law pertaining to broadcasting that has managed Parliamentary muster in over a decade. On at least eight occasions the Ministry's controlling drive ran aground in the face of thick opposition, but in cricket it found a populist catalyst that allowed it to build consensus. Its roots can be traced back to the 2004 India-Pakistan cricket series when the Ministry first forced Ten Sports, which had the broadcast rights, to share its live telecast of matches with Doordarshan to benefit non-satellite watchers. This seemed like a popular cause to espouse but apart from acquiring these sports broadcasts, ostensibly in the 'public interest', Doordarshan also wanted to make money by selling advertising spots. This was a serious threat to Ten Sport's advertising revenues and its parent company Taj TV protested in a bitterly contested case in the Supreme Court, where Prasar Bharti was forced to deposit a Rs500 million guarantee against possible revenue damages. It was also forbidden to sell advertising and forced to carry the Ten Sports' logo for the series broadcasts.[75] The Ministry countered in late 2005 through new downlinking guidelines that made it mandatory for private sport channels to share feeds of all major sports events of 'national and international importance'[76] in the larger 'public interest'. These guidelines went to the heart of free market considerations and private sports broadcasters who had paid large sums of money to acquire broadcast rights repeatedly challenged their legal validity. Through 2006 and early 2007, on at least three occasions, judicial rulings restrained the central government from interfering with their rights. On 9 May 2006, for example, the Supreme Court refused to force Ten Sports to share its coverage of India's cricket tour of the West Indies with the national broadcaster. A two-member bench of Justice Ashok Bhan and Justice L.K. Palta went so far as to ask the government to 'bring a law' on the matter, saying, 'You can't act on guidelines'.[77] Similarly in August 2006, the Supreme Court again ruled in favour of Ten Sports which contended that it would lose Rs80 million a day in advertising – for the July tri-series involving Sri Lanka, India and South Africa – if it was forced to share its signals with Doordarshan.[78] ESPN-STAR, which had exclusive rights for India's tour of South Africa in late 2006, also received protection from the Supreme Court for refusing to share its signals.[79]

By early 2007, the dispute between private sports broadcasters and the Ministry had reached boiling point. The immense confusion over legal structures meant that virtually every cricket series involving India was now accompanied by bitter court battles and tremendous uncertainty for viewers. In January 2007, Nimbus' initial refusal to share broadcasts with Prasar Bharti led to many cricket watchers missing the first few games of the India-West Indies series. Unlike ESPN-STAR or Ten Sports, Nimbus' new sports channel, Neo Sports, was still not available in all parts of India. Even viewers with satellite connections were unable to see it and the Delhi High Court finally asked Nimbus to share its feed with Doordarshan after a seven minute delay.[80] Counting on the anger of the average cricket fan, on 3 February 2007 the central government promulgated an Ordinance that turned its mandatory fee-sharing guidelines into a law. This became the *Sports Broadcasting Signals (Mandatory Sharing with Prasar Bharti) Bill* that was passed by Parliament on 9 March. It stipulated a 75:25 revenue split between the rights holder and Doordarshan[81] and the Parliamentary debate over the bill reflected two things: the serious concern in the government over the legal challenges to its guidelines, and the immense potential of cricket for building and harnessing public and political opinion. Harnessing political support for regulating broadcasting was difficult, but when it came to cricket, things were easier. When questioned about the infringement on the private market, Information and Broadcasting Minister Priyoranjan Dasmushi repeatedly pointed to the public's right to watch cricket, though the bill itself was not cricket-specific:

> Cricket is a popular game of the masses... A long battle continued in court to get the terrestrial rights. Fifty million T.V. homes depend on terrestrial in the villages, semi-urban areas, even in the rural areas to watch the matches ... It was, therefore, a bounden duty of the Government to think something which can justify the cause of the people in the greater public interest. We had to bring the Ordinance keeping in view that the World Cup Cricket is coming

up ... one should also appreciate that out of the total fund generated through tickets in the whole world, more than 75 per cent is generated from the Indian market alone. But, the tragedy is that the Indian common viewers cannot see the match.[82]

The appeal to the rights of the cricket-watching public found favour with most parliamentarians, cutting across party lines. The response of Dasmunshi's predecessor, the BJP's Ravishankar Prasad, was typical:

> Cricket, today, is not only a game, but it is almost a passion in India ... We are one with you that the ordinary people of the country, who have got a simple antenna of the terrestrial [*sic*] should have the right to see the cricket matches because cricket, today, is not only an elitist game, but it has reached in rural areas also ... If there are 4.5 crores of terrestrial homes in the country, the people must have the right to view the games ... So, many litigations are going on. Therefore, in that way, our party appreciate your concerns through this legislation. We are with you.[83]

The bill raised serious issues that were worthy of debate: the myth of Prasar Bharti's autonomy and its commercial advantages through state patronage, deeper questions about the validity of the state's right to rule on what constituted a sporting event of 'national importance' and the rights of private operators who had paid large amounts of money for broadcast rights through open market bidding. Nimbus, for instance, claimed it would lose 12% of the projected earnings from its $612 million dollar contract to broadcast Indian cricket over the next four years.[84] But there was hardly a dissenting voice in the Parliamentary debate as speaker after speaker reiterated cricket's 'uniting' potential and the 'rights of the common man' to watch the game.[85] In 1995, cricket had been the catalyst for the Supreme Court's landmark judgement that freed the airwaves for private players. In 2007, the national passion for the game was again a catalyst for a major change in broadcast law, but this time it allowed the government to gain back some measure of control.

## Conclusion

This essay began with Aaj Tak's aggressive reaffirmation with the Indian flag during the Twenty20 World Cup. It was the logical culmination of a process that began in the 1980s. Cricket's rise as the pre-eminent Indian game is intimately connected with Indian television. Television was consciously turned into a mass medium in the 1980s as a political/developmental strategy. This was accompanied by television advertising which augmented the creation of a 'new consumer class' and a new notion of collectivity expressed as 'the middle class'. The fact that these developments coincided with the 1983 World Cup win fundamentally changed the balance of power between cricket and other sports in India. Television was instrumental in creating conditions for cricket to become a central component of new notions of national identity and consumer spectacle.

The advent of satellite television in the 1990s pushed this linkage further. When television capitalists searched for 'national' publics in their quest to create a 'national' market, they ended up with cricket as the lowest denominator of Indian-ness. Satellite television is a cultural arena where the idea of India is debated and fought for every day and its focus on cricket since the 1990s has reinforced the centrality of cricket as a pan-Indian marker of 'Indian-ness'. A good example is that of the Sahara Group of companies which bought the telecast rights of the 2006 India-England cricket series. With Sahara One, the group's flagship entertainment channel, doing badly on the ratings, Sahara bought the television rights for the series hoping cricket would induce non-Sahara viewers to sample it. The network built a synergy between its entertainment programming and cricket by getting the lead actors of all its soap operas to talk about the cricket series during the shows. As Sahara One's CEO explained:

> The ingredients of cricket are quite similar to that of a show on a general entertainment channel. There is drama, there is entertainment, anger and cheerfulness in cricket, which is there in all our soaps, too. Therefore, there is bound to be a great synergy.[86]

Sahara One's advertisement line, *Television ke begum aur cricket ke badshah ek hee channel pe* [The queens of television and the kings of cricket, all on one channel], summed up this philosophy. Kerry Packer's 1977 World Series initiated the process of converting cricket into a television spectacle[87] but in India this process has evolved more than anywhere else with television networks turning cricket into a continuing soap opera, a spectacle far beyond the game itself.

This is a two-way process and world cricket itself has been transformed by the massive infusion of capital from Indian television. The enormous money that television has generated for cricket has also transformed India into the spiritual and financial heart of the global cricket industry. In this process, however, hockey and other sports have been left behind by the cold logic of capitalism and expanding markets.

## Notes

[1] Personal monitoring of television networks on 24 September 2007.
[2] The manager and the channel cannot be named for obvious reasons. However, I have permission to quote the conversation, without identifying the source.
[3] ESPN-STAR had the T-20 World Cup broadcast rights for India.
[4] Nalin Mehta, 'The Great Indian Willow Trick: Cricket, Nationalism and India's TV News Revolution, 1998–2005'.
[5] Appadurai, *Modernity at Large: Cultural Dimensions of Globalization*, 90. For Indian cricket and the nationalist imagination see, for example, Guha, *Corner of a Foreign Field: The Indian History of a British Sport*; Boria Majumdar, *22 Yards to Freedom: A Social History of Indian Cricket*; Nandy, *The Tao of Cricket*.
[6] Interview with Lalit Modi, Vice President, BCCI, October 12, 2006. http://content-usa.cricinfo.com/ci/content/story/262512.html.
[7] Samyabrata Ray Goswami, 'Man U Model for BCCI'. *The Telegraph*, December 28, 2005. http://www.telegraphindia.com/1051228/asp/nation/story_5652982.asp.
[8] India had 34,858,000 TV sets in 1992. Joshi and Trivedi, *Mass Media and Cross-Cultural Communication*, 16. The National Readership Studies Council 2006 survey estimated a total of 112 million television sets in India. NRS 2006, *Key Findings*, 4.
[9] PricewaterhouseCoopers, Federation of Indian Chambers of Commerce and Industry [hereafter PwC-FICCI], *The Indian Entertainment Industry*, 36.
[10] NRS 2006, *Key Findings*, 4, estimated 68 million satellite and cable households.
[11] India and China are not very big revenue earners for global corporations yet. For instance, Rupert Murdoch's pan-Asian network, STAR contributed less than 2% of News Corporation's total revenues until early 2005 but in strategic terms, the sheer numbers of China and India mean that these two countries are key focus areas for the corporation over the next decade. Personal Interview with Peter Mukerjea, Chief Executive, STAR India, 1999–2006, Mumbai: January 12, 2005. For Chinese television see, for example, Wang, Liu and Fore, 'Facing the Challenge: Chinese Television in the New Media Era'; Curtin, *Playing to the World's Biggest Audience*.
[12] The Union Ministry of Information and Broadcasting has a master list of 290 channels: 207 of these are licensed Indian private channels, 54 are foreign-owned and 27 are run by the state-controlled Doordarshan. http://mib.nic.in/informationb/CODES/frames.htm (November 5, 2005; November 11, 2006). Ministry of Information and Broadcasting, *Answer to Lok Sabha Unstarred Question No.2056*. March 9, 2006. http://164.100.24.208/lsq14/quest.asp?qref=26637, [hereafter MIB+date]. The actual numbers of channels is much higher because a large number of foreign and local channels are not covered by official data. A good example is the Delhi High

Court order of June 17, 2006 that restrained 92 cable operators in 11 states from telecasting the FIFA World Cup through free-to-air satellite channels like TV5, Cambodia TV, CC5 Channel, CCTV1, Super Sports, Multi-choice and Dream Satellite because none of them were registered with the MIB. 'Delhi High Court Restrains 92 Cable Operators From Unauthorized Telecast of the FIFA World Cup'. June 17, 2006. http://www.indiantelevision.com/headlines/y2k6/june/june240.htm.

[13] See for instance, Bandyopadhyay, '1911 in Retrospect: A Revisionist Perspective on a Famous Indian Sporting Victory', 27–47.

[14] *Amrit Bazar Patrika*, July 31, 1911.

[15] Quoted in *Mohun Bagan Platinum Jubilee Souvenir*, 25.

[16] *Nayak*, August 4, 1911.

[17] Swami Vivekanand, quoted in Majumdar and Bandyopadhyay, 'A Social History of Indian Football', 17.

[18] Majumdar and Bandyopadhyay, 'A Social History of Indian Football', 4.

[19] Bose, *A History of Indian Cricket*, 16–17.

[20] Majumdar, *Goalless: The Story of a Unique Footballing Nation*.

[21] Majumdar and Bandyopadhyay, 'A Social History of Indian Football', 173.

[22] Alarm bells rang in India when Helsinki, in 1949, expressed its unwillingness to host all hockey teams for 1952 because of lack of accommodation. The Indian Hockey Federation immediately proposed to the IOC to host the hockey event separately in Delhi. Eventually Helsinki did host the event but the Indian offer was indicative of how important hockey was to Indian sport. Letter from Dr A.C. Chatterji, Honorary Secretary, Indian Hockey Federation to Mr Demaurex, Honorary Secretary, Switzerland Hockey Federation, May 10, 1949.

[23] De Mello, *Portrait of Indian Sport*, 3.

[24] Ibid.

[25] Ibid.

[26] See Guha, *Corner of a Foreign Field*.

[27] See Majumdar, *22 Yards to Freedom*.

[28] De Mello, *Portrait of Indian Sport*, 9.

[29] Kumar, 'Whither Indian Hockey-I?'.

[30] This oft-repeated expression of Nehru's came to typify the Nehruvian economic model: a socialist model, but unlike the Soviet path, this 'mixed economy' model was presaged on a dominant public sector leading the march to development, a strong protectionist bias, a general pessimism over capitalism and a belief in the superiority of socialist planning. The Indian economic model, created by the statistician P.C. Mahalanobis, intellectually stemmed from Paul Baran's thesis, *The Political Economy of Growth*, which rejected capitalism as a model for development. See for instance Desai, 'Capitalism, Socialism and the Indian Economy', 186–90.

[31] The government required the Indian Broadcasting Company to collect licence fees and its share of import duties on radio equipment on its own. When the company collapsed, it was taken over by the government and renamed as the Indian State Broadcasting Service. The nomenclature of All India Radio was adopted in 1936. Until 1937, it functioned under the Department of Industries and Labour, whereupon it was transferred to the Department of Communication. The new Department of Information and Broadcasting assumed control over it in 1941 and upon independence in 1947, it became a new ministry. Chatterjee, *Broadcasting in India*, 39–41.

[32] Ninan, *Through the Magic Window*, 18–19.

[33] Doordarshan figures quoted in Bhatt, *Satellite Invasion of India*, Appendix VII, 281.

[34] Page and Crawley, *Satellites Over South Asia*, 53–6.

[35] Chatterjee, *Broadcasting in India*, 52–3.

[36] Fighting widespread opposition to her rule, Prime Minister Indira Gandhi declared an Emergency in 1975. It suspended democratic rights and remained in place until 1977 when she revoked it only to be swept out of power in a landslide verdict against her regime.

[37] Page and Crawley, *Satellites Over South Asia*, 54–6.

[38] Ninan, *Through the Magic Window*, 28–9.

[39] Mir Ranjan Negi's Interview with Shekhar Gupta, *The Indian Express*, September 17, 2007.

[40] Shekhar Gupta, 'Hockey Just Isn't Cricket'. *The Indian Express*, September 7, 2002.

[41] Guha, *India After Gandhi*, 736–7.

[42] Ninan, *Through the Magic Window*, 30.

[43] Page and Crawley, *Satellites Over South Asia*, 56.

44  Mazzarella, *Shoveling Smoke*, 98.
45  See, for example, Mankekar, *Screening Culture, Viewing Politics*; Rajagopal, *Politics After Television*.
46  Quoted in Mazzarella, *Shoveling Smoke*, 74–5.
47  Vir Sanghvi, 'A New Middle Class Fidelity?' *The Hindustan Times* (New Delhi), May 20, 2006. http://www.hindustantimes.com/news/181_1702508,00300001.htm.
48  Shalimar Mary, Letter to Editor. *Indian Express*, October 5, 1986. Quoted in Nandy, *The Tao of Cricket*, 1–2.
49  Harsha Bhogle, 'India Needs to Rediscover Another Sport'. *The Week*, July 27, 2003.
50  Ibid.
51  See for instance the interview by Dhanraj Pillai, India's most successful hockey player of the 1990s, 'They Don't Give a Damn'. *Tehelka* http://www.tehelka.com/story_main31.asp?filename= hub160607They_dont.asp.
52  Rohit Brijnath, 'The Lopsidedness in Indian Sports'. *Sportstar*, June 5–11, 2004.
53  Rupert Murdoch's News Corporation bought a controlling stake in Sky in 1983 and re-launched as Sky Television in 1989, but it made heavy losses until 1992 when BSkyB (Sky and BSB merged in 1990) acquired the rights to broadcast Premier League Soccer games for US$465 million. Almost a million subscribers signed up immediately and by 1993 BSkyB reached financial stability. Anand and Attea, *News Corporation*, 8. For a concise history of Sky Television and News Corporation's television operations, see also Ghemawat, *British Satellite Broadcasting Versus Sky Television*.
54  In 1999, for instance, News Corporation owned the Los Angeles Dodgers baseball club and had shares in the New York Knicks and Los Angeles Lakers basketball clubs, and the New York Rangers. In September 1998, BSkyB launched a take over bid for Manchester United, the world's richest football club, which was blocked by the British Mergers and Monopolies Commission on grounds that it was 'anti-competitive' in broadcasting. Rowe, 'To Serve and To Sell: Media Sport and Cultural Citizenship', 186.
55  Emphasis is mine. Rupert Murdoch to his shareholders in Adelaide, October 15, 1996. Quoted in S. Millar, 'Courtship Ends as Soccer and TV are United'. *The Guardian*, September 7, 1998.
56  Majumdar, *Twenty-Two Yards to Freedom*, 176. ESPN is part of ESPN-STAR which is jointly owned by News Corporation and Walt Disney.
57  Majumdar, *The Illustrated History of Indian Cricket*, 198.
58  *Supreme Court Case 161 before Justices, P.B. Sawant, S. Mohan and B.P. Jeevan Reddy, Civil Appeals Nos. 1429–30 of 1995, The Secretary Information & Broadcasting, Government of India & Others vs. Cricket Association of Bengal & Others, with Writ Petition (Civil) No.836 of 1993, Cricket Association of Bengal vs. Union of India and Others* (decided on February 9, 1995).
59  *The Indian Telegraph Act*, Act XIII of 1885, pt. II.
60  Section 7 of Act 47 of 1957, an amendment to the 1885 Act. There were five amendments to this Act from 1957 to 1974. Ninan, 'History of Indian Broadcasting Reform', 1–2.
61  The five nations that eventually participated in the Hero Cup were India, South Africa, West Indies, Sri Lanka and Zimbabwe.
62  Doordarshan put in a bid of Rs10 million (roughly US$318, 471 at 1993 exchange rates), as against TWI's vastly superior minimum guarantee of US$550,000. It was specified that if TWI received any sum in excess of the guaranteed sum, it would be split in a 70:30 ratio in favour of CAB. *Supreme Court Case 161 before Justices, P.B. Sawant, S. Mohan and B.P. Jeevan Reddy, Civil Appeals Nos. 1429–30 of 1995*.
63  Majumdar, 'Cricket, Television, Globalization: Defining India in the 1990s', 2.
64  VSNL was created as a public-sector undertaking in 1986. The Government of India first disinvested some stake in 1999 but remained a majority stakeholder till 2002. It is now managed by the Tatas.
65  *Supreme Court Case 161 before Justices, P.B. Sawant, S. Mohan and B.P. Jeevan Reddy, Civil Appeals Nos. 1429–30 of 1995*.
66  A senior Ministry official quoted in Majumdar, 'Cricket, Television, Globalization: Defining India in the 1990s', 7.
67  *Supreme Court Case 161 before Justices, P.B. Sawant, S. Mohan and B.P. Jeevan Reddy, Civil Appeals Nos. 1429–30 of 1995*.
68  C.R. Irani, 'Someone is Remembering Sanjay Gandhi'. *The Statesman*, November 13, 1993.
69  Majumdar, 'Cricket, Television, Globalization: Defining India in the 1990s', 8.

70 *Supreme Court Case 161 before Justices, P.B. Sawant, S. Mohan and B.P. Jeevan Reddy, Civil Appeals Nos. 1429–30 of 1995.*
71 Majumdar, 'Cricket, Television, Globalization: Defining India in the 1990s', 9–10.
72 *Supreme Court Case 161 before Justices, P.B. Sawant, S. Mohan and B.P. Jeevan Reddy, Civil Appeals Nos. 1429–30 of 1995.*
73 Meenal Baghel, 'Doordarshan Jams VSNL Plans to Uplink'. *The Asian Age*, September 19, 1994.
74 B.P.J. Reddy concurring, *Supreme Court Case 161 before Justices, P.B. Sawant, S. Mohan and B.P. Jeevan Reddy, Civil Appeals Nos. 1429–30 of 1995.*
75 Ten Sports estimated its initial damages to be worth Rs2.8 billion. 'DD to get Ten Sports Feed for all Matches'. *The Hindu Business Line*, March, 18, 2004.
76 Ministry of Information and Broadcasting, *Policy Guidelines for Downlinking of Television Channels.*
77 'Supreme Court Restrains DD from Interfering with Rights of Ten Sports'. *The Hindu*, May 10, 2006.
78 'Don't Interfere with Ten Sports' Rights: Court'. *The Hindu*, August 5, 2006.
79 UNI, 'SC Allows ESPN-STAR to Approach it if Coerced by the Centre'. January 8, 2007. http://www.indlawnews.com/2C829C337F2DBD858EAC77A54263988C.
80 PTI, 'Telecast India-WI Series with Delay: HC'. January 23, 2007. http://timesofindia.indiatimes.com/articleshow/1403569.cms.
81 The government contended that about 9–10% of Doordarshan's 25% share would pay for its expenditure in the broadcast while the remaining revenue would be ploughed back into national sports. Rajya Sabha, Synopsis of Debates (Proceedings other than Questions and Answers), *Statutory Resolution Seeking Disapproval of the Sports Broadcasting Signals (Mandatory Sharing with Prasar Bharati) Ordinance, 2007 and the Sports Broadcasting Signals (Mandatory Sharing with Prasar Bharati) Bill, 2007.*
82 Ibid.
83 Ibid.
84 The BCCI agreed to share half of the losses. PTI, 'BCCI to Share Nimbus Losses'. March 23, 2007. http://www.indianexpress.com/story/26365.html.
85 In the Rajya Sabha, for instance, only two speakers dissented. http://www.rajyasabha.nic.in/rsdebate/synopsis/210/09032007.htm.
86 Purnendu Bose, COO, SaharaOne, quoted in Latha Venkatraman and Ajita Shashidhar, 'Taking Refuge in Cricket'. *Business Line*, March 9, 2006.
87 When Kerry Packer's Channel 9 failed to win the broadcast rights to Australian cricket, he set up World Series Cricket as an independent cricket attraction. Channel 9's WSC signed up the world's top international players and introduced day-night one-day games, coloured clothing and aggressive marketing tactics to re-invent cricket as a television game. For details see Haigh, *The Cricket War.*

## References

Anand, Bharat, and Kate Attea. *News Corporation*. Harvard Business School Case No.9-702-425. Boston: Harvard Business School Publishing, Rev. June 27, 2003.
Appadurai, Arjun. *Modernity at Large: Cultural Dimensions of Globalization*. Minneapolis, MN: University of Minnesota Press, 1996.
Bandyopadhyay, Kausik, '1911 in Retrospect: A Revisionist Perspective on a Famous Indian Sporting Victory'. In *Sport in South Asian Society: Past and Present*, edited by Boria Majumdar and J.A. Mangan. London: Routledge, 2005.
Bhatt, S.C. *Satellite Invasion of India*. New Delhi: Gyan Publishing, 1994.
Bose, Mihir. *A History of Indian Cricket*. London: Andre Deutsch Ltd., 1990.
Chatterjee, P.C. *Broadcasting in India*. 2nd ed. New Delhi: Sage, 1991.
Curtin, Michael. *Playing to the World's Biggest Audience: The Globalization of Chinese Film and TV*. Berkeley, CA: University of California Press, 2007.
De Mello, Anthony. *Portrait of Indian Sport*. London: P.R. Macmillan, 1959.
Desai, Lord Meghnad. 'Capitalism, Socialism and the Indian Economy'. In *India: Joining the World Economy*, edited by Kalyan Bannerji and Tarjani Vakil, 183–200. New Delhi: Tata McGraw-Hill, 1995.

Ghemawat, Pankaj. *British Satellite Broadcasting Versus Sky Television*. Harvard Business School No.9-794-031. Boston: Harvard Business School Publishing, Rev. August 22, 1994.

Guha, Ramachandra. *Corner of a Foreign Field: The Indian History of a British Sport*. New Delhi: Pan Macmillan, 2002.

Guha, Ramachandra. *India After Gandhi: The History of the World's Largest Democracy*. New Delhi: Picador, 2007.

Haigh, Gideon. *The Cricket War: The Inside Story of Kerry Packer's World Series Cricket*. Melbourne: Text, 1993.

Joshi, S.R. *Asia Speaks Out: The Indian Television Landscape*, Report No.SRG-96-047. Ahmedabad: Development and Educational Communication Unit, Indian Space Research Organisation, April 1996.

Joshi, S.R., and Bela Trivedi. *Mass Media and Cross-Cultural Communication: A Study of Television in India*. Report No.SRG-94-041. Ahmedabad: Development and Educational Communication Unit, Indian Space Research Organisation, May 1994.

Kumar, Ashwini. 'Whither Indian Hockey-I?' *Indian Olympic Association Official Bulletin* 1, no. 2 (Jan.–Mar. 1960).

Majumdar, Boria. *22 Yards to Freedom: A Social History of Indian Cricket*. New Delhi: Penguin, 2004.

Majumdar, Boria. 'Cricket, Television, Globalization: Defining India in the 1990s'. Paper presented at the 'Television in Asia' conference, La Trobe University. Melbourne, December 14, 2005.

Majumdar, Boria. *The Illustrated History of Indian Cricket*. New Delhi: Roli, 2006.

Majumdar, Boria, and Kausik Bandyopadhyay. *A Social History of Indian Football: Striving to Score*. London: Routledge, 2006.

Majumdar, Boria, and Kausik Bandyopadhyay. *Goalless: The Story of a Unique Footballing Nation*. New Delhi: Penguin/Viking, 2006.

Mankekar, Purnima. *Screening Culture, Viewing Politics: An Ethnography of Television, Womanhood, and Nation in Postcolonial India*. Durham, NC: Duke University Press, 1999.

Mazzarella, William. *Shoveling Smoke: Advertising and Globalization in Contemporary India*. Durham, NC: Duke University Press, 2003.

Mehta, Nalin. 'The Great Indian Willow Trick: Cricket, Nationalism and India's TV News Revolution, 1998–2005', *The International Journal of the History of Sport* 24, no. 9 (2007): 1187–99.

*Mohun Bagan Platinum Jubilee Souvenir*. Calcutta: Mohun Bagan Club, 1964.

Nandy, Ashis. *The Tao of Cricket: On Games of Destiny and the Destiny of the Games*. New York: Viking, 1989.

National Readership Studies Council. *2006 – Key Findings*, Press Release. Mumbai: August 29, 2006.

Ninan, Sevanti. *Through the Magic Window: Television and Change in India*. New Delhi: Penguin, 1995.

Ninan, Sevanti. 'History of Indian Broadcasting Reform'. In *Broadcasting Reform in India: Media Law from a Global Perspective*, edited by Monroe E. Price and Stefaan G. Verhulst, 1–21. New Delhi: Oxford University Press, 1998.

Page, David, and Crawley William. *Satellites Over South Asia: Broadcasting, Culture and the Public Interest*. New Delhi: Sage, 2001.

PricewaterhouseCoopers, Federation of Indian Chambers of Commerce and Industry. *The Indian Entertainment Industry: An Unfolding Opportunity*. New Delhi: March 2005.

Rajagopal, Arvind. *Politics After Television: Religious Nationalism and the Reshaping of the Indian Public*. Cambridge: Cambridge University Press, 2001.

Rajya Sabha. Synopsis of Debates (Proceedings other than Questions and Answers). *Statutory Resolution Seeking Disapproval of the Sports Broadcasting Signals (Mandatory Sharing with Prasar Bharati) Ordinance, 2007 and the Sports Broadcasting Signals (Mandatory Sharing with Prasar Bharati) Bill, 2007*, (March 9, 2007). http://www.rajyasabha.nic.in/rsdebate/synopsis/210/09032007.htm

Rowe, David. 'To Serve and To Sell: Media Sport and Cultural Citizenship'. Paper presented at How you Play the Game: First International Conference on Sports and Human Rights, Sydney, September 1–3, 199. http://www.ausport.gov.au/fulltext/1999/nsw/p182-191.pdf.

*Supreme Court Case 161 before Justices, P.B. Sawant, S. Mohan and B.P. Jeevan Reddy, Civil Appeals Nos. 1429–30 of 1995, The Secretary Information & Broadcasting, Government of India & Others*

*vs. Cricket Association of Bengal & Others, with Writ Petition (Civil) No.836 of 1993, Cricket Association of Bengal vs. Union of India and Others* (decided on February 9, 1995) http://openarchive.in/judis/10896.htm.

*The Indian Telegraph Act*, Act XIII of 1885, pt. II. http://www.dot.gov.in/Acts/telegraphact.htm.

Wang, Zhenzi, Zhi-Qiang Liu, and Steve Fore. 'Facing the Challenge: Chinese Television in the New Media Era'. *Media International Australia Incorporating Culture and Policy*, 'Copyright, Media and Innovation' 114 (February 2005): 135–146.

# Different hats, different thinking? Technocracy, globalization and the Indian cricket team

Stephen Wagg[a]* and Sharda Ugra[b]

[a]Carnegie Faculty of Sport and Education, Leeds Metropolitan University, Leeds, UK; [b]Cricket Editor, India Today

The essay's title is taken from an exercise that Australian Greg Chappell and his assistant set for the Indian cricket squad in what amounted to their first professional meeting after Chappell took over as Indian coach in 2005. This essay is, at one level, about Chappell's tenure – which lasted around two years (2005–07) – and its significance for the world of professional international cricket which has recently seen the emergence of foreign coaches. The principal purpose of this essay is to interpret this pattern and to suggest that Chappell is a cardinal example of a growing trend.

At another level, though, the essay is about Indian cricket culture in the context of contemporary Indian society and, thus, about globalization; about relations between East and West within the global economy and about the way contemporary international cricket is conceived and practised. The argument will be that there are important elements in the practices of the Chappell regime that are to do, firstly, with what Edward Said disparaged as 'orientalism', secondly, with neo-liberalism and the embrace by India's ruling elite of the capitalist global economy and, thirdly, with the emergence, in parallel with this embrace, of a global cricket technocracy which flattens out, or threatens to flatten out, what have been perceived as historic differences between national cricket cultures.

## Tools for thinking?

Greg Chappell, former captain of Australia and son of that country's first cricketing family (his brothers Ian and Trevor both played for Australia and a stand at South Australia's Adelaide Oval is named after them), was appointed coach of the Indian cricket team in May of 2005. Others short listed for the post were Tom Moody of Australia, Desmond Haynes of West Indies and Mohinder Amarnath of India. 'No coaching assignment in the game has quite generated this kind of hype', wrote Ajit Parker of *India Daily* at the time.

'Speculation has been mounting ever since the outgoing coach, the former New Zealand captain and Kent coach John Wright, suggested in February that he would not renew his contract after a largely successful four-year stint.' The six-man selection panel, set up by the Indian cricket board, included three former India captains: Sunil Gavaskar, Ravi Shastri and Srinivas Venkataraghavan.[1]

Compared with other sports, coaches are comparatively new in international cricket. The Indian cricket team has only had one since 1989, when Bishen Bedi was employed to coach the team on its tour of New Zealand. The first six men to take the job were all Indians: Bedi, Ajit Wadekar (1992–96), Sandeep Patil (1996), Madan Lal (1996–97), Anshuman Gaekwad (1997–99) and Kapil Dev (1999–2000). After Kapil Dev departed, amid unsubstantiated rumours of his involvement in match-fixing, leading Indian players who had played on the English county circuit lobbied for the post to go to New Zealander John Wright. He was appointed, ahead of Chappell and Geoff Marsh, both Australians (the former was interviewed; the latter was not).[2]

As things stood in the early spring of 2007, all the 'eastern' international cricket teams had 'western' coaches: Chappell, the Englishman Bob Woolmer at Pakistan, Australian Tom Moody, who coached Sri Lanka and Dav Whatmore (a naturalised Australian born in what is now Sri Lanka) who was in charge of Bangladesh. It is difficult to dismiss this as coincidence, particularly since no 'western' national cricket sides are tutored by 'eastern' coaches. In 2004 the West Indies Cricket Board appointed an all-Australian coaching team of four, headed by Bennett King. King, the first non-Caribbean to have the job, had never played first class cricket. (He was replaced in June of 2007 by his deputy David Moore.) When Mickey Arthur was appointed in 2005 to coach his own national side of South Africa, Moody, Marsh and fellow Australian Steve Waugh are said to have been the other candidates.[3] New Zealand and, needless to say, Australia are coached in-house and, until the summer of 2007, England were coached by the Zimbabwean Duncan Fletcher.

Chappell's appointment was part of a larger pattern in international cricket. One of the factors said to have persuaded the appointment panel to take him on is said to have been Chappell's presentation on the theme of 'Commitment to excellence'.[4] In the following pages we outline some important aspects of this declared quest for excellence in Indian cricket and then attempt an analysis of it.

In mid-July 2005, two months into the new regime, *The Hindu* reported from Bangalore on Chappell's 'first formal interaction as coach with the Indian players', which took the form of a 'cricket skills camp'.[5] This report appears beneath the headline 'Chappell Asks Players to Make Their Own Destiny'[6] – on reflection, a powerful and heterodox request in a culture still at least partly wedded to the notion that destiny is given and not achieved. The first decisive step toward excellence and destiny had been taken under the tutelage of Shiva Subramaniam of Tata Consultancy Services, here described as 'among the world's 20 master teachers of the Edward de Bono method'. This method is said to have given the players 'tools for thinking'.

'You have tools for cutting vegetables', Shiva informed a sceptical media contingent, 'you have tools for communicating but we don't have tools for thinking'. These tools for thinking were to be imparted via de Bono's 'coloured hat' principle:

> the five hats, white hat for information, yellow hat for benefits, black hats for problems, green hat for creativity, and red hat for feelings and the last hat is the blue hat which controls my thinking. Which tells me to go from one hat to another. Essentially, we are talking about tools for thinking.[7]

At this press conference Chappell intervened forcefully to support his de Bono expert: 'The tools help in organised thinking, so that, in team sessions, we can get the players focussed on speaking about the same subject, rather than talking at cross purposes'.[8] The *Deccan Herald*, another leading paper, underlined Chappell's emphasis on 'mind games', continuing: 'the Aussie then admitted that de Bono will play a huge part in Team India's prospects in the coming season'.[9]

Two months on and there occurred a substantial public contretemps between the coach and the team captain, Sourav Ganguly. Ganguly, the son of a wealthy Kolkata family had, according to various cricket web pages, been nicknamed 'Bengal Tiger' and 'Prince of Calcutta' by his team-mates and 'Lord Snooty' by his opponents.[10] Chappell was reported to have said that Ganguly is 'mentally and physically unfit to lead the team' and that his 'attitude and outlook are not ideal'. He was also said to be 'miffed that the Indian captain does not follow the fitness regimen prescribed, and most of the time uses the false pretext of injury to exempt himself'.[11] Already, by late September, this was being described as 'the Sourav Ganguly – Greg Chappell saga' and Chappell had sent a lengthy email to the Board of Control for Cricket in India (BCCI) explaining his position. In it the coach claimed that Ganguly had been 'struggling as a player'. 'I also told him that his state of mind was fragile and it showed in the way that he made decisions on and off the field in relation to the team, especially team selection'. Chappell remarked later in the email, 'I told him of my own experiences toward the end of my career and cited other players such as Border, Taylor and Steve Waugh, all of whom struggled with batting form toward the end of their tenure as Australian captain'. He goes on: 'Greg King's [the team's trainer] reports continue to show Sourav as the person who does the least fitness and training work based on the criterion that has been developed by the support staff to monitor the work load of all the players'. He concludes: 'It is time that all players were treated with fairness and equity and that good behaviours and attitudes are rewarded at the selection table rather than punished'. The email was signed 'Greg Chappell MBE'.[12] Ganguly was omitted from the Indian team the following month.

In early October, Chappell's assistant, biomechanist Ian Frazer, entered the fray with another purported lesson in modern organizational methods for the Indian cricket authorities. The terms in which this lesson was couched were explicitly political and sociological. The *Express News Service* reported him as saying that the BCCI 'have to come to terms fast with making "hard decisions" when it came to a player's retirement'.[13] Frazer, said Indians, despite their diverse cultural background, had the ability to make such hard decisions. 'Indians have entered the business world, they are in the global market where they make decisions every day. It is a natural consequence. It can be done, and done professionally'.[14]

Chappell's email soon became public, as did Ganguly's lengthy rebuttal of its claims. In *India Today* Sharda Ugra announced an 'uneasy truce', with the headline 'Recipe for Disaster'.[15] 'He hears you out but sometimes you feel he is not listening to you', a player told her. 'Chappell has made it known that the anxiety he sees in the team is an exercise in weaning the weak from the strong'.[16] The article closed with a commentary by ex-Indian Test cricketer Sanjay Manjrekar. Manjrekar wrote,

> What would have been really sad was if Chappell had headed home ... That would have meant that we as a nation would have made a strong statement: that India was not a place for a man on a mission who wanted to make a difference and was willing to speak his mind at the risk of losing a highly lucrative job. That would have been a tragic portrayal of our country ... If Chappell succeeds, India will go to the next level.[17]

Two months later Chappell told *India Today*:

> The disciplines of what it takes to be successful are universal; it does not matter what environment you are in. We have obviously had to massage them [the players] to fit into a different culture. I mean Indians are not as used to the straightforward. We have had to speak more slowly for the boys to understand our accent.[18]

By January 2006 the *Indian Express* website reported that Indian opening batsman Virender Sehwag had been engaging in a 'simple schoolyard exercise devised to test and sharpen reflexes – But Ian Frazer, Team India's biomechanist has a more respectable name for it: Repositioning, or "neural stimuli"'.[19] Six months later, in June 2006, Chappell was interviewed for *Indian Express* by Ajay S. Shankar, who asked him the definitely leading questions, 'Have you ever encountered a clash of cultures during your stint? In India there's always a lot of sentiment attached to team selection, how have you handled that?' Here Chappell did not blink:

> No differently from any time in the past. I think honesty is the best policy. You need to deal with the truth if you want to be successful at this level. You have to be honest with yourself, you have to be honest with your teammates. I think, as coach, I have to be honest with the players. I don't know any other way, and that's the way I am going to be. I think, so far, the players have understood that and have respected it.[20]

In mid-October 2006, the Chandigarh-based paper *The Tribune* reported from New Delhi that Kapil Dev, recently appointed chair of the National cricket academy, did not know what the role entailed, thus calling into question BCCI claims of an enhanced professionalism in the commanding heights of Indian cricket. Dev, however, turned on Chappell. In a report headlined 'Chappell's methods foreign to Indians', *The Tribune* quoted the former Indian captain as disapproving of Chappell's policy of continuous experimentation with the composition and strategies of the Indian team, saying Indian players performed better when their place in the side was secure. 'Indians are not very comfortable with uncertainty. They need to be sure of their spot in the team to instill confidence in them', the World Cup-winning captain said. He attributed this factor to the culture and the general upbringing provided in the country. Kapil continued,

> We need our base to be strong. We are brought up that way. Even in other walks of life, Indians were not very amenable to change ... We don't change our bases readily for better jobs and higher salary. We want to stay close to home.[21]

On 25 November *Indian Express* reported that politicians were baying for Chappell's head, but that BCCI 'top guns' were considering asking him to stay on beyond the World Cup of 2007.[22] In December the *Calcutta Times* (the *Times of India*'s Calcutta city supplement) discussed the 'flak' that Chappell had drawn during his 18 months in the job. Among the opinions solicited here is that of former India opener and BJP (Bharatiya Janata Party, directly translated as Indian People's Party, is India's principal opposition party at the time of writing with a distinct ideology of right-wing Hindu nationalism) MP, Chetan Chauhan, who was 'not yet ready to label foreign coaches as unsuccessful'. Asked for his views, Chauhan, himself a former Test cricketer and a former Indian selector noted:

> It is too early to say that. Performance of the players is also a factor. The coaches have to be given a free hand and their strategy has to be right. One big problem with foreign coaches is that they haven't seen domestic cricket and are not accustomed to Indian conditions. Apart from the language and tradition of the country, the cricket culture is also very different. Here, the media and the public are hysteric, there is tremendous pressure, there are pressure groups in administration too ... Chappell is a great player but his experiments have boomeranged. In Australia and England the players are mentally very mature and independent. But that is not

the case in India. Some of the players are not yet ready for international cricket. The chopping and changing policy has not yielded results.[23]

Chappell ended the year still defending himself against growing criticism, resorting once again, like many spokespeople in this ongoing controversy, to a comparison of ethnicities. 'I'm an Australian', he told reporters, 'we are used to being blunt, saying things as they are. We can continue to be fine with each other after that too. In India, maybe people take it as a slight and don't forget it easily'.[24]

## The Chappell way: globalization and the politics of cricket coaching

In this final section we will try to make some sense of the Chappell furore and of the trend for 'eastern' cricket nations to seek 'western' coaches.

First of all, there have, perhaps inevitably, been postcolonial elements in the discourse over Chappell. Pranay Daryanani of the *Merinews* website recently compared the 'anti-Chappell' refrain to the angry reception Indians gave to Sir John Simon's commission on Indian governance which sat in 1942. Disparaged as 'Guru Greg', he is met, says Daryanani, with burnt effigies and 'Chappell, go back' placards everywhere he goes.[25] There is, in many Indian eyes, perhaps some substance to the notion of Chappell and his entourage as some kind of neo-colonial flagship.

Secondly, the wrangle over Chappell and his modus operandi is replete with ethnic stereotyping, but the picture here is complex and no clear-cut case can be made for an Orientalist discourse. To be sure, well-meaning, but intellectually unreliable, generalizations about Indian cricket are not hard to find in the international cricket world. The writer and commentator Simon Hughes, for example, wrote in 2000:

> The more I thought about it, the more I realised that Indian driving was like their cricket. Their batting was cheeky, pushy, risky, there was a general absence of braking. It was erratic and balls, like cars, had a habit of shooting off at odd angles. The hullabaloo their fielders made as they swarmed round the bat was no different to the chaos and commotion on the roads. In fact the rules about horning and appealing were identical.[26]

Generally speaking, Greg Chappell had resisted such Kiplingesque judgments, for the most part arguing simply that Indian players must not be afraid of change or bear grudges. This had applied even when he was posed pointedly leading questions about a 'clash of cultures'. The racial/ethnic generalizations in this chapter of Indian cricket history were at least as likely to come from Chappell's critics, whether Indians like Chetan Chauhan (England players are 'mentally very mature', Indian players are not) and Kapil Dev, as from Chappell's own country. Indeed the most wholehearted denunciation both of Chappell's methods and of the rush to appoint western coaches came from ex-Australian captain and coach, Bobby Simpson. In his 'Cricket Corner' column on the *Sportstar* web site, Simpson argued:

> The Indian selectors and Greg Chappell seem to be trying to change Indian cricket to fit in with their theory of how the game, and in particular one-day cricket, should be played. While more theories abound today than ever before, cricket is still a simple game that is only made more difficult by well meaning theorists.
> My whole theory on coaching the cricketers is based on improving the natural talents of the players and the culture of their game. Almost every country has its natural way of playing the game. Australia are different to England. South Africa and New Zealand are different to Australia and more like England. *The Asian countries are similar to each other, but have slightly different ways of using their incredibly flexible wrists while batting.* The West Indies have their own individual style, and thank goodness, this is what makes them so different and (more) exciting than the other countries. Unfortunately, the globalisation of world cricket and

the predominance of clipboard, biomechanical and scientific coaching have tended to muddle the natural skills of the players.

Equally unfortunate is that Australia seem to be the heartbeat of this movement and the Australian coaches now all the rage with Tom Moody (Sri Lanka), Greg Chappell (India) and Bennett King (West Indies). Fellow clipboard Englishman Bob Woolmer coaches Pakistan.

What worries me greatly is that in their desire for change and their faith in the so-called scientific approach, they will destroy the naturalness and culture of cricket in these lands.

Everybody now wants to jump the Australian bandwagon.[27] (emphasis added)

Hughes' and Simpson's observations, though undoubtedly well meant, would certainly have had Edward Said[28] reaching for his revolver. But, doubtful references to flexible wrists aside, Simpson's article recognizes something which is at the heart of the Chappell project, and of the appointment of similar coaches in similar situations elsewhere in the international cricket world: that it is about the attempted dismantling of national cricket cultures or the passage, to adopt Hilary Beckles' terms in relation to Caribbean cricket, from the nationalist phase of development to the age of globalization.[29] This transition has caused anguish in the West Indies, where writers such as Tim Hector sought to reconcile Caribbean cricket with science and modernity while maintaining it as a site of nationalist struggle.[30] In India, the minds of the national cricket team have similarly drifted on from thoughts of independence and national self-realization to a point where 'the symbolic undoing of colonial history is no longer a priority'.[31]

International cricket, especially given the growth in the importance of one-day cricket over the last 30 years, is a continuous, year-round affair. India's players, like comparable players of other countries, spend less and less time in their own countries and communities and more and more time on the international circuit. When they are in India, the Indian players have the status of celebrities – when he came to India, Chappell likened them to the Beatles[32] – and that status is, naturally, contingent on their performance as players. It is worth remembering that India's first foreign/western coach (John Wright, taken on in 2000) was appointed at the instigation of several of the Indian players, who knew him from the English county circuit. The aspirations of the players – to maintain and improve their performances on the international stage – marry with those of the BCCI. The Indian cricket team, as opposed to cricket in the regions and localities, is a massively popular culture in India and, since the early 1990s, its matches have been opened up to the commercial media. Here, and in the stadia, it commands huge audiences, but, in recent times,

the end result in favour or against the national team began to occupy the mind of the spectator, especially the one newly arrived to the game, to a greater extent than the quality of the cricket played ... the cricket match has become a barometer of national self worth.[33]

And the now-prevalent one-day cricket allows no draws.

This is where Chappell, or somebody like him, comes in. The people that run India, and Indian cricket, do not have unduly flexible wrists, nor are they congenitally incapable of driving a car in a straight line. They run call centres, finance companies, film studios and computer businesses and, like all Indian governments of the last 15 years, they are fierce advocates of neo-liberal economic policies, privatization and the global capitalist economy.

In this context, cricket is important in two ways. First, like cinema, it is a bridge between the country's elite and the masses – a shared national treasure and, like the nuclear bomb (successfully tested in May 1998), a visible means by which Indians might feel good about themselves in a globalized world. A thriving Indian team, then, is the basis for what we can still call hegemony. Second, it is a vehicle for the ideology of neo-liberalism itself and a means to the imparting of the stark disciplines that characterize the global marketplace. In a recent analysis of 'reality TV', sociologist Nick Couldry revived a notion of the historian E.P. Thompson, namely that 'every shift in economic organization ... (requires) new disciplines, new incentives, and a new human nature'.[34] Like 'reality TV' and other popular cultural manifestations, the Indian cricket team is becoming a theatre for the rehearsal of neo-liberal truths. The players in this theatre are coming under increased surveillance and must handle their 'workloads', they are flexible and will be laid off when their efficiency as economic units has diminished, they must clear their minds (with the enigmatic assistance of Edward de Bono) of unnecessary cultural baggage. As Couldry observes, neo-liberalism 'legitimates the market and de-legitimates the social'.[35] Indeed Ian Frazer, Chappell's right-hand man, said as much when calling for the laying off of cricketers past their best: 'Indians have entered the business world, they are in the global market where they make decisions every day. It is a natural consequence.'[36] Corroboration of this comes from leading Indian former cricketers turned commentators such as Manjrekar who already speak the restricted code of the global marketplace with its deadpan allusions to 'making a difference' and 'going to the next level'.

There is, almost certainly, a sense on the part of the 'modernizers' of Indian cricket (and Indian society) that these disciplines must come largely from outside India – from countries where sport and wider work cultures have travelled further in divesting themselves of tradition and restrictive practice. Chappell is a bringer of 'truths' and 'realities' defined outside of an India still weaning itself off the planned economy and the postcolonial nationalism of Nehru's Congress Party. Although he was India's second foreign coach, Chappell clearly regarded himself as the first bringer of these market truths.

Chappell's altercation with Ganguly was symbolic. While Wright had looked benignly back upon his relationship with the 'Prince of Kolkata', suggesting that the two of them had been united in seeking 'to create a new team culture and give the most passionate cricket nation in the world the team they deserved',[37] Chappell had made an example of Ganguly as a lazy, privileged token of the old order. In his famous email he rebuked Wright for his indulgence here,[38] and while he dispensed these new disciplines Chappell would run the gauntlet of a populist media, one minute comparing him to previous white invaders who sought to tamper with the Indian psyche, and the next, accusing him of failing to face down the senior players in the Indian dressing room, who stood between the nation and the beckoning world of cricket modernity.

But Chappell also related, and still relates, to the global marketplace on his own account. He has a global reputation derived from his gifted batsmanship, his captaincy of Australia and as author of the most pragmatic act in modern cricket history – when, as captain of Australia in a one-day international against New Zealand at the Melbourne Cricket Ground in February of 1981, he ordered his brother Trevor to bowl the final ball of the game under arm, so that New Zealand, needing six, could not win. Moreover, as an Australian, he is a leading representative of an aggressively competitive and successful national sport culture, within an equally aggressive, marketised economy. Chappell has had the attitudes to match, these being characterized by his biographer as 'a true conservatism – conservation is fine, but who paid for it?; erotica OK, pornography no; was Aboriginal rights back-door apartheid?; export uranium and retain the nuclear alliance'. Chappell was associated with the right wing Nationalist Party and, in the early 1980s, was briefly rumoured to be going into politics.[39] Chappell stayed with cricket but he undoubtedly saw, and wished to exploit, the market possibilities of a modernizing 'guru coach' in a cricket-crazy and increasingly entrepreneurial society.

Sunil Khilnani has described the emergence in India of a 'highly internationalised and entrepreneurial class – many with qualifications from America', the migration to India of foreign capital and multinational companies like Hewlett Packard in the 1990s, and the corresponding growth of cities like Bombay and Bangalore as the leading centres of 'Non Resident India'.[40] This rising entrepreneurial and cosmopolitan class, with its globalized aspirations and cultural horizons, is likely to provide a lucrative market for *The Chappell Way*, a training programme devised by Chappell and marketed via the Australian International Sports Academy (AISA) and an Indian marketing agency, The Flea. In India, The Flea has been appointed official affiliates of AISA. This programme is open to all boys between 12 and 20 years old, who wish to 'improve their game and learn what our national team is learning'. The Flea is also marketing AISA's coaching programmes for the Web and mobile phones. The official press release of the programme makes for instructive reading:

> The Chappell Way is a two-week programme that is meant to teach specialist skills to the participants, as well as inculcate a love for cricket. The training module takes into account a participant's individual strengths and weaknesses and hones them to perfection with personalized attention.
>
> 'We are proud to be associated with Greg Chappell and AISA and we hope to help them realize their vision of tapping the potential of talented youngsters all across India', says Sunil Shibad, Director, The Flea.
>
> Headquartered in Mumbai, with associates in Houston, St Louis, Brisbane and Pune, The Flea, India's first and only non-traditional marketing communication agency, is already carrying out viral and buzz marketing campaigns for clients such as Himalayan Natural Mineral Water, matrisearch.com, Idea Cellular, fropper.com, Jopasana Wildlife Conservation and Tain Construction. With AISA and The Chappell Way, the Flea is now entering the field of sports marketing.[41]

Frazer and Chappell are partners in what they call *The Chappell Way*. Tony Dell of AISA told India's *The Telegraph*, 'Right now our focus is largely India. The growing spending power of the middle class there is a big draw. And having Chappell there is a passport for us'.[42] We quote at length from this web story describing just how *The Chappell Way* functions:

> The camp, to which the first batch of students went in November, involves running, swimming, games and cricket training sessions peppered with sightseeing and lectures. With Chappell in India, most of the actual training is left to John Buchanan, the [current] coach of the Australian team, and Ian Healy, the former Australian wicketkeeper.
>
> For those that don't want to go all the way to Australia, The Chappell Way might soon come to India. 'We are hoping to start Greg Chappell Clinics in various schools and sports academies across India from June. There is talk also of an AISA team touring India, playing and conducting Chappell Way Clinics', said Dell ...
>
> Also in the pipeline is a reality TV show, from which the winner will get an all-expenses paid trip to Australia for The Chappell Way package, which Shibad describes as 'Greg's personally researched and patented mode of training'.
>
> 'Though The Chappell Way is generally brought to young cricketers through CD-ROMs and online interactive sessions, the Indian coach has designed a special in situ programme in Australia specifically for Indians. It shows his commitment towards India', Shibad said ...
>
> 'the cricket programme [is] brought to India by some of Australia's best coaches and communicators, people that have helped make Australia a great cricketing nation', he said ...
> 'For many youngsters hoping to sign up for the India coach's package, there's also the trip to Australia to look forward to, not counting the brag value among peers'.[43]

This is another key characteristic of life in the global economy – the commercially strategic presentation of self, using one's life, achievements and personal 'philosophy' as a purported navigational aid between newly enriched middle-class children and the dreams (cricket greatness, meeting/being coached by a celebrity, etc.) now held out to them. This seems to define the transition which Indian cricket is now undergoing: goodbye Pandit Nehru and Sunil Gavaskar – hello Edward de Bono, blue hats and buzz marketing.

### Afterword: goodbye Chappell, hello 'Australia'

In early April 2007, Greg Chappell let it be known that he had asked that his contract with the BCCI not be renewed. A post-mortem began in the Indian cricket media. During this post-mortem a number of important cultural political reassertions were made about India and its cricketers.

With the metaphorical ink scarcely dry on Chappell's resignation, the dispute between the departing coach and his senior players which had defined Chappell's stewardship of the Indian team, was now played out on the pages and websites of the Indian sports press, most notably in the *Times of India*. On 2 April it was reported that Chappell had told the BCCI that the senior players had 'absolutely no respect for the management and that they were too haughty to handle'.[44] Chappell, it was said, had found that these seniors floundered when 'out of their comfort zones', causing him to despair that 'you can't teach anything to someone who's not interested'.[45] Over the following 48 hours the players responded. They resented his use of the term 'mafia', they accused him of leaking confidential information to the media, and they insisted that it had been he, and not they, who had counselled that India bat first in the World Cup match against Bangladesh in Trinidad on 17 March. India had lost and Chappell's star had waned thereafter.[46]

Very soon, however, most of the journalists who were party to this controversy began to step outside of the paradigm of claim and counter-claim, and to reassert the importance of 'modernizing' the Indian Test team. Sumit Mukherjee, for example, accused the senior Indian players (those earning 'the real big bucks from endorsements') of 'an attitude problem'.[47] In *Express India* the BCCI were further tasked to combat

> the huge clout wielded by business interests in selection and team decisions, the conflicts of interest, the damage that a 'cartel', either in the form of the sponsor or a sports marketing agency, could do in undermining the process of selecting a XI strictly on merit.

Some kind of cap, it was argued, should be imposed on the endorsement of products by Indian Test players.[48] A month on and cricket journalist and former Australian fast bowler Geoff Lawson went on to the Web to style Chappell as a prophet without honour in the Babel of Indian cricket politics. 'Batting, bowling and fielding is only the tip of the iceberg when it comes to satisfying the myriad stakeholders of the sub-continent's cross culture religion', wrote Lawson. 'Maybe the cultural gap was too big to build any sort of bridge across. Perhaps the Indian players didn't have the stomach for hard work or the minds to allow for change'. Chappell, he concluded, would have 'a deal of sympathy from observers who feel that the job of perfecting India's cricket machine is as hard a task as getting a billion fanatics to agree on who should bat first wicket down'.[49] The alternative was spelled out in June by Rohit Brijnath, an Indian writer based in Australia:

> John Buchanan [coach to the Australian Test team 1999–2007] told this writer after the World Cup that Indian cricket had the potential to be the 'new Australia', that 'India would just dominate world cricket for so long'. Of course, only if it organised itself.

However, for Brijnath, along with a number of other writers this organizing capacity could reside equally in a captain as in a coach – India, after all, would now be travelling to England for a Test series without a coach.[50]

The signifiers here are, once again, quite clear. In the eyes of many of the commentators and principal actors in the Greg Chappell saga, religious fervour, fanaticism, a disinclination to work hard and/or a reluctance to move with the times marked out a country clinging to its traditions, unconvinced of the merits of the global marketplace and its attendant disciplines. Within this discourse, the 'Australia' of Buchanan's surmising is, in cricket terms, a metaphor for these disciplines: in the world of sport, and cricket in particular, 'Australia' is code for success and for doing the business, untrammelled by tradition, 'culture', sentiment or special pleading. Moreover, it springs from, and stands for, a political and social system fully wedded to the tenets of neo-liberalism.

On the Indian sub-continent, there has been specific cultural resistance to the 'Australianization' of local sporting practice. The anthropologist Michael Roberts, for example, recently called for Asian cricketers not to be drawn into the practice of 'sledging' (verbally taunting an opposing batsman) because it was, in effect, a cultural sacrifice that 'renders one into being an Australian (or British) clone. One is being turned into yet another western male, losing one's being as a Sri Lankan, Indian, Pakistani'.[51]

The Indian cricket team, however, is unlikely to heed this advice. They are caught between a populist national sports media, calling for an ever more professional approach and reproving lazy national celebrities, and an often militantly critical public demanding victory: the writer Ramachandra Guha wrote in 2002 that in India '[e]specially in the last decade, cricket nationalism has become more intense and ferocious ... Our side must win, at any cost'.[52] India's cricketers are, in any event, travellers on the global cricket circuit where sledging, sport science, computer print-outs and lap-top coaches are part of the cultural furniture. The signs, during the summer Test series in England in 2007, were that they were acquiring the aggression necessary to life in the global marketplace. In late July, following India's win in the Second Test at Nottingham,

> Ranjan Madugalle, the International Cricket Council match referee, reminded the captains of their responsibilities after a Test that featured sledging, a potentially lethal beamer, a possibly deliberate no-ball, and a fine for the Indian fast bowler Sreesanth, who lost half his match fee for aggressively brushing past Vaughan. 'The important thing is that the captains have got to remember they are responsible for the behaviour of their side', said Madugalle. 'I have had a chat with the two teams and I will be having a chat with them before the next game'.[53]

On the same tour, Rahul Dravid, the India captain, raised no objection to a prank in which England players had thrown jelly beans at the Indian bowler Zaheer, while he was batting. On the contrary: 'I'm more than happy if Zaheer gets upset', he said. 'I've never seen him so fired up'.[54]

Chappell's tenure as coach to the Indian cricket team represented, as we have argued, one possible future for cricket in India. Indeed the powerful political and economic impetus that has been placed behind it make this future more probable than not. In his recent history of post-war India, Guha remarks that cricket is,

> a game that privileges wrist-work rather than size or physical fitness; to be small and stocky is not always a disadvantage. Thus, Indians can compete with the rest of the world. Its slow pace and uninterrupted structure of play suits Indians.[55]

The language and expressed philosophy of Chappell and his backers run directly counter to this notion. For them cricket is a business conducted in an international marketplace. It is science-based and predicated, as we have seen, on optimal fitness levels and the technical consultancy of globetrotting 'lap-top' coaches, usually drawn from what were formerly the 'white' dominions of the old British Empire. He is backed by the burgeoning Indian business sector. There is no perceptible place in Chappell's vision for chubby, easygoing Indian players with flexible wrists. In this worldview Indian players should now strive to become part of a globalized elite of cricketers, whose skills have been honed since youth in academies around the world. These skills, it seems likely, will become less and less reducible to national character.

In the autumn of 2007 Chappell was back in India, reaffirming this philosophy and its explicit links to contemporary Indian capitalism. On 1 October it was announced that Chappell would be a consultant to a new cricket academy, run by Ian Frazer, his former assistant, in Jaipur, capital of Rajasthan in Northern India. This 'state-of-the-art Global Centre of Excellence', read a press release, 'is one of the most modern and well equipped academies in the world dedicated to improving the standards of cricketing talent across the globe and in India'.[56] While acknowledging that India had just won the Twenty20 Cricket World Cup and that 'talented cricketers are now breaking through [from] the unknown cricketing centres the likes of Bihar, Kerala and Jharkhand', Chappell asserted that,

> first class and international cricket is becoming demanding for players. Training methods of the past will not be suitable for the player of the future who will need to be fitter, stronger and more resilient, more flexible. Training programmes of and for the future will have to reflect that.[57]

As well as *The Making of Champions*, a book co-written by Chappell and Frazer, students would have the benefit of

> five indoor pitches, a full video analysis system and 24 outdoor practice wickets. It will accommodate 70 students and will have a state-of-the-art gymnasium provided by Cybex, the US-based fitness equipment manufacturers, with recreational and eating facilities and electronic data library.[58]

The academy will bear the name of its sponsors, the ironically named Future Group. The Future Group is one of India's leading business groups with presence in retail, consumer finance, capital, insurance, retail real estate development, media and logistics. Pantaloons, Central, Big Bazaar, Food Bazaar and Home Town are among the flagship retail chains that the company operates in 45 cities across the country. Commenting on the inauguration of the Future Cricket Academy, Future Group CEO Mr Kishore Biyani said:

> It is indeed a proud moment for all of us at the Future Group to associate ourselves with this truly world class cricketing facility that has been the brainchild of the Rajasthan Cricket Association. I think the Future Cricket Academy will play a significant role in unearthing new talent and shaping the future of Indian cricket. It has for long been our endeavour to promote sports at the grass roots levels in India and this association with the RCA is a step in that direction.[59]

Chappell's alliance with the Futures Group completed the circle of cricket, globalization and capitalism that came to typify his tenure as Indian team coach.

### Notes

[1]   Ajit Parker, 'Greg Chappell is India's new cricket coach'. http://www.indiadaily.com/editorial/2788.asp.
[2]   Suggested by co-author, Indian cricket writer Sharda Ugra, email to SW, February 18, 2007.
[3]   http://news.bbc.co.uk/sport1/hi/cricket/other_international/south_africa/4562945.stm.
[4]   Mike Selvey, 'Chappell Rides Bumps on Road Paved with Passion and Pop-star Idolatry'. http://sport.guardian.co.uk/englandinindia/story/0,,1720518,00.html.
[5]   'Chappell Asks Players to Make Their Own Destiny'. http://www.hindu.com/2005/07/14/stories/2005071404312000.htm.
[6]   Ibid.

[7] Ibid.

[8] Ibid.

[9] 'Team India readies for mind battles'. http://www.deccanherald.com/deccanherald/jul142005/sports1746312005713.asp.

[10] http://www.answers.com/topic/sourav-ganguly.

[11] http://in.rediff.com/cricket/2005/sep/23gang.htm.

[12] http://www.smh.com.au/news/cricket/text-of-greg-chappells-email/2005/09/26/1127586778800.html.

[13] http://cricket.expressindia.com/fulleistory.php?content_id=55946.

[14] Ibid.

[15] Sharda Ugra, 'Recipe for Disaster'. *India Today*, December 10, 2005, 70–1.

[16] Ibid., 76.

[17] Ibid., 78.

[18] Sharda Ugra, 'Team 2007 will be a Flexible One; We're Not trying to Sweep the Cupboard Clean' (interview with Greg Chappell and Rahul Dravid). *India Today*, December 12, 2005, 58.

[19] http://www.indianexpress.com/res/web/pIe/full_story.php?content_id=86108, January 18, 2006.

[20] http://www.indianexpress.com/printerFriendly/5825.html, June 6, 2006.

[21] http://www.tribuneindia.com/2006/20061013/sports.htm#2.

[22] Ajay S. Shankar, 'Politicians Bay for his Head but Chappell Looks to Future, Won't Say No to Post-World Cup Stint'. http://www.indianexpress.com/story/17276.html, November 25, 2006.

[23] Ashok Chatterjee, 'Lame Duck Pitch?'. *Calcutta Times*, December 5, 2006.

[24] http://cricket.expressindia.com/fulleistory.php?content_id=77982.

[25] http://www.merinews.com/catFull.jsp?articleID123885&category=Sports&catID=5.

[26] Hughes, *Yakking Around the World*, 209.

[27] http://www.sportstaronnet.com/stories/20061202010701200.htm, December 2, 2006.

[28] Said, *Orientalism*.

[29] Beckles, *The Development of West Indies Cricket*.

[30] See Hector, with Stephen Wagg, 'One Eye on the Ball, One Eye on the World: Cricket, West Indian Nationalism and the Spirit of C.L.R. James'.

[31] Ugra, 'Play Together, Live Apart: Religion, Politics and Markets in Indian Cricket since 1947', 89.

[32] Selvey, 'Chappell Rides Bumps on Road Paved with Passion and Pop-star Idolatry'.

[33] Ugra, 'Play Together, Live Apart: Religion, Politics and Markets in Indian Cricket since 1947', 86.

[34] Thompson, 'Time, Work-Discipline and Industrial Capitalism', 57. Quoted in Nick Couldry, 'Reality TV, or the Secret Theatre of Neoliberalism' available on Nick Couldry's web page http://www.goldsmiths.ac.uk/departments/media-communications/staff/couldry.php.

[35] Ibid.

[36] 'Money too good, Ian hints at Ganguly spot'. http://cricket.expressindia.com/fulleistory.php?content_id=55946, 5 December, 2006.

[37] Wright, with Ugra and Thomas, *John Wright's Indian Summers*, 241.

[38] http://www.smh.com.au/news/cricket/text-of-greg-chappells-email/2005/09/26/1127586778800.html.

[39] McGregor, *Greg Chappell*, 263.

[40] Khilnani, *The Idea of India*, 147–8.

[41] 'Cricket Legend Greg Chappell's Coaching is Now Available to All Indians'. http://www.1888pressrelease.com/cricket-legend-greg-chappell-s-coaching-is-now-available-to-pr-13ieu6u31.html, March 24, 2006.

[42] Samyabrata Ray Goswami, 'Pay & Chappell Way is Yours – Australian Company Sells Cricket Training Package'. http://www.telegraphindia.com/1060331/asp/frontpage/story_6038422.asp, March 31, 2006.

[43] Ibid.

[44] See, for example, Joseph Hoover, 'Chappell Blames "Haughty" Seniors'. *Times of India* (New Delhi Edition), April 2, 2007.

[45] Vinay Nayudu, 'Stranded on Chappellway'. *Times of India*, April 2, 2007.

[46] See Indranil Basu, 'Clean-Up Act? Seniors Join War of Words with Chappell'. *Times of India* (New Delhi Edition), April 3, 2007; Ajay Naidu, 'It Hurts if Coach Questions Our Attitude, says Tendulkar', and Ajay Naidu, 'Greg Pushed Indian Cricket Back', both in *Times of India* (New Delhi Edition), April 4, 2007.

[47] 'Indian board on horns of a dilemma'. *Times of India*, April 4, 2007.

48   Ajaysshankar, 'Dirt Piling Up, The Covers are being Drawn'. http://cricket.expressindia.com/fulliestory.php?content_id=27725, April 7, 2007.
49   Geoff Lawson, 'Drama and Greg!' http://www.mid-day.com/sports/international/2007/may/156675.htm, May 4, 2007.
50   Rohit Brijnath, 'Your Team, Skip!' http://www.mid-day.com/sports/national/2007/june/159705.htm, June 21, 2007.
51   Roberts, *Essaying Cricket: Sri Lanka and Beyond*, 2.
52   Guha, *A Corner of a Foreign Field: The Indian History of a British Sport*, 352.
53   Lawrence Booth, 'Vaughan Sorry After Bitter Defeat'. http://sport.guardian.co.uk/englandindia2007/story/0,,2138960,00.html, August 1, 2007.
54   Ibid.
55   Guha, *India After Gandhi: The History of the World's Largest Democracy*, 737.
56   Amit Jugran, Press Release: 'Greg Chappell Inaugurates the Future Cricket Academy on Behalf of Ad Factors'. October 1, 2007.
57   Ibid.
58   Ibid.
59   Ibid.

## References

Beckles, Hilary McD. *The Development of West Indies Cricket* (2 volumes). Kingston, Jamaica: The Press University of West Indies/London: Pluto Press, 1998.

Guha, Ramachandra. *A Corner of a Foreign Field: The Indian History of a British Sport*. London: Picador, 2003.

Guha, Ramachandra. *India After Gandhi: The History of the World's Largest Democracy*. Basingstoke: Macmillan, 2007.

Hector, Tim, with Stephen Wagg. 'One Eye on the Ball, One Eye on the World: Cricket, West Indian Nationalism and the Spirit of C.L.R. James'. In *Cricket and National Identity in the Postcolonial Age*, edited by Stephen Wagg, 159–77. London: Routledge, 2005.

Hughes, Simon. *Yakking Around the World*. London: Simon and Schuster, 2000.

Khilnani, Sunil. *The Idea of India*. London: Penguin, 1998.

McGregor, Adrian. *Greg Chappell*. London: Collins, 1985.

Roberts, Michael. *Essaying Cricket: Sri Lanka and Beyond*. Colombo: Vijitha Yapa Publishers, 2006.

Said, Edward W. *Orientalism*. Harmondsworth: Penguin, 1995.

Thompson, E.P. 'Time, Work-Discipline and Industrial Capitalism'. *Past and Present* 38 (1967): 56–97.

Ugra, Sharda. 'Play Together, Live Apart: Religion, Politics and Markets in Indian Cricket since 1947'. In *Cricket and National Identity in the Postcolonial Age*, edited by Stephen Wagg, 77–93. London: Routledge, 2005.

Wright, John, with Sharda Ugra, and Paul Thomas. *John Wright's Indian Summers*. New Delhi: Penguin/Viking, 2006.

# Malign or benign? English national identities and cricket

Dominic Malcolm*

*School of Sport and Exercise Sciences, Loughborough University, Loughborough, UK*

The ways in which English people perceive themselves and their relations with other UK nationalities appear to have undergone rapid and overt change in recent years as the traditional elision of English and British national identities has waned. Data from British Social Attitudes surveys indicate that whilst 31% of the population described themselves as English in 1992, by 2003 this figure had risen to 40%.[1] As a consequence of this, a number of leading government ministers – e.g. Jack Straw, David Blunkett and Gordon Brown – have each spoken publicly about the need for a debate about British and/or English national identities.[2] Whilst there have been increasing calls for St George's Day to be celebrated more formally and more widely to parallel the celebrations which mark the days allocated to the patron saints of Scotland, Ireland and Wales, others, such as Communities Secretary Ruth Kelly and Immigration Minister Liam Byrne, have called for the establishment of a 'Britain Day' to promote a stronger sense of British identity.[3]

The shifts in national identity which these tensions between Britishness and Englishness represent are generally attributed to several broader social processes. Commonly cited in this connection are the moves toward greater European integration,[4] globalization and the concomitant growth in the significance of local and regional identities,[5] and the growing importance of identity politics more generally. Such processes explain the more general rise of nationalism in Europe at the end of the twentieth century,[6] but a number of UK-specific processes are also believed to be significant. Debates about migrant labour from within an expanded EU, and the increasing number of people seeking asylum in the UK, have dispelled the 'powerful myth of the island fortress'.[7] Internally, Scottish and Welsh devolution firstly raised the issue of whether English regional parliaments should be established, and secondly about whether Scottish and Welsh MPs should be excluded from voting on particular issues in the House of Commons.[8]

Perhaps the most conspicuous displays of this changing sense of national identity have, however, occurred in relation to sport. Most notable in this regard has been the increased use of the flag of St George and, in particular, the phenomena of car-mounted flags which began during the 2002 Football World Cup. A number of writers have commented upon this phenomenon of 'celebratory patriotism'.[9] Polley argues that these developments indicate that 'English national identity in sport has been shifted to be more inclusive'. Crabbe, however, suggests that this trend is largely a 're-marketing' of the image of English football support, and Garland argues that 'whilst a new, more inclusive Englishness was evolving amongst England football supporters [in 2002], this was not reflected in associated tabloid coverage, where a narrower and more nostalgic Englishness was commonly observed'.[10] Further notes of caution are raised by Abell *et al.* and King. King argues that the transformed national identity evident in the 'interaction rituals' of sport may not necessarily be reflected in other spheres of social activity, whilst Abell *et al.*'s research similarly suggests that 'people can display immense emotional involvement in the fate of the England football team, without expressing any such concerns over the nation as an imagined community'.[11]

Though football has attracted considerably more attention from sociologists of sport, it could be argued that cricket provides a more revealing case study of English national identities, for analysts of sport and analysts of Englishness largely agree that cricket is inherently linked to notions of Englishness. Amongst the former, Joseph Maguire has argued that 'cricket is seen to represent what "England" is and gives meaning to the identity of being "English"'.[12] Richard Holt, in *Sport and the British*, notes that, 'To foreigners, cricket in particular was a uniquely English and imperial thing quite beyond ordinary understanding'; whilst Marqusee, author of the influential *Anyone but England*, notes that, 'everything [Americans] took, until recently, to be "English" – tradition, politeness, deference, gentle obscurantism – seems to be epitomised in "cricket"'.[13] Similarly, amongst analysts of Englishness Anthony Easthope has argued that, 'English national culture, profoundly secular as it is, seems to treat only two things as genuinely transcendental – cricket and its own sense of humour'.[14] Stephen Haseler, author of *The English Tribe*, argues that cricket is 'the most exalted icon' of 'theme park heritage Englishness ... a metaphor for the celebration of the English and rural nostalgia'.[15] Whilst football might be the more popular sport in England, the English share this game with the rest of the world, and various peoples (e.g. Brazilians, Italians, Nigerians, South Koreans) claim it as their 'national game'. Cricket, however, was not only 'invented' by the English, but became 'one of their most cherished institutions'.[16] Though cricket has not remained exclusive to the English (in contrast, say, to Gaelic games in Ireland) its diffusion has largely been restricted to the countries of the former British Empire.[17] This essay expands on existing analyses of English national identities exhibited in the context of sport through an examination of how English cricket has been depicted in the last 20 years. To what extent has popular discourse about cricket changed in recent years and what does this tell us about how the English, and spokespeople for the English, like to see themselves?

## English national identities

The sociological study of nations and nationalism is a sub-discipline which 'can appear esoteric, requiring specialized knowledge and using a language and conceptual apparatus entirely of its own'.[18] The core concept, obviously, is the nation. Increasingly however sociologists have questioned the commonsense assumptions used to define this term and, usefully in light of the present study, England provides an excellent illustrative example of many of the points of debate. Nations are often political units but this is not always the case, and hence nations (such as England) must be distinguished from nation-states (such as the United Kingdom). Nations are, inescapably, geographical units but rarely are boundaries fixed, uncontested or drawn with rational objectivity. Even in the case of England, where much of the border is dictated by sea, and where many people believe England's island status to be significant in generating an insular mentality (e.g. to the Europe Community),[19] the social construction of the nation is evident. The notion of the English as an 'island race' is, of course, a misnomer, for the English have always shared 'their' island with the Scots and the Welsh.

For some, the nation can be identified through similitudes, either biological (i.e. race), or cultural. The notion of a nation as a particular 'race' or blood line generally falters due to the false assumption of unity, and the English, made up of Angles, Saxons and Normans, not to mention any of the more recent commingling of peoples, illustrate that defining a nation in these terms is a highly subjective, if not untenable, process. Cultural similitudes also entail a false universalism. Take, for instance, language. On a general level language is clearly something that the English share, but the presence of regional accents (Brummies, Geordies, Scousers) and terms unique to different regions (e.g. Cockney rhyming slang), illustrate that English is not a uniform language within England. Moreover, the role of English as the language of the international community, with new words increasingly introduced by 'non-English' speakers (most notably Americans), and the extent to which English is spoken throughout the world, show that even this most obvious similitude cannot provide a clearly delineated nation.[20]

If defining what constitutes a nation is problematic, then defining national identity is likely to be contoured by similar debates. In this respect, Elias's conceptualization of national identity and habitus is useful. For Elias habitus is 'second nature' or embodied social learning.[21] Habitus develops throughout a person's life, albeit at different rates, and results from the specific networks of interdependence in which one is enmeshed. Habitus is therefore multilayered, an amalgam of the social characteristics of the multiple groups to which we belong – male, middle class, southerner – and moulded in contrast to the 'they' groups to which we don't belong – female, working class, northerner. One level of habitus is our national identity. National identity, therefore, is shaped by the relationships we form with those we see as belonging to 'our' nation, and those that we define as belonging somewhere else. At root national identity is a form of interdependence encompassing not just the 'imagined community' of cultural or biological similitudes to which Benedict Anderson refers,[22] but is defined (however imperfectly) by material factors such as geographic borders and political organization. The people of a nation, therefore, exhibit elements of both sameness (e.g. not being French) and difference (gender, class, region, political allegiance, etc.). The aforementioned changing relative sense of Englishness and Britishness is highly significant here. As increasing numbers of English people define themselves in opposition to other nationalities in the UK, different claims for sameness and difference are being made. The shifting interdependencies lead to shifting emphases in terms of what it means to belong to a nation – in this case, of what it means to be English – and what characteristics members of this national group are thought to share, and like to think of themselves as sharing.[23]

In the following empirical sections of this essay I want to argue that, just as others have detected shifts in notions and expressions of Englishness in recent years, so discourses of cricket reveal shifts in notions of English national identity. In order to chart these shifts I will draw upon the work of Edmunds and Turner who have suggested that in recent years it has been possible to identify two models of Englishness: malign and benign Englishness (see Table 1). Malign Englishness they define as closed (e.g. resentful of Scottish and Welsh nationalisms), insular (e.g. threatened by European identities and multiculturalism), earnest (e.g. seeing national identity as 'in the blood' and rejecting the notion of traditions as invented), masculine (e.g. aggressive) and reactive (e.g. defensive of traditional and nostalgic notions of Englishness). Benign Englishness is open (e.g. tolerant of Welsh/Scottish nationalism), cosmopolitan (e.g. enjoying the co-existence of different cultures and welcoming of multiculturalism), ironic (e.g. aware of the contingent character of national identities), feminine (e.g. pacifist), and creative (e.g. actively seeking to build an identity of openness, liberalism and tolerance).[24]

Whilst the model of malign and benign Englishness provides a useful heuristic device for organizing a wide range of empirical evidence, it is not without its weaknesses. There is much in Edmunds and Turner's model which replicates the somewhat false dichotomy of ethnic (malign) and civic (benign) nationalisms,[25] and in so doing seems to be underpinned by an explicit value judgement which distinguishes between 'good' and 'bad' nationalisms.[26] It is not my wish to replicate this value judgement here. Rather, (national) identities are conceptual tools which people use for organizing the social world into 'we' and 'they' groups, for '*all* identity to a degree practises insiderism together with an exclusionary force'.[27] With these conceptual caveats made, I hope to demonstrate that whilst a malign sense of Englishness was dominant in cricket discourse during the 1980s and 1990s, in the early years of the twenty-first century, a form of benign Englishness has become more prominent. Such a shift is not evidence of a changing habitus per se; rather it indicates that the openness and tolerance characteristic of benign Englishness is increasingly how the English, and sections of the media in particular, would like themselves to be seen.

## Malign Englishness

The development of cricket in the twentieth century is perhaps best described as a process of de-colonization and national self-assertion on the part of the cricket-playing nations of the former British Empire.[28] Gradually the English lost political control of the game. From the establishment of an international governing body for the sport in 1909 (the Imperial Cricket Conference, or ICC), the President and Secretary of the then British governing body of cricket, the Marylebone Cricket Club (MCC), were installed as ex-officio Chairman and ex-officio Secretary respectively. This practice ceased in 1989, with the presidency of the subsequently re-named *International* Cricket Council, now subject to a vote of the member nations.

Table 1.    Malign and benign Englishness.

| Malign | Benign |
| --- | --- |
| Closed (e.g. resentful of Scottish/Welsh nationalism | Open (e.g. tolerant of Welsh/Scottish nationalism) |
| Insular (e.g. threatened by European identity) | Cosmopolitan (e.g. open to European integration) |
| Earnest (e.g. sees national identity as 'sacred'/'in the blood') | Ironic (e.g. aware of contingency of national identity) |
| Masculine (e.g. aggressive) | Feminine (e.g. pacifist) |
| Reactive (nostalgic defence of traditional Englishness) | Creative (Englishness to be rebuilt around values of openness) |

Source: Edmunds and Turner, 'The Re-invention of National Identity'.

Moreover, starting with the so-called 'Bodyline' test series in 1932–33, the English gradually lost the unilateral right to define the way in which the game should be played. During this series of games the Australian Board of (Cricket) Control sent a telegram to the MCC complaining about the violent nature of the tactics employed by the MCC team. Crucially they complained that the tactics were 'unsportsmanlike', a remark that they were forced to retract. The retraction notwithstanding, the series was remarkable in that it represented the first time anyone 'challenged the imperial tradition that Britain set the standards for civilized behaviour'.[29] More recently the rise of Packer and other Australian- and Indian-driven attempts to commercialize the game have been met with English objections that the 'spirit of the game' would be lost.[30] The allegations of ball-tampering which accompanied Pakistan's emergence as a playing force in the early 1990s[31] can also be seen as a sign of English resistance to their waning power over the game and an increasing sense of insecurity in a politically changing world. Defeats on the pitch at the hands of the West Indies have largely been portrayed as more significant rejections of a colonial and subjugated past.[32]

Crabbe and Wagg argue that the English response to this was the development of 'an inward looking nationalism,' characterized by 'a preoccupation with "the enemy within"'.[33] It was in this context that Norman Tebbit introduced his so-called 'cricket test'. In 1990 Tebbit argued that if a British immigrant, or one of his/her descendants, chose to support a team such as India or the West Indies when that team was playing against England, this could, and indeed *should*, be used as a gauge of his/her level of assimilation into English society. Talking specifically about British-Asians (though he viewed the 'test' as more generally applicable) Tebbit asked, 'which side do they cheer for... were they still harking back to where they came from or where they were?'. He later explained that his remarks were not aimed at 'all immigrants', but particularly those 'second-generation' British-Blacks who had 'split loyalties'.[34] Echoing Tebbit, in 2001 the then England cricket captain Nasser Hussain complained that he 'couldn't understand' why British-born Asians continued not to support England.[35] During this period, therefore, English cricket was characterized by the kind of insularity Edmunds and Turner associate with malign Englishness.

The insularity of Englishness was particularly evident in the post-war treatment of (British resident) West Indian cricket supporters. Wagg, in his review of the English press's portrayal of England-West Indies cricket matches, notes that West Indian cricket supporters were initially received in a largely convivial and accommodating, albeit inquisitive, manner. The victory celebrations following the West Indian's landmark victory at Lord's in 1950 were, for example, described by the press as 'pleasantly strange'.[36] By 1976, however, West Indian supporters were not only being depicted as different or 'other' to English cricket spectatorship norms, but as intrusive and threatening. English cricket administrators asked Clive Lloyd, the West Indian captain, to urge supporters to be quieter. Despite such pleas, 'complaints about the "endless din", "mindless cacophony", "inescapable racket" of the West Indian fans ... became commonplace on "Test Match Special" and in the columns of *The Times* and *Telegraph*' throughout the 1970s and 1980s.[37] In 1984 it was claimed that an England player had been assaulted by West Indian supporters during after-match celebrations. Thus Wagg concludes, 'In 1950 and 1963, West Indian supporters celebrated; in 1976 they made intimidating noise and left debris; now, in 1984, they "attacked"'.[38] These public criticisms were supplemented by more substantive regulation during the 1980s. Restrictions were imposed on the use of musical instruments (especially drums, klaxons, whistles), the consumption of alcohol, and the display of flags and banners. For Searle, 'the British cricketing establishment and its watchdogs were attacking expressions of the enthusiasm, loyalty and wit of the Caribbean people'.[39] Marqusee likewise suggests that the message of integration was clear: 'unless they [West Indian supporters] behave like "English" people, they are not welcome at English cricket grounds'.[40]

Insularity was matched in some quarters by a sense of earnestness. In an article published in *Wisden Cricket Monthly*, a leading cricket magazine, Robert Henderson argued that the poor record of the England cricket team was connected to the prevalence of players who had been born overseas and/or had spent much of their childhood living in other countries. Players who had undergone such socializing experiences, Henderson claimed, could never be truly English and thus would never possess the same level of commitment as 'genuine' English players. Echoing Tebbit, Henderson claimed that the problem facing the England cricket selectors, 'were perhaps similar to that facing England as a nation'. Crucially Henderson suggested that player commitment was linked to ethnic/national purity. Whilst all players may well be trying at a conscious level, was that desire to succeed, he asked, '*instinctive*, a matter of biology? There lies the heart of the matter'.[41]

Henderson's views met with significant resistance. There was much criticism of editor David Frith's decision to publish the article, and a number of Black-British players threatened to sue Henderson for libel. The then captain of the England cricket team, Michael Atherton, resigned from his position on the magazine's editorial board and the broader debate acted as the stimulus for the establishment of a cricket-specific anti-racism pressure group, 'Hit Racism for Six'. That the article was published, and the passion of the subsequent debate, indicates the prominence of an insular and exclusionary Englishness, unsympathetic to the contingent character of national identities.

Research into the grassroots of cricket in the 1990s, indicated that this kind of insular nationalism not only permeated the game more broadly, but was also highly reactive.[42] A range of institutional and cultural barriers were identified which restricted the participation of migrant players in lower league and recreational cricket. The belief that different ethnic groups had radically different cricket cultures often served as the basis for cultural separation. Black and Asian players were viewed as 'flamboyant' and 'aggressive', their spectators as vociferous and partisan. Many white players contrasted this with a timeless, peaceful and ordered view of English cricket. Institutionally, teams with large numbers of black and Asian players were less likely to be affiliated to established leagues, and more likely to play on poor quality pitches hired from local authorities. Black and Asian cricketers complained about being denied access to particular leagues and of being discriminated against by umpires and disciplinary panels. Some stated that their requests for fixtures were sometimes refused because of the ethnicity of their players. Underpinning the institutional and cultural separation evident throughout English cricket was a romanticized, backward-looking stereotype of village green cricket which was viewed as quintessentially English. Critical of the cricket authorities' attempts to address racial discrimination in the game,[43] Malcolm argued that little would change 'if the central tenet in the reproduction of Englishness is allowed to remain uncontested'.[44]

Such was the exclusivity and reactive insularity of English cricket at the end of the millennium, that Paul Gilroy wrote:

> Men's cricket is in what appears to be terminal decline as a national spectator sport. Its old imperial logics lost and its civilizing codes increasingly anachronistic and unmoving in a world sharply and permanently divided into the two great camps: a select group of winners and an ever-expanding legion of losers. Few state schools have the time or the facilities to maintain teams. Tall boys want to play basketball rather than bowl and the fundamental idea

that a wholly satisfying contest can endure for five days and yet produce no result, increasingly defies comprehension. Meanwhile, the dead weight of a corrosive class culture prevents the decomposing game from re-inventing itself.[45]

As a consequence of being characterized by many of the features of what Edmunds and Turner define as malign Englishness, at the end of the twentieth century cultural commentators like Gilroy expressed concern that the game was about to implode. Insecure, insular, earnest, reactive and hostile if not aggressive to outsiders who threatened to disturb the status quo, the dominant discourse at this time argued for the restatement of tradition and a reversion to the historical traditions of the game. The insertion of a Preamble to the Laws of Cricket on the 'Spirit of the Game' in 2000 can be seen as a symbolic swansong of English influence over the international game.

## Benign Englishness

Counter to Gilroy's prediction, men's cricket is not in terminal decline. Events in 2005 indicate that English cricket has, certainly compared to recent decades, never been more popular or held greater social significance. As cricket journalist Mike Selvey argued, the 2005 Ashes victory 'captured the imagination of the public in a manner that hitherto could only be dreamed of'.[46] Newspapers reported increased sales of 5–10%.[47] The *BBC Sport* website had its busiest ever Saturday during the fourth test, 66% of the public said that members of the cricket team were 'much better role models' than England's footballers, and 80% of respondents to a *Radio 5Live* poll said that they now preferred cricket to football.[48] Manchester United manager Alex Ferguson noted that it was the first time in the history of the football Premiership that the start of the season had been overshadowed by Test cricket.[49] It seems reasonable to suppose that this celebratory patriotism is inherently linked to the displays of a changing sense of English national identity more commonly seen in relation to football in recent years. What evidence is there, however, to suggest that these celebrations of national identity have incorporated what Edmunds and Turner describe as benign Englishness?

Historically Englishness and Britishness have been blurred in the context of cricket. This blurring of nationalisms largely stemmed from the role of the MCC, a private members club rather than a conventional national governing body of sport with clearly delineated geographical boundaries, in selecting the 'England' team. Scottish players (e.g. Douglas Jardine, Mike Denness and more recently Dougie Brown and Gavin Hamilton), and Welsh players (e.g. Tony Lewis, Robert Croft and Simon Jones) were unproblematically and unquestioningly incorporated into the England cricket team. Thus the team that plays as 'England' is more properly a United Kingdom cricket team. The game's last major administrative re-organization, in 1997, saw the formation of the English and Welsh Cricket Board. Tellingly shortened to the initials ECB, the governing body's launch document, *Raising the Standard*, made no mention of cricket in Wales.[50] This blurring of Englishness and Britishness has historically been a consequence of the Scottish and Welsh simply being subsumed as part of 'greater England'.[51]

Increasingly, however, there is evidence that the English are both recognizing the separateness of Scottish and Welsh nationalisms, and being tolerant of their co-existence within cricket. Discussions amongst England cricket fans on the 'Barmy Army' website (www.barmyarmy.com), for instance, have focussed upon the appropriateness of the use of different flags by supporters. In March 2004 Pete, who's username was 'ENGLAND TILL I DIE' posted the question, 'St. George or Union Jack?' and asked, 'Is it OK to bring both along to England Games?' The consensus of the resulting correspondence seemed to be that either was 'perfectly acceptable'. Chris from London further pointed out that it was 'also acceptable (to bring) that spectacular flag with the dragon on a white and green background', pointedly adding, 'all ye supporters of the E&W cricket board'. There seems therefore to be an acceptance that, as Robert Croft has argued, playing cricket for England does not entail a clash of identities for a Welsh nationalist, but can be seen as representing a supra-national team, the equivalent of playing rugby union for the British Lions or for Europe in the Ryder Cup.[52]

Interestingly, there is a degree of reciprocity in this regard with, in particular, some Scots happy to support the England cricket team in a way unthinkable in other sports. In the aftermath of the 2005 Ashes victory, MSP Christine Grahame submitted a motion to the Scottish Parliament entitled 'It's Simply not Cricket', which 'lamented the overwhelming UK-wide coverage of a sport of only marginal interest in Scotland'.[53] This prompted four retaliatory motions condemning her 'petty and narrow minded nationalism' which was 'an insult to the thousands who play cricket in Scotland'. The critical voices in the ensuing public debate were largely directed at the London-based media rather than the English cricket establishment or the English per se. Many, like columnist Martin Hannan who described himself as a 'Fierce patriot ... cut me and I bleed Saltires', 'confessed' to cheering on England.[54] Craig Wright, captain of the Scottish cricket team, said that England's success had been 'celebrated by people all over Scotland'.[55] Television viewing figures seemed to support this, for whilst Scotland constitutes just 8.5% of the UK population, viewers in Scotland accounted for 18% of the total Channel 4 audience,[56] though it could be argued that for a significant proportion of viewers in Scotland this was not solely a manifestation of support, but equally borne out of the desire to see England lose.

Thus the relationship between the English and the Scottish appears to be more open and mutually supportive in cricket than it is in relation to other sports. Whilst Gordon Brown (a Scot) attracted considerable criticism for declaring his support for England during the 2006 Football World Cup, and for the English Football Association's bid to host the 2018 tournament, Scottish support for the England cricket team seems less problematic.[57] Tom English, writing in *Scotland on Sunday*, could revel in the aftermath of the England football team's defeat to Northern Ireland in September 2005, yet declare himself 'happy for the England cricket team ... because from a distance they seem an altogether agreeable lot. But we draw the line at [England football manager] Sven's men'.[58] Similarly broadcaster and columnist Nicky Campbell noted his (class-based) antipathy toward the England rugby union team – referring to 'Sir Clive's Smarmy Army' – and asked, 'What's different about Test Cricket?'. Campbell's answer was that, 'We don't play you and, if we are good, we play for you and occasionally captain you'.[59] English and Scottish nationalisms as manifest in the context of cricket can be seen as relatively open and non-exclusive.

Interestingly the formally incorporated Welsh appear to be rather more ambivalent. Writing in the *Western Mail*, Darren Devine argued that, 'Many of the fans delighted by news of Sven Goran Eriksson's setback [defeat to Northern Ireland] are happy to celebrate the triumphs of the British Lions or the English (and Welsh) cricket team'.[60] Others however declared themselves to be supporting Australia during the 2005 Ashes series, arguing that 'for those in charge of the [England] side, as well as most of those who commentate on it, the Welsh contribution has become the equivalent of a shameful family secret, the connection "that dares not speak its name"'.[61] Though perhaps not as clear cut as the Scottish case, it remains the case that Welsh attitudes towards supporting the English cricket team are qualitatively different to Welsh attitudes towards English football or rugby teams.

This greater openness in English cricket was underscored during the 2006 series against Pakistan. During the series Saj Mahmood, a Bolton-born, British-Pakistani, Muslim was selected to play for England. Mahmood publicly spoke about the split loyalties of his father who, he said, had not been sure whether to support his son or the country of his birth. Such comments from a British minority ethnic sportsperson would have been unthinkable 15 years ago in the wake of the Tebbit test. Moreover, when England played Pakistan at Headingley in Leeds, Mahmood was barracked by sections of the crowd with chants of 'traitor' and 'reject'.[62] Though one would not wish to suggest that these incidents were reflective of the closed and insular character of British Pakistanis more generally, or that the lack of reports of the abuse of Mahmood from English cricket supporters is indicative of a universal welcoming of multiculturalism, what is interesting about these events is that they contribute to the depiction of the English as open and cosmopolitan, and thus support the model of benign Englishness proposed by Edmunds and Turner. Mahmood's reception is indicative of the conceptual repositioning of the English as a fundamentally inclusive, open and tolerant people.

Similar comments could be made about the attention given to, and the popularity of, Monty Panesar, the first Sikh to play cricket for England. Panesar's public reception again stands in marked contrast to the 1990s debate about players born or raised overseas. It might be argued that the focus on Panesar's 'visual otherness' – his wearing of a turban and growth of a full beard – and the focus on his sometimes inept fielding, betrays a lack of respect for difference and thus exposes an undercurrent of racism. However, in the context of comparing malign and benign forms of Englishness, the most significant aspect of Panesar's reception is the broad feeling of affection for the player, and the absence of expressions of hostility. His shortlisting for the 2006 BBC Sports Personality of the Year award is indicative of the breadth of his public appeal. Moreover, the stance of the press over the racial abuse of Panesar during the early stages of England's 2006–07 tour to Australia is indicative of how the zeitgeist has changed in recent years.[63] When Cricket Australia's James Sutherland was reported to have called Panesar 'a stupid Indian', *The Sun*, traditionally a newspaper relatively antipathetic to multiculturalism, retorted, 'For your information, A – Monty's not stupid, B – He isn't Indian'.[64] Whilst 10 to 20 years ago it was English supporters and administrators who were alleged to have racially abused minority ethnic cricketers,[65] in the twenty-first century racism started to be depicted as something others inflicted upon the English.

The championing of Panesar has largely been driven by cricket supporters who align themselves with the Barmy Army. Parry and Malcolm have discussed the reasons why this relatively small but vocal band of cricket supporters have come to wield so much influence in English cricket, and have detailed the particular style of the spectatorship that the Barmy Army embodies. Whilst there is not scope in this essay for a more extensive discussion of this form of cricket spectatorship which may 'represent a new variant of English national identity', two particular points are worthy of address here.[66]

First it should be stressed that the Barmy Army support is strongly influenced by a cosmopolitan ideology, which stresses the enjoyment of the co-existence of different cultures. Many aspects of the Barmy Army's style of support are borrowed. The carnivalesque elements of the Barmy Army's support, exemplified by the wearing of fancy dress, and the use of face paints and inflatables, are arguably originally appropriated from the styles of Dutch and Danish football fans. In terms of cricket, the Barmy Army appear to have 'borrowed' the use of musical instruments from the traditions of cricket spectatorship in the Caribbean, the barracking of opposition players from Australian traditions, and exuberance from the sub-continent. The rise of the

Barmy Army is underpinned by the rejection of the traditions of English cricket spectatorship, and the commingling of cosmopolitan influences. Moreover, when abroad the Barmy Army is strongly influenced by a 'back packing' ethos, and an 'identity which emphasizes that being a fan abroad involves a responsibility to actively and positively experience foreign cultures, and to socialize with opposing fans'.[67] The Barmy Army often stages its own cricket matches whilst on tour, and when in South Africa, for instance, has sought to use these events to raise money to support the development of cricket in townships.

Second, it should be noted that the Barmy Army exhibit strong elements of irony. One of the common elements of Barmy Army support has been the ironic inversion of the longstanding tradition of applauding a successful bowler at the end of his over. Instead the Barmy Army vociferously applaud opposing bowlers *only* if they have bowled badly. Moreover, as Parry and Malcolm argue, the behaviour of the Barmy Army is closely aligned to the 'New Laddism', defined as a reversion to traditional masculine working-class values as a reaction to the 'New Man' phenomenon. A significant aspect of New Laddism is, according to Whelehan, the use of irony to shield essentially sexist behaviour and attitudes.[68] Finally, unlike the many 'barmy armies' which follow club football teams and which derive their name from the self-perception of the fanaticism of their support, the Barmy Army which follows the England cricket team acquired its name from the apparent irrationality of spending so much time and money following a team which was so rarely successful. Whilst following England in New Zealand in 1999, the Barmy Army modified the football chant 'Only sing when you're winning', to become 'We only lose when we're playing'.

This sense of irony is evident in relation to national identity. Whilst characterized by a more overt championing of Englishness than other groups of cricket spectators, the Barmy Army recognizes the contingent nature of such sporting/national allegiances. According to the Barmy Army website, 'anybody can join the Barmy Army on tour, there isn't a membership scheme and anybody who wants to support England, sing some songs, party hard and enjoy themselves is welcome to join in'.[69] Moreover, there appears to be a greater acceptance of the diversity of backgrounds of players than in the past. The South African-born Kevin Pietersen has qualified to play for England through residency and has become one of the most popular current England players. Andrew Strauss, also South African-born and married to an Australian, qualifies to play for England because he has an English mother. Interestingly, in Strauss's case, his educational experience (Radley College and Durham University), has helped him acquire many of the characteristics of traditional, upper-class conceptions of Englishness. The contingent nature of national identities has most explicitly been commented upon by Ed Joyce, a Dublin born former Ireland cricketer who subsequently qualified and chose to play for England. Reflecting on his shift of national identity Joyce has stated,

> there's no doubt ... [once] you supported anyone other than England. That's changing now.
> I think its just time, a new generation. And the England team now have an interesting mix of
> people. There was Geraint Jones [born in Papua New Guinea of Welsh parents], and there's
> Kevin Pietersen and Monty Panesar and Sajid Mahmood. If you look at England and Britain as
> a whole it is a brilliant mix. I look at the team and see a progressive country here.[70]

In addition to cosmopolitanism and irony, there is evidence to suggest that elements of the cricket community are becoming 'creative' in their outlook, actively seeking to build an identity of openness, liberalism and tolerance. It was notable in the wake of the 2005 Ashes series victory that, in sharp contrast to the traditional notions of cricket, the apparent classlessness of the current England cricket team was celebrated. BBC correspondent

Benjamin Dirs described the victory parade in Trafalgar Square as 'one big coming out party ... this is a very modern England with very modern fans'. The team were depicted as 'normal blokes'; 'these are men that you might like to have a few beers with ... Can you imagine going for a drink with [English footballers] Becks, Rooney and Rio? No, neither can I. England's footballers are remote by comparison and increasingly difficult to identify with'.[71] The cricketers were seen as down to earth and non-aspirational in material terms. As one *Guardian* journalist noted of England's leading player, Andrew Flintoff, 'there seems to be an ordinary man trying to break out of the superman carapace and retire to a quiet corner of the pub'.[72] A reporter in the Scottish *Evening News*, argued that the idea that cricket was 'only for sissies or for toffs from private schools ... is fast going out the window. Cricket is becoming a "normal" game'.[73] Andrew Collier in *The Scotsman* similarly argued that these events had radically altered the image of cricket: 'A piece of traditional England died this week, the notion of cricket as a game for gentlemen'.[74] Centrally, therefore, this discourse portrayed the social hierarchies which have traditionally underpinned both cricket and Englishness as defunct. It was noticeable, moreover, that it was Scottish journalists in particular who stressed the significance of the changing class base of the game. It appears that the democratization of English cricket has been important in popularizing cricket among the other nationalities of the UK.

Finally in relation to benign Englishness, we can detect some elements of the feminization of cricket. Television audiences grew significantly during the summer of 2005, with female viewers being one of the most significant growth areas. On the first morning of the first test only a quarter of viewers were female, but by the final day of the fifth test, that figure had grown to 39%. The increase in the actual number of female viewers therefore was from approximately 500,000 to around 3.25m.[75] The England women's cricket team (who also defeated their Australian counterparts that summer) were included in the Ashes victory parade and were similarly entertained at Downing Street by Prime Minister Tony Blair.

In this regard it is interesting to note that post-Ashes victory Mark Lawson suggested that England's Andrew Flintoff represented, 'a new kind of sporting masculinity'. The basis for this claim was that Flintoff drank gin and tonic (which, of course, no traditionally masculine cricketer would have done) and, more significantly, because of Flintoff's obvious affection for his daughter Holly: 'for most of the two mile victory parade, he held his baby daughter Holly, as if she were the trophy that really mattered'.[76] But Flintoff was portrayed as feminized not only in the sense of nurturing and family-oriented, but also as caring and compassionate. When the England team celebrated victory in the second test, much media attention focussed on Flintoff's comforting of the Australian player Brett Lee who had been central in getting Australia to within two runs of an unlikely victory. Whilst it is important to note that Flintoff's masculine imagery is in part based around heavy drinking, and the humour of New Laddism, a comparison between Flintoff and previous English cricketing celebrities – e.g. Ian Botham, Fred Trueman (see Williams in this volume) – indicates a desire to depict cricketing masculinities in more feminized terms than in the past, or at least a propensity to celebrate such feminine characteristics and overlook the more traditional, aggressive aspects of male cricket culture. It was revealing that the image of Flintoff putting his arm around Lee became the biggest selling sports picture of 2005, rather than, for instance, the image of Australian captain Ricky Ponting bleeding from the face having been hit by a ball bowled by Steve Harmison. After losing to the Australians in 2006, England bowler Matthew Hoggard could confess to needing 'a good hug' from his wife, and Flintoff to being reduced to tears: 'I wasn't boo-hooing or anything like that – but the tears were there'.[77]

## Conclusion

Recent cricket discourse has, therefore, been characterized by many elements of what Edmunds and Turner describe as benign Englishness. Whilst some elements are stronger than others, this trend has been interdependent with a de-emphasizing of elements of malign Englishness. *Pace* Gilroy, men's cricket in England is not in terminal decline, but is perhaps more popular now than at any time in the recent past. The extent to which the decline of one form of Englishness and the rise of another has been responsible for the game's growing popularity is, however, difficult to assess.

What does this shift in discourse mean in terms of English people's shifting sense of self identity? I would not wish to argue that there has been such a rapid and radical shift in national consciousness as the evidence presented above appears to imply; indeed Elias's concept of habitus would suggest that rapid changes in personality structure are extremely rare. Rather, I think that it is highly likely that benign Englishness was relatively widespread at the end of the twentieth century (and hence the debate which followed the Tebbit and Henderson affairs), but that those who held such views were not sufficiently powerful to dictate the sport and national identity agenda. Likewise it is unrealistic to suggest that insular and backward-looking malign Englishness has simply disappeared in recent years. Indeed concern over the growth of Islamaphobia post-9/11 is compelling evidence of this. What I think we are seeing, however, is a growing perception that the openness and tolerance characteristic of benign Englishness is more palatable (to many English people) than the cricketing discourse of 10–15 years ago, and conducive to the modernizing and democratizing of the game, and thus will enable its popularity to increase. There appears, that is to say, an active attempt to promote these character traits, and downplay the exclusivity and insularity of the recent past.

To some extent the 2005 Ashes-winning celebrations closely paralleled the dominant themes of that summer's other major news events. The London bombings were largely framed (by London Mayor Ken Livingstone in particular) not as an attack on the British/English but, as a consequence of London's multiculturalism, as an attack on the people of the world. The Gleneagles G8 summit, the *Make Poverty History* campaign and the Live Aid concert in Hyde Park were seen as indicators of Britain/England's role in leading the social conscience of Western nations. If I am right, the English obsession with what it means to be English has led to the 'rebranding' of the nation and the characteristics of its people. It remains to be seen, however, to what extent the English people follow.

## Acknowledgements

I am grateful to Daniel Burdsey for his comments regarding the interpretation of Monty Panesar's representation and popular appeal, and to Alan Bairner for challenging what he saw as some of my anglocentric readings of data.

## Notes

[1]  Blunkett, *A New England*.
[2]  See 'Straw Calls for "Rounded Sense of Englishness"'. *The Guardian*, January 11, 2000; Blunkett, *A New England*; and Brown's 2004 British Council Annual Lecture reproduced at *Guardian Unlimited*, July 8, 2004. http://politics.guardian.co.uk/labour/story/0,9061,1256550,00.html.
[3]  'Ministers Proposing "Britain Day"'. BBC News, June 5, 2007. http://news.bbc.co.uk/1/hi/uk/6721239.stm.
[4]  Smith, '"Set in the Silver Sea": English National Identity and European Integration'; Kumar, 'Britain, England and Europe'.
[5]  King, 'Nationalism and Sport'.

[6] Spencer and Wollman, 'Introduction'; Day and Thompson, *Theorizing Nationalism*, ix.

[7] Bassnett, 'Discovering Englands', 3.

[8] Nairn, *After Britain*. See Kumar, *The Making of English National Identity*, Chap. 8, for an overview.

[9] Perryman, 'Going Oriental', 30.

[10] Polley, 'Sport and National Identity in Contemporary England', 18; Crabbe, '*englandfans* – A New Club for a New England?', 63; Garland, 'The Same Old Story? Englishness, the Tabloid Press and the 2002 Football World Cup', 79.

[11] King, 'Nationalism and Sport', 250; Abell *et al.*, 'Who ate all the Pride? Patriotic Sentiment and English National Football Support', 113.

[12] Maguire, 'Sport, Identity Politics, and Globalization', 414.

[13] Holt, *Sport and the British*, 1; Marqusee, *Anyone but England: Cricket, Race and Class*, 15.

[14] Easthope, *Englishness and National Culture*, 162.

[15] Haselar, *The English Tribe: Identity, Nation and Europe*, 59.

[16] Birley, *A Social History of English Cricket*, ix.

[17] Stoddart and Sandiford, *The Imperial Game: Cricket, Culture and Society*. See Bairner, *Sport, Nationalism, and Globalization*, for a discussion of national sports.

[18] Day and Thompson, *Theorizing Nationalism*, 2.

[19] Paxman, *The English*; Smith, '"Set in the Silver Sea"'.

[20] Haselar, *The English Tribe*, 114.

[21] Elias, *The Society of Individuals*.

[22] Anderson, *Imagined Communities*.

[23] See Tuck, 'The Men in White: Reflections on Rugby Union, the Media and Englishness', for a discussion of Elias, habitus and national identity.

[24] Edmunds and Turner, 'The Re-invention of National Identity'.

[25] McCrone, *The Sociology of Nationalism*.

[26] Spencer and Wollman, 'Good and Bad Nationalisms'.

[27] Easthope, *Englishness and National Culture*, 24.

[28] Malcolm, 'Cricket: Civilizing and De-civilizing Processes in the Imperial Game'.

[29] Stoddart, 'Cricket's Imperial Crisis: the 1932–33 MCC Tour of Australia', 126.

[30] Wright, *Betrayal: The Struggle for Cricket's Soul*.

[31] Williams, *Cricket and Race*, Chap. 6.

[32] Beckles and Stoddart, *Liberation Cricket: West Indies Cricket Culture*.

[33] Crabbe and Wagg, '"A Carnival of Cricket"?', 70.

[34] Maguire, 'Globalisation, Sport and National Identities'; Marqusee, *Anyone but England*, 157.

[35] Vivek Chaudhury, 'A Question of Support'. *The Guardian*, May 29, 2001.

[36] Wagg, 'Calypso Kings, Dark Destroyers: England-West Indies Test Cricket and the English Press, 1950–1984', 171.

[37] Marqusee, *Anyone but England*, 171.

[38] Wagg, 'Calypso Kings, Dark Destroyers', 198.

[39] Searle, 'Towards a Cricket of the Future', 49.

[40] Marqusee, *Anyone but England*, 171.

[41] Henderson, 'Is it in the Blood', 10; Marqusee, *Anyone but England*, 290.

[42] Greenfield and Osborn, 'Oh to be in England? Mythology and Identity in English Cricket', Long *et al.*, *Crossing the Boundary: A Study of the Nature and Extent of Racism in Local League Cricket*; McDonald and Ugra, *Anyone for Cricket? Equal Opportunities and Changing Cricket Cultures in Essex and East London*.

[43] ECB, *Going Forward Together: A Report on Racial Equality in Cricket*.

[44] Malcolm, '"Clean Bowled?" Cricket, Racism and Equal Opportunities', 322.

[45] Gilroy, Foreword, xv.

[46] Mike Selvey, 'Flintoff Makes Glorious Summer for Old Romantics and First Time Fans', *The Guardian*, December 21, 2005.

[47] Peter Preston, 'Stifling a Yawn at the Beautiful Game'. *The Observer*, September 18, 2005.

[48] 'Ashes Fever'. BBC News, September 5, 2005. http://news.bbc.co.uk/go/pr/fr/-/sport1/hi/cricket/england/4206016.stm; David Brook, 'Bowling the Nation Over', *The Guardian*, August 22, 2005.

[49] David Brook, 'Bowling the Nation Over', *The Guardian*, August 22, 2005.

[50] ECB, *Raising the Standard*.

[51] Haselar, *The English Tribe*, 30.

[52] 'Sports Talk: you quizzed Robert Croft'. BBC Online Sports Talk, April 12, 2001. http://news.bbc.co.uk/sport1/low/sports_talk/1274017.stm.

[53] 'Cricket Motion is Stumped by MSP's Backlash', *The Scotsman*, September 15, 2005.

[54] Martin Hannan, 'Breaking the Boundaries', *Scotland on Sunday*, September 18, 2005.

[55] Hamish MacDonell, 'SNP Cricket Critic Hit for Six', *The Scotsman*, September 15, 2005.

[56] Murdo MacLeod, 'Scots Officially Bowled Over by the Ashes', *Scotland on Sunday*, September 18, 2005.

[57] *The Scotsman*, May 22, 2006; 'World Cup Own Goal for Chancellor', BBC News, January 19, 2007. http://news.bbc.co.uk/go/pr/fr/-/1/hi/scotland/6280663.stm.

[58] Tom English, 'Great Week to be a Scot: My Sporting Week', *Scotland on Sunday*, September 11, 2005.

[59] Nicky Campbell, 'Confessions of a Scotsman – Caught Mills, Bowled Boon', *The Guardian*, September 15, 2005.

[60] Darren Devine, 'So Where do your Sporting Loyalties Lie?', *Western Mail*, September 6, 2005.

[61] Mario Basini, 'I'm Supporting Australia for the Fifth Test', *Western Mail*, September 3, 2005.

[62] 'Mahmood Dismisses "Traitor" Abuse'. BBC Sport, August 9, 2006. http://news.bbc.co.uk/sport1/hi/cricket/england/4775149.stm.

[63] 'Panesar Targeted for Racial Abuse'. BBC Sport, November 13, 2006. http://news.bbc.co.uk/sport1/hi/cricket/england/6145104.stm.

[64] John Etheridge, 'Barmy Harmy Baffles Fletcher', *The Sun*, November 18, 2006.

[65] Malcolm, '"Clean Bowled?"', 316–17.

[66] Parry and Malcolm, 'England's Barmy Army: Commercialization, Masculinity and Nationalism', 82.

[67] Ibid., 81–2.

[68] Whelehan, *Overloaded: Popular Culture and the Future of Feminisms*.

[69] Parry and Malcolm, 'England's Barmy Army', 78.

[70] 'Ed Joyce: The Irishman Happy to be at the Heart of a New England'. *The Independent* Online, March 11, 2007. http://news.independent.co.uk/people/profiles/article2347483.ece.

[71] Benjamin Dirs, 'Cricket's Turn in the Sun'. BBC News, September 13, 2005. http://news.bbc.co.uk/sport1/hi/cricket/ashes_2005/4242220.stm.

[72] 'An Old Fashioned Kind of Hero', *The Guardian*, October 15, 2005.

[73] Elizabeth Smith, 'Has Cricket knocked you for Six this Year', *Evening News*, August 20, 2005.

[74] Andrew Collier, 'A Big, Boisterous, Booze Binge? It's Just not Cricket', *The Scotsman*, September 15, 2005.

[75] Owen Gibson, 'Women Tune in to Become Growth Market', *The Guardian*, November 3, 2005.

[76] Mark Lawson, 'Giants on a Dinky', *The Guardian*, September 14, 2005.

[77] Matthew Hoggard, 'From Seventh Heaven to Sheer Hell', *The Times*, December 6, 2006; Chris Maume, 'A Sporting Year in Quotes', *The Independent*, December 28, 2006.

## References

Abell, Jackie, Susan Candor, Robert Lowe, Stephen Gibson, and Clifford Stevenson. 'Who Ate All the Pride? Patriotic Sentiment and English National Football Support'. *Nations and Nationalism* 13, no. 1 (2007): 97–116.

Anderson, Benedict. *Imagined Communities: Reflections on the Origin and Spread of Nationalism*. London: Verso, 1983.

Bairner, Alan. *Sport, Nationalism, and Globalization: European and North American Perspectives*. New York: SUNY Press, 2001.

Bassnett, Susan. 'Discovering Englands'. *British Studies Now Special Report: Looking into England* 13 (2000): 3.

Beckles, Hilary, and Brian Stoddart, eds. *Liberation Cricket: West Indies Cricket Culture*. Manchester: Manchester University Press, 1995.

Birley, Derek. *A Social History of English Cricket*. London: Aurum Press, 1999.

Blunkett, David. *A New England. An English Identity within Britain*. London: Institute of Public Policy Research, 2005.

Crabbe, Tim. '*englandfans* – A New Club for a New England? Social Inclusion, Authenticity and the Performance of Englishness at "Home" and "Away"'. *Leisure Studies* 23, no. 1 (2004): 63–78.

Crabbe, Tim, and Stephen Wagg. '"A Carnival of Cricket"? The Cricket World Cup, "Race" and the Politics of Carnival'. *Culture, Sport, Society* 3, no. 2 (2000): 70–88.

Day, Graham, and Andrew Thompson. *Theorizing Nationalism*. Basingstoke, UK: Palgrave MacMillan, 2004.

Easthope, Anthony. *Englishness and National Culture*. London: Routledge, 1999.

ECB. *Raising the Standard*. London: England and Wales Cricket Board, 1997.

ECB. *Going Forward Together: A Report on Racial Equality in Cricket*. London: England and Wales Cricket Board, Racism Study Group, 1999.

Edmunds, June, and Bryan Turner. 'The Re-invention of National Identity'. *Ethnicities* 1, no. 1 (2001): 83–108.

Elias, Norbert. *The Society of Individuals*. Oxford: Basil Blackwell, 1991.

Garland, Jon. 'The Same Old Story? Englishness, the Tabloid Press and the 2002 Football World Cup'. *Leisure Studies* 23, no. 1 (2004): 79–92.

Gilroy, Paul. Foreword. *'Race', Sport and British Society*, edited by Ben Carrington and Ian MacDonald, xi–xvii. London: Routledge, 2001.

Greenfield, Steve, and Gary Osborn. 'Oh to be in England? Mythology and Identity in English Cricket'. *Social Identities* 2, no. 2 (1996): 271–91.

Haselar, Stephen. *The English Tribe: Identity, Nation and Europe*. London: Macmillan, 1996.

Henderson, Robert. 'Is it in the Blood?'. *Wisden Cricket Monthly* 17, no. 2 (1995): 9–10.

Holt, Richard. *Sport and the British*. Oxford: Oxford University Press, 1989.

King, Anthony. 'Nationalism and Sport'. In *The Sage Handbook of Nations and Nationalism*, edited by Gerard Delanty and Krishan Kumar, 249–59. London: Sage, 2006.

Kumar, Krishan. *The Making of English National Identity*. Cambridge: Cambridge University Press, 2003.

Kumar, Krishan. 'Britain, England and Europe'. *European Journal of Social Theory* 6, no. 1 (2003): 5–23.

Long, Jonathon, Mark Nesti, Ben Carrington, and Nicola Gibson. *Crossing the Boundary: A Study of the Nature and Extent of Racism in Local League Cricket*. Leeds: Working Papers in Leisure and Sport, Leeds Metropolitan University, 1997.

MacDonald, Ian, and Sharda Ugra. *Anyone for Cricket? Equal Opportunities and Changing Cricket Cultures in Essex and East London*. London: Centre for Sport Development Research, Roehampton Institute and Centre for New Ethnicities Research, University of East London, 1998.

Maguire, Joseph. 'Globalisation, Sport and National Identities: "The Empires Strike Back"?' *Society and Leisure* 16, no. 2 (1993): 293–322.

Maguire, Joseph. 'Sport, Identity Politics, and Globalization: Diminishing Contrasts and Increasing Varieties'. *Sociology of Sport Journal* 11, no. 4 (1994): 398–427.

Malcolm, Dominic. '"Clean Bowled?" Cricket, Racism and Equal Opportunities'. *Journal of Ethnic and Migration Studies* 28, no. 2 (2002): 307–25.

Malcolm, Dominic. 'Cricket: Civilizing and De-civilizing Processes in the Imperial Game'. In *Sport Histories: Figurational Studies of the Development of Modern Sports*, edited by Eric Dunning, Dominic Malcolm and Ivan Waddington, 71–87. London: Routledge, 2004.

Marqusee, Mike. *Anyone but England: Cricket, Race and Class*. 2nd ed. London: Two Heads Publishing, 1998.

McCrone, David. *The Sociology of Nationalism: Tomorrow's Ancestors*. London: Routledge, 1998.

Nairn, Tom. *After Britain*. London: Granta Books, 2000.

Parry, Matt, and Dominic Malcolm. 'England's Barmy Army: Commercialization, Masculinity and Nationalism'. *International Review for the Sociology of Sport* 39, no. 1 (2004): 73–92.

Paxman, Jeremy. *The English: A Portrait of a People*. London: Penguin Books, 1999.

Perryman, Mark. 'Going Oriental'. In *Going Oriental*, edited by Mark Perryman, 17–38. Edinburgh: Mainstream, 2002.

Polley, Martin. 'Sport and National Identity in Contemporary England'. In *Sport and National Identity in the Post-War World*, edited by Dilwyn Porter and Adrian Smith, 10–30. London: Routledge, 2003.

Searle, Chris. 'Towards a Cricket of the Future'. *Race and Class* 37, no. 4 (1996): 45–59.

Smith, Anthony. '"Set in the Silver Sea": English National Identity and European Integration'. *Nations and Nationalism* 12, no. 3 (2006): 433–52.

Spencer, Philip, and Howard Wollman. 'Introduction'. In *Nations and Nationalism: A Reader*, edited by Philip Spencer and Howard Wollman, 1–19. Edinburgh: Edinburgh University Press, 2005.

Spencer, Philip, and Howard Wollman. 'Good and Bad Nationalisms'. In *Nations and Nationalism: A Reader*, edited by Philip Spencer and Howard Wollman, 197–217. Edinburgh: Edinburgh University Press, 2005.

Stoddart, Brian. 'Cricket's Imperial Crisis: the 1932–33 MCC Tour of Australia'. In *Sport in History*, edited by Richard Cashman and Michael McKernan, 124–47. Queensland: University of Queensland Press, 1979.

Stoddart, Brian, and Keith Sandiford, eds. *The Imperial Game: Cricket, Culture and Society*. Manchester: Manchester University Press, 1998.

Tuck, Jason. 'The Men in White: Reflections on Rugby Union, the Media and Englishness'. *International Review for the Sociology of Sport* 38, no. 2 (2003): 177–99.

Wagg, Stephen. 'Calypso Kings, Dark Destroyers: England-West Indies Test Cricket and the English Press, 1950–1984'. In *Cricket and National Identity in a Postcolonial World*, edited by Stephen Wagg, 181–203. London: Routledge, 2005.

Whelehan, Imelda. *Overloaded: Popular Culture and the Future of Feminisms*. London: Women's Press, 2000.

Williams, Jack. *Cricket and Race*. Oxford: Berg, 2001.

Wright, Graeme. *Betrayal: The Struggle for Cricket's Soul*. London: H.F. & G. Witherby, 1993.

# 'Look, it's a girl': cricket and gender relations in the UK

Philippa Velija[a]* and Dominic Malcolm[b]

[a]Faculty of Health and Life Sciences, York St John University, York, UK; [b]School of Sport and Exercise Sciences, Loughborough University, Loughborough, UK

It is widely accepted that there are now more opportunities for females to be involved in playing sport than at any time in the recent past. Not only have we seen the development of female participation in activities viewed as 'female-appropriate' (e.g. aerobics[1]) but also in the sports which have traditionally been male preserves, such as rugby, football and cricket.[2] Evidence for this can be seen in a recent survey published by Sport England that demonstrates that female involvement in sports such as football has doubled since 1994.[3] In sports traditionally seen as 'male-appropriate', the longstanding separation and institutional barriers to greater contact between the sexes have come under increasing social pressure. Thus, women have successfully begun to enter these male sporting arenas, despite persistent ideologies around gender and sexuality.[4] The merger of the Women's Cricket Association (WCA) and the England and Wales Cricket Board (ECB) can be understood as part of a wider trend in which female sports organizations have moved closer to their male counterparts (i.e. the Women's Football Association merged with the Football Association in 1994/95, and the All England Women's Hockey Association merged with the England Hockey Association in 1996).[5] Founded in 1928, the WCA remained separate from the governing body for male cricket until 1998 when it was absorbed by the newly formed ECB, partly due to fears that the WCA faced bankruptcy (and no 'responsible' governing body could be seen to allow this to happen), and partly because the establishment of the National Lottery in Britain meant that public funding increased for those sports governing bodies which complied with equity guidelines. This merger was encouraged as part of governmental pressure to enhance sexual equality through forcing organizations to provide a greater range of opportunities for females to participate in sport.

Despite research which indicates that females' involvement in sport has increased in general terms, there is some disagreement over data related to cricket. The ECB suggest that there were in excess of two million girls playing cricket in 2003,[6] a growth they attributed to the merger with the WCA and the subsequent increased funding and restructuring of the women's game. Sport England surveys conducted in 1994, 1999 and 2002 suggest a rather different story however. Despite demonstrating a clear increase in female involvement in sports such as football, these surveys indicate that girls' involvement in cricket did not change significantly between 1994 and 2002. In 1994, for instance, 20% of boys regularly played cricket in school compared to 7% of girls. Whilst in 1999 this had increased to 24% of boys and 8% of girls, in 2002 figures dropped back to 20% and 7% respectively.[7] Out of school participation in cricket demonstrates a similar trend. In 1994, 27% of boys aged 6–11 regularly participated in cricket out of school in comparison to just 6% of girls. Again there were slight increases in 1999 with 29% of boys and 8% of girls regularly involved in playing cricket but by 2002 these figures had also decreased to just 22% of boys and 5% of girls. Given the size of the Sport England surveys (charting the physical activities of some 3,000 6–16 year olds), their production of standardized time series data, and given that Sport England has no vested interest in portraying individual sports in a particularly positive light, it is likely that these figures are the most reliable. The overall picture, therefore, is of considerable differences in the number of girls and boys playing the game and, in contrast to many other sports, no evidence that this gap has narrowed in recent years.

A further indication of the limited scale of female participation in cricket can be seen in the recent UKSport publication, *Women and Sport: The State of Play*. Within this report it is claimed that cricket remains among the top ten sports in which men aged over 16 participate.[8] Comparatively, female involvement in cricket is too low to merit a mention. The report also signals the extent to which cricket remains an overwhelmingly male sport with just 1% of the ECB's 533,000 affiliated members being female and all ten members of the ECB's board/executive committee being male.[9] According to White and Kay this is similar to football and rugby organizations where women are rarely found in positions of governance.[10] Again, these figures suggest that the involvement of females in cricket, in a variety of forms, has not increased significantly since the WCA and the ECB merged in 1998.

The purpose of the essay, therefore, is to explore this apparent lack of change to the number of females involved in the game. In order to do this we examine a number of contexts in which gender relations are played out: that is to say, when females play cricket within predominantly male cricket teams; when female cricketers, living their everyday lives, encounter males with entrenched attitudes about the sport; and when female cricketers are part of an organizational restructuring which entails closer formal collaboration with their male counterparts. Finally we examine female cricketers' perceptions of the relative strengths and weaknesses of the male and female games, and conclude by suggesting that women's experiences of playing cricket lead to a habitus characterized by the internalization of a negative we-group image.[11]

## The theory of established-outsider relations

In this essay we adopt a figurational perspective, in particular utilizing Elias's theory of established-outsider relations.[12] The theory of established-outsider relations first appeared in Elias's *The Civilizing Process* but is most clearly expressed in Elias's joint work with John Scotson, *The Established and the Outsiders*.[13] Mennell argues that although the theory of civilizing processes has rather overshadowed the theory of established-outsider relations, one is essentially an extension of the other; that is to say, both are centrally concerned with connections between 'changing power ratios between groups ... (and) the social habitus of group members'.[14]

Elias and Scotson's study focused on a community which consisted of three clearly distinguishable neighbourhoods. Zone 1 was relatively affluent, predominantly middle class, and commonly regarded as the 'best' residential area. The largely working-class communities of Zones 2 and 3 were very similar in terms of income, occupational structure and social class but, crucially, the inhabitants of these two communities viewed themselves as being very different from each other.[15] More particularly, those in Zone 2 (the 'village') perceived themselves to be superior to those in Zone 3 (the 'estate'). 'Villagers' described those in Zone 3 as rough, unclean, promiscuous and unable to control their children. Though only true of a small minority of families on the estate, those in Zone 3 largely accepted this characterization of themselves as a group. Elias and Scotson explained this perceptual difference partly in terms of the length of residency (hence the terms 'established' and 'outsiders') but more particularly in terms of how differences in group cohesion and patterns of interdependency ties had developed over time. Gossip, which worked more effectively in the closely bonded group, played a central role in the creation and perpetuation of a 'highly simplified presentation of social reality'.[16] Thus, Elias and Scotson reflected,

> in this small setting one encountered and, to some extent, learned to understand an optical illusion characteristic of the making of social images in many other much wider social settings: the image which the 'established', which powerful ruling sections of a society have of themselves and communicate to others tends to be modelled on the 'minority of the best'; it inclines towards idealisation. The image of 'outsiders', of groups who have in relation to the 'established' sections relatively little power tends to be modelled on the 'minority of the worst'; it inclines towards denigration.[17]

Consequently, though inhabitants of Zones 2 and 3 were very similar on any conventional or 'objective' measure of social stratification, differences could be identified in their respective habituses. A collective, largely positive, 'we-image' was incorporated into the self-image of 'villagers' and a collective, largely negative, 'we-image' was internalized by those living on the estate. Elias and Scotson used the twin terms 'group charisma' and 'group disgrace' to describe these self-images, but significantly note that the group charisma of the established is inseparable from the creation, and unquestioning acceptance of, the outsiders' group disgrace.

Mennell provides a useful summary of the ways in which the theory of established-outsider relations has been used to elucidate broader social processes such as the civilizing of the working class and the rise of the welfare state.[18] Within the sociology of sport the theory of established-outsider relations has been used to examine race relations, gender relations, globalization and the use of performance-enhancing drugs.[19] Most pertinent for present purposes however, is Van Stolk and Wouters' work which compared and contrasted the mutual balance of power and respective group identities in two established-outsider case studies: relations between women (outsiders) who had left their abusive male (established) partners, and relations between heterosexuals (established) and homosexuals (outsiders).[20]

The theory of established-outsider relations was developed to explore how dominant groups create and maintain feelings of superiority over subordinates who, as a result of the interdependent relationships in which they are enmeshed, come to internalize and normalize their inferior status. It is, therefore, particularly useful as a framework for understanding power relations between men and women in contemporary sport because it emphasizes not the material barriers which perpetuate inequality (such as organizational separation), and which are increasingly coming under attack, but the ideological barriers which are less tangible but – in the case of cricket at least – seemingly more enduring. These ideological barriers, it is suggested, help us to explain why changes to rates of female participation in the game have been so limited. This essay seeks to illuminate how females, through the acceptance rather than the rejection of their subordinate status, are more deeply embedded in a network of unequal social relations than is recognized in many policies designed to promote gender equity in sports participation.

## Methods

The data presented in this essay were collected as part of a wider PhD project on females' experiences of playing cricket.[21] Data gathering was confined to a single UK county (hereafter County A). The county is widely recognized as having one of the strongest and longest traditions of organized (male) cricket in England.

A qualitative approach was used throughout the data collection, with a mixture of ethnographic and interview techniques employed. Between March and September 2004, 15 semi-structured interviews were conducted with girls aged 13–15 who played for the U15 county team. The first named author also travelled with the girls to matches during the season and spent time with the girls during games. A further 16 interviews were conducted with adult female cricketers between October 2004 and June 2005. The adult interviewees were all club players of various standards and experience, and ranged in age from 19–45. Interviews were taped and lasted an average of 45 minutes.

All interviews were transcribed within two weeks of them taking place and interviewees were given pseudonyms to ensure anonymity. The transcribed data were read and re-read before a thematic data analysis began.[22] During this process of familiarization emerging patterns were identified and the subsequent analysis took the form of organizing data into thematic files. A considerable amount of data was collected during the research but for the purposes of this study we will focus specifically on four themes: female cricketers' experiences of playing cricket with males; the reactions of males who encounter female cricketers in everyday settings; female cricketers' experiences of an organizational merger with a male team; and female cricketers' views of the status of women's cricket relative to the men's game.

## Playing with the boys

Almost half of those interviewed had experience of playing in cricket teams alongside males. Whilst in part this is a consequence of the lack of clubs providing cricket exclusively for females (at the time this research was undertaken there were 193 male clubs and only three female clubs in County A), it also demonstrates a broader, formal acceptance of female cricketers within otherwise all-male teams. Unlike football in which there are restrictions on females playing with males after the age of 11,[23] in cricket there are no formal restrictions on females playing alongside males. The decision to allow females to play alongside males is largely dependent on committees within individual clubs or, within schools, upon the decisions of individual teachers. It is only recently that the ECB has published guidelines regarding girls' participation in otherwise all-boy leagues. These guidelines state:

> The ECB wishes to encourage the development of girl cricketers and is happy for them to participate in boy's cricket. Team managers and coaches have a duty of care to all players and girls should only be allowed to participate if the responsible adults are satisfied that they are competent to do so. Suitable arrangements need to be in place, particularly relating to changing facilities and transportation arrangements, if applicable. In ECB national competitions the age group requirements apply to all players regardless of their sex. In local Leagues and other competitions it is up to each League or competition to specify the age group requirements. If girls who are older than the specified age group are allowed to play the League must specify a maximum age for the girl players and confirm how many older girls can play in any team. The same regulations must apply to all clubs in that League or competition. For the sake of clarity it should be understood that boys cannot play in girls' leagues or competitions unless explicit provision for this is included in the rules of that League or competition. Boys cannot play in the ECB girls' competitions.[24]

These organizational arrangements formally enable a more integrated context in which the sexes can play the sport. It should be noted however that the underlying tenor of these guidelines is not so much designed to treat sex as an irrelevant category for participation, but to make provision for a limited number of suitably talented girls to play in what will essentially remain 'boys' teams'. The exclusion of boys from 'girls' competitions' is premised upon assumptions of differential sporting ability being inherently linked, we would suggest, to biological sex. The character of the integrated playing context which stems from these organizational arrangements has particular consequences for female cricketers' identities and thus their experiences of participation.

Interviewees expressed a mixture of negative and positive experiences of playing with 'the boys'. Some of the U15 girls found that playing in the context of a male team allowed them to demonstrate their ability to play cricket and challenge common perceptions about female fragility and physicality.[25] Megan, Harriet, Sarah and Natalie made the following comments about playing alongside boys: 'It's fine, they respect me' (Megan); 'its fine, at primary school most of my friends were boys anyway' (Harriet); 'We prove we are as good as they are, as long as you can do that you won't get any stick' (Sarah); 'once they can see a girl can play to a serious standard they are quite welcoming' (Natalie). For these girls the experience of playing cricket with boys seemed to heighten their self-esteem and confidence in their own abilities. Whilst the girls enjoyed playing cricket in this context the potential to pose a broader challenge to gender relations was limited because the girl normally remained isolated as the only female in this male space. Moreover, as Sarah and Natalie note, acceptance in this context was contingent on being able to play to a 'serious standard', as indeed the reference to competence in the ECB guidelines suggests should be the case. By implication, however, this is the standard to which the boys perceive themselves to play. The emphasis therefore is on girls integrating into the 'male' game, rather than the organization of the game being altered to reflect a mixed-sex sport.

Such positive experiences were not universal for a number of girls who, whilst playing in mixed-sex cricket teams, had found themselves stigmatized due to others' perceptions of their playing ability. Natalie, for instance said that, 'Sometimes I feel like I don't get any respect at all, they expect me to get out straightaway', and Phoebe noted that whilst 'Some of the boys were nice. Some thought we [girls] were basically crap and that cricket wasn't our sport.' The experiences of Nicki are also enlightening. Nicki started playing club cricket at the age of 10 (she was 15 at the time of the interview), but gave up because people, both spectators and opponents, would often shout comments such as, 'hit it to her, she is a girl, she won't get it'. On joining her school team, she found the teachers and the majority of the boys supportive but ultimately she dropped out of that team too because, in her view, 'I just felt I shouldn't be there'. Reflecting on these experiences Nicki noted that it was rarely the case that people aimed their comments directly towards her, but that the sense of exclusion came from what males said to each other in gossip networks: 'I used to play for the boys but then I realised everywhere I went people were saying things like, '"look it's a girl" … people think girls shouldn't play cricket. They don't say it, you just get that impression'.

Despite organizational arrangements which enable males and females to play cricket together, deep-seated ideological beliefs about the essential distinctiveness of males and females remain. Sometimes this takes the form of open prejudice based on the assumed 'group disgrace' of the natural physical inferiority of females. Because they are the 'established', having numerical dominance, longevity of association and, due to most female cricketers' isolation, a more closely bonded character, male cricketers are able to use gossip and innuendo to reinforce this outsider status. This leads some female cricketers to be strongly aware that their physical appearance categorizes them as 'outsiders' to this male space. Interviewees' comments are illustrative of the degree to which the girls internalize and normalize this relationship and thus do not contest male 'ownership' of the game. For instance, Phoebe identifies the perception that cricket is not 'our sport' and Nicki refers to herself as having played *for* the boys, rather than *with* them. The girls do not, therefore, perceive themselves as sharing this space, but as being granted access; their participation is not viewed as a right but as an exemption in exceptional circumstances. The overt and covert resistance to their involvement by some males reinforces to them that in the context of cricket they are, and remain, *outsiders*.

The adult interviewees also expressed both positive and negative experiences of mixed-sex cricket. Sarah recalled the experience of playing alongside boys as being largely positive, arguing that it had helped her to become a better player: 'my running between the wickets is good compared to other girls'. Tellingly however the positive aspects of this experience do not relate to the breaking down of barriers between the sexes but of the personal advantage for Sarah, an advantage she experienced relative to the females she now plays against.

More commonly adult interviewees expressed negative experiences of mixed-sex cricket. Neve, like many of the U15 girls, described the mechanisms by which her outsider status was both intentionally and unwittingly reinforced. At times, male opponents had used physical aggression which, she felt, would have led to some females withdrawing from the game: 'There was some intimidation at times, but I desperately wanted to play. But I knew some other people who weren't quite as brave as me and wouldn't have played. It would have put them off.' At other times, however, her sense of difference and exclusion came through less personal, but ultimately equally divisive, channels. Neve recalled,

> I was the only girl that played on the boys' team. I didn't get to play in all the games. Some of the league games I wasn't allowed to play in so I could only play friendlies. When it gets to that level girls aren't allowed to play against boys. We didn't have a girls' team. (Neve)

Once again, therefore, a female's membership of this male space is marked out by difference. Whilst, as noted above, currently there are no national restrictions preventing mixed-sex cricket, leagues are free to make their own rules. Allowing a female to join the team, but then restricting the type and number matches in which she is able to play, flags up and reaffirms outsider status. Her restricted participation is inherently linked to her sex and limits not just the scope to develop cricketing skills but, more importantly, the scope to develop a sense of identity and belonging.

## Beyond a boundary: perceptions of female cricketers in everyday life

Due to their more extensive and varied life experience, adult interviewees were more likely to have had these negative reactions to their involvement in cricket and thus their outsider status reinforced from a wider variety of sources. As Donnelly and Young indicate in their classic study of socialization into sport subcultures, possession and appropriate use of relevant sporting equipment is crucial in signalling and negotiating group membership.[26] Katie, however, indicated some of the problems females may experience when entering another male domain – the sports shop – to buy equipment to play the game:

> I was trying on a pair of shoes, which is hard because I have small feet, so I found a pair and I asked to try them on. The guy said, 'are these for your brother?' I said, 'no they are for me'. He was like, 'oh, but they are cricket shoes you know?' I was like, 'yes, I know'.

The adult interviewees regularly reported male responses to their playing cricket which were patronizing and perplexed, but which had the (unintended) consequence of undermining their developing identity as a cricketer. In a similar vein, Eleanor explained that her involvement in cricket was something which tended to provoke further questioning during job interviews. She recalled:

> Whenever you say you play women's cricket people laugh at you ... it's on my CV that I played at county girls' level and when I go for interview it always comes up, they ask, 'what do you mean you play cricket? Are you having a laugh?'

In part such incredulous responses, and the frequency with which they are experienced, serve to reinforce the notion that female participation in cricket is at best a curiosity and at worst inappropriate. But the nature of the questions, and in particular the response that this must be some kind of a joke, also serves to trivialize Eleanor's achievement within county cricket and convey the message that female sport is, relative to male sport, of little value. Later on in the interview Eleanor expressed her frustration at men's responses to her involvement in cricket:

> People say 'what you actually play?' They think you mean you watch it on telly and I say 'no I actually play', they say 'do you bat and bowl?' They get this image of girls standing in whites and they laugh ... sometimes I just want to say 'grow up'. I think it's that perception again. They expect you to play a girl's sport.

Within various social contexts, therefore, female cricketers experience views which suggest that playing cricket is an unusual activity for a female. Often these prejudices do not seem to stem from conscious attempts to discriminate or exclude, but are intentional and stem from ignorance. They are, we could say, part of the second nature of many males, part of a habitus moulded within a particular context of power relations, and based on assumptions about the tastes and dispositions of the 'outsider' group. In many ways these deep-seated, 'normalized', beliefs create barriers to female participation in sport which remain even when the formal or explicit barriers to participation are being dismantled. Moreover, as we shall see, the views of the established males become internalized by female cricketers and thus an integral part of their outsider habitus.

## Merging men's and women's teams

The social processes leading to the merger of the WCA and the ECB have, of course, been experienced at lower levels of the game. Just as the national governing body's ability to access public money has been enhanced by conforming to gender equity policies, so has the access of individual clubs to such funding. Thus, in addition to mixed-sex teams at younger age levels, cricket clubs which have traditionally only catered for men have either established teams for women or, on occasion, merged with all-female clubs.

Females from a club which had recently undergone a merger were interviewed as part of the research reported here. The women's side had a long history, originally being formed in 1946. However, over the years the club had failed to establish a permanent base for itself, and had led an itinerant existence being based at various places at various times. The inability of the club to control access to a satisfactory playing venue informed the decision to merge, for the players deemed the club's facilities immediately prior to the merger to be unsuitable, and the club did not have sufficient money to secure better ones. According to one of the players, 'we had heard that a men's club were looking to form a ladies' side so we had negotiations' (Julie). The women were able to provide the club with a ready-made female team and for the women, to be 'part of an established male club (with) all the benefits that it brings' was the main motivation. Thus the women's desire to merge largely stemmed from the dominance over resources which males have traditionally had in the sport and they therefore entered into the merger with this legacy of long-term disadvantage.

As in the cases of mixed-sex cricket teams, however, organizational changes bringing the sexes closer together had not led to a significant degree of equalizing of playing opportunities. The women pointed to a number of promises which had been made during the merger negotiations which remained unfulfilled. Neve noted that, 'they said we would get matches on the green, (but) ... we have only had one match'. Jane recalled that, 'we were told we would get a coach, but I have never seen one'. Emma, a new club member also noted that, 'there is no proper coaching at all'. Thus, whilst the merger was supposed to ensure that the females were able to access a wider range of facilities than had been available to them as an independent club, this had not materialized. Other members recognized the impoverished status of the women's team; as Helen pointed out, 'we don't have much'.

There was, however, a certain resignation to, and a concomitant lack of resentment towards, the women's resultant position. Juliet, secretary of the women's section at the club noted that there was, 'no point complaining – it falls on deaf ears'. Despite their formal integration into the administration of the merged club, and the direct opportunity to raise issues at club committee meetings, the women ultimately felt powerless. In part this was due to their minority status (numerically speaking), but their inability or unwillingness to challenge their subordinate position was also directly related to the respective positions of the male and female sections when they merged. Because they feared for what might happen should the merger collapse – that the women would not be able to resurrect their former club and would thus not be in a position to continue playing – the women's committee representatives were reluctant to more forcefully raise issues of concern. The women thus felt resigned to their outsider status, unable to secure what had been promised to them, and reluctant to petition more strongly for its delivery.

The extent of the women's resistance was to state that the merger had been a backward step and to verbalize the negative impact it had on playing opportunities. Juliet noted:

> Personally I wouldn't encourage a club to amalgamate. It's easier to be independent, you can make your own decisions if you have your facilities, the other clubs have their own pitches. There are pro and cons to everything, the worst thing is the lack of independence; you are guided by what they (the men's section) tell you to do, e.g. they run a very good Saturday side so we can never use either home ground on a Saturday so that means if you want a Sat game you have to hire somewhere. We have given up playing Saturday cricket, so we have missed out there, we have to play Sundays. There are people who don't want to play Sunday, but getting Saturday pitches is extremely difficult.

Thus because of the balance of power between the respective parties when the male and female clubs merged, the new administrative arrangement had in fact been an absorption of the women rather than the creation of a new, joint entity. Ultimately the only tangible links between the women and the men were that they wore the same club colours and shared a club name. Katie reinforced this point noting that despite Juliet writing a report for the club handbook about the women's section, 'it's never put in'. Katie also noted that the merger could have been beneficial for the women by helping them to recruit members through advertising, but again the women did not find that this had occurred; as Katie summed up, 'they could advertise for us, but nothing.'

Prior ownership of facilities and dominance of positions on club committees meant that the men were both literally the established, but also the established in terms of their relative power within the club. The taken-for-granted status of the men's section and relatively unchallenged character of the relationship was manifest in the expectation that the men's team would have priority when pitches were allocated. There seemed to be little or no compensation for the women's loss of independence for they continued only to have access to facilities located away from the club and which they felt were poor.

Characteristic of established-outsider group relations more generally, there was evidence of the internalization of the outsiders' group disgrace and the acceptance of the group charisma of the established. That Juliet's resentment is not focussed so much on the fact that the women are dictated to, but rather the specifics of the arrangements dictated, reveals the limited extent to which the existing balance of power is seen as illegitimate. Similarly Katie argued that the treatment of the women's side was in some ways understandable and a consequence of the women's own behaviour: 'We are a hindrance to them, we don't bring money in over the bar, they think we are a pain ... they haven't given us much but then we haven't done much for them either'. The tendency among the women to blame themselves is indicative of their loosely bonded character as a group, and a lack of collective identity. Thus we can see how broader power relations are deeply imprinted in the habitus of different social groups. As Van Stolk and Wouters noted, the abused wives in their study viewed emancipation from their husbands ambivalently because they had so deeply internalized their partners' views. Commonly, 'She takes more notice of him than he of her, she is more sensitive to his whims than he to hers'.[27] In a similar though less extreme way, the broader experience of being a cricket outsider leads female cricketers to internalize a negative self-image, which in turn acts to limit the extent to which inequalities are challenged.

## Cricketing identities: group charisma and group disgrace

As noted above, Elias and Scotson's study emphasized the way in which established groups were able to convey an image of themselves that was relatively idealized, whilst outsiders came to internalize a view of themselves which emphasized negative traits. According to Elias and Scotson these respective group images are highly interdependent. In the context of cricket, and indeed sports more generally, the relative group charisma and group disgrace of males and females has historically rested on beliefs about innate biological abilities. As Messner notes, in reality men's and women's bodies exist on a continuum of difference with some men stronger than some women and vice versa, but hegemonic masculinity is based on the belief that men are stronger than women per se.[28] This ideology is derived, in Elias's terms, from an extrapolation of the abilities of 'the minority of the best'. The 'naturalness' of sport in general as a male-appropriate activity, and of certain sports as 'categorically unacceptable' for women,[29] largely rests on the assumptions underlying this ideology. To this end, a gauge of the degree to which female cricketers internalize their 'group disgrace' is the extent to which they attribute differences between the male and female game to biological difference. Conversely, the degree to which female cricketers' cite social factors as the primary cause for the relative weakness of the women's game indicates the degree to which the outsiders' group disgrace is challenged or rejected.

An interesting feature of the research data was the greater propensity of the younger females, when discussing the differences between male and female players, to cite the different social conditions under which boys and girls develop as cricketers. Of course many of the girls perceived that they were different from boys because males are stronger than females. Ella stated that, 'I think boys are stronger than girls'; Maddie noted that 'Boys are bigger and stronger'; whilst Nicki suggested that, 'we play different because we aren't strong enough, or fast enough'. In addition to this, however, a number of girls cited 'social' reasons why they believed that men's/boy's cricket was different/superior. Having highlighted biological differences Nicki went on to note that, 'the boys train at a younger age'. Not only did they start earlier but, according to Sophie, 'they get better training'. Moreover, the culture in which boys played cricket was deemed to be different; 'boy's cricket is more competitive and the coaches put more pressure on to make sure you get it right' (Phoebe).

In contrast the majority of adult interviewees understood the differences between the men's and women's games as the manifestation of biological differences between the sexes. For example, Eleanor argued that, 'there is a huge difference between a man's ability to play cricket and a girl's; a guy can hit the ball harder than a girl'. Emma echoed this view, simply saying that, 'the difference (between men and women) is strength'. These strength differentials meant that, 'there is a difference in the speed of bowling and people's ability to throw' (Heather), and because, 'women aren't as strong as men, they rely on timing' (Fiona). Even when women were forced to reassess these 'commonsense' assumptions, such as when females had successfully played with males, this was considered as a 'one-off' example of exceptional female ability as opposed to evidence that females can successfully compete with males. According to Susie, 'I think if you are an excellent bat you can compete with them (men) but for the bowlers women struggle because you don't bowl as quick. A quick bowler in women's cricket is a slow bowler in men's.'

Only three of the adult women mentioned socially constructed differences between male and female cricketers. Like the younger players the adults drew attention to the provision of coaching. Juliet, for instance, stated that, 'I think the coaching and the organization they get [is significant], they have colts, the men are practising and helping the colts ... the parents get involved'. She went on to further highlight the younger age at which males tended to take up the game, the fact that boys may have opportunities to take up the game at both clubs and at school, and 'the sheer numbers' taking up the game from which a more talented pool of players would almost inevitably emerge.

Similar to other research in this area,[30] female participants were not unwilling to describe their sport in positive terms but, in so doing, they did not directly challenge perceptions of biological difference head-on but chose, rather, to stress alternative qualities in the women's game. For instance, in their research with female footballers, Mennesson and Clement found that it is not uncommon for female athletes to argue that their sport is a more tactical or skilful version of men's sport.[31] Whilst Molly was amongst those adult female cricketers who expressed similar sentiments – 'I think women are more technically able than the blokes ... women have to be more technical because the guys can use brute strength' – it was telling that even this endorsement of the game was predicated on an internalization of a negative 'we-group' image based on relative biological ability.

There was, therefore, considerable evidence of an internalization of the group disgrace of females based on biological inferiority. This aspect of their personality structure is, of course, contoured by the relationship networks in which they are enmeshed, and stems from their interactions with others both in the direct context of playing cricket and in society more widely. The differences between the older and younger females could in part be attributed to generational differences and the increasing number of challenges posed to the 'female frailty myth'. On the other hand, these differences may also be indicative of the relatively limited or insubstantial challenge to notions of male dominance which are posed by mixed-sex sporting experiences. Whilst some of the adult players were relative newcomers to cricket, and therefore did not necessarily have extensive playing experiences to draw upon, almost all had been involved in other sports, such as hockey and football, and therefore had related experiences to draw upon. In sum, there was little evidence to suggest that female sports participation led to a broader ideological challenge to the 'naturalness' of sport as a male-appropriate and female-inappropriate activity, and some evidence to suggest that the very opposite was a more common outcome.

## Conclusion

In this study we have sought to explain why, despite organizational changes which would appear to have been conducive to expansion, the growth of female participation in cricket in recent years can at best be described as stilted. Our evidence suggests that experiences of mixed-sex cricket, a common route by which young females come to the game, are often negative. Acceptance within otherwise all-male teams is in part policed by existing (male) members' perceptions of playing ability and even then may be problematized by the rules of individual leagues. Male resistance to female involvement may come in the form of verbal abuse, physical intimidation or gossip and innuendo. These experiences, and the broader questioning of the appropriateness of cricket as an activity for females which occurs in everyday life, underscore the marginal status of women in the game and thus limit the development of a stronger sense of 'we' group identity. Consequently when broader social circumstances push males and females into organizational arrangements which, on the face of it, entail heightened levels of interdependence and thus more even power balances, female cricketers are reluctant to make more radical challenges to their disadvantaged status, and express high degrees of resignation towards their unequal status. The degree to which female cricketers accept male sporting superiority, and the focus on biological rather than social explanations of the causes of this inequality, is indicative of the extent to which female cricketers internalize their 'group disgrace' as part of their habitus. In turn, the degree to which the positive group image of the established and the negative group image of outsiders is internalized is, according to Elias, indicative of the gulf in power between the two groups, and a constraint on the ability of the outsider group to successfully challenge such inequality in the future. Thus increased participation may not necessarily follow from organizational changes, such as mergers between male and female governing bodies but, rather, is more likely to stem from changes to attitudes and ideologies which may be deeply embedded in the habitus of individuals.

The essay has utilized theoretical tools developed by Elias, and in particular his theory of established-outsider relations. A broader consideration of theoretical perspectives on gender is beyond the remit of this essay and in the absence of a broader evaluation, it would be wrong to claim that the insights and conclusions drawn here could *only* have developed out of this model. We would however suggest that when seeking to understand a context (one might say a figuration) in which material and organizational changes have not resulted in as significant a shift in the balance of power as one might otherwise have expected, it is vital to consider the social habitus of group members and, in particular, the degree to which negative self-images have been internalized by the subordinate or outsider group. In this respect, we think that use of this Eliasian model has been very useful in explaining why female cricketers continue to exist on the boundaries of the sport.

## Notes

[1]   See Maguire and Mansfield, '"No-Body's Perfect": Women, Aerobics, and the Body Beautiful'; Markula, 'Firm but Shapely, Fit but Sexy, Strong but Thin: the Postmodern Aerobicizing Female Bodies'.
[2]   Howe, 'Women's Rugby and the Nexus Between Embodiment, Professionalism and Sexuality: an Ethnographic Account'; Malcolm and Velija, 'Female Cricketers and Male Preserves'; Mennesson and Clement, 'Homosociability and Homosexuality: The Case of Soccer Played by Women'; Scraton *et al.*, 'Is it Still a Man's Game? The Experiences of Top Level European Women Footballers'.
[3]   Sport England, *Young People and Sport in England: A Survey of Young People and PE Teachers*; Sport England, *Young People and Sport in England 1999*; Sport England, *Young People and Sport in England; Trends in Participation 1994–2002*.
[4]   Aitchison, *Sport and Gender Identities*.
[5]   http://www.ecb.co.uk/womens/domestic/womens-cricket-history,264,BP.html; http://www. thefa.com/Womens/EnglandSenior/History/; http://www.englandhockey.co.uk/text.asp? section = 000100010003.
[6]   http://www.ecb.co.uk/womens/.
[7]   Sport England, *Young People and Sport in England*; Sport England, *Young People and Sport in England 1999*; Sport England, *Young People and Sport in England; Trends in Participation*.
[8]   UKSport, *Women in Sport: The State of Play 2006*.
[9]   http://www.ecb.co.uk/ecb/about/ecb-structure,28,BP.html.
[10]  White and Kay, 'Who Rules Sport Now?'. White and Kay discuss how women's position with sports governance has increased significantly in the last 20 years, but this is predominantly within the context of women's sport. In sports such as rugby and football women hold relatively few senior governance positions.
[11]  The concept of habitus used in this essay is drawn from the work of Elias. Elias defines habitus as 'second nature' or embodied social learning and argues that each person develops an individual habitus which is relatively unique, as well as a series of social habituses related, for instance to class, gender or nationality. Whilst we recognize that the concept is more normally associated with Bourdieu, Bourdieu's formulation of habitus can, at times, be criticized for being somewhat deterministic, with little scope for human agency. For this reason, and in line with the broader theoretical position of the paper, we prefer to use Elias in this context.
[12]  Elias and Scotson, *The Established and the Outsiders*.
[13]  Elias, *The Civilizing Process*; Elias and Scotson, *The Established and the Outsiders*.
[14]  Mennell, *Norbert Elias*, 116.
[15]  Elias and Scotson, *The Established and the Outsiders*, 16.
[16]  Ibid., 81.
[17]  Ibid., 7.
[18]  Mennell, *Norbert Elias*.
[19]  Dunning, *Sport Matters*; Liston, 'Established-outsider Relations between Males and Females in the Field of Sports in Ireland'; Maguire and Mansfield, 'No-Body's Perfect'; Maguire, *Global Sport*; Dunning and Waddington, 'Sport as a Drug and Drugs in Sport'.
[20]  Van Stolk and Wouters, 'Power Changes and Self Respect: A Comparison of Two Cases of Established-Outsider Relations'.
[21]  Velija, 'Women, Cricket and Gender Relations; A Sociological Analysis of the Experiences of Female Cricketers'.

[22] Patton, *Qualitative Research and Evaluation Methods*.
[23] The FA state: 'Save for matches in a playing season in the age ranges Under 7, Under 8, Under 9, Under 10 and Under 11 players in a match must be of the same gender'. http://www.thefa.com/Womens/GettingInvolved/NewsAndFeatures/Postings/2007/06.
[24] http://www.ecb.co.uk/ecb/publications/girls-playing-in-boys-age-group-leagues-and-competitions, 598,BP.html.
[25] See, for example, Dowling, *The Frailty Myth*; Young, 'Throwing Like A Girl: A Phenomenology of Feminine Body Comportment, Motility and Spatiality'.
[26] Donnelly and Young, 'The Construction and Confirmation of Identity in Sport Subcultures'.
[27] Van Stolk and Wouters, 'Power Changes and Self Respect', 479.
[28] Messner, *Taking the Field: Women, Men and Sport*.
[29] Snyder and Spreitzer, *Social Aspects of Sport*.
[30] See for example, McGinnis, McQuillan and Chapple, 'I Just Want to Play: Women, Sexism and Persistence in Golf', an account of female golfers, and also Henry and Comeaux, 'Gender Egalitarianism in Coed Sport: A Case Study of American Soccer', an account of females playing coed soccer.
[31] Mennesson and Clement, 'Homosociability and Homosexuality'.

## References

Aitchison, Cara. *Sport and Gender Identities: Masculinities, Femininities and Sexualities*. London: Routledge, 2007.

Donnelly, Peter, and Kevin Young. 'The Construction and Confirmation of Identity in Sport Subcultures'. *Sociology of Sport Journal* 5, no. 3 (1988): 223–40.

Dowling, Colette. *The Frailty Myth*. New York: Random House, 2000.

Dunning, Eric. *Sport Matters: Sociological Studies of Sport, Violence and Civilization*. London: Routledge, 1999.

Dunning, Eric, and Ivan Waddington. 'Sport as a Drug and Drugs in Sport'. *International Review for the Sociology of Sport* 38, no. 3 (2003): 351–68.

Elias, Norbert. *The Civilizing Process*. London: Blackwell, 2000.

Elias, Norbert, and John Scotson. *The Established and the Outsiders*. London: Sage, 1994.

Henry, M. Jacques, and P. Howard Comeaux. 'Gender Egalitarianism in Coed Sport: A Case Study of American Soccer'. *International Review for the Sociology of Sport* 34, no. 3 (1999): 277–90.

Howe, P. David. 'Women's Rugby and the Nexus Between Embodiment, Professionalism and Sexuality: an Ethnographic Account'. *Football Studies* 4, no. 2 (2001): 77–92.

Liston, Katie. 'Established-outsider Relations between Males and Females in the Field of Sports in Ireland'. *Irish Journal of Sociology* 14, no. 1 (2005): 66–85.

Maguire, Joseph. *Global Sport*. Cambridge: Polity Press, 1999.

Maguire, Joseph, and Mansfield, Louise. '"No-Body's Perfect": Women, Aerobics, and the Body Beautiful'. *Sociology of Sport Journal* 15 (1998): 109–37.

Malcolm, Dominic, and Philippa Velija. 'Female Cricketers and Male Preserves'. In *Tribal Play: Sport Subcultures And Countercultures*, edited by Michael Atkinson and Kevin Young, 217–35. London: Elsevier Press, 2008.

Markula, Pirkko. 'Firm but Shapely, Fit but Sexy, Strong but Thin: the Postmodern Aerobicizing Female Bodies'. *Sociology of Sport Journal* 12, no. 4 (1995): 424–53.

McGinnis, Lee, Julia McQuillan, and Chapple L. Constance. 'I Just Want to Play: Women, Sexism and Persistence in Golf'. *Journal of Sport and Social Issues* 29, no. 3 (2005): 313–37.

Mennell, Stephen. *Norbert Elias*. Dublin: University College Dublin Press, 2000.

Mennesson, Christine, and John-Paul Clement. 'Homosociability and Homosexuality: The Case of Soccer Played by Women'. *International Review for Sociology of Sport* 38, no. 3 (2003): 311–30.

Messner, Michael. *Taking the Field: Women, Men and Sport*. London: University of Minnesota Press, 2002.

Patton, Chris. *Qualitative Research and Evaluation Methods*. London: Sage Publications, 2002.

Scraton, Sheila, Ana Bunuel, Kari Fasting, and Gertrud Pfister. 'Is it still a Man's Game? The Experiences of Top Level European Women Footballers'. *International Review for the Sociology of Sport* 34, no. 2 (1999): 99–111.

Snyder, Eldon, and Elmer Spreitzer. *Social Aspects of Sport*. Englewood Cliffs, NJ: Prentice Hall, 1989.

Sport England. *Young People and Sport in England: A Survey of Young People and PE Teachers.* London: Sport England, 1994.

Sport England. *Young People and Sport in England 1999: A Survey of Young People and PE Teachers.* London: Sport England, 2001.

Sport England. *Young People and Sport in England; Trends in Participation 1994–2002.* London: Sport England, 2003.

UKSport. *Women in Sport: The State of Play 2006.* London: UKSport, 2006.

Van Stolk, Bram, and Cas Wouters. 'Power Changes and Self Respect: A Comparison of Two Cases of Established-Outsider Relations'. *Theory, Culture and Society* 4, no. 4 (1987): 477–88.

Velija, Philippa. 'Women, Cricket and Gender Relations; A Sociological Analysis of the Experiences of Female Cricketers'. PhD Diss., Brunel University, 2007.

White, Michelle, and Joyce Kay. 'Who Rules Sport Now?: White and Brackenridge Revisited'. *International Review for the Sociology of Sport* 41, no. 3 (2006): 465–73.

Young, Irene. 'Throwing Like A Girl: A Phenomenology of Feminine Body Comportment, Motility and Spatiality'. In *Throwing Like a Girl and Other Essays in Feminists Philosophy and Social Theory*, edited by I. Young. Bloomington, IN: Indiana University Press, 1990.

# International cricket – the hegemony of commerce, the decline of government interest and the end of morality?

Russell Holden*

*Director, In the Zone, Sport and Politics Consultancy*

## Introduction

In capturing the imagination of the British public during the summer of 2005 the England cricket team's remarkable Ashes victory did much to redeem the bruised image of a sport that had been poorly served in recent times by its governing body's handling of cricketing relations with Zimbabwe. Despite widespread oppression in Zimbabwe and the persecution of opponents of the Mugabe regime, cricket has continued there, although allegations concerning political interference, intimidation of players and mismanagement of the game remain rife. The question of whether to play cricket in, and with, Zimbabwe involves issues of ethics and morality and the granting of legitimacy to a regime that engages in fundamental breaches of human rights similar to that which occurred in South Africa during the apartheid era.

To explore the complexity of the Zimbabwe question, the role and actions of the governing body of international cricket, the International Cricket Council (ICC), and its response to this issue, must be examined. However, this only becomes meaningful when viewed in the context of the impact of the ICC's behaviour on a national cricket authority, which in this instance is the England and Wales Cricket Board (EWCB).[1] Furthermore, this investigation has to be conducted in the context of the changing nature of international sport where the new commercial realities of a game (cricket) that is ever more global is reflected in the power centre having re-located to South Asia from its longstanding base in England. This has presented an additional challenge to those who formerly controlled the game, as it overturns the orthodox model of globalization and economic development which maintains that the dynamics of globalization are spurred on by the forces of wealth from traditional geographical locations: namely the developed economies. With the power base of cricket now firmly entrenched in South Asia, the old order has been overthrown in both sporting and commercial terms. Furthermore, as Berry comments, the game is no longer dominated by white people.[2]

Consequently, this essay seeks to explore this changing reality by focusing on the growing dominance of commercial interests and how, in coping with these, two major cricket authorities have struggled to understand and reconcile the clash between the commercial instincts and ethical considerations that riddle international sport.

This investigation will be undertaken by using the England-Zimbabwe cricket crisis (2002–05) as the focus of the study with the emphasis of the inquiry looking at the England-Zimbabwe fixture in Harare during the 2003 World Cup hosted by South Africa, and the later tour of Zimbabwe by the England team in 2004. Throughout, it will also be necessary to consider whether the British government displayed any culpability in failing to provide leadership in responding to one of the most controversial issues for the government and cricket authorities in the United Kingdom since the cancellation of the South African cricket tour to England in 1970. However, due acknowledgement will have to be made in this study to the fact that government interest and action is constrained by the pressures of advancing globalization. The investigation will also consider whether it is the case, as Calder and Dain suggest, that 'sporting relations are somehow beyond the range of the moral compass'.[3]

In seeking to address the aforementioned objectives, this essay will consist of four distinct sections. These will explore the development of international cricket as it relates to politics in the twenty-first century, the growing significance of globalization as it applies to cricket, the lack of government leadership (in this instance that of the United Kingdom government's response to the Zimbabwe crisis), and finally whether the aforementioned concerns reveal an increasing absence of morality on the part of cricket's decision-makers in the management of their game as they are ever more cognizant of sport being firmly embedded in the global economy. This has generated the perception that this marks the death of morality in sport for reasons of realpolitik whilst acknowledging that financial reward has penetrated to the core of professional sport.[4]

Throughout the following discussion, analysis will be conducted on the premise that politics and sport are not autonomous phenomena.[5] This essay will argue that sporting bodies cannot divorce themselves from the political environments in which they are located because, as Barnes maintains, sport and politics 'have been blood brothers since the first national anthem was played at a sporting event'.[6]

## The Development of International Cricket

As Anil Gupta perceptively remarks:

> International cricket has not followed the path of other transnational sporting events. It is a game where the non-western countries have begun to dominate not just on the field, but, more importantly, in shaping the economics and politics of the game.[7]

Consequently, any examination of the realities of international cricket, whether it be in terms of issues of principal or realpolitik, must acknowledge a distinctiveness of the game in comparison to that of other sports. However, critical to the development of the game has been the rise of a transnational community able to support its favoured team across national boundaries. The spread of technology now enables the provision of real-time coverage of the sport, be it via satellite, cable, web or podcast, and this helps to satisfy the increasing demands of the Indian diaspora. This is a far cry from the beginnings of modern day international cricket.

The origins of the international game date back to 1909 and the birth of the Imperial Cricket Conference (ICC). The new governing body of cricket began life with a grand vision: the setting up of a triangular tournament involving England, South Africa and Australia in 1909. Although the competition failed, this initiative marked the start of regular meetings between representatives of a growing number of Test cricket playing countries, which became an annual event in 1929. However, as Haigh suggests, the organization remained an adjunct of the MCC. For many years, the ICC operated on the basis that unspoken codes of behaviour, rather than rules and statutes, were deemed sufficient in overseeing the game. Even as international cricket expanded, Haigh reminds us that 'its management remained as simple as a post-office box and filing cabinet at Lords'.[8]

In 1929, the ICC began to meet annually at Lord's (London) and while it gradually extended its membership to include the West Indies, India, Pakistan and New Zealand, it remained an adjunct of the MCC. The president and secretary of the MCC doubled up as chair and secretary of the ICC. The ICC agenda remained routine for many years: however, in 1960 it addressed the 'chucking' pandemic and shortly afterwards it expelled South Africa following its decision to leave the Commonwealth.

It was not until the emergence of Australian business tycoon Kerry Packer that the ICC's cosy existence was challenged. Although the ICC took a major blow with the emergence of World Series Cricket in the second half of the 1970s, which represented a hostile take-over of international cricket by a wealthy outsider, Kerry Packer's ultimate objective was not to own international cricket but to secure the broadcasting rights for cricket in Australia. For the ICC this was a small price to pay in turn for the restoration of peace in the international game.

However, there was already evidence of the ICC failing to keep up with the changing needs of cricket. It had failed to realize the potential benefits of one-day international cricket until the 1970s and then chose to grant the staging of the first four World Cup competitions to England and Australia. With respect to the distribution of broadcasting rights, the ICC was again conservative in its handling of an issue vital to the game's global development. Even in the late 1980s it was difficult to receive telecasts of some major international games - notably in Australia, as national broadcasting corporations which transmitted live broadcasts were paid very poorly for the privilege of so doing. Although Packer had revolutionized the playing style of the game, moving it towards realizing its potential for providing a livelihood as well as in terms of marketing and administration, the running of the game was lagging behind in terms of the professional ethos.

As regards cricket in southern Africa, once the ICC expelled South Africa after its decision to leave the Commonwealth in 1961, it was loathe to interfere in the responses of national cricket authorities to the apartheid regime. However, in 1979, an ICC delegation visiting the Republic appeared impressed with changes afoot and recommended that a team of players from a range of countries tour South Africa.[9] In 1981, it unanimously passed a resolution supporting the view that cricket should be given every form of encouragement to become more multi-racial. However, in realizing this objective it was not willing to endorse rebel tours which contravened the 1977 Gleneagles Agreement (a measure agreed by all Commonwealth member states ensuring the sporting isolation of South Africa). All of this indicated a desire by the ICC to exclude itself from involvement in political matters whenever it could, and this set down markers for the ICC's later policy stance over Zimbabwe. Yet in 1989, fearing a schism over the South African issue, the ICC set down a series of guidelines that provided a set of minimum sanctions to which each Test playing country was urged to adhere. All member countries accepted these though there were elements within the Test and County Cricket Board, the forerunner of the EWCB, who were very reluctant to do so, yet it feared a loss of revenue and power caused by maintaining South African connections. This response also contributed to the drawing up of the battle lines that emerged within the ICC during the 1990s continuing into the new century that have served to weaken England's negotiating position within the ICC power structure.[10]

Belatedly in 1989, the MCC surrendered its role in the management of international cricket and the International Cricket Conference became the International Cricket Council, although the voting structure that was introduced privileged the entitlements of the foundation members (England and Australia). England suffered a dramatic loss of administrative supremacy within the game, though this was far from being a revolutionary event. It was only in 1993, when India wrested the hosting of the 1996 World Cup from England, that real change came, with power being taken from English officials in the running of the game. This event marked what Haigh has termed 'the first significant bust-up at the ICC twixt East and West'.[11]

As a consequence the ICC obtained its first full-time secretariat, and a non-English chair and chief executive. Irrespective of its strength or lack of it, the individual national cricketing boards remained in hock to what the ICC determined. This has culminated not just in the financial control of the game that India now holds (a development spurred on by the Presidency of Jagmohan Dalmiya, the first non-westerner to occupy this position) but also in the assertion of power that displayed in 2006 by forcing the ICC to re-jig its future tours programme to reflect the demands of its consumer market combined with its ability to generate 75% of cricket's global revenue.[12]

In showing a weakness in understanding the financial potential of the game, the ICC failed to learn from sporting bodies such as the Fédération Internationale de Football Association (FIFA) which had made tremendous efforts to reach out to non-western and non-traditional playing countries in its efforts to widen the appeal and marketability of the game. This generated a reaction from a new power source – South Asia – which was willing to develop the game to a new level, encouraging more interest, new talent and most critical of all, locating new sources of finance, with Dalmiya very much to the fore in this process.

### Hegemony of commerce

Having noted how the administrators of international cricket have struggled to keep pace with the changing commercial imperative, it is necessary to view cricket in terms of the globalization thesis. This will help to determine an understanding of how globalization has impacted on the game even if it is only viewed as a continuation or extension of the modernization processes. A much respected view suggests this process in terms of cricket has passed through three stages, with the globalized period having followed those of colonialism and nationalism.[13] However, as the investigation contained within this essay unfolds, the division between the nationalist and globalized periods is not always easy to detect.

The development of sport in both competitive and commercial terms has to be seen in the context of globalization, namely the speeding up and deepening impact of transcontinental flows and patterns of social interaction. However, this remains a very uneven process that has its origins in trade and commercial activities dating back over 500 years.

A substantial literature exists on globalization, and more specifically on the globalization of sport.[14] In essence, however, this material can be distilled into two distinct perspectives. The first concentrates on the imperialist rationale emphasizing the unequal relationship between the culturally dominant capitalist, and predominantly western, economies and the developing countries. The emergence of this relationship is spurred on by the wish of the western economies to extend markets for capitalist products, which include sport. The upshot of this is that the peripheral nations are left as 'more the taker than the giver' of meaning and meaningful form. However, this perspective is increasingly challenged by the view that some of the underlying ideals of cultural imperialism are open to question, notably those concerning what Allison refers to as 'the uni-directional flow of culture and the coercive nature of the relationship'.[15]

Consequently, an alternative theoretical perspective on globalization has evolved which places increased emphasis on the interconnection and interdependency of all global areas and the weakening of cultural coherence of individual states. Maguire takes this further by suggesting that sport is now bound up with a network of interdependent chains marked by uneven power relations.[16] As a result of this, sport is best perceived as a set of global power networks in which the practice and consumption of elite modern sport can best be understood. Cricket is now locked into a set of global networks largely driven by commercial interests, thus intensifying the commodification of the game. For cricket, the apex of this development is the World Cup competition held every four years. Cricket features amongst a list of sports including baseball, basketball, ice hockey and rugby union which may appear to be globalized in terms of intensity and impact but in reality only have a grip on certain geographical areas rather than having a universal popular presence. Thus, the globalization of sport is an uneven process within which the place of cricket is distinct, reminding us that the rhetoric of globalization reflects the drive of global capital to extend and deepen its dominion.[17] Yet sport's constant use of the nation as a rallying point and focus, creates an uneasy tension when advocating the globalization argument. The globalization of sporting practices, in terms of the spread of certain games around the world, has paradoxically fuelled nationalism, which has manifested itself within cricket's governing body, the ICC.

A key element of globalization has been the flow of wealth, technology and ideas from the core to the periphery. Yet cricket disproves this model with the non-western nations now in a position to determine the format of the game, its content (international touring schedules) and venues whilst conceivably moving to reshape the rules of the international game through its voting power within the ICC. When coupled with the lack of United States involvement in the sport, despite efforts to bring 2007 World Cup fixtures there, and the comparative decline of English cricket until recently, the challenge to Asian dominance was minimal. With even the heroes of Australia's cricketing dominance over the past decade having taken the sub-continent to heart (notably Steve Waugh, Shane Warne and Brett Lee), the increasing commodification of the game provided yet more opportunities for profits to be realized.

Even though sport is less sympathetic to globalization than other cultural forms such as music and film because of its dependence on passionate national differentiation, the commodification of cricket has led to a geographical, if not an ideological, relocation of power with the activities of operatives like the Murdoch Global Cricket Corporation (MGCC) being the driving mechanism.[18] The MGCC has capitalized on the migration of labour, with the spread of technology helping to extend the notion of global entertainment. Indeed it was the actions of the Indian media mogul Mark Mascarenhas, who was able to secure the true market value for international cricket when he was successful in his bid of $8.5m by his company World Tel for broadcasting rights of the 1996 World Cup, that took cricket to a new level of commercial activity. His efforts were undoubtedly boosted by the rapid growth of technology, the interest of transnational TV networks, the commercial possibilities of the one-day game and the opportunity to have an advertisement screened at the end of each over. The payment of $22.5m to secure the television rights for India for the 2003 and 2007 World Cups and three ICC Champions Trophies in 2002, 2004 and 2006, was seven times more than the amount paid by Murdoch's STAR Sports network. Marqusee goes further in noting the significance of South Asia in terms of the globalization of sports broadcasting industry (via global networks such as ESPN and STAR) remarking that 'because of its vast popular base, cricket in the subcontinent is an ideal vehicle for multinational corporations seeking to penetrate emerging markets'.[19]

## The government and the cricket administrators – who takes responsibility?

To date, the thrust of this essay has argued that the administration of international cricket has evolved slowly. Now, in offering an illustration of how the game has responded to the changing nature of international sport driven by the dynamics of globalization, a case study approach will be pursued.

In focusing on the England-Zimbabwe episodes of 2002–05, it is possible to combine the consideration of a number of critical issues. Firstly, there is an opportunity to explore the implications of the commodification of cricket; secondly we must look at how and when the financial imperative is questioned by moral considerations; and lastly, we must examine whether the game's governing bodies and national government absolve themselves of wider responsibilities and whether they too are restricted by the dictates of commercial needs and budgetary constraints whilst struggling to secure a satisfactory balance between morality, justice and politics.

In using a case study with two points of reference (the 2003 World Cup fixture and the 2004 tour of Zimbabwe), it becomes possible to gauge whether the attitudes of the main protagonists altered. In terms of the EWCB, it becomes clear, from a consideration of the events, that its room for diplomatic manoeuvring was constrained by the actions of the ICC, yet the British government became more alarmed (albeit exhibited more through rhetoric than action) by the behaviour of a regime that was employing ever-more brutal tactics against its own subjects. However, as the government and anyone associated with the game in England and Wales had long realized, the English game was totally dependent on the earnings received from international cricket.[20]

Although cricket's international schedule has been curtailed during the past 20 years by both domestic politics and conflict between member states, the Zimbabwe issue was more complicated. The country was experiencing increasing violence as a result of the outcome of the March 2002 rigged election won by President Mugabe, who subsequently imprisoned the main opposition leader on a fabricated charge of plotting to assassinate him. The on-going process of land reform which amounted to blatant anti-white racism generated tremendous suffering, which was compounded by a food crisis with the World Food Programme claiming that approximately five million people would be facing famine by February 2003.[21] Though, as Calder and Dain note about cricket through the ages, 'has there ever been a point at which cricket has been left untarnished by politics given the importance of class and empire through history?'[22]

The England-Zimbabwe issue exemplifies this reality and the fact that Britain was the former colonial power until Rhodesia's Universal Declaration of Independence (see the contribution of Little to this collection) in 1965 placed higher expectations on a team representing England as well as on the domestic cricket authorities. In this context, the EWCB and the British government had a case for lobbying the ICC for a change of venue as the former colonial power, yet this resembled a veto which could be utilized in matches in other countries. However, one has to question whether this was something the ICC took account of in the context of their stance on separating sport from politics. President Mugabe had championed cricket in his native country since the mid 1980s, capitalizing on Zimbabwe's success in qualifying for the 1983 Cricket World Cup. Mugabe went further commenting that cricket 'civilizes people and creates good gentlemen. I want everyone in Zimbabwe to play cricket in Zimbabwe. I want ours to be a nation of gentlemen'.[23]

In effect Mugabe was happy to exploit the game for his own ends, yet as the former Zimbabwe cricket captain Andy Flower confirms, cricket had been displaced by football as the chief sporting past-time of the majority population.[24]

### The 2003 World Cup

The 2003 Harare fixture focused attention on an issue that had been brewing since February 2001 when the World Cup schedule was first drawn up by the ICC. The later tour of 2004, however, appears to have been undertaken by the EWCB with a view to securing goodwill within the broader family of cricket whilst paving the way for an injection of much-needed funding into the Zimbabwe Cricket Union (ZCU) as compensation for the cancellation of the scheduled Test matches.

One of the dominant themes evident in each of these episodes was the deep-rooted belief of many sports administrators that they have no right or obligation to interfere in the activities of a sovereign state. This represents an upholding of the amateur ethos that ignores the interlocking issues of politics and sport despite the enormous impact of both on financing existing and future commitments. However, it is important to note that previous experience could have been drawn on for lessons in how to respond to a similar episode.

In January 1969, the MCC Cricket Council recommended that South Africa be invited to tour England and Wales in 1970, a decision that it confirmed in May 1970. However, there was an acknowledgement by the MCC Cricket Council that there were political connotations to the tour and that these were best resolved by the state, providing the government with an opportunity to intervene. The Sports Council, chaired by the Minister of Sport, maintained that the responsibilities of governing bodies were first to their own sport, secondly to sport in general, whilst thirdly, account should be taken of the influence this action would have on the wider community. The Home Secretary James Callaghan notified the cricket authorities of his concerns about the impact of the tour on relations with other Commonwealth countries, domestic race relations and the threat to law and order. The government thus came to the conclusion that on grounds of broad public policy, it should request that the cricket authorities cancel the tour. This decision was taken by the Cricket Council within 24 hours of Callaghan's comments as it believed that it had no option but to accede to the request.

Such decisive action was not evident in the handling of the Harare fixture, yet neither were the broader concerns. From late December 2002, the government applied pressure on the England cricket team, initially via Foreign Office Minister Mike O'Brien, with the endorsement of the Prime Minister's Office, that England should not play in Harare. However, all the comments emanating from the government were couched in terms that the final decision lay with the EWCB and that the government's role was advisory and not that of ordering or instructing an independent sporting body to opt out of its match in Harare, which was accompanied by the danger that its presence would endorse the Mugabe regime. This also sparked an ethical dilemma for the cricket authorities in Australia because they too had a fixture to fulfil in Bulawayo, though eventually Cricket Australia accepted the ICC's assurances regarding their own safety and chose to play their match.

In so doing, they chose not to confront the issue of playing in a country ruled by an autocrat who was both the Patron and President of the Zimbabwe Cricket Union.

The EWCB made its position very clear in its statement of January 14:

> We are fully aware of what is happening in Zimbabwe and we do not in any way condone the policies and actions of the political regime in that country. However, we do not believe that the cancellation of one cricket match in Zimbabwe will make any difference to the leaders of that regime.[25]

For the EWCB, which, from the outset, was keen to fulfil the World Cup fixture for both financial and internal political reasons, a dilemma was evident. If England played, the British government was being defied and the Mugabe administration was being gifted a symbolic victory likely to generate substantial opposition in the United Kingdom. By choosing to boycott the fixture, goodwill in the international cricket community was likely to be sacrificed, with the ICC likely to impose a fine of approximately £1m. As regards progress in the tournament, choosing not to play the fixture meant sacrificing probable progress to the later stages. There was also a strong likelihood that Zimbabwe could cancel their projected tour of England in the summer of 2003 with South Africa following suit, thus costing the EWCB yet more in lost revenue. Ironically, this debate was continuing at a time when Zimbabwe was still banned from the Commonwealth, although its athletes had been permitted to take part in the 2002 Commonwealth Games that had been staged in Manchester. The government was far less vocal about the Commonwealth Games as it was keen not to disrupt a successful sporting event which it believed could help to sway the International Olympic Committee in deciding whether the London was capable of hosting a summer Olympiad.

The ICC, through the office of its Chair Malcolm Gray, made it clear that political gestures should not concern its members, and that it should focus purely on cricketing matters (which included issues of security). He further remarked at that point that the cricket establishment in Zimbabwe was not an ally of the government and therefore was deserving of support (even though it remained a bastion of the white minority). As ICC Chief Executive Malcolm Speed commented, 'While some countries have imposed sanctions on Zimbabwe, no government in any part of the world has identified sporting sanctions as an appropriate tool to achieve a political outcome'.[26]

As far as the ICC was concerned, the only anxiety was security as this was deemed to fall under what was classified as a cricket or a sport-related issue. In no way did it wish to fulfil a wider policy vacuum left by national government. It at no point expressed a willingness to reflect on the realities of starvation and repression, believing itself unable and unwilling to provide a moral lead. As Malcolm Speed remarked, 'it is not our function to evaluate the political regime of any country'.[27]

The ICC's sole concern was the security of the players, yet it also wished to spread the game to new territories. As cricket's governing body it also took every opportunity to remind everyone that it remained cricket's senior body concerned with cricket alone, although every hint of normality as portrayed to the outside world by playing the Harare fixture would make the task of Mugabe's opponents even tougher. The EWCB was placed in a quandary as it was fully aware of previous instances of Australia and New Zealand cancelling tours to Sri Lanka and Pakistan on grounds of security, yet in this instance the security fears were being allayed by personnel at the EWCB responsible for England's World Cup arrangements, though the cocktail of dissent and injustice had the potential to implode in Zimbabwe at any moment. This was a view that was echoed by the EWCB who took very seriously the threats of the 'Sons and Daughters of Zimbabwe' who were on a list of targeted suspects from Interpol. The security issue provided a useful smokescreen for both the ICC and EWCB. However, the EWCB was able to view this crisis in wider terms than the ICC, as the following EWCB Press Release reveals: 'playing this match in Harare does not mean that we are endorsing the Mugabe regime any more than playing in Pakistan means that we are endorsing military rule in preference to democracy'.[28]

In the England-Zimbabwe instance the relations between the EWCB and the British government were strained. It was only with growing public displeasure stirred by the media that government activity increased. As far as the EWCB were concerned they could only call off the match if instructions were forthcoming from the government; however the government was reluctant to do this as they did not feel that this was their responsibility. Neither did the government wish to issue instructions to the business community forbidding trade with Zimbabwe. This dilemma was further compounded by the substantial leverage available to it because of the provision of public and lottery funding which the EWCB believed could be utilized in addressing the losses that the EWCB were to sustain through the fixture cancellation. The EWCB was ever-more aware of the need to address commercial pressures and as a consequence of the decision to refuse to play in Zimbabwe in 2003, and the unwillingness of the government to compensate for the losses incurred, the EWCB announced a £4m budget cut to accommodate the losses incurred in Harare, a move in line with the commercial instincts that the Chief Executive Tim Lamb had sought to instil: 'like all responsible businesses we need to balance our books. We will further renew our efforts to run cricket on the most cost efficient basis'.[29]

**The 2004 tour**

As Zimbabwe, according to the Foreign Office,[30] slipped further into tyranny, the EWCB continued to maintain that it was correct to send an England team to this hostile destination. In early 2004, the EWCB began focusing on how to handle the planned visit to Zimbabwe later the same year. With the appointment of Des Wilson as Chair of the EWCB Corporate Affairs and Marketing Advisory Committee, the Board sought to avoid a repetition of the debacle of the previous year. Wilson advocated the cancellation of England's tour in 2004 on moral grounds as it was intended that the EWCB would publish a framework and follow-up paper for taking decisions about controversial tours. This would help to provide an intellectual and moral basis for taking decisions on all future tours.

A tour could be cancelled if a government issued clear instructions under the auspices of *force majeure*. As far as the British government was concerned, it responded to the EWCB's request for advice by declaring in a letter from Foreign Secretary Jack Straw that the EWCB should take note of the efforts of the international community in seeking to isolate a country with an appalling human rights record: 'you may wish to consider whether a high-profile England cricket tour at this time is consistent with that approach'.[31]

The letter also stated that the government believed that the overall situation in Zimbabwe had worsened since 2003. This represented the form of advice that would have been welcomed one year previously. However, the final decision in 2004 lay with the EWCB. Throughout this episode, the government clearly declared that the decision to tour had to be that of the EWCB (as had been the case the previous year), despite the desire from the EWCB to hear something stronger from the government.[32] Whereas this may have been sufficient for the domestic media, it was never likely to be enough for the ICC, as was confirmed when David Morgan took the framework paper (with the good wishes of the Commonwealth Secretariat) to the ICC spring meeting in Auckland and argued the *force majeure* case, but without success. The framework identified five factors that could lead to the abandonment of a tour – threats to the safety and security of players, impacts on the integrity of the tour, the link with British foreign policy, the views of the cricket world and moral considerations such as whether the tour would give succour to a despotic ruler. However, the ICC had already confirmed in January 2004 that it did not permit cancellation on the basis of political or moral considerations, a view that was endorsed by ICC President Ehsan Mani.[33]

The Auckland meeting agreed that countries could only cancel a tour for security reasons or if ordered to do so by governments, with any unilateral decision taken incurring a $2m fine. Furthermore, the ICC responded with hostility to the Straw letter (22 January 2004) implying that it constituted specific advice not to proceed with the tour which represented a challenge to their authority. When the Chair of Cricket Australia proposed an additional penalty for abandoning a tour – the suspension of the offending country from the international game – the EWCB was aghast. With the meeting confirming the international cricket schedule for the foreseeable future, the EWCB was left with two options, but it decided to go ahead with the tour. This was a decision that David Morgan was happy to endorse on behalf of the EWCB. However, at the eleventh hour, more obstacles were laid in England's path with the failure of the Zimbabwe government to offer accreditation for 13 journalists who intended to cover the tour. Through a combination of delicate handling and appropriate rhetoric by the conciliatory David Morgan, the crisis was defused and the tour went ahead. The essence of the EWCB's thinking is accurately summed up by Morgan's remark that:

> it has been very clear to me and our board for a considerable time that moral or political objections to touring are totally unacceptable within the international cricket community. Our business or trade is cricket, and our revenue earner is international cricket. If we want to trade in international cricket then we have to do so by the rules of the ICC.[34]

The EWCB's decision to tour undoubtedly helped to restore some of its lost status within the ICC. However, had the EWCB decided not to go ahead, it is highly questionable how far the ICC would have gone in punishing the EWCB (it had withheld England's World Cup share of £2.33m for their refusal to play in Harare). The moral dilemma remained, as the cancellation of one tour in isolation despite its value in symbolic terms was not enough when compared to organized and systematic mass action. Yet as Andy Flower, the former Zimbabwe cricket captain, maintains, sometimes limited action provides the arrant regime with an opportunity to provoke dissension amongst its opponents which may prolong its own life-time.[35]

### The end of morality?

Beneath the conjecture surrounding the recent difficulties in England–Zimbabwe cricketing relations, the fundamental issue remains: whether, as Des Wilson remarks, cricket should still be beyond moral and political activity? 'To seek to isolate sport as an activity that stands alone in human affairs, untouched by "politics" or "moral considerations" and unconcerned for the fate of those deprived of human rights is as unrealistic as it is (self-destructively) self-serving'.[36] However, to Ali Bacher, the Executive Director of the Cricket World Cup 2003, (who during the 1980s had organized rebel tours to South Africa), the reality was different: 'cricket is not qualified to do the job of politicians'.[37]

This critical discussion is complicated by the commodification of the game referred to earlier. The 2003 World Cup marked cricket as a global spectacle played by gladiators and governed by entrepreneurs. The crux of the matter was not whether the players simply desired a switch of venue from Harare to one outside Zimbabwe in 2003, but rather whether they wished to boycott the game altogether, as the then England captain Nasser Hussain explains in his autobiography.[38]

In a climate far removed from the Ashes euphoria of 2005, the hands of the EWCB were tied, as it realized how dependent it was on revenue from Test matches and how this restricted its bargaining position within the ICC, the undoubted masters of the game. The ICC opted to side with the ZCU, realizing that this move would be endorsed by the majority of the ICC membership, and it was therefore spared the prospect of having to compensate both the MGCC and ZCU. As Williamson commented, finance was victorious over principle:

> The decision was as good as made when the British government refused to compensate English cricket for the potential loss of income and fines likely to result from any boycott of the match in Harare. The choice was reduced to either losing £10m or taking a moral stand. If only it were that straightforward.[39]

The furore surrounding the World Cup fixture and the 2004 tour revolved around the issue of whether to have sporting relationships with a country stained by massive injustice (although business dealings were continuing regardless). Despite the horrors of the apartheid era and its enforcement of segregation, the Zimbabwean situation was different, with a tyrannical system operating and punishing anyone who dared to oppose the government. However, it was still possible for opponents of the tour to adopt the mantra used by those condemning white-led cricket in South Africa – namely that of 'No normal sport in an abnormal society'. In pursuing this path, however, as Flower maintains, there was always the risk of destroying a game that was already undermined by the expansion of global football. Former England captain Mike Brearley noted:

> Does it not go against the grain, to play [cricket] with a country whose opponents are too frightened to go into hospital to have wounds inflicted by the security forces treated for fear that they will be injected with slow-acting poisons by the Central Intelligence Organization.[40]

However, the magnitude of Brearley's comments was and continues to be ignored. By agreeing to forgo the tournament points available, the EWCB's decision to boycott the Harare game showed the cricketers in a good light but at the same time presented problems for the domestic administrators. On 2 April 2003, the EWCB announced that a £4 million budget cut was needed to accommodate the losses for England not having played in Zimbabwe. However, the strongest sentiment voiced by the EWCB was the need to run the game as a business rather than an as an organization dedicated to making political and moral decisions, as Brearley certainly would have preferred. As human-rights activist Peter Tatchell suggests, a situation had been reached where 'sporting values such as friendship and fair play have been displaced by the cash register mentality'. The commercialization of cricket means maximizing investment returns. Ethical considerations are a low priority.[41]

With the EWCB losing out financially and in terms of maintaining allies within the higher echelons of the ICC, it became obvious that a new strategy to recover and mend relations with its cricketing fraternal brothers was of the essence, even if a further tour to Zimbabwe had to happen. At least this time the procedure available to the EWCB for handling it would be more carefully planned as a consequence of Wilson's blueprint.

Consequently, the EWCB was not going to challenge the muted response of the ICC to the Olonga-Flower decision to don black arm-bands as a symbol of the death of democracy in Zimbabwe during their country's World Cup fixture with Namibia. Their action, a cross-colour display of solidarity against the government's intention of stirring racial animosity, blurred the lines between political issues and the sporting arena. On numerous occasions since, Olonga has spoken out on the need for cricket to have moral leadership from the ICC rather than the apparent apathy and inaction in the face of sport's most divisive confrontations. Such comments are understandable following the lack of support provided by the ICC to him and his former Test Match cricketing colleague.

The ICC's attitude to the making of political statements is best summed up by the ICC President Eshan Mani:

> The ICC recognizes that in certain circumstances, politicians may exercise their right to use sporting sanctions as a foreign policy tool. It is not something that is particularly welcome but the reality is that from time to time it does happen … if governments take this action, their decision will be accepted by the ICC and there would be no impact on the individual board … The actions or inactions of politicians do not drive the policy of the ICC.[42]

Such remarks categorically reveal how the ICC has acted and continues to act over the Zimbabwe issue. In managing a set of diverging interests and needs as articulated by its membership, the path that the ICC chooses to take in respect of policy and principle is difficult to determine, yet it appears that finance remains the key factor in the decision-making process, even when it is the principle of racism that ultimately underpins the unravelling of cricket in Zimbabwe.[43]

As regards the British government, it took until August 2005 for Jack Straw and Tessa Jowell, in a letter to the Chair of the ICC, to jointly call for Zimbabwe to be banned from international cricket because of widespread human rights abuses.[44] This followed earlier requests from the Foreign Ministers of Australia and New Zealand for the ICC to intervene in the activities of the ZCU. However, at all times it must be remembered that depriving people of sport does not hurt governments but does affect the coffers of the administrators and the media. As part of a wider diplomatic and economic process, sanctions do, however, contribute to the sapping of morale and the eventual undermining of government.


## Conclusion

International cricket at the start of the twenty-first century suffers from a moral vacuum with the desire to expand the game taking precedence over all other concerns, as manifest in the ICC's handling of the England-Zimbabwe issue. With the payment of £132,000 compensation to the ZCU by the EWCB (a lower figure than the EWCB sought) for the two Test matches postponed in 2004, this was deemed to mark an end to three years of acrimony. However, all this represented was an opportunity to defer this matter, as England are not scheduled to play in Zimbabwe until 2009, by which time it is hoped that Mugabe will no longer be in power.

Although the ICC has shown itself incapable of displaying sensitivity to issues of injustice, some of the EWCB's own pronouncements during the unfolding of this affair rest on the implied assumption that sport and politics do mix.[45] It has asked for assurances from the British government that other sportsmen and women will be obliged to take the same political stance as the national government. It has questioned the effectiveness of cricket adopting one stance – that of boycotting Zimbabwe – over another – their own preferred option of going ahead regardless.

Although since the end of the American Civil War cricket has not been a significant sport on the American cultural landscape, the commodification of sport perfected in the United States has provided a model increasingly followed within cricket. This is possible as the game is able to link in with an international economy driven by consumers, markets and revenues that places ever-higher value on sport entertainment and technological attributes that cricket encompasses. As ICC President Eshan Mani recently commented, in a competitive economic environment 'we are all looking to attract the public's dollar'.[46]

Ultimately, however, the question remains how heinous a regime must be before it is banned from international cricket.[47] In a climate of commodification, sport administrators increasingly tend to isolate themselves from addressing such issues. As governmental authority declines in comparison with that of a small number of multinational enterprises, issues of morality do not alter even if the power, location and commercial base of the game has shifted, with India (steered by the Board of Cricket Control in India) and, more generally, Asia having taken control of the game. Morality, like globalization, has no geographical boundaries and cricket now faces a situation in which new masters are confronting long-established challenges. They have not, however, so far, shown themselves able to provide a new response to those challenges and this could permanently threaten the credibility of the game.

## Notes

[1] The England and Wales Cricket Board controversially uses the abbreviation ECB and hence omits the W for Wales from its official acronym.
[2] Berry notes in 'A Real Eye Opener' that three fifths of the top positions within the ICC are in Asian hands and that two fifths of the full membership are Asian.
[3] Calder and Dain, 'Not Cricket? Ethics, Rhetoric and Sporting Boycotts', 96.
[4] Majumdar and Mangan, *Cricketing Cultures in Conflict: World Cup 2003*, 2–5.
[5] Gemmell, *The Politics of South African Cricket*, 20–1.
[6] Simon Barnes, 'Truth and the Latest Casualty as the ICC Bends to Mugabe', *The Times*, December 20, 2002.
[7] Gupta, 'The Globalization of Cricket: The Rise of the Non-West', 257.
[8] Haigh, Gideon. *The Mandarins*. The New Ball Vol 6, 2001 p. 16.
[9] Only representatives of three white member states, plus Bermuda and the United States, were in this delegation.
[10] David Morgan, Chairperson of the ECB, interview by author, February 21, 2006.
[11] Haigh, *The Mandarins. The New Ball*, 20.
[12] Abbasi, 'Cricket's New Order'. http://content.cricinfo.com/i/content/story/234092.html.
[13] Beckles, *Development of West Indies Cricket: Volume 2, The Age of Globalization*, 21–2.
[14] Allison, *Taking Sport Seriously*, 77–8.
[15] Allison, *Taking Sport Seriously*, 78.
[16] See Bairner, 'Sport and the Nation in the Global Era'.
[17] Rowe, 'Sport and the Repudiation of the Global', 287.
[18] Ibid., 292.
[19] Marqusee, 'For the Love of the Game', 21.
[20] David Morgan, Chairperson of the ECB, interview by author, February 21, 2006.
[21] Malcolm Grey, 'Government Criticism – What is the Big Concern', *The Guardian*, December 12, 2002.
[22] Calder and Dain, 'Not Cricket? Ethics, Rhetoric and Sporting Boycotts', 97.
[23] Chesterfield, *'Zimbabwe Cricket: A Challenge almost Won.' Cricketing Cultures in Conflict: World Cup 2003*, 131.
[24] Andy Flower, former Captain of Zimbabwe, interview by author, October 20, 2005.
[25] ECB Press Release, January 14, 2003.
[26] Malcolm Speed, 'Lamb Recognition of no Support. Power Structures and the role of the ICC', *The Guardian*, November 16, 2002.
[27] Ibid.
[28] ECB Press Release, January 14, 2003.
[29] Majumdar and Mangan, *Cricketing Cultures in Conflict*, 240.
[30] David Morgan, Chairperson of the ECB, interview by author, February 21, 2006.
[31] Jack Straw, correspondence with ECB, January 22, 2004. This was confirmed in correspondence between the Foreign Office and the ECB. Further detail is available in the letter from the Foreign Secretary to the ECB in *ECB News*, January 14, 2004.
[32] This was regardless of whether the comments came from Richard Caborn, Minister of Sport, Tessa Jowell, Secretary of State for Culture, Media and Sport, Mike O'Brien, Foreign Office Minister, Baroness Amos, Junior Foreign Office Minister, or the Prime Minister.

[33] Williamson, 'Our Remit is Cricket'.
[34] David Morgan, ECB Press Statement, November 27, 2004.
[35] Andy Flower, former Captain of Zimbabwe, interview by author, October 20, 2005.
[36] Wilson, 'Cricket's Shame: The Inside Story', 23.
[37] Ali Bacher, BBCNewsWebsite. 2003. news,http:/wwwbbc.co.uk/sport/hi/cricket/2657323.stm.
[38] Discussion amongst the England team was lengthy and sometimes heated: however, Nasser Hussein notes the greater contribution from players who arrived in South Africa, having spent the proceeding weeks in England where they immersed themselves in the detail of Zimbabwe's unfolding political crisis. Hussain, *Playing with Fire*.
[39] Williamson, 'Counting the Cost of Zimbabwe'.
[40] Mike Brearley, Zimbabwe's Tour Runs Counter to the Moral Gain'. *The Observer*, May 25, 2003.
[41] Peter Tatchell, 'English Cricket puts Money before Morality'. *The Observer*, April 27, 2003.
[42] Eshan Mahni, ICC Press Release, March 10, 2004.
[43] Henry Olonga has articulated his beliefs on this question widely since his retirement from first class cricket, notably in *The Independent on Sunday,* November 28, 2004 and *The Guardian*, December 16, 2003.
[44] ICC Press Release, March 10, 2004. Andrew Cuff, 'MPs Attack Belated Call for Zimbabwe Cricket Ban'. *The Guardian*, August 22, 2005.
[45] Calder and Dain, 'Not Cricket? Ethics, Rhetoric and Sporting Boycotts', 96.
[46] Williamson, 'Our Remit is Cricket, not Internal Politics'.
[47] Steve James, former Captain of Glamorgan who also played in Zimbabwe in the late 1980s and early 1990s, interview by author, August 20, 2005.

## References

Abbasi, Kamran. 'Cricket's New Order'. January 23, 2006. http://content.cricinfo.com/i/content/story/234092.html

Allison, Lincoln. *Taking Sport Seriously*. Aachen: Meyer & Meyer, 1998.

Bacher Ali. BBCNewsWebsite. 2003. http:/wwwbbc.co.uk/sport/hi/cricket/2657323.stm.

Bairner, Alan. 'Sport and the Nation in the Global Era'. In *The Global Politics of Sport*, edited by L. Allison, 87–99. Abingdon: Routledge, 2005.

Beckles, Hilary. *The Development of West Indies Cricket: Volume 2, The Age of Globalization*. Kingston: The University of West Indies Press, 1998.

Berry, Scyld. 'A Real Eye Opener'. *Wisden Cricket*, April (2005): 22–25.

Calder, Gideon, and Edward Dain. 'Not Cricket? Ethics, Rhetoric and Sporting Boycotts'. *Journal of Applied Philosophy* 24, no. 1 (2007): 95–109.

Chesterfield, Trevor. '*Zimbabwe Cricket: A Challenge almost Won', Cricketing Cultures in Conflict: World Cup 2003*. London: Routledge, 2004.

Gemmell, John. *The Politics of South African Cricket*. London: Routledge, 2004.

Gupta, Anil. 'The Globalization of Cricket: The Rise of the Non-West'. *The International Journal of the History of Sport* 21, no. 2 (2004): 257–73.

Haigh, Gideon. *The Mandarins. The New Ball Vol 6*. London: Sports Books Direct, 2001.

Hussain, Nasser. *Playing with Fire*. London: Penguin, 2004.

Majumdar, Boria, and John Mangan. *Cricketing Cultures in Conflict: World Cup 2003*. London: Routledge, 2004.

Marqusee, Mike. 'For the Love of the Game'. *New Statesman and Society* (March 15, 1996): 32–35.

Rowe, David. 'Sport and the Repudiation of the Global'. *International Review for the Sociology of Sport* 38, no. 3 (2003): 281–94.

Williamson, Martin. 'Counting the Cost of Zimbabwe'. February 13, 2003. http://www.wisden.com.

Williamson, Martin. 'Our Remit is Cricket, not Internal Politics'. November 1, 2005. http://www.cricinfo.com.

Wilson, Des. 'Cricket's Shame: The Inside Story'. *New Statesman and Society* (December 6, 2004): 27–29.

# A legacy deeply mired in contradiction: World Cup 2007 in retrospect

Boria Majumdar*

*Department of Sport, Tourism and Hospitality Management, La Trobe University, Melbourne, Australia*

> In the end, I had a choice between selling the Finals tickets for 50% less and holding onto them as souvenirs. I preferred the latter. That is all I have to show for my huge investment in the [2007] World Cup. I plan to frame them and keep them as the one World Cup that I was happy to miss.
>
> Velu Palaparthi, Indian cricket fan, 2007[1]

> For a tournament that lurched on the edge of disaster before it began and almost toppled over before it got past the first week, World Cup 2003 is a roaring success. Never mind, England's ridiculous prevarication over Zimbabwe (with what started as a moral issue ending, bizarrely, as a security one); New Zealand's less publicised, but equally unwarranted, decision to skip Kenya; the tragic end to Jonty Rhodes's career; Allan Donald's no show; and Shane Warne's deadly folly (or sin, was it), the cricket has been resplendent.
>
> Wisden Asia, 2003[2]

The contrasting viewpoints expressed above sum it up beautifully. If CWC 2003 was the best, CWC 2007 might easily rank among the worst. Soon after the World Cup had concluded amidst considerable chaos and confusion, I travelled to Canada, to the University of Toronto, for a one day conference on the theme: *A Sport in Crisis: The Future of Cricket after World Cup 2007*.[3] The title said it all. It was indication enough that the legacy of the Cup was 'depressing' and the conference, initially planned to discuss the impact of the event, was transformed into a forum to discuss possible remedies for cricket and the Caribbean post-CWC 2007. In fact, to set facts in order, the conference had been conceived a year before to discuss the impact of CWC 2007 on the Caribbean and the rest of the world. The principal organizer, Professor Bruce Kidd, noted social scientist and Dean at the University of Toronto, called me at the end of March 2007, to suggest that the happenings in India after the defeat against Sri Lanka and Bob Woolmer's death were signals of alarm for world cricket, issues worth discussing at the symposium. When we spoke once again from the Caribbean around the middle of April, we decided to add the question of the impact of the World Cup on the economies of the Caribbean, knowing full well that such stock taking would be critical, hence the insistence to ensure that one of the speakers on the occasion was Derek Jones, Senior Legal Counsel for CWC 2007. Jones had been involved in the planning and implementation of the Sunset legislation and in the conduct of the tournament from very close quarters.

Soon after Jones had finished with his keynote address at the convention, an erudite rendition about how difficult it was to run a tournament of this nature in the Caribbean with multiple sovereign states involved, he was barraged with questions like; 'What will happen to the newly constructed stadiums in future?', 'Will the money spent turn out prudent investments in the end?', 'How will the investment impact the ordinary tax payer in the islands?', and 'Will the Owen Arthur and Portia Simpson Miller governments in Barbados and Jamaica respectively survive the negative impact of the world cup in the forthcoming elections?'

Jones, who has his way with words, to his credit, did not drop his guard. His answers to most of the questions were anecdotal, which hardly gave away the real picture. To be fair to him, as an insider it must have been awfully difficult for him to blurt out the real truth – that the World Cup might indeed leave behind a negative legacy in the long or medium term. He did smilingly say, however, that CWC 2007, the company formed to run the World Cup, would be closed down at the end of June 2007 and thereafter 'these white elephants (the stadiums) will be the responsibilities of the individual governments of the islands'. It was incredulous to note that the Vivian Richards Stadium in Antigua, constructed at a cost of approximately US$60 million and which has a capacity of 20,000, is meant to cater to a population of 75,000 Antiguans. A tournament that stood on the margins of disaster before it commenced and ultimately plummeted into complete chaos in the last minutes of the final, may well end up transforming the Caribbean for all times to come. Only the transformation is expected to severely impact the well being of an already poor Caribbean population, the Cup's lasting legacy.

From an organizational perspective, the tumultuous build up, it appears in hindsight, was not so bad after all. It is pertinent perhaps to go back briefly to my experiences in the West Indies in February, when the final touches to the preparations were underway. As my flight was about to touch down at the Grantley Adams International Airport in Barbados on 15 February 2007, I was trying to absorb every possible glimpse available of the beautiful island from my window seat to see if the Barbados I was coming back to was different.[4] This was because the Barbados I had been to in 2005 and 2006 was a thoroughly enjoyable tourist destination, but was certainly not a nation ready to host the cricket World Cup final – counted as one of the top ten sporting events of the world. Soon after the flight had taxied and reached the parking stand, an announcement was made asking me to meet the ground staff on disembarkation. I was thrilled. Friends from Barbados Tourism had come to the airport and I would have no problem in getting my television equipment cleared through customs. Barbados had indeed changed.

However, that ecstasy could change to despair in a matter of seconds was brilliantly borne out to me on disembarkation. The announcement was made that our equipment had been left behind at Gatwick airport in London and would only make it to Barbados in the evening of the following day! On reaching the arrival hall and having cleared immigration without much fuss, we were a little taken aback in finding out that there were no trolleys for arriving passengers. There were a handful of porters, but with passengers coming in by the hundreds, if not thousands, for the formal opening of the Kensington Oval stadium, the venue for the Cup final, they were soon lost in the crowd. To their credit, none of these teething problems, except luggage issues, confronted visitors to Barbados during the Cup.

During the final phase of the build up, from the last days in February to the middle of March, news of under-preparedness was emanating from all over the Caribbean. When asked what he felt about the dismal traffic situation in Barbados, David Allan, former West Indian cricketer, came up with the most intriguing of answers: 'I know the traffic is horrible and it might take you hours to travel to the stadium, a nightmare for international tourists. So what have I done? I have bought a new speedboat. That way it will not take me more than 15 minutes to travel!'[5]

While Allan was intent on travelling to the stadium in his newly bought boat to avoid the nightmarish traffic, the cricket world had braced itself for chaos. Everybody knew it would be rough. Since nine sovereign states were involved, countries that normally do not always see eye to eye, teething problems were only to be expected. *The Australian* on 3 March 2007 rounded off the alarm rather nicely:

> A disastrous World Cup, blighted by bad organization, crime, or some other misfortune, could bankrupt local cricket bodies, set the islands quarrelling and leave disgruntled visitors vowing never to spend another dollar in that part of the world ... Jamaica's new airport is not finished [it is still not finished in fact], the new Sabina Park stadium has been bogged down with construction delays and millions of dollars of promised beautification works never happened ... A cover-all visa, which officials say was designed to allow free passage between the islands for the duration of the tournament – but has been seen in some sectors as an exploitative tax on cricket fans – has been an administrative and public relations disaster. Only Australian, New Zealander, Indian and Pakistani fans had been asked to pay $130 for the visa that took months to issue and prompted one official, Trinidad and Tobago honorary consul in Australia Mike Agostini, to resign in protest ... The Australian government has issued a travel warning advising tourists to be cautious of violent crime and a high incidence of AIDS in the islands, while the US State Department went further and said large gatherings there carried a danger of terrorism or other violence.[6]

However, there still had not happened a Woolmer that would transform world cricket forever. India and Pakistan had not yet let the organizers down, nor had West Indian hopes of a revival been dashed. With these back-to-back punches landing in a matter of days, the Cup's legacy had been scripted in stone even before the half way stage had been reached. The expected boost to tourism never happened, jobs weren't generated for the economically underprivileged and by the time of the final most projects geared for the World Cup had been shelved. The desire to use the profits from the Cup to develop disadvantaged sections of the Caribbean and ignite cricketing passion among the local population had been replaced by the urge to ensure that the mega event didn't end up rendering the islands bankrupt.

**Expectations**

> This World Cup will be a stand out one. Yes, there are teething problems, but we have it in us to overcome all of these problems. And the spirit that you will see and experience here is unparalleled.

> Wes Hall, on the eve of the World Cup in Barbados[7]

> This World Cup will be an unique event. Never before has such excitement been seen here in the Caribbean.

> Charlie Griffith, on the eve of the World Cup in Barbados[8]

The long or medium term impact of a major international sporting event on host societies is perhaps its most venerable legacy. To echo and adapt a celebrated comment by Renaud Donnedieu de Valises, French Minister of Culture, on the legacy of the modern Olympic games: Each Olympic city has had appropriate pride in its national, regional and urban traditions and roots, while at the same time it has shared a common global Olympic heritage of creativity, innovation and positive purpose.

It was expected that the cricket World Cup in the Caribbean would be no exception. In fact, it was perceived as the most significant event in Caribbean history in terms of establishing international reputation with a longstanding impact. Accordingly, even before the tournament had started, a meeting to discuss the legacy of the mega event had been fixed for 29 May 2007.[9]

When asked what the World Cup meant to Barbados, Steven Alleyne, CEO of the Barbados World Cup Organizing committee, emphasized a seven-part legacy vision, which included improving the standard of living for the ordinary Bajan, involving the youth in new activities of earning, converting Barbados into an export economy and engendering a huge boost to tourism, the island's major commercial activity. In trying to achieve these aims, more than US$120 million, he emphasized, had been pumped into the Bajan economy in giving the nation a facelift ahead of the Cup.[10]

Multiple organizations with overlapping responsibilities, the Barbados Tourism Authority, the CWC local organizing committee, the local television network, corporate sponsors, media organizations, human rights organizations – as well as the politicians led by the PM Owen Arthur and Deputy PM Mia Mottley – positioned themselves to affect or control the paradigms through which the tournament was to be understood worldwide, often with a high degree of symbolism.

CWC 2007, it was argued, was an opportunity to project the image of a united global Caribbean community while also creating opportunities to force more tangible intra West Indian diplomatic and business networks. As articulated by Reverend Wes Hall, it was expected to create new possibilities for re-examining the structure of Caricom and help in the integration of the Caribbean on the same model as the European Union.[11]

Most West Indian professionals were looking to emphasize the point that the World Cup would help overcome the major struggles that have plagued Caricom since inception in 1972 and help examine ways in which key actors from within could come together as a strong economic and political entity.

**Ground reality**

Cricket World Cup 2007, it has been predicted by the International Monetary Fund (IMF), could hit the Caribbean economies hard. This was suggested in a report released by the International Monetary Fund on 16 April 2007, which is sceptical that the US$500 million spent in construction costs by the nine host venues are unlikely to result in positive economic benefits.[12]

The economic legacy of the World Cup, declared the IMF, would depend on the Caribbean countries' ability to market themselves as key tourism destinations following the event. This, it can be suggested, necessitates the opening up of new tourist markets, for the Caribbean already gets its fair share of tourists from the UK, USA and Canada. While the Barbados Tourism Authority is doing much to open up the Indian market, negotiations with the Indian Chamber of Commerce and Industry and Air India are cases in point, little has been done by the other islands so far.

The IMF report is sceptical about whether the positive effects on the tourism sector could extend into the medium or long term. There is further concern that the overall legacy of CWC 2007 could well be negative in light of its heavy fiscal costs and already high public debt burdens in the region.[13]

Padamja Khandelwal, the IMF economist who drew up the report, is of the opinion that the economic benefits of the event may water down because matches were spread across multiple countries, and were taking place in the midst of the peak winter tourist season when occupancy rates were already very high in most of the Caribbean islands. According to Khandelwal,

> In general, Caribbean public investment has shown a relatively weak link with growth, suggesting the need to increase the efficiency of these outlays. Over the longer term, prospects for growth will hinge critically on the region's ability to continue to market itself successfully as a tourist destination, to realize incremental revenues from the additional hotel rooms that have been constructed, and to address macro-economic vulnerabilities, including high levels of public debt.[14]

According to the report, preparations for the Cup led to accelerated economic activity in the region, particularly since 2005, but have been costly in terms of direct government expenditure and provisions for new tax concessions. Five new stadiums were built and others were upgraded, and construction costs are estimated at US$250 million. Additional public expenditures have also been incurred in improving infrastructure (roads, airports, hotels). As a result, primary balances have deteriorated in most countries, and average public debt remained over 100% of GDP at the end of 2006 in all the host nations.

Finally, the report suggests that the Caribbean countries had banked on significant economic benefits from the World Cup based on the expectations of selling close to 800,000 tickets spread over the 51 matches, a two billion international television audience, and about 100,000 additional (non-Caribbean) visitors.[15]

The reality was starkly different from the projections. Average attendance at the World Cup, according to data released by the CWC organizing committee midway through the tournament, stood at an average of 9,000 spectators per match, implying a total ticket sale of 490,000–500,000 for the whole tournament. This equates to a deficit of 300,000 from the projected sales figure.[16] However, figures subsequently released by the former WICB President Ken Gordon suggested that a total of 672,000 tickets were sold during CWC 2007. This figure, which takes the average attendance to almost 13,500 per game, needs verification. Even if it only includes net sales, it falls 128,000 short of the original projection.[17] The estimated international TV audience too had drastically fallen after the exits of India and Pakistan, and the number of non-Caribbean visitors certainly did not exceed 40,000. For example, the Barbados Tourism Authority had estimated 4,000 visitors coming from India to enjoy the World Cup. With India crashing out in the first round itself, only 800 turned up, a 70% drop from the original projection.[18]

A strange problem that plagued the Cup organizers was that there were multiple occasions when tickets were sold out but spectators did not physically turn up to watch the matches. Robert Bryan, head of the local organizing committee in Jamaica, for example, was insistent that the first semi-final between Sri Lanka and New Zealand was sold out in November 2006. On the day of the contest, 24 April 2007, the stadium was hardly more than half full. In fact, the joint press release from the LOC and ICC mentioned that just under 16,000 of the 16,161 seats available for sale were sold for the clash.[19] It also stated that 17,000 tickets had been sold for the semi-final between Australia and South Africa in St Lucia.

In such a situation, the only explanation is that people had bought tickets before they found out who would be playing and eventually opted not to come. It also draws attention to the difference between attendance and tickets sold. While purchase of tickets or tickets sold benefits the organizers, absentee purchasers hurt the local economy. People who had bought tickets were expected to turn up and boost the local economy in the process.

Their absence may not have hurt the organizers much but did cardinal damage to the economy centring on the World Cup, especially to the possibility of return visits. It is well documented that every time a sports fan travels to a tourist destination he or she likes, there is a possibility of a revisit some time in future. During the World Cup, those that rented hotel rooms or bought air tickets were able to cancel for a partial refund or postpone their visits – so they might yet travel to the Caribbean some day, but for those that rented villas had to pay up the whole amount leaving a bad taste.

To add to the organizers' woes, a *Sunday Sun* report on 22 April made the point that even within the Caribbean there is talk of an independent probe being headed by researchers at the University of West Indies 'to determine why so much went wrong since our successful bid to host the historic event back in 1998?' The report states that leaders of Caricom, on whose support depended the successful hosting of the World Cup, did not receive a copy of the host agreement signed between the ICC, WICB and CWC 2007 Inc. until rather late. Also, the final handing over of the Host Agreement had already been preceded by the signing of a Master Rights Agreement between the ICC, GCC and the CWC 2007 Inc. for exclusive broadcasting and commercial rights, to which no changes could legally be made. Warnings by the former President of CWC 2007 Inc. Rawle Brancker that the ICC was enjoying too much of a free ride over its demands for compliance were also left unheeded. In fact, responding to Brancker's criticisms in September 2005, President of CWC 2007 Chris Dehring had declared that he had 'no time for such peripheral issues' and was intent 'on delivering the Cricket World Cup'. While he has indeed delivered, the possible alarming impact of the delivery has forced Caricom leaders to demand copies of vital documents 'that were being kept from them – whether by default or design'.[20]

People peripherally associated with the World Cup were also badly hit. Citi-world-travel, an ICC appointed Official Travel Agent based in the US has incurred a loss of approximately US$400,000 from the event. Pramod Mistry, Managing Director of Citi-world-travel lamented on 7 May 2007, 'I am not even thinking of my losses. I am travelling to India in May-June to sell a property I have in Juhu in Mumbai to meet the costs. It has been a disaster.'[21]

In an article for the *Financial Express* on the eve of the tournament, Mistry had written that he had spent more than US$2 million on the event. His company had reserved hundreds of rooms, cruises, match tickets and flight seats to serve people, especially Indians settled in the US, during the World Cup.

> When it finally dawned on me that the World Cup was being organized just next door to us in the US, I was determined that this was the best opportunity I will have to showcase my passion for a game that continuously reminds me of a land still considered home by many in my family. Having played cricket as a child and having lived with it via the internet every day since moving to the US, it was an easy decision for me to appeal to the ICC seeking permission to be recognized as an OTA (Official Travel Operator). The US$50,000 I had to submit at the very initial stage to be considered eligible was indeed a substantial sum, but not big enough to desist me or douse my enthusiasm. My decision was strengthened by marketing reports that spoke about the manifold expansion in the cricket market in North America over the last decade. This growth, largely a handiwork of Indian expatriates settled in the US, made me immensely confident about selling all my packages.[22]

He expected to transport more than 3,000 cricket fans to the West Indies from around the US. Such high numbers were ascribed to the fact that compared to other countries of the world the cost of travel between the US and the Caribbean was fairly reasonable. Also, while fans from other countries like the UK, India-Pakistan or Australia get to see competitive cricket regularly, cricket fans in US are often forced to quench their thirst with 'masala matches', which are hardly ever played in the same competitive spirit. In such circumstances, the organization of the world cup in the Caribbean, Mistry argued, 'was like a lottery win, not only do you get to see your favourite stars, but also the very best in the world at cricket's biggest ever stage'.[23]

Unfortunately for him, most of his clients were Indians and Pakistanis. These men and women cancelled their trips after both countries crashed out unexpectedly in the first round of the tournament which meant that they wouldn't get to see their favourite icons in action. Mistry had rounded off his piece with the words,

> The final point about being an OTA in America is that the job is fraught with plenty of uncertainties. An early Indian loss will inevitably lead the expatriates to turn their backs at the tournament. In such a situation I am prepared to be loaded with multiple requests to cancel the tour midway and return home.[24]

The vagaries, it appears in hindsight, are far more dangerous.

The politico-social legacy isn't something to be proud of either. The Cup hardly fulfilled the professed ambitions. Nor has it been successful in integrating the Caribbean in the way it was expected to. Most locals I spoke to in the West Indies hadn't been to the stadium to watch the matches. Roy Drake, a Barbadian who works in the transport sector in London, was intent on returning his tickets after he found out that the 'tournament had been robbed of Caribbean flavour'. Munching his burger at the local fast food chain in Barbados, he appeared dejected:

> I would not have undertaken this costly trip. I expected this to be our World Cup, a Caribbean World Cup. This is an ICC event and we are like tenants running it. It is not for the poor people. Not many locals are travelling between islands to watch the matches. What it will do is it will urge kids to stay away from cricket even more. It has harmed West Indian cricket in the long term.[25]

His sentiment found support among locals like Rickey Singh and Susan Joseph. Singh, a Barbadian journalist, declared, 'It looks like the World Cup was a bad joke – to have imposed exorbitant ticket fees, treat musical instruments as weapons of terror, restrict drinks and food containers at matches.'[26] 'It's not for us, it's for the foreigners', lamented taxi driver Joseph.[27]

Bajan immigration and customs officials and other locals were more scathing:

> Using the free movement clause during the World Cup, many from the poor islands have entered Barbados and it will be a challenge to identify them after the Cup is over. In fact, we are worried the number of illegal immigrants in Barbados would swell significantly because of this event.[28]

Also, the Free Movement Clause has significantly altered the reputation of higher-end places like Barbados. A close friend based in New Jersey who went there during the Cup and stayed at a rented villa in a rather nice part of town experienced a burglary. He lost two laptops and a video camera and a still camera. The police were at a loss to explain this. Who could have stolen the gadgets is a question that continues to haunt them. Some years ago, when I was in Barbados, the police boasted that they did not need to carry weapons. There was simply no need for weapons in some of the more prosperous islands. The World Cup, unfortunately, has transformed the situation for all times to come. Soon after the tournament had ended, the game of one-upmanship between the islands started. For example, Bajans were quick to point out why the Cup was a success in Barbados and not in neighbouring Trinidad: 'The Trinis thought they would get away smuggling alcohol into the World Cup matches in sun block bottles. They did not realize that the ICC, which cares for big bucks far more than cricket, was far shrewder than them.'[29]

I experienced the intra-island jealousy first hand while finishing a BBC Bengali radio interview soon after the first semi-final was over in Jamaica. It exposed the deep-rooted hatred the Jamaicans continue to nurture against the Bajans. I was speaking in Bengali and had mentioned Barbados a couple of times in the course of the interview only because the final was to be played in Barbados. A local Jamaican lady, inebriated as most people at the stadium were, heard me saying Barbados and immediately turned abusive. She even tried to push me on more than one occasion and finally seeing I was not deterred went and complained to her husband that while in Jamaica I was talking of Barbados! Thereafter he too joined the hate party and I had to flee to the safe haven of my cricket logistics transport to avoid being smashed!

Far more significant was the concern expressed by DCP Mark Shields, chief investigator in the Woolmer case. Shields was candid in declaring that, 'The Cup has been a distraction. Deployment of police personnel for the World Cup to Sabina Park was a distraction and it affected the crime situation in Jamaica.'[30] For the record, there had already been more than 300 murders in Jamaica in 2007, an increase of more than 10% since 2006. With police personnel not available to patrol the dangerous inner-city areas, gang wars went up significantly between January and March. Efforts to cleanse the inner cities of serious crime led to nothing and there were random tourist muggings at Kingston before the first semi-final. 'They targeted our mobile phones. If we refused to comply with their orders they would not hesitate in taking out arms. It was dangerous even in the area around the Hilton hotel', recounted an elderly Kiwi supporter.[31]

## Vexed issue of Caribbean flavour

The most disappointing aspect of CWC 2007 was half-full venues across the Caribbean.[32] The primary reason behind poor attendance, it has been argued, was the organizers' determination to try things that were hardly commensurate with Caribbean culture. While speaking to the ordinary West Indian on the street it was apparent that he or she isn't internet savvy. The number of internet cafés across the Caribbean is also an indication. While every neighbourhood in Delhi has a handful of internet cafés, Barbados, the showpiece among the islands, has some 20 or so. The number is fewer in Jamaica and even fewer in Antigua. An organizational faux pas ensured that World Cup tickets were mostly available on the net. Says Avinash Ketwaroo, a Jamaican national completing medical school at Harvard,

> It is part of our culture to decide at the very last moment. The information conveyed to us was that tickets were sold out and there was little chance of getting tickets on match days. This is why West Indians decided to stay away. It is not in our culture to book things a year in advance. More, not all of us here are net savvy. Buying tickets on the net is still alien and many West Indians just stayed away failing to understand how to go about things.[33]

Though the organizers made available internet facilities for the media, in most venues except Barbados (where it was free) prices were prohibitively expensive. For a day of internet access at Sabina Park in Jamaica the amount charged was US$24.

Yet another decision that had initially robbed the tournament of local flavour was the restriction imposed on musical instruments. While this was removed mid way into the tournament, the damage had already been done. Attesting to this unfortunate outcome, the owner of the No. 1 record shop in Barbados declared, 'Our singers have been practicing for years for this event. Now if you tell them you aren't allowed to take your instruments to the ground a backlash is inevitable.'[34] The common West Indian, she emphasized, felt betrayed, a sentiment supported by *New Statesman* columnist Darcus Howe,

> Every hindrance was placed in the way of the Caribbean peoples. The traditional picnic basket, which was an integral part of cricket attendance, was reduced to a 12x12-inch bag. Alcohol had to be bought at the ground; brand names had to be scraped off commodities; punters had to remove tops from plastic bottles. The advertising brand names on billboards brooked no competition. No musical instruments were permitted, no sounds of freedom, no rhythms – all these are fundamental parts of Caribbean cricket watching. It was as though a Nazi regime had engulfed Caribbean cricket.[35]

The ones who most compellingly felt betrayed were the former residents of Pickwick Gap, who were forced to relocate to Barbarees Gardens on account of the Kensington Oval makeover. Most of them, vendors and small business owners, pointed out that not only had their sales dropped because Barbarees Gardens had no direct proximity to the Oval, but they also missed the entire nostalgia associated with the Oval. After the *Nation* of 20 April 2007 exposed the plight of these hapless Bajans, I followed up the story to end up feeling acutely frustrated for these passionate cricket fans. One of them, Linda Waterman, a small time vendor, bemoaned her plight:

> I miss it. I continue to conduct business from here in Barbarees Gardens but it is hardly the same. I am aware that the World Cup is being played in Barbados these days but if I don't look at the television to find out what is going on, I wouldn't know that cricket is on. At Pickwick Gap I was always in the throes of action.

Waterman was born in Pickwick Gap and had converted part of her house and backyard to accommodate diners. During the cup she refused to sign on with the Kensington vendors' programme saying she had been cheated and disrespected.

> I was there long before any of the other vendors and they forced me to move. Now that the island is on show they want me to go back and beg. For them my business stands ruined. I have only prepared lunch for a dozen people by special request and am down to one employee from the nine I employed at Pickwick Gap.[36]

Her former customers came from the Barbados Port Authority and other surrounding businesses, but most of them are unwilling to travel to Barbarees Gardens. Her compatriot Margaret Grant recounts a similar tale. 'It hurts because I miss the action. 16 months ago I would just open my backyard and car owners would park there. I would also sell T shirts, caps and other memorabilia.' As reported by the *Nation*, 'she had the privileged spot next to the John Goddard gate and from time to time got a "living color" view of the game'.[37]

A third resident who had an ideal vantage point before she was forced to relocate was Asefa Kariya. Her two-storey house next door to the Oval is no more. Prior to the remodelling she could watch the action from home and would invite relatives to pay a visit during cricket matches. 'We would have family over, especially during England-West Indies contests', recounts Asefa.[38]

While none of them traditionally make the cut as cricket fanatics, they were as much part of the Oval as any cricketer or avid cricket follower. And the harsh truth is that for the world cup their lives have been transformed forever.

Others who got an equally raw deal are the members of the Pickwick Club, which stood at the Kensington Oval for over 120 years. The remodelling has forced the club, founded in 1882, to seek a new home at Foursquare, St Phillip, a forced move that has caused much ill will among the members. One of the members speaking on conditions of anonymity blurted out the truth, 'We were compelled to vacate Kensington. It was certainly not a voluntary decision.' As consolation, the walkway to the new 3W's stand has been named the Pickwick Walk, in recognition to the club's contribution to Kensington and its history.

The old Pickwick pavilion was torn down to make way for the new 3W's stand. Voicing the discontent felt by the members, club President Philip Nichols declared, 'Given the decision that was made, our members feel badly let down. They are extremely disappointed in what they feel has been scant regard paid to the history of the club.' A long standing member, Brigitte Bethell Laurayne best portrayed the hapless situation, 'I am appalled and saddened that this part of the history of Kensington has been so quickly erased and forgotten in the name of progress and development for Cricket World Cup 2007. It is as though Pickwick never existed.'[39]

However, the worst affected in the World Cup bargain are the three elderly Bajans, Anthony Chandler, Patron Burrowes and Antoinette Taylor. While the other residents of Pickwick Gap were at least paid compensation and granted housing, these three aged people were left in the cold after the completion of the Kensington resettlement project. Despite multiple promises of compensation and newer employment opportunities, nothing was done.[40] So much so that the opposition party led by Patrick Todd is keen to appropriate the cause of these three Bajans as an electoral issue in an attempt to garner support against the Owen Arthur government.

In Jamaica, too, the failed World Cup has now turned into a political issue. The Jamaica Labour Party (JLP) has repeatedly called on the Government to provide details on whether the country received value for money from the $9 billion spent on the tournament. Soon after the first semi-final in Jamaica was over, the JLP demanded explanations from the government on the benefits received. In an official media release, opposition spokesperson Ted Bartlett declared, '(We need to find out) To what extent the smaller entrepreneurs and the small concessionaires who put out some huge investments in order to pay for concessionaire stands and rights and so on realized a profit.' The seriousness of the World Cup disaster was finally evident when the Portia Simpson Miller government of the People's Nationalist Party lost the national election on 3 September to the JLP.[41]

**Voices in isolation**

However, as always, there are positive voices. A survey titled, 'Residents' Perception of the Impacts of the Cricket World Cup 2007 on Barbados', conducted by three researchers from the University of West Indies, Troy Lorde, Dwayne Devonish and Dion Greenidge, concluded that 'the Barbadians believe the millions of dollars spent on the event was worth it and there will be eventual revenue trickling down for local businesses after the event'. The researchers declared that, 'the perception about the increase in prices as a result of hosting the event could be mitigated by the Government if it puts plans in place to ensure that facilities constructed for the event generate income after the event'.[42]

Their observations find support in the survey on the impact of the World Cup conducted by Scotia Bank. The report, which was made public soon after the tournament was over, suggests that the Caribbean host countries spent more than US$800 million on the upgrading of infrastructure; airports, roads, power generation and information technology systems and on the development of stadia and temporary facilities in preparation for the event. Conducted by the economic research department of Scotia Bank, it affirms that direct foreign investment in the region in the wake of the Cup would vary between US$500 million and US$700 million. The study concludes that the infrastructure left behind in the wake of CWC augurs well for the future of the region's development.

According to its findings, the anticipated 5.5 per cent growth rate in the Caribbean region's economy this year is due in large measure to the economic benefits that the region will derive from its hosting of CWC. It also noted that CWC-related projects provided employment for more than 10,000 people.[43]

There has also been a claim that the World Cup has successfully opened up Barbados to newer tourist markets across the world. Petra Roach, Vice President of the Barbados Tourism Authority, was emphatic about the positives to come out of CWC 2007 when we met at her Tottenham Court Road office on 11 June:

> Let me say Barbados has seen a 1,000% increase in tourist influx in May and June 2007, months after the world cup ended. It is the best ever tourist boom that we have had in the history of Barbados and the World Cup is the reason behind this ... We in Barbados are thrilled with the outcome. Traditionally Barbados gets tourists from the UK and Europe and some from the United States. This year our reach has increased and we have started getting tourists from far away destinations including your country. This is a tremendous thing for us and we are looking to consolidate these links in the coming years. We were looking to expand our base beyond the traditional domains and the World Cup has helped us achieve this objective.[44]

Ken Gordon too has praised the CWC 2007 organizing committee, suggesting that CWC 2007 has done much to alleviate the financial crisis facing the West Indies cricket board:

> We sold more tickets [672,000] than the last two World Cups in South Africa [625,000] and England [476,000] and garnered $32 million in ticket revenue, which the ICC [International Cricket Council] has told us is the highest gate ever ... The directors are very satisfied with the overall results of the tournament.[45]

Finally, the organizers and the ICC can derive some consolation from the fact that the World Cup was drug free. The World Anti-Doping Agency (WADA) cleared all 68 cricketers randomly tested during the World Cup. Expressing delight at the results, ICC Chief Executive Malcolm Speed declared, 'The fact that all drug tests at the World Cup proved negative is a great result for the game. It sends out a very positive message, something everyone connected with the game can be very proud of.' Speed also said that the tests confirmed cricket's low-risk reputation when it comes to the use of performance-enhancing drugs, an issue that had marred the start of the World Cup four years ago with the legendary Shane Warne pulled out for the use of a banned diuretic.[46]

## Two way traffic

Hazel Coward, a small business owner in Barbados, while concurring somewhat with the above analysis, suggested that the legacy of the World Cup has been mixed.

> The fact that Banks Breweries reported that they had Christmas in April indicates some sectors benefited more than others ... As a small business owner myself, the World Cup made little difference to my operations. Seeing visitors pass through Bridgetown drunk on match days was testimony that only some sectors benefited from the tournament.[47]

Senior management staff at Banks, the biggest Barbadian brewery, agreed that cricket fans helped boost beer revenue. The brewery executive suggested that Banks sales during the World Cup had outpaced the traditionally high 'Crop Over' season and this could largely be ascribed to Banks signing a pour deal with the ICC for the Kensington Oval as part of a joint tender with five other regional breweries under the banner of the Caribbean Brewers Association. At the Oval, BHL reported booming sales of its signature beer, Banks. The limited sponsorship deal, which cost BHL more than US$100,000, was based on a cost split on a pro rata basis between the regional breweries based on the beer sold in the match venues – except in Jamaica and Antigua, which were secured separately by Jamaican brewery Red Stripe. This deal, however, did not carry with it rights of signage at Kensington, something BHL wasn't interested in:

> We were always adamant that we never saw the value in the signage, especially fixed signage on the grounds and so on, beaming to an audience in markets where we don't have a presence. We wanted a contract that reflected pouring rather than signage.[48]

It was this limited contract that eventually helped swell Banks coffers, an opportunity most other corporate concerns, big or small, did not have.

## Conclusion

Post-CWC 2007, world cricket is very delicately poised and a satisfactory balance between morality, politics and monetary considerations is an urgent need. Cricket is, indeed, at a crossroad, with cricketing cultures across the globe in serious conflict with each other, the Cup's heartrending legacy. Even the ICC chief executive Malcolm Speed conceded soon after the conclusion of the World Cup that the 2007 tournament would be chiefly remembered for the death of coach Bob Woolmer and the chaotic finish to Australia's final victory. According to Speed,

> It's too early to predict how history will view the tournament, but certainly Bob Woolmer's tragic death and the finish of the final are two things that will be uppermost in the minds of people who followed the event ... It was disappointing there were not a great number of matches that stayed in the minds.[49]

To leave the last words to Hazel Coward, 'At the end of the day when all the drama dies down we must all be able to live having made a profit. After all that's what we were all expecting when the World Cup came here.'[50] Sadly, that has not happened.

## Notes

[1]  Venu Palaparthi, avid cricket fan and Director of Dreamcricket Pavilionshop based in New Jersey, interviewed by author, August 16, 2007.
[2]  'Editorial'. *Wisden Asia Cricket*.
[3]  The conference was held at the University of Toronto on 3 May 2007.
[4]  I travelled to Barbados in February to attend the formal opening of the Kensington Oval stadium on 17 February 2007.
[5]  David Allan, interviewed by author, February 17, 2007.
[6]  Peter Wilson, 'Caribbean Chaos'. *The Australian*, March 3, 2007.
[7]  Wes Hall, interviewed by author, Barbados, February 18, 2007.
[8]  Charlie Griffith, interviewed by author, Barbados, February 20, 2007.
[9]  This was revealed by Steven Alleyne, CEO, Barbados Local World Cup Organizing Committee at the formal opening of the Kensington Oval on 17 February 2007.
[10]  Steven Alleyne, interviewed by author, Barbados, February 20, 2007.
[11]  Wes Hall, interviewed by author, Barbados, February 18, 2007.
[12]  'World Economic and Financial Surveys: Economic and Regional Outlook – Western Hemisphere'. *Report of the International Monetary Fund*.
[13]  Ibid.
[14]  Ibid.
[15]  Ibid.
[16]  The World Cup Organizing Committee released this data on 17 April 2007.
[17]  http://content-usa.cricinfo.com/westindies/content/current/story/301516.html.
[18]  Petra Roach, Vice President, Barbados Tourism Authority, interviewed by author, London, June 11, 2007.
[19]  Robert Bryan, interviewed by author, Kingston, Jamaica, April 25, 2007.
[20]  *The Sunday Sun*, April 22, 2007.
[21]  Pramod Mistry, telephone interview with author, May 7, 2007.

22  Pramod Mistry, *The Financial Express* World Cup Special Supplement, March 11, 2007.
23  Ibid.
24  Ibid.
25  Roy Drake, interviewed by author at the Independence Square in Barbados, April 15, 2007.
26  Ibid.
27  Ibid.
28  Personal interview with a series of customs officials at the Grantley Adams Airport, April 28, 2007.
29  *The Nation*, April 22, 2007.
30  Mark Shields, interviewed by author, Kingston, Jamaica, April 26, 2007.
31  Personal interview by author, April 27, 2007.
32  Not a single match, except the final and the England–West Indies game on 19 April, which was Brian Lara's last international match, resulted in a packed house.
33  Avinash Ketwaroo, interviewed by author, April 24, 2007.
34  Personal interview by author, April 20, 2007.
35  Darcus Howe, 'The Cricket World Cup: A Farce in the Dark'. *New Statesman*, May 7, 2007.
36  Linda Waterman, interviewed by author, April 21, 2007.
37  *The Nation*, April 20, 2007.
38  Asefa Kariya, interviewed by author, April 21, 2007.
39  Brigitte Bethell Laurayne, interviewed by author, 29 April, 2007
40  Ibid.
41  http://jamaica-elections.com/general/2007/.
42  Extracts of the Survey were published in *The Nation*, April 21, 2007.
43  Scotia Bank World Cup Report distributed at the Toronto Cricket Conference, 3 May 2007.
44  Petra Roach, Vice President, Barbados Tourism Authority, interviewed by author, London, June 11, 2007.
45  http://content-usa.cricinfo.com/westindies/content/current/story/301516.html.
46  Malcolm Speed, interviewed by author, July 17, 2007.
47  Hazel Coward, interviewed by author, May 31, 2007.
48  Interview with BHL staff in Barbados, 27 April, 2007.
49  Malcolm Speed, interviewed by author, August 4, 2007.
50  Hazel Coward, interviewed by author, May 31, 2007.

## References

'Editorial'. *Wisden Asia Cricket*, March 2003.
'World Economic and Financial Surveys: Economic and Regional Outlook – Western Hemisphere.' *Report of the International Monetary Fund*, April 2007.

# Burning down the house

Rob Steen*

*Senior Lecturer, Chelsea School, University of Brighton, Sussex, UK*

Call me irresponsible; feel free to cast aspersions about the tint of my glasses and my sanity, but I sincerely believe cricket has been as vibrant, adventurous and stimulating over the past decade as it can ever have been. I do freely confess, mind, that this conviction is deeply embedded in soil of richest gratitude.

After all, had I, three decades ago, shortly before another World Cup, the first such event, predicted that five-day Test matches would be still be a going concern in 2007, I would have been branded a hopeless romantic. Had I predicted that these contests would be flourishing as never before in terms of frequency, media coverage and global interest, the precise number of marbles at my disposal would have been a brief, entirely one-sided debate. Had I predicted that 30-hour games would be attracting record crowds in Australia, packed congregations for every Test played in England and the chequebook of the world's most accomplished media magnate, I probably would have been censored for bringing the game into disrepute.

I don't think it is an exaggeration to state that cricket was the least likely major spectator sport to survive the twentieth century, nor that it is in better fettle than any of us dared dream prior to that afternoon at Lord's in June 1975, when West Indies defeated Australia in that magnificent first World Cup final. I was there, a teenager fearful that my obsession, Test cricket, was living on time borrowed at prohibitive interest rates. I was also frightened that, as soon as my father's generation passed on, the last generation to whom patience was a virtue, remote controls a luxury and Old Father Time occasionally paused to smell the coffee, the game's highest form of expression would enter irreversible decline. Oh me of little faith.

That full house at Lord's, for a match *not* involving the hosts, was the first indication to the international community that *serious* money could be made from cricket, even if it had to be made via a bastardised form. Australians, in particular, took note. Kerry Packer's advisers above all. Triggered by a bitter dispute over a TV contract, the Packer Revolution followed inside two years. The eventual, mutually self-improving pact, between Packer's Channel 9 and the Australian Cricket Board, would be the first major step in cricket's profitable partnership with broadcasters.

Three decades on, I think it fair to claim – for all the frustrations, delays, detours and hopelessly wrong turnings, and for all the deep wounds left by match-fixing – that the ensuing new world is a far, far better one than any of us suspected or feared. It is certainly a rather better future than the one sketched out in strictest monochrome by the doom-and-gloom mongers of the anti-Packer lobby. It is even brighter than the one painted by Packer's marketing team, because Test cricket has regained its primacy.

Not that this is the only reason to be cheerful. When I started writing about cricket for a living, I did so with missionary zeal and a preservationist's passion: I wanted my children to experience what I had experienced; to have the opportunity to fall in love with what I had fallen in love with. Less than a quarter of a century later, I love the fact that the politics of race and class, which poisoned the game for so long – and English cricket in particular – have receded; however, much progress is still to be made.[1] I love that cricket, in this respect, seems to be so far ahead of so many other sports. For all the manifest and manifold growing pains, I love the fact that India, rather than England or Australia, is now the game's economic powerhouse. I love the fact that the Caribbean, home to the game's most joyous and delightful crowds, had the opportunity to spread the gospel to a more sceptical generation by hosting the (2007) World Cup, even more than I lament that the event was a shoddy advert for the game – and even more than I regret the ill-conceived hotel and ticket pricing, and astronomic construction costs, that prevented the regenerative windfall politicians and business leaders assured those at the sharp end of those beleaguered island economies would be theirs.[2] I love the fact that television replays have been accepted as a valid aid to umpires in the quest for justice. I love the fact that, on a frightful January Friday in blustery East Sussex, I could watch a Test match from South Africa live on TV, and that the following week I could watch internationals from India, Africa and Australia live on the same day. Above all, I love the fact that, on that Friday, the hosts bowled out Pakistan primarily by dint of the sterling efforts of a black fast bowler, Makhaya Ntini, and were then saved from a batting collapse by a Muslim batsman, Hashim Amla, and his Cape Coloured partners, Ashwell Prince and Herschelle Gibbs. Oh my Vorster and my Botha of not all that long ago . . .

The boy in me also loves the fact that so many astonishing Test records have been challenged and broken in recent times. The past four years have brought the two highest individual innings, three of the top four, the second-fastest century, the highest score by a nightwatchman, the highest partnership for any wicket, the second-highest opening stand, and, perhaps most magical of all, the highest successful fourth-innings chase, 418 by West Indies, *against* Australia. You want drama? Since January 1999 we have witnessed four of Test cricket's one-wicket wins, five of its 16 two-wicket margins, one by two runs, one by seven and two by twelve; not to mention three of the most gripping series on record, the 2005 Ashes and those epic scraps between India and Australia in 2001 and 2004. Of the 25 biggest first-innings deficits that have been conjured into victory, 15 have occurred in the past decade; ten since the end of the last century. During that span we have also revelled in that rarest of cricketing triumphs: the third instance of a side winning a Test after following-on. It might be considered greedy to ask for more.

The blot on the landscape, though, is threatening to become a permanent stain: namely, the greed and short-termism of the ten national boards that comprise the decision-making heart of the International Cricket Council. Understandably tempted as they are by the willingness of broadcasters to dole out sums of GNP proportions for the exclusive right to transmit live sport, the bloated fixture list is damaging the men to whom they owe their salaries, namely the players, and primarily the faster bowlers. That the list of recent record-busting focuses almost exclusively on batting feats is assuredly no coincidence. Nor the sad fact that genuinely fast bowlers are becoming scarcer than pandas. In the medium-term this will undermine the game's credibility; in the longer term, to use language familiar to those administrators and moguls, it will lose audience share and erode the product's value.

To realize what that would spell, one has only to see the acres of empty seats evident in Tests played everywhere outside England and Australia. Even in Perth and Sydney those seats are now, rather astutely, painted in colours that might easily delude the viewer into imagining they are occupied. Cricket's greatest secret is that the column inches, airtime, web pages and SMS texts devoted to Test scores in no way reflect the number of people willing or able to click through the turnstiles. The unsociable playing hours and admission prices don't help, of course. What cannot be denied, therefore, is that it is the shorter forms of the game, increasingly played after the end of the working day, that financially support Test matches. How gorgeously ironic that a game perennially criticized for gross conservatism has been the only major sport to adapt to times and tastes by giving birth to what might be called a 'Mini Me'.

A comparison of the workloads of players past and present is illustrative. The first 500 Test matches spanned 83 years, an average, overall, of barely six per year. The next 1,000 arrived 40 years later, the annual mean having leapt to 31. Over the next six and a half years, to January 2007, thanks largely to the inception of the World Test Championship table and the Future Tours Programme designed to make it credible, there were no fewer than 327, a yearly average of 50. In the 12 months from May 2005 to April 2006, 64 were scheduled (see Table 1).

As if that were not enough, leading performers are also expected to play around two dozen one-day internationals per year. Starting in 1971, the first 1,000 of these spanned 17 years; since then the rate has increased sixfold (see Table 2). These games may be done and dusted a great deal quicker, but the sheer pace at which they are played, and the inordinate amount of travel required, heightens the physical pressures and thus aggravates the risk of injury, fatigue, stress or simply loss of appetite.

Until Kerry Packer's timely, if not entirely advertent, intrusion, only England and Australia played more than one Test series a year; some nations went a year or more between fixtures. Tours, moreover, were worthy of the name, spanning seasons rather than weeks. These days, a team may play five five-dayers in as many weeks or otherwise have

Table 1.   The development of Test match cricket

| |
|---|
| 500th Test Australia v West Indies Melbourne 1960 |
| 1,000th Test Pakistan v New Zealand Hyderabad 1984 |
| 1,500th Test England v West Indies Edgbaston 2000 |
| Total Tests to January 16, 2007 = 1827 |

Table 2.   The development of one day international cricket.

| |
|---|
| 500th ODI played 1988 (17 years after 1st) |
| 1,000th ODI played May 1995 |
| 1,500th ODI played August 1999 |
| 2,000th ODI played April 2003 |
| Total ODIs to December 10, 2006 = 2,463 |

their plate full of one-day internationals; and each XI will number at least five or six players considered to be automatic choices in both forms. For representatives of England, the only Test nation whose home season extends from April to September and hence the only one that plays every month of the year, the demands are almost unrelenting, for all the advantages engendered by central contracts. The cause of Marcus Trescothick's withdrawal from the 2006–07 Ashes series prompted several interpretations and countless scientific names, but stress seemed much the most appropriate. He appeared, indeed, to have suffered something close to a nervous breakdown. That said, the journalist in me feels obliged to point out that the chief reason, which I understand to be domestic in origin, might dilute sympathy.

Yet it was not an Englishman but an Australian, Steve Waugh, the toughest and most determined sportsman I have ever met, who bemoaned the state of play as long ago as 2002:

> There will be players saying 'I don't think I can continue playing this amount of cricket'. I don't think you can pick and choose tours – there's too many good players out there – but you might be able to pick which form of cricket you play.[3]

At the same time as Waugh made his comments, his countryman Shane Warne urged his national board to limit the international schedule, as he put it, 'if it wants to keep the better players in all the teams playing for longer'.[4] Small wonder Jonty Rhodes, the world's best fielder, and Wasim Akram, Pakistan's leading all-rounder, confined themselves to one-day duty in the lead-up to the 2003 World Cup.

By the same token, attested David Richardson, the ICC's general manager for cricket, of the ten national captains at a meeting in 2003, 'Three said there was too much cricket; three or four said that the volume was about right and three said that there was not enough'.[5] This struck me as highly disingenuous. An educated guess would suggest that the captains wishing to play more were from Zimbabwe, Bangladesh and Sri Lanka or New Zealand, the Test nations with the least box-office appeal and hence lowest workload. Sri Lanka, for instance, played just two Tests in their 2006–07 summer. In late 2003, according to Richardson, the ICC was 'aware that the workload on the players must be carefully managed and that a surfeit of cricket risks turning the international game into a commodity'.[6] He also offered a surprisingly frank personal view: 'We have come very close to reaching saturation point'.[7] Since then, the going has grown ever more gruelling, prompting protests from the players which have been acknowledged, to a limited but insufficient extent, by the ICC. Last year, its executive board was persuaded to recommend lengthening that cycle of reciprocal home-and-away series between all nations from five years to six. The casualties, though, have already begun to form an orderly queue.

His commitment may be questioned, but it was still alarming when Steve Harmison, a fast bowler who has never made any bones about how much he hates travelling and being away from family, hearth and football team, decided to retire from one-day internationals at the comparatively tender age of 28. That he did so in the run-up to a World Cup – an event to which, one would have thought, he should have been looking forward with some relish – seemed even more indicative of a workforce in pain. Small wonder Duncan Fletcher, then Harmison's national coach, recently joined the chorus of dismay. Asked for his thoughts on Australia's request to play six Tests when England next tour in 2010–11, Fletcher insisted something had to give: 'Either we limit the amount of one-day cricket or Test matches, but it is a difficult decision to make because of all the history in the game and the sides we play against'.[8]

Table 3.    The decline of older international cricketers.

|  | Overall | 1/1/1979 to present | 1/1/2000 to present |
|---|---|---|---|
| Test Players Aged 35+ | 469 | n/a | 35 |
| Test Players Aged 40+ | 102 | 13 | 1 |

One measure of the players' vulnerability lies in the ages at which they are now retiring. Until the Second World War, tours were few and far enough between to enable players to continue into their mid-40s. Overall, 102 men have played Test cricket at 40, but only one since 1997. Despite the greater financial incentives, between the beginning of 2000 and the end of 2007, only 35 Test players have played beyond the age of 34 – less than 8% of the overall figure of 469. This figure is all the more remarkable given that nearly 20% of all Tests have been played during the period. Cricket has never been such a young man's business (see Table 3).

Admittedly, there are other contributory factors. Because salaries, sponsorships, endorsements and pension funds have soared over the past decade, again courtesy of those deep, hungry and far-reaching pockets belonging to Mr Murdoch and his rivals, it is now easier to retire earlier, in a more secure frame of mind. Here, too, the media as a whole, propelled by television, has exerted a significant influence: more airtime and sports sections mean more prospects in commentary booth and press box for former players. As coffers swell, so the benefits to these achievers and stalwarts can also be found in coaching, management and administration.

Let us turn again, though, to those hard-pressed bowlers. Sting further drawn by the pitches, they are nothing like as economic as they were. Of the 79 bowlers who had taken 100 Test wickets at under 30 runs apiece to December 2006, 35 have played in the past 20 years – yet only one, Matthew Hoggard, made his debut this century. The 2001 *Wisden* lists 15 such achievers still plying their trade, only three of whom are still doing so; the most recent edition listed 13, three of whom have played their final Test and four of whom are considerably closer to final curtain than first night. Meanwhile, the number of batsmen averaging 50 has risen enormously. The 1986 *Wisden* listed four active Test players averaging between 50 and 55; the 2006 edition listed ten, including four averages of *over* 55. True, cricket needs runs as much as its spectators need air, yet such an oppressive rule of bat cannot possibly be healthy. As the journalist Simon Briggs observed, this growing workload 'is tilting everything towards the bully with the three-foot plank'.[9] I know of at least one member of the MCC Working Party currently re-examining the laws of the game who not only believes something must be done, but, privately, that some form of ball-tampering could be legitimized.

I recently had the pleasure, shortly before his death, of discussing this vexing issue with that wise owl Tom Cartwright, the former England seamer without whose coaching wisdom Ian Botham would probably have never taken a wicket for Somerset, much less one on his country's behalf. As spirited and humanitarian a soul in his late 60s as he was when he refused to coach in Ian Smith's Rhodesia three decades ago, Cartwright cited one-day cricket as a major factor in the imbalance between bat and ball. 'It has detracted enormously from excellence', he fumed. 'Batsmen used to try to work out what the bowlers were trying to do: now it's the other way round'.[10] It was refreshing to find somebody else who firmly believes the first step to remedy matters should be to scrap the restriction on the number of overs a bowler can deliver in a one-day match.

Another measure of the endemic problems can be gleaned from the capacity of players to stay fit and perform with consistency, notably fast or fast-medium bowlers, whose exertions are subject to the greatest demands. The most consecutive Test appearances made by such a bowler is 66, by India's Kapil Dev, and there have been four other instances of 50 or more; between January 2003 and March 2007, the best has been 42 by England's Hoggard, whose run ended when he missed the final Test of the 2006/07 Ashes series. Among truly fast bowlers, the best since the start of 2000 has been 35 by Makhaya Ntini, with Harmison next on 29. Shoaib Akhtar's most durable sequence has been six; the most managed by Simon Jones, such a key man in that 2005 Ashes series, is seven. Shane Bond, the fast bowler who troubles Australia most, won his first 15 caps over a period of five years, and has yet to play a complete three-Test series (see Table 4).

It is plain – and surely no coincidence - that Test cricket has never been played at a faster lick. This has been primarily due to a combination of good and bad: on the one hand, positive, urgent and even impatient batsmanship, allied to enterprising, aggressive captaincy; on the other, benign pitches, a negation and betrayal of the competitive arts which can be at least partly attributed – no matter what the groundsmen might claim – to the desire of administrators to make matches last the full five days and hence please their broadcasting pals. The draw, as a consequence, has been going out of fashion (see Table 5). Overall, in matches played between the eight most senior nations – Australia, England, South Africa, West Indies, New Zealand, India, Pakistan and Sri Lanka – there have been 179 more draws than decisive outcomes; since January 2004 there have been 17 more victories. This has something to do with the impatience of modern society. Might it not also have something to do with the inability of the tired brain and jaded body to summon the focus and discipline required to turn defeat into honours shared, however unequally? Yet according to the modern mindset, failing to win is as grievous a sin as losing.

Table 4. Most consecutive Test appearances by fast bowlers.

| Overall | | Since 1/1/2003 | |
|---|---|---|---|
| Kapil Dev | 66 | Matthew Hoggard | 42 |
| Kapil Dev | 65 | Andrew Flintoff | 36 |
| Ian Botham | 65 | Steve Harmison | 29 |
| Glenn McGrath | 54 | Chaminda Vaas | 28 |
| Courtney Walsh | 53 | Shaun Pollock | 25 |
| Wes Hall | 44 | Heath Streak | 24 |

Table 5. The decline of the draw in test match cricket.

| Country | Overall | Since 1/1/2004 |
|---|---|---|
| Australia | 9 | 4 |
| England | 6 | 1 |
| West Indies | 10 | 11 |
| South Africa | 13 | 2 |
| Pakistan | 55 | 4 |
| Sri Lanka | 6 | 5 |
| India | 53 | 5 |
| New Zealand | 9 | 5 |
| Total | 179 | 17 |

As highlighted by Tim May, instigator and long-time chief executive of the Federation of International Cricket Associations (FICA), drug use is becoming another unhappy consequence of this fixture overload.[11] Last year, Shoaib Akhtar and his new Pakistan partner, Mohammad Asif, became the first international players suspended for such an infraction, though the bans were controversially overturned. Not only are they both fast bowlers – Shoaib is probably the fastest the game has ever seen – but the drug in question was nandrolone, the healer of choice among those seeking speedier recovery from breaks, aches and strains.

So what can be done? All the fingers in my possession point to the ICC and the individual boards, some of whom have a nasty and divisive habit of pursuing their own agenda regardless of collective interest or greater good. These text-messaging mandarins must recognize the primacy of the players, re-examine their workloads, peer beyond the end of their noses and adjust that fixture list accordingly.

Progress, I am delighted to report, is being made, however sluggishly. 'Players are not sufficiently involved in the administration of the game and ownership of the problems... Consideration should be given to enhancing the role of the players and their representative bodies'. Thus averred Recommendation 10 of The Condon Report into the match-fixing crisis that enfeebled cricket's reputation in the last decade of the twentieth century.[12] A couple of years later, in May 2003, I interviewed Tim May, then in the midst of some major shuttle-diplomacy in seeking recognition for FICA. How did he respond to Lord Condon's statement? 'We're not just employees – we're the *product*', May insisted. 'The game is a *shared* responsibility'.[13]

Nearly four years later, thanks in the main to the Indian board of control's belated, if grudging, recognition of that sprawling nation's players' association, we are a lot further down the road. While it would be stretching things to say that ICC and FICA are now singing in rhythm and harmony, at least they are following a similar melody line. The next step is for the conductors to listen more attentively and consistently to the musicians.

## The Twenty20 solution

And the cricketing solution? Perverse as it may seem, I would like to advocate something that would almost certainly ensure the extinction of the draw. And for me, the advent of Twenty20 cricket, with its two-hour games and consequent attraction for the young and the North American, offers a passport to this higher plane of cricketing existence.

First, though, something does indeed have to give, and, if the players' wishes are to be considered, that something is the traditional one-day format. I know I am far from alone in finding 50-over games increasingly tedious and predictable, as the recent World Cup bore out so painfully. The 20-over variant strips away the fat and is thus easier to swallow. One-sided cricket matches are an affront to the spirit, and genuinely dramatic 50-over finishes are almost as lesser-spotted as the dodo: the briefer the match, the longer the odds against boredom. Every ball counts, and there is no need for the plasticity of powerplays or fielding restrictions. There is no room for passengers either but oodles of openings for quick-thinking strategists, breathtaking fielders, clever gap-finders, brave hitters and, best of all, canny, flexible and creative spinners. Can 50-over cricket survive such a challenge from its own Mini-Me? I sincerely doubt it. Indeed, in 2006, it was decided to stage the inaugural Twenty20 World Cup in September 2007; the plan is to hold one every other year.

Prior to the 2004 Champions Trophy, I was commissioned to research an article on this subject for the magazine *India Today*. I am not quoting it to show off my credentials as an apprentice soothsayer, merely to stress my qualifications as an unapologetic, hopelessly unreconstructed, hopeful romantic:

> The possibilities, as mirrored by [Twenty20] Finals Day, featuring both semi-finals and final, are enticing. Imagine an India-Pakistan tripleheader. Imagine an entire Pepsi/Honda/Samsung series being done and dusted in a week, or a World Cup compressed into a fortnight. Imagine the impact such brevity and conciseness could have . . . Imagine the impact on the longevity of the players obliged to bear that burden.[14]

Since single innings matches are 'cricket lite', however, I would urge a further tweak and a more elegant variation: two innings of 20 overs per side. (Admittedly, this is not a unique concept. It is merely an extension of Cricket Max, the short-lived yet uncannily prescient innovation devised by Martin Crowe a decade ago, featuring two innings per side spanning ten overs apiece.) While the single innings format could co-exist, this would certainly prepare younger observers for the dramatic possibilities of the Test match. This brought me to a seductive, probably excessively fanciful conclusion: 'Imagine the possibilities for Test cricket, the game's highest form of expression. Within the context of a looser schedule, it could revert to its unbound, unexpurgated, timeless form'.[15]

A return to 'timeless' Tests, if perhaps only for the concluding chapter of an undecided series or a World Championship final, would be a tantalizing proposition. Of course, such is the pace of scoring, together with that universal shortening of attention spans, that it is unlikely that more than a handful of matches could be stretched beyond five days. Global warming, meanwhile, is bound to offset the climactic obstacles. By the same token, the reduction in fatigue and stress rendered possible by a less onerous schedule could be beneficial to fitness and hence endurance levels. Those excessively batsman-friendly pitches, moreover, might well prove less of a handicap to bowlers in general, and spinners in particular.

In an unsound, 'sound-bitten' world, a world of tabloid mentalities and a beast known deceptively as 'reality' TV, what better way to maintain and prolong cricket's anachronistic grip on a couple of billion imaginations than to revive a variant that thumbs its nose so resolutely at virtually every commandment engraved on broadcasting's tablets of stone. Bar, of course, the one referring to television's holy grail: the quite decent soap opera.

## Postscript

October 3, 2007. It is now just over a week since the end of the inaugural World Twenty20 in South Africa, an event hailed as a rousing success on virtually every front. Granted, some purists held their noses to evade the aesthetic pong, and there were dire warnings about overkill, yet the contrast with the 50-over World Cup was refreshing in its starkness. This time we were graced with close contests, high drama, plenty of crowd-pleasing batsmanship (including, courtesy of India's Yuvraj Singh, the first instance of a player from one senior Test nation hitting six sixes in an over against a senior rival) and twice as many (albeit only two) instances of giant-killing.

The impact was such that *The Times* ran a four-day 'special'[16] featuring post-mortems from four diverse contributors, ranging from the newly-retired former captain of Kent, David Fulton, to the paper's own former cricket correspondent John Woodcock, who has been writing about the international game for more than half a century. Only Woodcock tempered his enthusiasm. What made this attention all the more remarkable was that *The Times* feature had been competing for column inches with a Rugby World Cup, the climax of an historic Formula 1 of especial interest to British readers, José Mourinho's departure from Chelsea and the retirement of a national sporting icon, Tim Henman.

To Malcolm Speed, the ICC chief executive, Twenty20 may prove to be the key to unlocking the potential of two major markets, China and the USA. The latter has been the game's holiest grail since the advent of Babe Ruth shoved cricket into the nation's nooks and crannies. Speed noted, 'I heard about an article in one of the Washington papers that was talking about the phenomenon of Twenty20 cricket. It has been televised in the USA and it's been televised in China, so it's the perfect vehicle for cricket to develop in new countries'.[17]

From Australia, meanwhile, came a typically imaginative response from John Buchanan, the former Australia coach. The older abbreviated format, he contended, should be overhauled to make it more attractive to spectators who have acquired a thirst for the longueur-free frills of Twenty20. His proposals included giving two sides two innings each within 50 overs, bonus points for high scoring rates, and freer use of substitutes.[18]

It was inevitable, and understandable, that Tim May should express renewed concerns about the players' workload:

> Twenty20's success may work against the game in the medium-to long-term because it might dilute the role of 50-over cricket, which is the financial base for international cricket. It might in fact replace that and the financial models that are going around tell you that no matter how popular Twenty20 is at the moment, it doesn't produce the financial returns that the 50-over game does.[19]

On the other hand, that last comment may in due course be seen merely as a reflection of incomplete 'financial models': the appeal of the first international Twenty20 event took even the organizers by surprise. Although the sheer pace of the game works against convenient advertising breaks, it is hard to believe that staging two or even three matches a day will not suit the broadcasters better. The benefit in terms of live attendances may also be felt, as it has been in Britain, where Twenty20 crowds far exceed those for the average 40- or 50-over contest.

May went part of the way towards a two-format solution. For the players' sake, and hence that of the game itself, he argued, administrators must accept that some 'meaningless' limited-overs tours should be scrapped as Twenty20 gains in popularity. Delivered just as Australia headed straight from the World Twenty20 to India for a seven-ODI series, his summary was inarguable: 'Something has got to give somewhere along the line, something must give'.[20]

Not for the first time, some thoughtful solutions emanated from the laptop of Ian Chappell, one of the shrewdest men ever to captain Australia as well as an early and vocal advocate of players' rights. In doing so, he also turned the spotlight back on match-fixing, a closely-related subject ignored and suppressed in polite company for some time now:

> With the urge for globalization catered for in the Twenty20 format, the 50-overs World Cup could return to being the elite tournament it was initially intended to be. The number of teams could be reduced to ten, with a schedule that replicated the one used in the 1991–92 tournament where each team played every other in the round-robin stage. Then, rather than a semi-final and final, a best-of-three final series could decide the best 50-over team in the game. That way a truly competitive World Cup could be completed in around a month with the best team unearthed in the fairest manner.
>
> Freed from the albatross that is the need for globalization, the ICC could address the dilution of Test cricket that has occurred in recent times. This has resulted from granting top-level status to teams that don't warrant the accolade. By reducing the number of accredited teams to the eight major playing nations, the ICC could then run a viable Test world championship that would unveil the best side in the game's premier format...
>
> By restructuring in such a way, the ICC would then be better placed to produce a balanced playing schedule that caters for the need to finance the development of the game without working the star players into the ground. What is called for is a simple change

of focus from quantity to quality in cricket matches. If the problem of players being overworked isn't addressed, the fans are likely to become disillusioned with the game and the players susceptible to quick, easy money from either rich entrepreneurs or greedy gamblers.[21]

The match-fixing crisis is purportedly over, yet doubts persist. The more tired, hurt and resentful the players become, the more likely they are to succumb to temptation. The shadow cast by Hansie Cronje and others who consorted with gamblers to deceive and betray the public looms far too large to ignore Chappell's sound recommendations. Even if they don't go quite as far as this writer would like.

## Notes

Note: All statistics courtesy of Crickstats, a subscription-only database run by statistician Ric Finlay in Tasmania. Figures correct to March 2, 2007.

1  Examples of recent literature about the politics and racial aspects of cricket include: Beckles, *The Development of West Indies Cricket. Volume 2: The Age of Globalization*; Carrington and McDonald, 'Whose Game is it Anyway? Racism in Local League Cricket'; Malcolm, 'It's not Cricket: Colonial Legacies and Contemporary Inequalities'; Marqusee, *Anyone But England: Cricket, Race and Class*; Murray and Merrett, *Caught Behind: Race and Politics in Springbok Cricket*; Williams, *Cricket and Race*; Steen, 'Whatever Happened to the Black Cricketer?', an article published in *The Wisden Cricketer* in August 2004, and subsequently adapted for the *Evening Standard* and *The Observer*, which won the UK section of the 2005 EU 'For diversity, against discrimination' Journalism Award.
2  Shawn Cumberbatch, 'IMF CWC Warning'. *Barbados Advocate*, April 17, 2007. http://dlpbarbados.wordpress.com/2007/04/17/caribbean-economies-whiplash-from-cwc.
3  Briggs, 'Burned Out or Fired Up?', 47.
4  Ibid., 48
5  John, 'Excess fare', 49.
6  Ibid., 49.
7  Ibid., 49.
8  Richard Hobson, 'Schofield to Lead the Inquest into England's Debacle Down Under'. *Times Online*, January 16, 2007. http://www.timesonline.co.uk/tol/sport/cricket/article1293353.ece.
9  Briggs, 'Burned Out or Fired Up?', 47.
10 Steen, 'The Oval And After', 77.
11 Steen, 'Leading the Way to Player Power'.
12 Condon *et al.*, *Report on Corruption in International Cricket*. http://www.rediff.com/cricket/2001/may/23paul6.htm (section 120).
13 Steen, 'Leading the Way to Player Power', 37.
14 Steen, 'Pitched Right', *India Today*, August 4, 2003, 27.
15 Ibid., 27.
16 *The Times*, Main Section, London Edition, September 25–28, 2007.
17 England and Wales Cricket Board, 'Speed admits Twenty20 hope'.
18 Crincifo, 'Twenty20 Won't Bring in the Money – FICA'.
19 'May Calls for Cautious Approach from ICC'. *Daily Times*, Pakistan, September 29, 2007, www.dailytimes.com.pk/default.asp?page=2007%5C09%5C29%5Cstory_29-9-2007_pg2_4.
20 Ibid.
21 Chappell, 'A Cure for Cricket's Cancer'.

## References

Beckles, Hilary. *The Development of West Indies Cricket. Volume 2: The Age of Globalization*. Kingston: University of West Indies Press, 1998.
Briggs, Simon. 'Burned Out or Fired Up?' *Wisden Cricket Monthly* (January 2003): 47–49.
Carrington, Ben, and Ian McDonald. 'Whose Game is it Anyway? Racism in Local League Cricket'. *Race, Sport and British Society* 49/69 (2001).
Chappell, Ian. 'A Cure for Cricket's Cancer'. Cricinfo, September 16, 2007. http://content-ind.cricinfo.com/extracover/content/current/story/311030.html.

Condon, Sir Paul. *Report on Corruption in International Cricket.* Anti-Corruption Unit, April 2001.

Crincifo. 'Twenty20 Won't Bring in the Money – FICA'. Cricinfo, September 28, 2007. http://content-www.cricinfo.com/ci/content/story/312829.html.

England and Wates Cricket Board. 'Speed Admits Twenty20 Hope'. Ecb.co.uk, October 3, 2007. http://www.ecb.co.uk/england/series-tours-archive/icc-world-twenty20/news-archive/speed-admits-twenty20-hope,15167,EN.html.

John, Emma. 'Excess Fare'. *The Wisden Cricketer* (January 2004): 46–50.

Malcolm, Dominic. 'It's not Cricket: Colonial Legacies and Contemporary Inequalities'. *Journal of Historical Sociology* 14, no. 3 (2001): 253–75.

Marqusee, Mike. *Anyone But England: Cricket, Race and Class.* London: Two Heads, 1998.

Murray, Bruce, and Christopher Merrett. *Caught Behind: Race and Politics in Springbok Cricket.* Johannesburg: Wits University Press, 2004.

Steen, Rob. 'Leading the Way to Player Power'. *Wisden Cricket Monthly* (August 2003): 36–37.

Steen, Rob. 'Whatever Happened to the Black Cricketer?' *The Wisden Cricketer* (August 2004): 22–28.

Steen, Rob. 'Pitched Right'. *India Today* (August 4, 2003), 25–27.

Steen, Rob. 'The Oval And After'. In *Wisden Cricketers' Almanack 2007*, edited by Matthew Engel, 76–78. Hampshire: John Wisden, 2007.

Williams, Jack. *Cricket and Race.* Oxford: Berg, 2001.

# A strong sport growing stronger: a perspective on the growth, development and future of international cricket

Ehsan Mani*

*Chairman, ICC Global Cricket Academy*

## Introduction

Cricket is currently at the strongest point in its history. There are more players, men and women, from more countries involved in the game than ever before; cricket is followed by more people on television and the internet, in more parts of the world than could have been imagined ten years ago. Most importantly, high quality, innovative and exciting cricket is being played at the international level. In its numerical support base, cricket is the second most popular sport in the world, after football. After years of limited development the game has evolved rapidly in the past decade, bringing with it the promise of a truly global sport played in all regions of the world.

It is important to place the game today in context. In order to know where the game will go from now, we need to examine how it has got here in the first place.

## History

For a sport which is so well chronicled, cricket's earliest origins are unclear. The roots of the game, some people believe, can be traced to ancient shepherds playing with their crook standing in front of a field gate with stones being bowled at them. The shepherds' crook was called a 'cricce'. *Wisden* tells us that an early form of the game probably evolved between the end of the Roman Empire and the start of the Norman invasion of England in 1066. More than 500 years then passed before references to cricket became more frequent. In 1709 the first county game had been played between Kent and Surrey. The first laws of cricket were drawn up in 1744, and the famous Hambledon Club was formed in Hampshire in 1767, followed by the Marylebone Cricket Club in 1787.

In the eighteenth century cricket was taken up by the aristocracy. Surrey was supported by the Prince of Wales who became passionately fond of the game and to this day the Surrey emblem is the Prince of Wales' feathers. Even today, the Prince of Wales is the landlord of Surrey's home, the Oval, in South London. Soon cricket gained a reputation as a sport for the upper classes, played at grand country house venues; the matches were big social events, often involving the wagering of substantial amounts of money on the outcome of individual games.

As cricket established itself in England it was introduced to all parts of the British Empire by British traders, settlers, administrators and the British Army. As early as 1676 there is mention of cricket being played by British residents in Aleppo,[1] Syria. By 1730 cricket is mentioned being played by the Honourable Artillery Company at the Artillery Ground in the City of London, where it continues to be played to this day. In 1841 General Lord Hill, commander-in-chief of the British Army ordered a cricket ground to be made an adjunct of every military barrack.[2]

Initially the game was played overseas by the British between themselves. In Australia and New Zealand the indigenous population were on the whole excluded from society and the game. Over the years there have been a few aborigine cricketers in Australia. In South Africa and Rhodesia (now Zimbabwe) the British settlers, soldiers and administrators introduced the game in the first half of the nineteenth century. However, it was initially very much a British sport and did not, at least initially, appeal to the Boers. Black Africans were not encouraged to play the game; as one former colonial administrator told me, 'cricket was considered too complicated for the African mind; they were encouraged to play football instead on the premise that anyone could kick a ball'![3] In other colonies, particularly the Indian subcontinent and the West Indies, the native population took to the game first by watching the British play, but gradually discovered this alien pastime was something very special, involving skill and guile. The beauty and the passion of the game appealed to their temperament. In India the game first captivated the Indian princes and then consumed the whole of the subcontinent.

The first known official international match took place in 1844 between Canada and the United States in New York and was attended by over 10,000 spectators. The first touring team from England played in both these countries in 1859. The Civil War disrupted the game in the United States and in time the game in North America was marginalized as baseball, American football and other sports developed. In 1877 the first Test match between England and Australia took place in Melbourne, which Australia won by 45 runs. Australia toured England for the first time in 1880. South Africa played its first Test match in 1889.

International cricket remained a sport of the select. It was not until 1926 that India, New Zealand and West Indies received international recognition. Following partition, 26 years later Pakistan became a member of the ICC in 1952. The ICC did not elect any Full Member for the next 29 years until Sri Lanka was granted membership in 1981. Membership for South Africa (re-admitted in 1991), Zimbabwe (1992) and Bangladesh (2000) completed the ten Full Members of the ICC.

By 1997, when the ICC Development Strategy was put in place, the ICC had nine Full Members and 38 Associate Members in its 88 years as the governing body of the sport – an average of about one new member being added every two years. In the late 1980s I was struck by the reluctance to admit new members. This was for a number of reasons: lack of funding to promote the game and concerns over the long term implications on the voting structure of the ICC, which carried with it the possibility of a change in the balance of power within the governing body. On paper, 38 Associate Member countries looked good but in reality cricket was very much a game played by a small number of expatriates in the Associate countries. There was no clear pathway for an Associate who aspired to the higher status of One Day or Test cricket. Any development in the Associate Member countries depended on the enthusiasm and passion of volunteers who loved the game and wanted to play it but did not necessarily have the resources or the expertise to promote, develop and sell the sport to the masses. All that was about to change and the next section elaborates on how that change came about

## Lord's to Dubai: origins and evolution of the International Cricket Council

As cricket flourished, the MCC and Lord's cricket ground became synonymous as the home of cricket. It was at Lord's that the Imperial Cricket Conference was established by England, Australia and South Africa in 1909. The MCC, a private members club, took responsibility for the game throughout the world. The President of the MCC, or his nominee, chaired all ICC meetings and its secretariat handled the administration. The MCC ceded control of the game in the United Kingdom to the Test and County Cricket Board (since renamed the England and Wales Cricket Board) in 1968 but retained a virtual stranglehold over international cricket for another 25 years until 1993.

Interestingly, when the ICC was first formed, membership was limited to only the governing bodies of cricket in countries within the British Commonwealth. The ICC was an exclusive club. One wonders if the first rules of the ICC were drafted specifically to exclude the United States of America. Certainly cricket and politics do mix. In recent years the political climate between India and Pakistan has determined whether the governments of these two Asian cricket giants were prepared to allow cricket matches to take place between them. Nor have the governments of the United Kingdom, Australia and New Zealand been shy of asking the ICC to boycott Zimbabwe and in some cases not allowing their national team to play against Zimbabwe.

In 1965, the name of the ICC was changed to the International Cricket Conference. New rules were adopted to allow election of countries from outside the Commonwealth, and the USA and Fiji were elected as the first Associate Members with limited rights. South Africa had left the Commonwealth in 1961 and had ceased to be a member but now the ground had been prepared to re-admit South Africa without it necessarily re-joining the Commonwealth. England and Australia, known as the Foundation Members, were given a veto over all resolutions. In 1989 the organization was renamed as the International Cricket Council and the ICC was given the authority for the first time to make binding decisions rather than making recommendations to national governing bodies. However England and Australia still retained the veto, resulting in only those binding decisions going forward which had their approval. It was only in 1993 that the Foundation Members were persuaded to give up their veto when it became apparent that the other Full Members were no longer prepared to accept that some Full Members were more equal than others.

The surrender of the veto was one of the first issues to test the unity of the ICC members. England and Australia eventually accepted that times had changed. Not only had the membership of the ICC expanded but the performance on the field of West Indies, India and Pakistan meant that the game was no longer dominated by the founding countries. This was the first step in the change of the balance of power within the international governing body. Wisely it was accompanied by the adoption of an excellent governance structure with appropriate checks and balances; this saw the ICC appoint its first non-British President, Sir Clyde Walcott and its first Chief Executive. The member countries finally took over control of the ICC from the MCC, some 84 years after it was formed.

The office of the ICC was moved from a filing cabinet in the office of the Secretary of the MCC to a small corner of Lord's behind the Compton Stand. The offices were meant to accommodate a staff of eight. Some 12 years later, when the ICC moved to larger premises in Dubai, about 25 people were crammed in these modest offices.

The most recent chapter in the evolution of the ICC into a world governing body with real resource and influence came with the decision to relocate from Lord's to a new home in Dubai. It was a decision which was not taken lightly; after being based at the spiritual home of the game since 1909 this was a momentous decision which recognized the need to move with the times and become more readily accessible and relevant to more of its members.

While the Government of the United Kingdom baulked at granting the ICC exemption from tax on its worldwide income, other countries such as Singapore, Monaco, Ireland, Malaysia and Dubai stepped forward to offer not only favourable tax treatment but also other incentives such as cash grants and premises at subsidised rates to host the ICC. Dubai was ultimately chosen due to its excellent location and increasingly impressive infrastructure.

In Dubai the ICC is today in modern offices and is in the process of building its own state-of-the-art head office; it is closer to eight of its ten Full Members than it was in England. This means it is better positioned to do face-to-face business with many of them, such as Bangladesh, India, Pakistan and Sri Lanka, who between them possess almost 20% of the world's population and an insatiable appetite for the game. It also brought the governing body closer to Africa, one of the most important regions for the ICC Development Programme.

The move in 2005 to Dubai has also resulted in a change in the profile of the ICC staff. Today the organization's management team is more representative of the diversity of its membership and includes people from Australia, South Africa, Pakistan, England, India, New Zealand and other member countries.

## The ICC's challenges: growth, money and development

In July 1993, with the founding members agreeing to greater democratization, the ICC became a truly independent body but one that was facing a serious financial crisis. It had its own President, Chief Executive and three other employees, but virtually no money.

The annual operating budget for 1993 was less than $250,000. By 1996/97 it had grown to about $1,000,000 of which $400,000 was accounted for by sponsorship for umpires and referees. Full Members complained about their annual ICC subscriptions of $15,000 each and how this was taking valuable resources away from the development of the sport in their countries. The financial muscle of the governing body of international cricket was hardly the stuff that would change the cricket world.

While cricket was no longer played only in stately homes or exclusively by the privileged classes, and the distinction between amateurs and professionals had disappeared, cricket was still a sport of the elite in many of the Full Member countries. The Packer revolution of 1977[4] had resulted in players, who were paid a pittance for representing their countries, receiving substantially more than they had been before Packer showed that cricket and money did mix. However, it still lagged behind a number of major sports in terms of what the players received. In Associate Member countries it was still an expatriate sport and would continue that way unless considerable investment in grounds, equipment, administrators, curators, coaches, umpires and much more was made to enable it to reach out as a sport for the masses.

With inadequate financial resources the game was not going to develop beyond its traditional boundaries. Even in the Test playing nations the game was under threat from other sports; in England, Australia and New Zealand young talented sportsmen had alternatives; they could opt for soccer or rugby and increase their earning potential considerably. Similarly, in the West Indies the lure of American sports such as basketball and baseball was attractive when compared with the rewards offered by cricket and was drawing youngsters away from the game. Clearly cricket needed a serious amount of money to nurture the sport in countries where it had taken root and invest in other countries to develop and survive.

1997 was the landmark year. The ICC Development Committee, chaired by Dr Ali Bacher, produced a Global Development Plan which would have far reaching effects on the way cricket was promoted as a global sport. However, implementation of the development programme was only made possible by the then ICC President, Jagmohan Dalmiya, with his vision of globalization, of taking the game beyond its traditional colonial boundaries. To finance the development programme Dalmiya proposed holding a knock-out tournament (later to be adapted to become the Champion's Trophy). The inaugural tournament was held in Dhaka in 1998 and raised approximately $13 million which was all ear-marked for the development of the game.

As Chairman of the ICC Finance and Marketing Committee at that time it was clear to me that ad-hoc tournaments would not provide the sustainable resources to run a truly global development programme, let alone a truly global sport. The ICC needed to raise much larger sums of money to invest not only in the developing nations, but also in the Full Member countries, some of whom were seriously lacking the infrastructure to sustain the game in the long term.

The ICC had pledged itself to making cricket a stronger sport, to reach outside its traditional frontiers and compete effectively as a major sport with football, rugby, tennis, golf, motor racing and other sports. There were many elements that needed to come together to achieve this. One of the most important was to secure a sound and sustainable financial base for the game.

In 2000, therefore, the ICC reached a landmark media and sponsorship rights agreement with an affiliate of News Corp, which has interests in Sky, ESPN-Star Sports, Star TV and other major sports channels around the world.[5] The ICC sold cricket rights for a seven-year period for US$550 million, a sum that brought with it a new level of financial security.

This was only made possible by the ICC taking control of the media and sponsorship rights to the events owned by it and selling them as a bundle covering more than one event. This was more difficult than it sounded. There was considerable debate within the ICC over this move and it had to overcome the concerns of the host of the 2003 World Cup, South Africa, and also the West Indies, who were to host the 2007 event. Up to this time each host country of an ICC event was left to exploit the commercial value on its own, in return offering the participating countries a minimum guaranteed fee. Both initially felt that the commercial rights belonged to them and any change would impact on their ability to maximize the financial windfall they anticipated from holding the event. In 1996, India and Pakistan had each made around $20 million. Under the revised arrangement South Africa received approximately $80 million as hosting fees and West Indies over $100 million. For the 1996 World Cup in the subcontinent each Full Member received $500,000, compared to nearly $10m from the 2007 World Cup.

At the end of 2006 a new commercial media rights agreement was concluded with ESPN-Star Sports covering the period from the conclusion of the 2007 Cricket World Cup to 2015. This, together with the potential sponsorship income, will deliver in the region of $1.5 billion to the members of the ICC. Of this amount approximately $350 million will be invested in Associate and Affiliate Member countries.

The Test playing countries support the game in their countries primarily from the sale of their media rights, sponsorship, gate-money and, increasingly, from the distributions from ICC-held events. In the case of Associate Members, revenue distribution by the ICC is the most important, and in some cases the sole, source of funding.

Advancements in new media technology including digital television, internet, broadband broadcast, on demand viewing and mobile technology have greatly increased the demand for content by broadcasters around the world. Cricket is a relatively cheap content provider and in the subcontinent an excellent tool for companies to promote their goods and services by advertising on the electronic media to an increasingly affluent society. While the ICC has entered into arrangements which will deliver unprecedented financial benefits for its members, the Test playing nations have all also benefited greatly when marketing their commercial rights to international and domestic cricket. The Board of Control for Cricket in India (BCCI) substantially increased its revenue from the sale of its broadcast rights, as have Australia and England, and this trend is expected to continue when other countries return to the market to renew their rights.

Critics have accused the ICC of being motivated by money to the detriment of the game. I do not agree and would counter those claims by saying that the financial certainty and security which cricket enjoys today is essential for the health of the game. While there is more money in the game than ever before, it is still not enough. Cricket is an expensive game to run with huge investment required in stadiums, grounds and the playing infrastructure. Even in the Full Member countries such as India and Pakistan tens of millions of dollars are being belatedly spent on improving stadiums that host international matches which currently lack basic spectator facilities. The governments of the West Indies spent over $300 million in upgrading the grounds in the lead up to the 2007 World Cup. For the majority of members, ICC revenue is the difference between profit and loss; it is the difference between being able to pay players their true market value and it is the difference in making cricket a viable and rewarding career for officials and administrators around the world. It has also made cricket relevant in countries where it was a marginal sport.

It is important, though, that the ICC and its members have the proper governance structures in place to ensure that the money generated for the benefit of the game is spent for just that purpose with absolute transparency and accountability.

Ten years ago, at the start of the ICC Development Programme, the ICC membership stood at 47 countries; a tiny market penetration for a sport with global potential. Today, the ICC has 101 members. This has been made possible because there have been the financial resources available together with a sound and cohesive development programme.

Recruiting new members has been exciting and rewarding and has demonstrated that cricket's athletic and emotional appeal really does translate on a global sporting basis. Cricket now has an established infrastructure in countries as diverse as Afghanistan, Argentina, Brazil, China, Croatia, Fiji, Indonesia, Japan, Malawi and Tanzania and increasingly it is being introduced at grass-roots levels to the non expatriate population.

Having made such spectacular progress in expanding its membership base, the priority of the ICC has now moved towards consolidating and strengthening the infrastructure of the sport across 101 individual countries and territories around the world.

Traditionally, ICC membership has been based on a pyramid structure, with a small elite group of ten Test playing nations and a large base of Associate and Affiliate Members. Now there is greater emphasis on moving to an inverse pyramid structure, with focus on improving the quality and playing standards of the game rather than a drive to recruit new ones. The ICC today has a substantial global membership base which gives it a superb platform from which to take the sport forward.

## Twenty20 and innovation

Innovation is a vital aspect of the game's continued development to remain relevant and to attract new fans and supporters. Cricket is adapting to reach out in countries where there is no tradition of the game. The ICC has not been afraid to innovate and experiment.

Cricket's traditional image hides the fact that it is a sport which has welcomed innovation. The new Twenty20 format is an excellent example of this; it is probably the most significant development in the game since Packer introduced what was then dismissed as 'pyjama cricket' to the world. Just a few years since its introduction in English domestic cricket, the ICC has staged the first Twenty20 World Cup in South Africa. India has changed its position dramatically from publicly refusing to play this form of the game to setting up an official professional league. Twenty20 has had an enormous positive influence on the game in the United Kingdom, South Africa and Australia; it has attracted new audiences and increased participation numbers. In some developing countries, such as China and the United States, it could be the ideal form to promote cricket.

Innovation at the international level also includes the use of technology to assist umpires improve on the 94% of correct decisions they already achieve. Cricket really has taken a lead role among major sports in this respect. For example, the 2007 World Cup saw earpieces being used by officials to pick up sound from the stump microphones, in addition to the standard referrals to the third umpire for line call decisions. Certainly, cricket as a spectator sport has become more exciting through the use of technology.

Not all innovations have been successful; the 2006 Super Series in Australia looked good on paper and was supported by all the Test playing nations but failed to capture the public's imagination. Another less than successful innovation was the use of the super-subs in one day matches. None of these should stop cricket from trying out new ideas first in domestic cricket and, if successful, at the international level. We have seen in the past with Packer and more recently with the rebel Indian Cricket League that unless the ICC and the national governing bodies lead from the front others will step in.

## Cricket: the path ahead

### *Bridging the gulf*

One cannot pretend that there is anything other than a huge gulf in playing standards between the elite Test playing nations and those below them at Associate and Affiliate level. There has been the occasional upset in one day games, but by and large the developing nations cannot compete with the Test playing countries.

For the first time in the history of the sport, the ICC has introduced a system which aims to narrow the gulf in standards and eventually expand the base of teams playing at the highest level. The top six associate countries benefit through a high performance programme, giving them the chance to play official one day internationals and working to improve their administrative and coaching structures. Also, importantly the ICC is aware that these countries must be supported financially to ensure that improvements in standards can be sustained. In addition to the distributions these countries receive from the ICC events, each of the six Associate Members who took part in the 2007 World Cup received a grant of $500,000 and this amount will increase to $1 million in 2011.

There is also an annual winter training camp for the best players from the top Associate Members and the World Cricket League that offers all 91 Associates and Affiliates a path to qualify for the World Cup. Bermuda, Canada, Ireland, Kenya, the Netherlands and Scotland all played in the Caribbean in the 2007 World Cup.

The late Bob Woolmer, a past High Performance manager of the ICC, was adamant that for the teams below Test playing level to improve, they had to play the longer version of the game. The ICC launched the Intercontinental Cup a few years ago, which gives the best Associate sides the chance to play 3- and 4-day cricket at first-class level for the first time.

Another substantial step forward in this area is the opening of the ICC Global Cricket Academy in Dubai. This magnificent facility offers players, umpires, coaches and groundsmen from all member countries the chance to hone skills with the best coaches in the world, in a world-class environment that will be a model of best practice. Led by head coach Rod Marsh, it will be absolutely state-of-the-art in every sense.

Perhaps the most important step has been the decision that the top six Associate Members will play regular one day international matches each year against the Full Members. This will not only give them exposure against the world's top teams but will also provide the ICC High Performance department with the opportunity to assess the playing standards of these countries.

### Women's cricket

Women's cricket is another area of the game where great progress is being made. The ICC could not lead international cricket unless it represented all its stakeholders. In 2005 the ICC merged with the International Women's Cricket Council (IWCC). At the time of the merger there were only 15 IWCC members, but by 2007 there were 42 countries with organized women's structures, and another 23 with junior development initiatives.

The new broadcasting agreement mentioned earlier includes a commitment to televise future Women's World Cups, starting with the next event in Australia in 2009. This will further assist in the promotion of the women's game.

An example of the way cricket is expanding among women is the Women's World Cup qualifying event in Pakistan in November 2007. This included sides from Zimbabwe and Bermuda which, a year ago, did not have women's national teams at all. In the recent Asian Cricket Council (ACC) Women's tournament, teams from the United Arab Emirates, Hong Kong, Singapore, Malaysia, China, Thailand, Bangladesh and Nepal took part for the first time and Bangladesh, which only recently formed a women's team, won this tournament. Women's cricket will continue to gain in popularity and will play an increasingly important part in the development of the game around the world.

### USA and China

Although consolidation is a priority for the ICC after a decade of impressive growth, there are two countries where cricket's expansion could dramatically increase its global representation. These are the United States and China.

There is a huge appetite for cricket in the United States; it is one of the oldest cricket playing nations in the world. Cricket, for example, has been played in Philadelphia for over two centuries and Haverford College has played cricket since 1833. Sadly, the game has been neglected in the United States. Over the past couple of decades there has been resurgence in the game due to the influx of West Indian, Indian, Pakistani and Sri Lankan immigrants. New Jersey, for example, is home to over a million people from the subcontinent as well as about 200,000 West Indians; it has more than 100 cricket clubs playing in four leagues. In all, the United States has over 20,000 active cricketers. The game has enormous potential, but for cricket to become an established sport it must be introduced at junior school and grass roots levels and must target the whole spectrum of the American population. The ICC has in the past offered to set up the administrative structure required to develop cricket as an officially recognized sport which would attract local government support in terms of facilities and funding. Unfortunately, local politics and strife within the USA Cricket Association have prevented this from happening. It is incredibly frustrating that those mandated to promote the game in the United States have held it back for personal agendas. In the long term there is reason to hope for a more constructive future. Even without the stimulus of high quality domestic or international cricket, the USA is now one of the largest markets for broadcast rights deals. Recently the BCCI rights were sold in the United States for about $50 million and it is a significant contributor to the ICC media rights.

China is the other country with literally untapped potential. When I was first approached, as President of the ICC, regarding China's application for ICC Membership my immediate reaction was 'why cricket?' I was told that the Chinese had been following cricket since Sri Lanka's triumph in the 1996 Cricket World Cup and had come to the conclusion that it was a game that they could, in time, excel at. On further enquiry I was told that their analysis had shown that it was a game of skill, of strategy and of the mind; it was not a contact or physical sport and the Chinese saw no reason, given the right support, why they could not adapt to the game.

The Asian Cricket Council and the ICC have been working together in promoting the game in China through financial and technical support. From no organized cricket at all in mainland China two years ago, it is exciting to see China in the Junior ACC tournaments and the women's team participating in Malaysia last July. The biggest challenge is the lack of cricket culture in the country, but I have no doubt that the small steps being taken in China will lead to big strides in the future. The 2007 Twenty20 World Cup was broadcast live on television in China; this, and the exposure to international cricket events in the future, will help build an understanding of the game in the country.

When the then ICC chief executive Malcolm Speed visited Beijing and Shanghai in 2006 on a fact-finding tour, he described his trip as one of the most interesting he had experienced in ten years of cricket administration. Malcolm believes that over the next five years women's cricket in China will emerge strongly, with the possibility of qualification for the 2013 Women's World Cup in India. For the men's game anything is possible, even the prospect of China playing in the 2019 World Cup in England. These are incredible possibilities but, with the right level of external support and commitment from the Chinese authorities, anything is within reach.

**Challenges for the game**

In financial terms, in membership strength, in public interest and in playing standards, cricket is in great shape. But no business and no sport can be immune from threats to undermine it. The world is changing at a bewildering pace and there is no guarantee that future generations will share their predecessors' fondness for the game unless cricket stays relevant as an athletic pursuit to attract players. It has to also stay relevant as a form of entertainment to attract spectators and global media coverage.

The challenge is to find the balance between innovation and change to maintain cricket's intrinsic qualities of fairness, competition and integrity, without losing its contemporary appeal. Twenty20 cricket is part of the answer at the moment, combining great skills with fantastic entertainment, which has proved popular with a younger audience who may not have seen a cricket match a few years ago. However, innovation and game development must not be at the expense of Test cricket which itself has been more lively and entertaining in the past few years than ever before. Test cricket is the purest form of the game and requires techniques and skills which are not necessarily tested or exposed in a Twenty20 game or a 50-over match. Fortunately, Test cricket today is as popular as it has ever been; it is essential that the ICC and its member boards ensure that a proper balance is maintained between the different forms of the game, and that the integrity of Test cricket is preserved.

Maintaining high standards of conduct on the field of play has always been a cornerstone of cricket's reputation. Compared to any other sport, these standards are very high and there are processes in place to make sure they stay that way. The ICC has a strong code of conduct to ensure that standards are maintained. The MCC and the ICC have championed the drive to maintain the unique culture of cricket through their Spirit of Cricket initiative. From time to time I am asked what the Spirit of the Game is. Cricket is unique in that it should be played not only within the Laws but also within the Spirit of the Game. This includes the players behaving in a manner which should not bring the game into disrepute, not disputing the umpires decision, respect for not only one's own team but also the opponents, not to indulge in cheating or sharp practice, to respect the game's traditional values and much more which make cricket so special. Lord Harris, Captain of England in 1878–79 summed this up:

> You do well to love cricket, because it is more free from anything sordid, anything dishonourable than any game in the world. To play it keenly, generously, self-sacrificingly is a moral lesson in itself, and the classroom is God's air and sunshine. Foster it, my brothers, so that it may attract all who find time to play it, protect it from anything that will sully it, so it may grow in favour with all men.[6]

Cricket must continue to strive to preserve its unique culture.

The ICC and its members acknowledge that cricket has a social responsibility to play a positive role in the societies in which it operates. The ICC works closely with UNAIDS to promote awareness of issues surrounding HIV and AIDS, using the sport as a platform. Cricket is a powerful platform and is supported by iconic cricketers such as Sachin Tendulkar, Muttiah Muralitharan and others who have freely given their time to help overcome the social stigma of HIV and AIDS imbedded in some societies. Cricket was the first international sport to come forward to raise money for the victims of the Asian Tsunami and the earthquake which devastated parts of South Asia in recent years. Cricket must continue to reach out to help make a difference to the lives of millions of the under privileged around the world who love the sport.

Other sports, notably football, have suffered problems with racism among players and spectators. Fortunately, cricket has not had to deal with this apart from rare and isolated incidents. Even so, these have resulted in the ICC strengthening its anti-racism code and adopting a zero tolerance approach.

Drugs have pervaded and diminished several other high profile sports. Fortunately, cricket is deemed to be a low risk sport for drug abuse, but there have been occasions when high profile players have failed drugs tests. The ICC is a signatory to the WADA code for the events it organizes and is working with members to educate their players, who are role models for millions of children, to play clean and stay clean.

Player workload is an issue that has to be carefully managed by national cricket boards. Players are the most valuable stakeholders in the game and spectators want to see the biggest stars and the most exciting players performing at their peak. There has to be a proper balance between the volume of cricket each country plays and the financial benefits flowing to the members from staging matches. There is now a future tours programme which maps out the international fixtures the ten Full Member countries will play each year up to 2012. This should allow the Boards, coaches and managers to manage the workloads of their players by incorporating appropriate rest and recovery time into the fixture schedules, or by expanding the pool of players they select from for different playing commitments. Too many senior players have recently complained of work load pressures; their Boards ignore these concerns at their peril.

The ICC membership is a rich mix of cultural diversity, which is a real strength of the game and a massive unifying factor. Cricket cuts across social and political divides and should be used as a tool to foster goodwill and to break down barriers. As Nelson Mandela said, 'Cricket speaks in languages far beyond that of politicians.'[7] The resumption of cricketing ties between India and Pakistan is a superb example of this and the cooperation and collective will demonstrated by the countries of the Caribbean coming together for the 2007 Cricket World Cup is another.

It is inevitable that because of its enormous popularity cricket and politics will mix and cricket will be used as a political tool by governments from time to time. One of my first challenges as President of the ICC was to bring about the resumption of cricketing ties between India and Pakistan: the two nations had not played against each other for a long time and there was genuine concern in India about playing in Pakistan. My message to the boards and politicians was simple: 'start playing cricket and you will see that the game will take over'. Another challenge was the pressure from a number of governments on the ICC to suspend Zimbabwe from international cricket. The ICC refused to bow to these pressures. These governments were not prepared, at that time, to stop their players from playing against Zimbabwe but wanted the ICC to take a political decision on a matter which went far beyond the game. I was clear in my mind that it was for politicians to make political decisions; the ICC's mandate is to protect and promote the game.

## Conclusion

Cricket is a sport with centuries of tradition and a rich history. But a brief look at that history at international level shows that until recently it has mostly been confined to competition between a handful of nations. Even 100 years since the ICC was formed, there are only ten countries in the world that play Test cricket.

Cricket has ambitions to become a truly global game and is now being played by more men and women in more countries than at any time in its history. But it still needs to be nurtured and managed by the ICC to make sure the vast potential can be captured and sustained.

Bridging the divide between the best playing nations and the developing nations will be extremely difficult. Unlike, say, football, cricket requires the learning of new skills that do not come as naturally as running, jumping and kicking a ball. But there is now an infrastructure in place to reduce the gulf and encourage new nations to reach for the top.

Today, cricket in all Full Member countries, with the exception of Zimbabwe, is stronger than ever before. England's Ashes win in 2005 hugely increased the interest in the game not only in the United Kingdom but around the world. Every India and Pakistan match is watched by over 500 million television viewers, and punters bet over $300 million on the outcome of each one day match. Australia's continued dominance in the game has been incredible and it has set standards for other countries to aspire to. A lot of people have complained about Bangladesh's elevation to Test status: history has shown that teams playing Test cricket for the first time struggle for many years at this level. I have no doubt that with the passion and the fanatical following that exists for the game in the country it will be only a matter of time before Bangladesh's performance becomes more competitive and consistent. South Africa, New Zealand and Sri Lanka all continue to enjoy increased support and the popularity of the game continues to grow. West Indies has gone through a drought, unable to win a Test series in recent years, unlike the 1970s and 1980s when they dominated world cricket. I believe that the legacy of the 2007 World Cup has started a process which will see the gradual resurgence of the West Indies as one of the most exciting and attractive teams in the world. Even in Zimbabwe, where the game has been embroiled in the political strife within the country, cricket is being played by more children, mostly black, then ever before and the young Zimbabwe team will continue to improve and increasingly challenge the other Full Members in the one day game. However, I do not believe that Zimbabwe should return to Test cricket until its players have had sufficient exposure to 3- and 4-day first class matches against 'A' and first class teams from the Test playing countries and start winning against these sides.

The game is in good shape. It has overcome the stigma of corruption from the early 2000s; it is played fiercely but in good spirit and the curses of racism and drugs are marginal threats.

There is huge demand from broadcaster, sponsors and the cricket-watching public for exciting cricket. While the one day game and Twenty20 are popular with fans, Test cricket remains strong. Cricket today is being followed and played by more people and in more countries than ever before. What better barometer could there be to gauge the health of the game?

## Notes

[1] See Bailey, *A History of Cricket.*
[2] All historical details above are from volumes of the *Wisden Cricketers Almanack.*
[3] As told to the author by a former Colonial Administrator in 2006.
[4] See, for example, Haigh, *The Cricket War.*
[5] Rupert Murdoch's News Corporation bought a controlling stake in Sky in 1983 and re-launched as Sky Television in 1989, but it made heavy losses until 1992 when BSkyB (Sky and BSB merged in 1990) acquired the rights to broadcast Premier League Soccer games for US$465 million. Anand and Attea, 'News Corporation', 8. Murdoch has always placed great emphasis on sport. In 1999, for instance, News Corporation owned the Los Angeles Dodgers baseball club and had shares in the New York Knicks and Los Angeles Lakers basketball clubs, and the New York Rangers. In September 1998, BSkyB launched a take over bid for Manchester United, the world's richest football club, which was blocked by the British Mergers and Monopolies Commission on grounds that it was 'anti-competitive' in broadcasting. Rowe, 'To Serve and To Sell: Media Sport and Cultural Citizenship', 186.
[6] Lord Harris, founder member of Imperial Cricket Council and Governor General of Bombay (1890–95), quoted in Roberts, 'Cricket as Global as Honourable', 6.
[7] Nelson Mandela addressing the England cricket team in Soweto in 1995.

## References

Anand, Bharat and Kate Attea. 'News Corporation'. Harvard Business School Case No. 9-702-425. Boston, MA: Harvard Business School Publishing, Rev. June 27, 2003.
Bailey, Trevor. *A History of Cricket*. London: George Allen & Unwin, 1979.
Haigh, Gideon. *The Cricket War: The Inside Story of Kerry Packer's World*. Melbourne: Text, 1993.

Roberts, Michael, 'Cricket as Global as Honourable'. In *Essaying Cricket: Sri Lanka and Beyond*, edited by Michael Roberts. Colombo: Vijitha Yapa, 2006.

Rowe, David, 'To Serve and To Sell: Media Sport and Cultural Citizenship.' Paper presented at How you Play the Game: First International Conference on Sports and Human Rights, Sydney, September 1–3, 1999.

# 'Bombay Sport Exchange': cricket, globalization and the future

Nalin Mehta[a]*, Jon Gemmell[b] and Dominic Malcolm[c]

[a]School of Social Sciences, La Trobe University, Melbourne, Australia; [b]Kennet School, Thatcham, Berkshire, UK; [c]School of Sport and Exercise Sciences, Loughborough University, Loughborough, UK

## Indian Rupees and 'God's Air': cricket and the Indian Premier League

Lord Harris, Governor General of colonial Bombay (1890–95) and co-founder of what was then the Imperial Cricket Conference captured for posterity the centrality of cricket in the British Empire when he declared that to play 'cricket is more remote than anything sordid, anything dishonourable than any game in the world. To play it... honorably... is a moral lesson in itself and the classroom is god's air and sunshine.'[1] As the essays in this collection delineate, cricket had a special place in the idea of the Empire, encompassing notions of muscular Christianity, 'gentlemanliness' and what was later called the 'games ethic'. Cricket's early lineage continues to define its present form across the former Empire, though the meanings attached to it differ between locales. Had he been alive today, Lord Harris would have fond that the 'god's air' of cricket now smells of Indian rupees. That India has controlled the purse strings of global cricket for the past decade is well documented.[2] On February 20, 2008, India Inc., in one of the most visible manifestations of the growing influence of the Indian economy, bought into the Board of Control for Cricket in India's (BCCI) new Indian Premier League (IPL) in an audacious manoeuvre that could completely change the global dynamics of the game on several registers. The IPL experiment has deep implications for debates about post-colonialism and globalization touched upon in this collection.

The facts speak for themselves. The genesis of IPL – a Twenty20 club League composed of players from across the cricket playing world – is the Indian Board's response to the rebel Indian Cricket League (ICL) of television mogul Subhash Chandra.[3] Frustrated at being denied broadcasting rights in India by the BCCI, Subhash Chandra, who runs India's largest private television network, did 'a Kerry Packer'.[4] Just like the Australian tycoon who, denied television rights by the Australian Cricket Board in 1977, hit back with a new cricket tournament to fuel his Channel 9, Chandra in 2007 kick-started his own private cricket Twenty20 league for his Zee TV. The ICL, with headhunters like former England captain Tony Grieg and former Indian captain Kapil Dev, hired young Indian players from across the country and about 60 non-Indian players in a total player pool of 135. The League is as global as it is national, consisting of big names from the West Indies, New Zealand, Australia, Zimbabwe and an entire team made up of international Pakistani stars.[5] In and of itself, the rebel ICL was a stark illustration of the fact that the financial centre of the game has shifted from the Anglo-Saxon boardrooms of England and Australia to a new home in the dusty plains of India. In 1977, Packer's revolt, riding on Australian dollars and the muscle of Australian television, had given birth to day-night games, coloured clothing and an entirely new capitalist orientation that was at first derided as 'pyjama cricket' but was later to define the game itself.[6] In 1977, India did not have a truly national television network, let alone a television mogul.[7] By 2007, India had emerged as a new global 'media capital', its television industry, along with China, increasingly becoming a centre of global televisual flows. Subhash Chandra's gambit to change cricket rode on the money power of this new and burgeoning industry.[8] Where, in 1977, the best international cricketers had been bought with Australian dollars, now they were bought with Indian rupees. Just as Packer had bet on the then emerging one-day format of the game, Chandra was placing his confidence in the innovation of Twenty20 cricket.

The BCCI, sensing the immense challenge, responded by banning ICL-contracted players – a stance that has the potential to change the nature of the game worldwide. The progress of its IPL so far, 'cricket's biggest money-spinner of all time',[9] sheds more light on the wider trends of globalization and post-colonial discourse that this collection has outlined. The IPL, built around eight Indian city-based clubs, borrows its format from World Series Baseball, the NFL draft and the English Premier League.[10] The sheer money numbers, all generated from within India, make for mind-boggling reading. By February 2008, $1.7 billion had been committed from the sale of global media rights and team franchises.[11] Sony Entertainment Television and World Sports Group bought the television rights for $1.03 billion for ten years and the construction company DLF bought the title and trophy sponsorship for $50 million for five years.[12] The eight team-owners – among them India's richest tycoon, Mukesh Ambani of Reliance Industries, Bollywood's reigning superstar Shahrukh Khan,[13] and UB Group's Vijay Mallya, a liquor baron who already owns an airline and a Formula-1 team – combined to pay the BCCI $723.69 million for ten-year franchises,[14] and further paid in the region of another $32 million in the first round of cricket's inaugural player auction to decide the composition of the eight teams.[15] Held in a five-star hotel in India's financial capital of Mumbai on 20 February 2008, the auction captured the imagination of India's media, with all the major newspapers making it the lead story the next day. The headlines are revealing. Tapping into the perceived national frenzy over cricket, *The Times of India's* front page declared that, 'Cricket Just Got Even Bigger',[16] *The Indian Express* announced that, 'It Doesn't Get Any Bigger'[17] and *The Asian Age* noted that 'Stars Shine at Pathbreaking Cricket Auction in Mumbai'.[18] But in the city that houses the Bombay Stock Exchange, it was *The Hindustan Times* edition that best captured the linkage between the new Indian economy and cricket, its front-page headline writer dubbing the cricket auction as the new 'Bombay Sport Exchange'.[19] In a game that has intrinsically been linked to notions of gentlemanliness and morality, with commercial factors their antithesis,[20] this was capitalism at its best, but capitalism Indian style. Despite the protestations of purists, there is no doubt that cricket has long since been turned into a consumer sport and the IPL auction where players were sold as commodities completes the circle. The buying and selling of players is hardly a novel innovation in sport – the IPL is only following the lead of football and, to some extent, the commercial practices of baseball and basketball– but in cricket, with its immense cultural baggage, this is unprecedented.

The make-up of the auction and the price that Indian and non-Indian players commanded at the end of the 7.5 hour-long first auction make for interesting reading. Of the 78 players that went under the hammer, 51 were not Indian. The team owners spent as much as $14 million on the 27 Indians – an average of $518,518 per player.[21] The 51 foreign players attracted $18 million – an average of $352,941 per player.[22] The stark difference between the prices commanded by Indians as opposed to foreign players is revealing, for not even the best apologists of Indian cricket argue that India's cricketers are inherently more talented simply by virtue of their being Indian. In a country where cricket is an intrinsically nationalistic activity – and hence domestic-level cricket competitions run to empty stadiums and virtually zero television coverage – the buyers of cricket were simply off-setting the challenge of establishing new club loyalties by investing in the one thing they knew works: Indian nationalism. Though partly a consequence of league rules which restricted franchises to just four overseas players per season, this explains why six of the top ten most expensive players were Indians and even young players like Rohit Sharma, Manoj Tiwary, Robin Uthappa and Gautam Gambhir – who between them have played just one international season – commanded higher prices than legends of the game like Australian captain Ricky Ponting, Mathew Hayden and Adam Gilchrist. As *The Indian Express* noted:

> The biggest pointer towards the bidders going by nationalist sentiments is the case of Ishant Sharma. The [19-year-old] Delhi fast bowler, who has come up by leaps and bounds over the last couple of months [in India's 2007–08 tour of Australia] went for an incredible Rs. 3.7 crore [$925,000]. Chaminda Vaas, one of the stingiest bowlers world cricket has known over the last decade was picked up by Hyderabad for Rs. 80 lakh [$200,000].[23]

This explains why in an auction of the world's best players, India's one-day and Twenty20 World Cup winning captain Mahendra Singh Dhoni emerged with the highest individual price tag of $1.5 million.[24] In a country where cricketers are the biggest brand names in the consumer economy,[25] the IPL's team managers were gambling more on the brand value that their stars could command, than on their cricket skills. As another reporter noted:

> The verdict was unanimous. Be Indian, Buy Indian. In a trend that is sure to startle even those who have been tracking this business closely, and anger some Australian cricketers, India's cricketers lapped up the lion's share of the money that was spent. It defied cricketing logic that Yusuf Pathan was sold for more than Ponting, that someone like Ishant Sharma ... very much a greenhorn still, went close to a million dollars.[26]

But the ethics of the consumer economy had at least as much to do with the auction as pure nationalism. The fact that Australian Andrew Symonds commanded the second highest price of $1.3 million, well above other greats of the game, is significant. The auction was held in the middle of a bitter international series between India and Australia where Andrew Symonds' allegation of racist slurs by the Indian bowler Harbhajan Singh almost resulted in the tour being called off. The implications of that episode are examined later, but for now it is enough to note that Symonds, who emerged as the 'villain' of the piece in Indian media discourse, was valued by the IPL's buyers at least as much for his brand recall value as for his cricket skills. As the *Times of India* noted, 'it was a good day for the bad boys who make headlines and attract eyeballs'.[27]

A second auction was held on 11 March 2008 for U-19 players and non-Indians left over in the first round. In the second round 18 additional players were sold and the implications of the two auctions for cricket are immense.[28] In a country which only embraced the free market in 1991 with then Finance Minister Manmohan Singh's policy of economic liberalization,[29] the auction was seen as yet another offshoot of an economy that has been booming ever since. As senior BCCI official I.S. Bindra put it: 'This is the first time that market forces are determining the price of a player and not the selectors. This is how free market economy works.'[30] Long before the IPL, the 'free market economy' had already made Indian cricketers the highest paid in the world, but the IPL dwarfed everything that came before. As the *Times of India* noted:

> [Mahendra Singh] Dhoni [Indian one-day captain] will get Rs. 37.5 lakh [Rs. 3.7 million] for one T20 match [in the Indian Premier League] – over ten times what he gets for every Test he plays [for India]. Looked at another way, a Delhi University professor would earn a total of Rs. 2.2 crore [Rs. 22 million] over a career of about 35 years. Dhoni will make twice that amount for a fortnight of match play.[31]

The response to the IPL and ICL by non-Indian players is particularly instructive. Both these Leagues are based on the short Twenty20 format which until recently was decried by Australian players (and indeed Indian officials), so much so that in the middle of the first Twenty20 World Cup in 2007, Adam Gilchrist argued that Australia had so far not taken the format too seriously.[32] Yet, just five months later Gilchrist, after having announced his retirement from the international game, was arguing in favour of the League:

> I have come to realize the importance of the Twenty20 format in cricket, and would like to be involved in it. This is a format for the future, and the IPL would help launch this version in world cricket, just like the World Series in the late 1970s launched One-Day cricket. I understand the concerns of various boards, who do not want to see promising careers being cut short by the league, and am certain that the concerned boards will be able to handle the situation sensibly.[33]

Gilchrist, of course, was to win a $700,000 pay packet from the IPL just a week later,[34] a factor which may well explain why leading international cricketers are now embracing the new format. Another former Australian player, Michael Kasprowicz, has made it clear that joining the Indian Cricket League was a 'no-brainer', on account of its financial incentives.

The movement of international players to Indian shores brings with it deeper dilemmas for the global game. Countries like New Zealand, for instance, which have a small base of cricketers, are already reeling from the adverse impact their players moving to India will have on the domestic game. As David Lloyd points out:

> I can tell you that the whole country [New Zealand] is reeling with the news that it is going to lose so many players and so many experienced players. I don't think New Zealand is a country that can lose all that expertise and experience.
>   I think there are a lot of questions that need to be asked … it seems at this stage that it is going to be very disruptive to the rest of cricket.
>   It may be early days and we may find out the whys and wherefores of the IPL and where it fits into the global scheme of things. But it will isolate the vulnerable countries … West Indies and New Zealand. All of us in cricket are watching this space: what are you going to do in India to compensate the rest of the game and to legislate the rest of the game to ensure that it is ongoing?[35]

That this statement was no exaggeration was proved when the rebel ICL virtually broke the back of Bangladeshi cricket by signing up 13 of its international players to create a new team called Dhaka Warriors in September 2008. The players, who signed up for roughly $200,000 each for a three-year period, essentially did so for the financial benefits that were hard to come by in their home country.[36] Under pressure from the BCCI, though, the Bangladesh Board banned them for ten years, effectively ending their international careers.[37] It was the latest indication yet that what is essentially a feud between two private leagues in India – albeit one with official patronage from the BCCI – is now threatening the future of global cricket, at least as we know it.

Similar concerns have also been expressed by Darren Lehmann in Australia who has argued that if Cricket Australia continues to ban those signing up for the rebel ICL, Australian cricket will end up losing large numbers of players.[38] In this context, there is also a great deal of concern in Pakistan. Pakistani banks, traditionally the main employers of Pakistani cricketers, have already told players that they will not be paid salaries for the period that they play for the ICL, effectively banishing them from first-class Pakistani cricket. As Osman Samiuddin notes:

> 'The BCCI is the only board to benefit financially from the IPL and it is the only board to stand to lose if the ICL thrives ... This is the insanity of it, that a TV rights tangle in an overcharged, loud, brash industry is threatening relations between players and boards, players' livelihoods and domestic cricket around the world.'[39]

The pitfalls in the new Leagues are many, but so are the opportunities. From a historical perspective, it is too early to pass judgment but certainly the fact that an entire team of Pakistani players – Lahore Badshahs [Kings] – will now virtually permanently play in India, after years of absolutely no cricket due to political rivalries, is not without social and cultural significance.

It is also noteworthy that in the 2008 season, England, the original home of cricket, was the only country to have stayed away from the two Indian Leagues. The reluctance among England's cricket administrators to embrace the Indian Leagues is at least as much to do with reluctance to embrace the new era of Indian control over cricket as with genuine problems over scheduling. As Mike Marqusee put it: 'On the English side, there's an incredible resentment of the Indians' rise. The English need to accept this demographic reality, which inevitably translates into superior financial power.'[40] On the other hand, Andrew Flintoff says, the IPL was not a priority for English players because it interfered with county cricket during the summer and England's international commitments in winter.[41] That may well change in the future. England's most flamboyant player, Kevin Peitersen, made no secret of his ire at being denied the chance of playing in the lucrative IPL[42] and the pressure put by the players, in particular the UK's Professional Cricketers' Association, forced the England and Wales Cricket Board to allow its players to play in IPL's 2009 season, subject to an agreement on scheduling.[43] A new English Premier League is also on the cards.

With the IPL emerging as a clear success after its first season,[44] one thing is clear: whilst talented non-English cricketers looking to make money once gravitated towards the English county circuit, now they will turn towards India and its new Leagues. The IPL's future depended on whether it could succeed in creating club loyalties in a land where cricket has always been identified by its nationalist affiliations. Critics asked questions like whether Mumbai crowds, for instance, would be persuaded to cheer for a Shane Warne against a Sachin Tendulkar at the Wankhede?[45] That question now seems to have been answered. At least, in the first season, the IPL was a huge commercial success and most IPL crowds did cheer for their city teams but it is perhaps too early to make a definitive judgment. The bigger question is what would happen to the longer and traditional forms of the game after the IPL's success.[46] There are no easy answers and there are no predictive models, but the fact that the IPL could be invented in India in 2008 offers a unique case study for the processes of globalization.[47]

Already, talks have been held between the ICC and the rebel ICL for a merger of the two Indian leagues, and an international Champions League Twenty20 tournament with the best ranked club sides from the five main cricket playing countries was planned for December 2008. This was eventually cancelled due to the terrorist attack on Mumbai on November 26 2008 but the planning process for this event was instructive. Building upon

IPL's marketing success, the Australian, Indian and South African boards invited the two top teams from five countries to compete and ESPN-Star Sports paid $975 million for broadcast and marketing rights for the Champions League for ten years – the most ever for a cricket tournament on a per-game basis. The fact that Indians control the levers of power was underscored once again when England's Kent County Cricket Club, which qualified for the tournament, could not participate because of the BCCI's ban on Indian Cricket League players. Kent has two of them playing for it and despite the England's board's protests, Kent was left out.[48]

### 'Indian Cricket Council': The 'Asian Bloc' and 'Tough Luck Globalization'

West Indians, as Hilary McD. Beckles tells us (see also Westall in this collection), are fond of proclaiming that 'cricket is we', 'an expression laden with ontological significance that is richly supported by the writings of their most gifted intellectuals'.[49] The essays contained herein illustrate the validity of that statement to the global cricket world. The IPL, in that sense, can also be seen as a derivative of changing economic equations in the global order of power. Paul Kennedy has noted that in 1790 India accounted for 23% of world manufacturing output and Britain just 1.8%. By 1947, when the British left India, Britain accounted for 23% of the world's manufacturing output while India's share had been reduced to 1.8%.[50] In some respects we are in the midst of a gradual shift back to the old global economic order. It is no accident that these figures were alluded to by Indian Finance Minister P. Chidambaram in the presentation of the Union Budget in Parliament on February 29, 2008, as he spelt out his economic vision for India in the current financial year.[51] India's growing financial power is the bedrock of its increased control over world cricket. This is not to argue that India's growing economic power automatically translates into sporting power. That would be manifestly untrue. For instance, India's economic power does not translate in to power in soccer, hockey or other sports. But in cricket it has found a vehicle for post-colonial assertion. India has money but the aggressiveness of its cricket managers grows fundamentally from a belief that the time has come to change the old order which they see as a vestige of the colonial past. This is why the BCCI's Vice President and the brains behind the IPL, Lalit Modi, explains his gambit in one sentence: 'We are trying to change the world order.'[52]

For the International Cricket Council, this is nothing short of revolutionary. The ICC, after all, was called the Imperial Cricket Conference until 1965. Its founding members, England and Australia enjoyed veto powers until as late as 1992. In such an organization, so closely rooted in its colonial past, the new Indian challenge has not surprisingly been met with a great deal of initial resentment from the old power centres. This is a fact noted by many Australian and English commentators.[53] Writing, for instance, on the power of the 'new Asian bloc' and the possibility of BCCI president Sharad Pawar taking over the ICC, one English journalist typified unease by decrying what he called the rise of the 'Asian bloc' as 'bad for cricket':

> With the Asian bloc unbreakable, *all it would take for a Pawar victory would be a shifting of support of the African contingent, and then Pandora's Box really would be cracked open … With Pawar installed at the head of the ICC, the way would be cleared for the takeover of the ICC* that has long been threatened by the frustrated Indians, who represent 70% of the game's income and whose early exit from the World Cup conveniently distanced them from most – if not all – of the tournament's myriad failings.[54] (Emphasis is original)

He was alluding to the commercial problems of the 2007 World Cup, outlined by Boria Majumdar in this collection, but it is a comment that typifies the ongoing debates within cricket over power and hegemony. As one Indian novelist responded immediately in the blogosphere:

This is a remarkable sentence: the first half is unexamined prejudice and the second half is incoherent ... India has held the presidency of the ICC before, when Jagmohan Dalmiya occupied that post, and the end of his tenure saw the ICC become a much richer body without becoming an Indian principality. So 'The Indians are coming' motif is silly. The second half of the sentence seems to be based on the odd proposition that the more successful a team was in the last World Cup, the more responsible it was for the tournament's shortcomings. If India is conveniently distanced from the tournament's failings because it got knocked out so quickly, the Australians who won the World Cup, must, on this argument, be closely associated with its failure. How does that work? (Perhaps the Indians knew, in their sly Oriental way, that the tournament was going to be a disaster and artfully lost early to avoid prolonged association.)

> ... *The genteel, unequal world of the MCC and the Imperial Cricket Conference isn't one that Indians feel nostalgic about.* It contributed nothing to the development of the modern game ... *For a discussion of the qualities most needed to manage the contemporary game, the 'old world' is not a good place to begin.*[55] (Emphasis is original).

He concluded by writing, 'The Indians are not coming. They are already here.'[56] That one sentence brings within it the entire gamut of post-colonial politics and tensions that continue to define modern cricket.

When Jagmohan Dalmiya became the ICC's Chairman in 1997, he drastically changed the balance of power, first by uncorking the consumer potential of the Indian cricket economy by piggybacking on the satellite revolution of India, and secondly by drastically increasing the voting power of the Associate Members. In the ICC, the permanent members had always enjoyed two votes each, as opposed to the single vote enjoyed by the Associate Member countries. Dalmiya increased his political influence by increasing the membership of associate countries manifold. When Dalmiya became head of the ICC, the body had 20 Associate Members, only five of which were from Asia. By the time his tenure ended, the ICC had more than 70 Associate Members, 14 of which were from Asia. His rationale for the expansion was that he wanted to globalize cricket. As he put it:

> Cricket has a potential to be a global game but for 90 years it was left to the individual national associations to come up to world standards so they could be given Test status. Only Zimbabwe made the cut and later Bangladesh under my tenure. Unless money was spent on the newer countries the game would not go anywhere. I thought it was necessary to (go) continent-by-continent to fuse funds into the national associations to spread the game and that helped us (the ICC) out.[57]

What he does not say is that the new globalization strategy also 'helped' the Indian administrators to increase their influence within the ICC because the newer members were beholden to them for their position in the new structure of international cricket. Dalmiya saw the traditional power centres of the game – England and Australia – as hindrances from the colonial past and it is clear that he was driven by a post-colonial impulse to overturn the power order of the ICC. According to him:

> At that time we [India and Pakistan] almost never received our due share ... They [the ICC] were a corrupt kind of a setup ... basically it was England, Australia and New Zealand. India and Pakistan were just two members. South Africa was in exile at that time. It was more a colony or more a small kind of a club and we felt it was necessary to change all that.[58]

This was a clear strategy. International tournaments began to be organized in countries like Canada and Malaysia simply to keep the Associate Members happy. While they were meant to spread the game in new catchment areas, they were also meant to increase the voting power of the Indian contingent.[59] Of the International Cricket Council's total earnings, 80% are now estimated to come from India[60] and the Indian cricket board is now the richest cricket body in the world.[61] The BCCI, for instance, has begun to organize international cricket tournaments primarily for Indian television audiences. A good example of this was the September 2006 one-day international tri-series at Kuala Lumpur, Malaysia, which the Indian board organized after spending US$4 million to install floodlights in a stadium with a capacity of only 7,000, and then paid the Australian and West Indian cricket boards US$1 million each for every match in which their teams played.[62] Similarly, in May 2006, the BCCI won the hosting rights for the 2011 World Cup out of turn because of its financial muscle. According to media reports, the BCCI out-witted the Australian Board by offering financial help to the West Indies Cricket Board in return for its vote in the bidding process.[63]

In analysing India's rise as the centre of world cricket, it is possible to draw a parallel from theoretical frameworks in studies of the media and globalization, and in particular, the work of Michael Curtin's notion of what he calls 'media capitals'. At the heart of debates over media capitalism are concerns over location – centres with concentration of resources and their spheres of circulation which lead to concerns over culture, identity and power. Curtin's 'media capitals' are geographic centres which transcend national boundaries and become global. These are places where resources, talent and production processes concentrate based on the inherent logic of capitalism: the accumulation of capital. Creative talent migrates towards 'media capitals' and the ruthless logic of efficiency fuels perpetual circuits of expansion. There is a socio-cultural dimension to this. For the logic of capitalist expansion to work, it needs to address local variations such as language, cultural issues, identities, communal imaginaries, etc., but primarily this is a process central to capitalism. Curtin uses extensive research on the Chinese media industry to show the emergence of cities like Hong Kong as new 'media capitals' and a re-ordering of global flows of information. Within the same framework is a city like Mumbai which each year produces more films than Hollywood, though its financial output is smaller. There are different reasons for different cities emerging as centres of global capitalism but 'capitals' wax and wane. For instance, Curtin says, it was unthinkable in 1960s America that Detroit would cease to be the centre of the world's car industry, but the rise of Japanese industry changed the balance irrevocably. In the same vein, he argues that the global media industry is witnessing the rise of new 'media capitals' which are shifting the balance from America to new centres in Asia. Curtin's theory of 'media capitals' is specific to cities and he confines himself essentially to China. However, if we stretch the same principle to cricket then there is no doubt that India is now the new 'cricket capital' of the world. Nalin Mehta has argued elsewhere that India is now a new 'media capital' in a global world and, in this collection, that its rise as a 'cricket capital' is intrinsically linked to this development.[64] Its capitalist base has turned it into a new centre which cricketing talent migrates towards (in terms of players as well as coaches; see Wagg and Ugra in this collection) and its financial strength underpins the economy of the game. This is why Australian players like Brett Lee have begun to learn Hindi to become more marketable in Indian television commercials.[65] In that sense, Boria Majumdar has a point when he argues that:

> modern Indian cricket is far closer to being a postcolonial sport after having disengaged itself from the colonial past. Given that the nerve-centre of world cricket has firmly shifted to the east, that the subcontinent can easily overpower Western nations to win rights to host the World Cup competitions and the fact that cricket in India has a financial muscle comparable to no one else demonstrates that cricket in India has discontinued all connections to the colonial world.[66]

But the colonial past is not easy to wish away. And what of the other cricket nations? Cricket is certainly not an Indian monopoly. The power balances may have changed, but cricketing nations remain interdependently linked. In this respect, it is instructive to look at the narratives surrounding the two biggest controversies that have hit international cricket since 2007: the Pakistani 'walkout' in August 2006, and the charges made by Australian cricketers in 2008 of racism against Indian bowler Harbhajan Singh.

Let us look at these chronologically. When Pakistan forfeited the fourth Test match at the Oval against England on 21 August 2006, citing discrimination by Australian umpire Darrell Hair, it ignited a row that split the cricket world down the middle. This was the first time that an international side had forfeited a game by walking out of the ground after a dispute with an umpire. Hair and West Indian umpire Billy Doctrove had accused the Pakistani bowlers of ball-tampering, a charge later found specious by an ICC committee, but when he was penalized and removed from the ICC's elite panel of umpires for this decision, his defence was instructive. At a tribunal hearing in London, his lawyer, Robert Griffiths QC, accused the ICC of bowing to the power of the Asian bloc (led by India) and went so far as to accuse the Indian and Pakistani Boards of racism. As he argued:

> Darrell Hair's case is that he was treated the way he was because the ICC bowed to the racially discriminatory pressure that was brought to bear on it by the Asian bloc. The Asian bloc is dominant in cricket, sometimes it uses that dominance inappropriately. Everyone knows it, but most are afraid to say so.[67]

Griffith was referring to the fact that the ICC's three-man panel that penalized Hair consisted of then Pakistan Board chairman Nasim Ashraf, the New Zealand Board chairman who had earlier supported action against the Australian, and the then Zimbabwe Cricket President Peter Chingoka.[68] The ICC immediately refuted the charges of racism and bias and whether the charges had substance or not need not detain us here. For our purposes the very fact that such a charge could be made against the 'Asian bloc' by an Australian umpire in 2006 is itself a reflection of the complete changeover in power equations in a body where the Australians held veto powers until just a decade before.

The second example is that of the racism row ignited by Australia's Andrew Symonds who accused the Indian spinner Harbhajan Singh of calling him a 'monkey' in the third Test at Sydney on 2–6 January 2008. After a hearing by the ICC match referee Mike Proctor, Singh was found guilty on charges of racism and faced a short-term ban. The Indians responded by arguing that there was no evidence of Singh's guilt. Sachin Tendulkar, the only other Indian within earshot when the alleged slur occurred, vouched for his team-mate and there was no video or audio evidence to substantiate the charges, although three of Symonds' colleagues testified to hearing the comment. Singh, in fact, argued that instead of calling Symonds a 'monkey' he had uttered an Indian profanity, *teri maa kee* [your mother's . . . ] which sounded similar to the word 'monkey'. Of course, it is possible to argue that this was worse and there is also a debate about what constitutes a racist slur itself. In the post-match hearing though it ultimately boiled down to the testimony of Australian players against the testimony of Indian players, and Proctor decided against Singh after a marathon eight-hour hearing that went on into the early hours of the morning.[69] The guilty verdict created such uproar in India over the next few days that in virtually all news channels and newspapers this became the primary story of national import. As with the Hair ball-tampering incident at the Oval, what started off as a small spat on the cricket field became a question of national honour.[70] Faced with such media pressure, the Indian Board and the team dug in and refused to continue on to the next tour game in Canberra.[71] To save the tour, the ICC was forced to suspend the sentence, pending a final appeal hearing which was scheduled for three weeks later despite an ICC stipulation for such appeals to be held within seven days.[72] A judge from New Zealand was especially appointed to hear the appeal in a federal court in Adelaide and what followed is instructive. Australian and Indian officials worked behind the scenes to defuse the crisis but the Indian Board made it clear that if the racism charges were not dropped the tour would be off. It was speculated that the BCCI had chartered a plane to take its players home in case the hearing did not result in a favourable verdict. It was even suggested that the Sri Lankans, who made up the third team in a triangular tournament, would also abandon the tour in support of the Indians.[73]

Cricket Australia found itself in a difficult situation because if the Indians carried out their threat, the Australians faced the prospect of a $60 million lawsuit from broadcast partner ESPN. This was ESPN's Indian arm and if it sued successfully, Cricket Australia told its players, it would take another ten years to recoup the losses. Therefore, the five Australian players who were witnesses in the case were forced to change their stand and Singh was let off. As one player told a newspaper on conditions of anonymity:

> The thing that pisses us off is that it shows how much power India has. The Aussie guys aren't going to make it up. The players are frustrated because this shows how much influence India has, because of the wealth they generate. Money talks.[74]

What influenced the Australian U-turn was the possibility of their wages being slashed after an Indian walk-out plus the 'welcome mat of the lucrative Indian Premier League being withdrawn'.[75] The media discourse in England and Australia followed the same lines as that in the row between Pakistan and Darrell Hair. Once again the motif of this discourse was the spectre of 'Indian/Asian' control over the game. *The Sydney Morning Herald* described the Australian retreat as 'Cricket's Day of Shame'[76] and one writer went so far as to sarcastically announce, 'welcome to the era of the Indian Cricket Council'.[77] As Chloe Saltau and Alex Brown wrote: 'World cricket authorities have caved in to the game's financial superpower, India, and Cricket Australia has incurred the wrath of its own Test players by pressuring them to drop a racial slur charge against Harbhajan Singh.'[78]

Of course, the Indian media saw it differently. All Indian newspapers and television channels applauded the verdict and many even castigated the Indian Board for not pressing for counter-charges against Andrew Symonds. The Indians saw the racism charges as part of a sustained campaign of attrition against the Indian players, a component of a calculated strategy on the playing field.[79] It was a crisis that split world cricket down the middle along the lines of Asians versus the Rest. Pakistan and Sri Lanka, for instance, supported the Indians. As Sri Lankan Board President Arjuna Ranatunga said, 'Australia have had these issues with touring sides. History shows whenever they get it back, they struggle. Sometimes they also need to learn a lesson.'[80]

The debate around the cricket world fed on, and reflected, the anxieties of the colonial past, postcolonial assertion and the profound changes afflicted by the processes of globalization. It can be seen in the context of what Alan Klein has termed 'tough-love globalization'. As Klein puts it, this includes not only the cardinal features of contemporary globalization (for example, time and space contraction) but also a degree of decentralization of power:

> Tough-love globalization is inclusive of corporations and nations – encouraging the have-nots to enter into the matrix if they can – it stops short of institutionally seeking to distribute power and wealth. Tough love is about merit, and though it opens the door to opportunity, it brooks no failure. This is not to be confused with a utopian vision, concerned primarily with distributing the benefits of globalization. Tough-love globalization merely allows entry to those that can take advantage of it, turning its back on all others.[81]

The IPL and ICL are products of this 'tough-love globalization'. When the English introduced cricket to the different parts of the Empire, they expected it to perform a normative function in terms of inculcating what were seen as English values that defined the British Empire. As the essays in this collection have shown, the game took a different form in different countries, each dictated by its local conditions. The discomfort in the older centres of cricket power about the changing global power equations partly stems from a discomfort with what they see as a failure to conform to what were seen as the 'original' notions that underpinned cricket. In a different context, Meaghan Morris, for instance, has argued that too often narratives of change recount 'a *known history*, something which has *already happened elsewhere*, and which is to be reproduced, mechanically or otherwise, with a local content'.[82] The direction that contemporary cricket is taking though is very different from that which came before. This new direction needs new perspectives and new mind-sets if we are to understand it. As Stephen Wagg has noted elsewhere, despite honourable exceptions and,

> the presence of a small, if growing, literature on the politics of the game, the ring of mainstream cricket discourse is still held by the 'Test Match Special' types. We can't really look to Christopher Martin-Jenkins or Michael Atherton or Mark Nicholas for a sentient discussion of Tamil bombings, sledging, racism or the proposed boycott of Zimbabwean cricket.[83]

A new politics of the game needs new voices.

One thing though is certain. Postcolonial studies for more than two decades has been focused on answering a cardinal question by Gayatri Chakraborty Spivak, 'Can the subaltern speak?'[84] The evidence from cricket in this collection makes it possible to raise a counter-question: Is the subaltern a subaltern any more?

## Notes

[1] Lord Harris, founder member of Imperial Cricket Council and Governor General of Bombay (1890–95), quoted in Roberts, 'Cricket as Global as Honourable', 6.

[2] See, for example, Majumdar, *The Illustrated History of Indian Cricket.*

[3] Subhash Chandra's Zee TV was India's first private satellite TV network in 1992. Zee has now grown into a global satellite empire with 17 international and 25 domestic channels. Vinay Kamath and Archana Venkat, 'Zee Plans Russian Channel Foray'. *Business Line*, June 23, 2006. Television is only one part of Chandra's business portfolio. One of his companies Essel Propack, for instance, is the world's largest producer of laminated tubes, claiming 30 per cent of the global share by 2004 and operating in 11 countries. In 2003, the company made it to the Forbes 200 Best Small Companies list. Swami, 'Chandra Shining', 58.

[4] When Kerry Packer's Channel 9 failed to win the broadcast rights to Australian cricket, he set up World Series Cricket as an independent cricket attraction. Channel 9's WSC signed up the world's top international players and introduced day-night one-day games, coloured clothing and aggressive marketing tactics to re-invent cricket as a television game. For details see Haigh, *The Cricket War.*

[5] Sixty of ICL's 135 players are non-Indian (I am grateful to Boria Majumdar for this information). ICL's first leg had six teams but two more teams were added for its second leg called ICL 20's Grand Championship between 9 March and 7 April 2008. The eight teams for this second leg were Chennai Superstars, Delhi Giants, Mumbai Champs, Hyderabad Heroes, Kolkata Tigers, Chandigarh Lions, Ahmedabad Rockets and Lahore Badshahs. *Impact: The Marketing Advertising and Media Weekly*, 14.

[6] See Haigh, *The Cricket War.*

[7] See Mehta, *India on Television.*

[8] For more on India's centrality as a new media centre and the notion of new 'media capitals' in Asia see Ibid. For the Chinese television industry see Curtin, *Playing to the World's Biggest Audience.*

[9] Arindam Mukherjee and Shuchi Srivastava, 'The Roaring 20s'. *Outlook*, February 11, 2008, 38.

[10] Interview with Lalit Modi, Vice President, BCCI, 'Competing with the Saas-Bahu Soap Operas'; Goswami, 'Cricket's New Innings', 48–9.

[11] Mukherjee and Srivastava, 'The Roaring 20s', 38–9.

[12] Goswami, 'Cricket's New Innings', 47.

[13] The IPL teams are owned by Shahrukh Khan's Red Chillies Entertainment (Kolkata), Deccan Chronicle (Hyderabad), Reliance Industries Ltd (Mumbai), Bollywood star Preity

Zinta, Ness Wadia and Mohit Burman (Chandigarh), Emerging Media (Jaipur), India Cements (Chennai), GMR Holdings (Delhi) and the UB Group (Bangalore). Nair, 'Beaming Smiles', 18.

[14] Mukherjee and Srivastava, 'The Roaring 20s', 38–9.

[15] In Indian terms, the total spent on players was Rs. 1,280,000,000 in the first auction. By a rough calculation this amounts to $32 million at February 2008 exchange rates. K. Shriniwas Rao, 'It Doesn't Get Any Bigger: Auction Becomes an Indian Parade, Even Rookies Get Twice as Ponting'. *The Indian Express* (Mumbai), February 21, 2008, 1.

[16] Team TOI, 'Cricket Just Got Even Bigger'. *Times of India* (Mumbai), February 21, 2008, 1.

[17] Rao, 'It Doesn't Get Any Bigger: Auction Becomes an Indian Parade, Even Rookies Get Twice as Ponting', 1.

[18] Sundari Iyer, 'Stars Shine at Pathbreaking Cricket Auction in Mumbai: Dhoni Bags Rs 6 Crores'. *The Asian Age* (Mumbai), February 21, 2008, 1.

[19] 'Bombay Stock Exchange', *The Hindustan Times* (Mumbai), February 21, 2008.

[20] Parry and Malcolm, 'England's Barmy Army', 77.

[21] In Indian terms, Rs 560,000,000 was spent on Indian players, at an average of Rs. 21,000,000 per player. The rough conversion is ours at February 2008 exchange rates. Much more money was spent in the Rao, 'It Doesn't Get Any Bigger', 1.

[22] In Indian terms, Rs 720,000,000 was spent on foreign players, at an average of Rs. 14,000,000 per player. The rough conversion is ours at February 2008 exchange rates. Ibid., 1.

[23] Ibid., 1.

[24] Iyer, 'Stars Shine at Pathbreaking Cricket Auction in Mumbai: Dhoni Bags Rs 6 Crores', 1.

[25] See Goswami, 'Cricket's New Innings', 48–9.

[26] Anand Vasu, 'Be Indian, Buy Indian'. *The Hindustan Times* (Mumbai), February 21, 2008, 18.

[27] Team TOI, 'Making Sense of the Bids'. *Times of India* (Mumbai), February 21, 2008, 1.

[28] The second auction was held because teams had money left over from the first round. The amounts left over were $374,000 with Bangalore, $23,750 with Chennai, $71,250 with Delhi, $262,500 with Hyderabad, $1,700,000 with Jaipur, $107,500 with Kolkata, $292,250 with Mohali and $53,750 with Mumbai. Qaiser Mohammad Ali, IANS, March 9, 2008. http://www.indiaenews.com/sports/20080309/103000.htm.

[29] For a detailed analysis of the reforms see Joshi and Little, *India's Economic Reforms 1991–2001*. For a range of perspectives see Ahluwalia and Little (eds.), *India's Economic Reforms and Development*; Cassen and Joshi, eds, *India: The Future of Economic Reform*. Most economists agree that the measures of 1991 were fundamentally different from previous reforms in the 1980s. In contrast, Deepak Nayyar, for instance, has argued that 1991 was not a fundamental turning point, that economic performance had been good from 1980 onwards and that the failure had been in translating growth into well-being. Nayyar, 'India's Unfinished Journey: Translating Growth into Development'.

[30] I.S. Bindra quoted in 'Quote-Unquote', *The Asian Age* (Mumbai), February 21, 2008, 17.

[31] Team TOI, 'Cricket Just Got Even Bigger', 1.

[32] Interview with Adam Gilchrist, telecast on Times Now, September 2007.

[33] Adam Gilchrist, 'IPL Not Distracting Me in Tri-Series'. *Times of India* (Mumbai), February 10, 2008, 28.

[34] Iyer, 'Stars Shine at Pathbreaking Cricket Auction in Mumbai: Dhoni Bags Rs 6 Crores', 1.

[35] David Lloyd in Roundtable discussion 'The IPL has to be Governed Globally'. March 4, 2008. Transcript posted at http://content-ind.cricinfo.com/talk/content/multimedia/340986.html?view=transcript.

[36] Anam Arsala, 'Dhaka Warriors Step Into the ICL Ring'. *The Hindustan Times*, September 16, 2008. http://www.hindustantimes.com/StoryPage/StoryPage.aspx?sectionName=&id=a77160f9-7db1-47d6-b35e-f1724a538da9&&IsCricket=true&Headline=Dhaka+Warriors+step+into+the+ICL+ring.

[37] AFP, 'Bangladesh ICL Rebels Banned for Ten Years'. *The Nation*, September 18, 2008. http://www.nation.com.pk/pakistan-news-newspaper-daily-english-online/Sports/18-Sep-2008/Bangladesh-ICL-rebels-banned-for-10-years.

[38] 'Player Drain an Issue: Lehmann'. *Mumbai Mirror*, March 2, 2008, 2.

[39] Osman Samiuddin, 'Welcome to the Inquisition'. March 1, 2005. http://content-www.cricinfo.com/magazine/content/story/340430.html.

40 Richard Tomlinson and Abhay Singh, 'India's Twenty20 Cricket Imports Cheerleaders, Grabs UK Stars'. September 26, 2008. http://www.bloomberg.com/apps/news?pid=20601085&sid= agXm3oIJqEUA&refer=europe.

41 'Flintoff Says IPL Not on Priority List'. *The Asian Age*, February 21, 2008, 17.

42 IANS, 'Kevin Pietersen Wants to Play for IPL'. April 9, 2008. http://sports.in.msn.com/cricket/ stories/article.aspx?cp-documentid=1330824.

43 Tomlinson and Singh, 'India's Twenty20 Cricket Imports Cheerleaders, Grabs UK Stars'. http:// www.bloomberg.com/apps/news?pid=20601085&sid=agXm3oIJqEUA&refer=europe.

44 See, for example, Ashwin Pinto, 'IPL Lived Up the Hype'. June 7, 2008. http://www. indiantelevision.com/special/y2k8/ipl_main_spl_1.php.

45 See for instance Kunal Pradhan, 'Batting for Sachin in Jaipur'. *The Indian Express*, February 22, 2008, 10.

46 See, for example, Ian Chappell, 'IPL Impact: Future Imperfect'. *The Hindustan Times* (Mumbai), March 2, 2008, 20.

47 For details on the challenges faced by IPL see Majumdar, 'Commercial Cricket'.

48 Tomlinson and Singh, 'India's Twenty20 Cricket Imports Cheerleaders, Grabs UK Stars'.

49 Beckles, 'Introduction', 1.

50 Kennedy, *The Rise and Fall of Great Powers*.

51 P. Chidambaram's budget speech, telecast on Doordarshan, February 29, 2008.

52 Quoted in Roundtable discussion, 'The IPL has to be Governed Globally'.

53 Ian Chappell and David Lloyd in Roundtable discussion, 'The IPL has to be Governed Globally', March 4, 2008. Transcript posted at http://content-ind.cricinfo.com/talk/content/multimedia/ 340986.html?view=transcript.

54 Emphasis is ours. Andrew Miller, 'Worse to Follow'. March 29, 2007. http://content-ind.cricinfo. com/ci/content/story/296258.html.

55 Emphasis is original. Mukul Keswan, 'The Indians are Coming'. June 4, 2007. http://blogs. cricinfo.com/meninwhite/archives/2007/06/.

56 Ibid.

57 Jagmohan Dalmiya, Chairman, ICC (1997–2000), interviewed by Nalin Mehta, Kolkata, March 17, 2008.

58 Ibid.

59 See in this context, Boria Majumdar, 'The Pied Piper's Magic Flute'. *Outlook* internet edition, September 12, 2006. http://www.outlookindia.com/full.asp?fodname=20060912&fname= boria&sid=1.

60 Interview with Lalit Modi, Vice President, BCCI, October 12, 2006. http://content-usa.cricinfo. com/ci/content/story/262512.html.

61 Samyabrata Ray Goswami, 'Man U Model for BCCI'. *The Telegraph*, December 28, 2005. http:// www.telegraphindia.com/1051228/asp/nation/story_5652982.asp.

62 Majumdar, 'The Pied Piper's Magic Flute'.

63 Majumdar, 'Nationalist Romance to Postcolonial Sport', 96.

64 Mehta, *India on Television*.

65 We are grateful to Boria Majumdar for this information.

66 Majumdar, 'Nationalist Romance to Postcolonial Sport: Cricket in 2006 India', 91.

67 Cricinfo staff, 'Asian Bloc Forced ICC's Hand Claims Hair QC'. October 1, 2007. http:// content-www.cricinfo.com/ci-icc/content/story/313231.html.

68 Ibid.

69 News Reports telecast on Times Now, January 7–8, 2008.

70 On Times Now, NDTV and CNN-IBN this was the primary news story till the issue was resolved. Nalin Mehta's monitoring of Indian newspapers and television news channels for the second week of January 2008.

71 Information from Sunder Iyer, Sports Editor, Times Now, who was present when the Indian team off-loaded its bags from the team bus to Canberra on 7 January 2008.

72 Chloe Saltau and Alex Brown, 'Cricket's Day of Shame'. *The Sydney Morning Herald*, January 30, 2008. http://www.smh.com.au/news/cricket/crickets-day-of-shame/2008/01/29/ 1201369135083.html.

73 Alex Brown, 'Sri Lanka May Have Quit One-day Series Too'. *Sydney Morning Herald*, January 30, 2008.

74 Quoted in Ibid.

75 Alex Brown, 'Australian Players Irate After the Board Yields to Pressure'. *The Sydney Morning Herald*, January 30, 2008. http://www.smh.com.au/news/cricket/australian-players-irate-after-board-yields-to-pressure/2008/01/29/1201369135077.html.

76 Saltau and Brown, 'Cricket's Day of Shame'.

77 Alex Brown, January 30, 2008. http://blogs.smh.com.au/sport/archives/2008/01/welcome_to_the_era_of_the_indi.html.

78 Saltau and Brown, 'Cricket's Day of Shame'.

79 This was the line taken by news channels like Times Now which para-phrased its coverage with the headline, 'Is this justice enough'. See also the coverage in the news magazine *Tehelka*, 5, no.2, January 19, 2008.

80 Arjuna Ranatunga quoted in Cricinfo Staff, 'Australia Incensed by Harbhajan Reprieve'. January 29, 2008. http://content-ind.cricinfo.com/ausvind/content/current/story/334111.html.

81 Klein, quoted in Majumdar, 'Nationalist Romance to Postcolonial Sport: Cricket in 2006 India', 94.

82 Morris, 'Metamorposes at Sydney Tower', 10. Quoted in Chakrabarty, 'Post Coloniality and the Artifice of History: Who Speaks for "Indian" Pasts?', p.17.

83 Wagg, Review of Michael Roberts, *Essaying Cricket: Sri Lanka and Beyond*.

84 For a comprehensive discussion on Spivak's question see Gandhi, *Postcolonial Theory*, 2.

## References

Ahluwalia, Isher Judge, and I.M.D. Little, eds. *India's Economic Reforms and Development: Essays for Manmohan Singh*. New Delhi: Oxford University Press, 1998.

Beckles, Hillary. 'Introduction'. In *Liberation Cricket: West Indian Cricket Culture*, edited by Hillary Beckles and Brian Stoddart, 1–8. Manchester: Manchester University Press, 1995.

Cassen, Robert, and Vijay Joshi, eds. *India: The Future of Economic Reform*. Delhi: Oxford University Press, 1995.

Chakrabarty, Dipesh. 'Post Coloniality and the Artifice of History: Who Speaks for "Indian" Pasts?'. *Representations*, Special Issue: Imperial Fantasies and Postcolonial Histories, 37 (Winter 1992): 1–26.

Curtin, Michael. *Playing to the World's Biggest Audience: The Globalization of Chinese Film and TV*. Berkeley, CA: University of California Press, 2007.

Gandhi, Leela. *Postcolonial Theory: A Critical Introduction*. Edinburgh: Edinburgh University Press, 1998.

Goswami, Anupam. 'Cricket's New Innings'. *Business India* (March 23, 2008): 45–48.

Haigh, Gideon. *The Cricket War: The Inside Story of Kerry Packer's World Series Cricket*. Melbourne: Text, 1993.

*Impact: The Marketing Advertising and Media Weekly* 14, no. 37 (3–9 March 2008): 14.

Joshi, Vijay, and I.M.D. Little. *India's Economic Reforms 1991–2001*. Oxford: Clarendon, 1996.

Kennedy, Paul. *The Rise and Fall of the Great Powers: Economic Change and Military Conflict From 1500 to 2000*. New York: Random House, 1987.

Majumdar, Boria. *The Illustrated History of Indian Cricket*. New Delhi: Roli, 2007.

Majumdar, Boria. 'Nationalist Romance to Postcolonial Sport: Cricket in 2006 India'. In 'Cricket, Race and the 2007 World Cup', edited by Jon Gemmell and Boria Majumdar, special issue *Sport and Society: Culture, Commerce, Media, Politics* 10, no.1 (2007): 88–100.

Majumdar, Boria. 'Commercial Cricket'. *Himal: South Asian* 21, no. 4 (2008).

Mehta, Nalin. *India on Television*. New Delhi: Harper Collins, 2008.

Morris, Meaghan. 'Metamorposes at Sydney Tower'. *New Formations* 11 (Summer 1990): 5–18.

Nair, Sapna. 'Beaming Smiles'. *The Brand Reporter* (March 1–15, 2008): 18–19.

Nayyar, Deepak. 'India's Unfinished Journey: Translating Growth into Development'. *Modern Asian Studies* 40, no. 3 (2006): 797–832.

Parry, Matthew, and Dominic Malcolm. 'England's Barmy Army: Commercialization, Masculinity and Nationalism'. *International Review for the Sociology of Sport* 39, no. 1 (2004): 75–94.

Roberts, Michael. 'Cricket as Global as Honourable'. In *Essaying Cricket: Sri Lanka and Beyond*, edited by Michael Roberts. Colombo: Vijitha Yapa, 2006.

Swami, Parthasarthy. 'Chandra Shining'. *Business India* (March 15–28, 2004): 58.

Wagg, Stephen. Review of Michael Roberts, *Essaying Cricket: Sri Lanka and Beyond*. (Colombo: Vijitha Yapa, 2006) [unpublished].

# Index